TAVARES STRACHAN

MICHELE ROBECCHI
GAVIN DELAHUNTY
EMMA DABIRI
JASON SCHMIDT

Φ

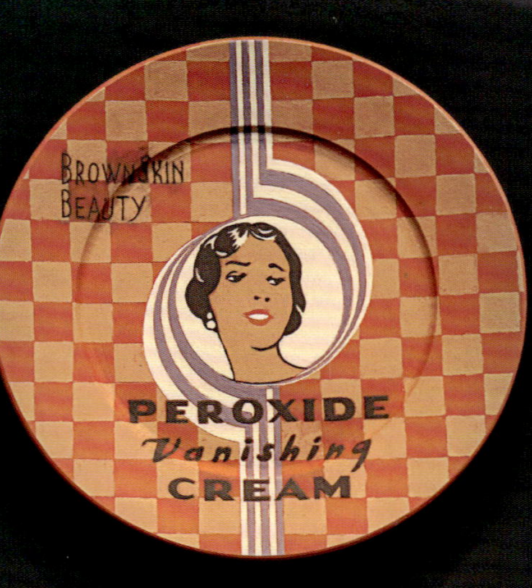
BROWN SKIN BEAUTY
PEROXIDE
Vanishing
CREAM

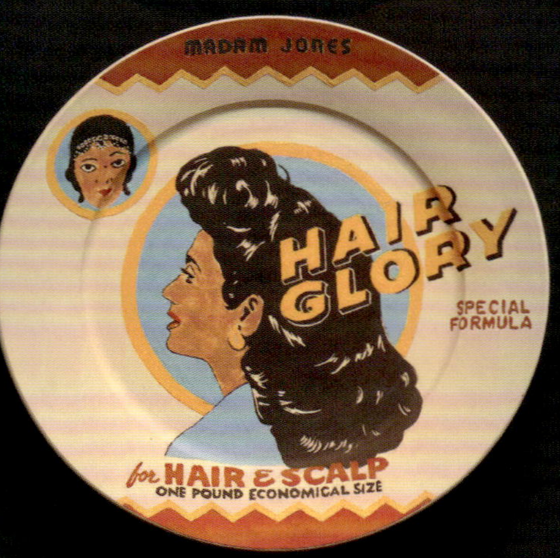
MADAM JONES
HAIR GLORY
SPECIAL FORMULA
for HAIR & SCALP
ONE POUND ECONOMICAL SIZE

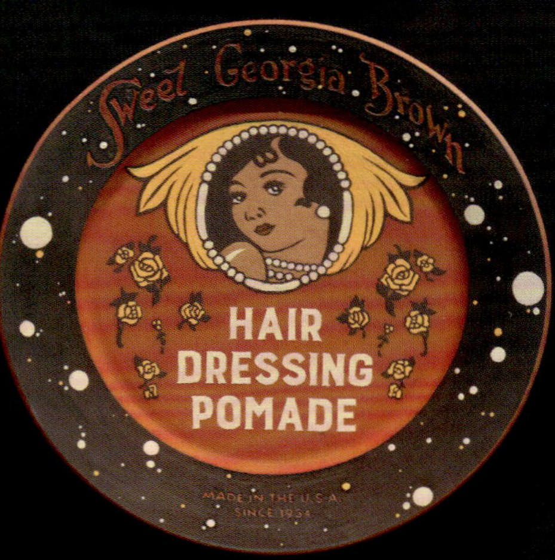
Sweet Georgia Brown
HAIR
DRESSING
POMADE

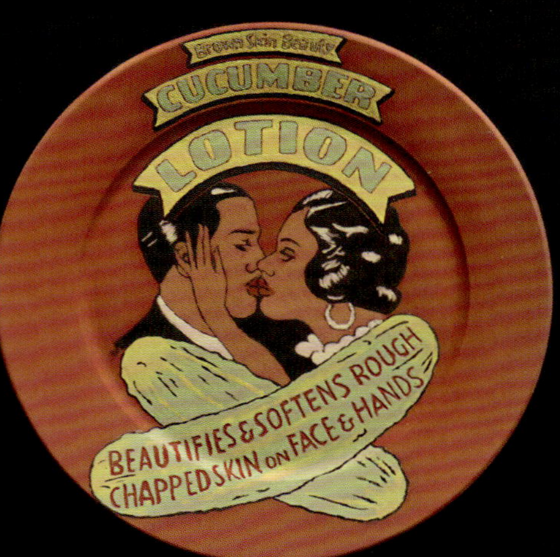
Brown Skin Beauty
CUCUMBER
LOTION
BEAUTIFIES & SOFTENS ROUGH
CHAPPED SKIN ON FACE & HANDS

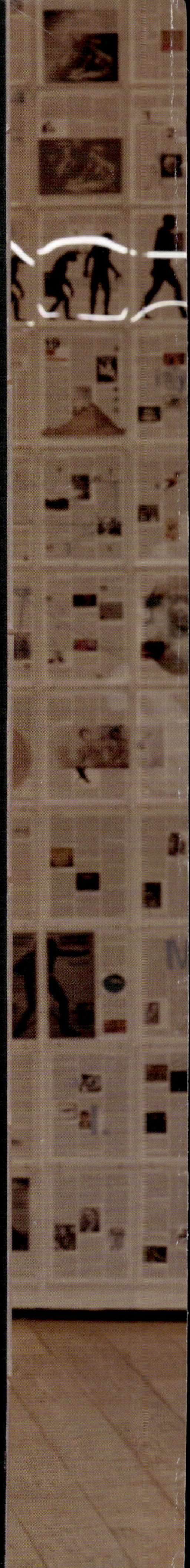

from top,
SWEET GEORGIA BROWN, 2025
CERAMIC
6 X Ø 36 CM

HAIR GLORY, 2025
CERAMIC
6 X Ø 36 CM

VANISHING CREAM, 2025
CERAMIC
6 X Ø 36 CM

BEAUTIFIES AND SOFTENS, 2025
CERAMIC
6 X Ø 36 CM

INSTALLATION VIEW AT THE LOS ANGELES COUNTY MUSEUM OF ART, 2025

CONTENTS

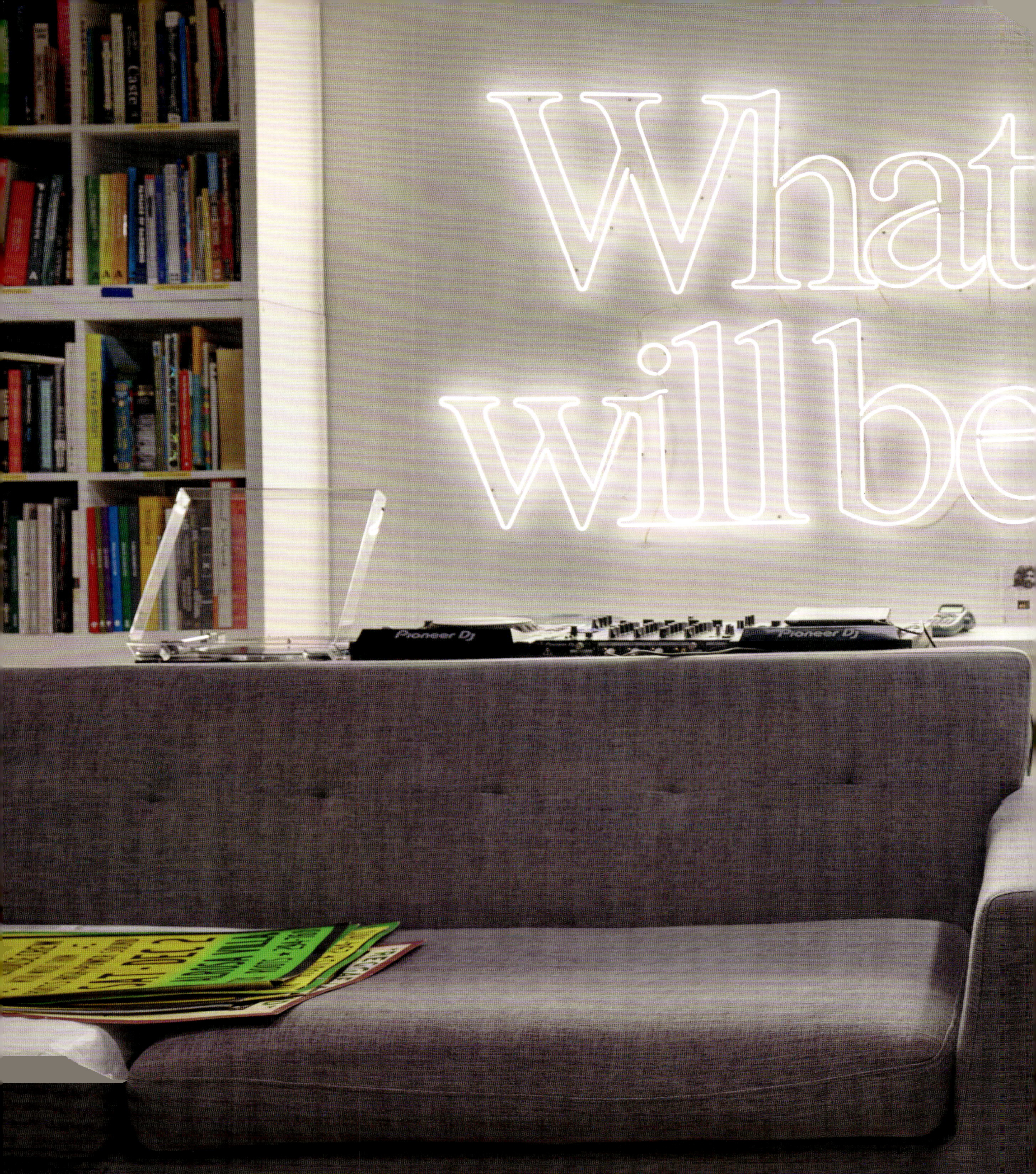

What
will
Pioneer DJ
Pioneer DJ

005 INTERVIEW

Michele Robecchi in conversation with Tavares Strachan

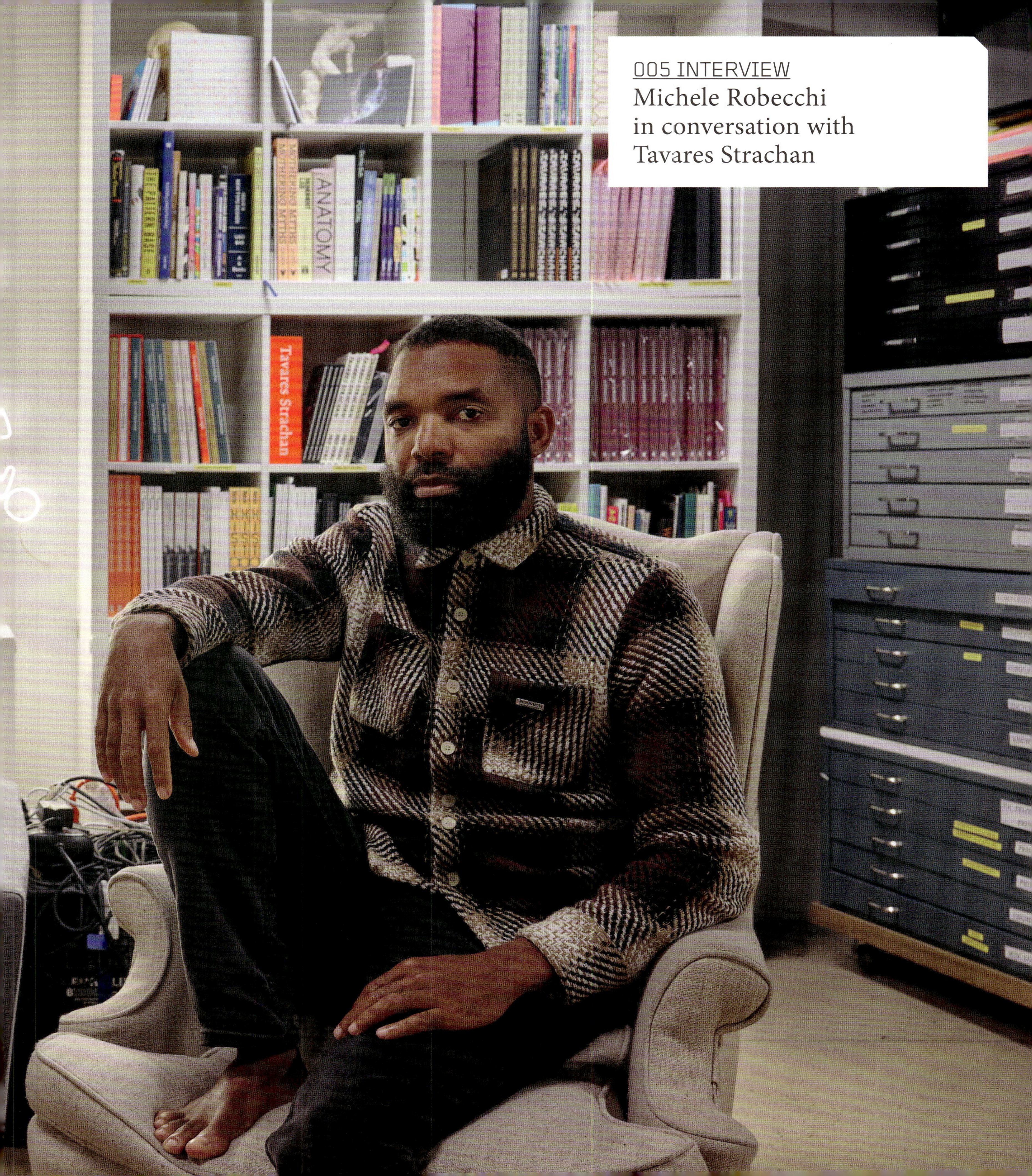

previous pages,
TAVARES STRACHAN, ISOLATED
LABS, NEW YORK, 2025

opposite,
EVERY TONGUE SHALL CONFESS, 2023
OIL, ENAMEL, PGIMENT AND ACRYLIC ON TWO PANELS
213 X 213 CM

below,
LETTER E, 1999
HOUSE PAINT ON WOOD
122 X 61 CM

MICHELE ROBECCHI: *Like most artists, you started as a painter. There's not a lot around from that period of your life, but one thing I came across is this painting you made of the letter 'E'. This is pre-Rhode Island School of Design, this is pre-Yale School of Art – this is the UB (University of Bahamas) in Nassau in 1999, when presumably representational painting was predominant within the faculty's discourse. It seems to me that already at that age you were making a deliberate decision to stray from the pack. What are your recollections of that time? Where were you at when you were making that painting?*

TAVARES STRACHAN: That painting was made on my mother's porch. I must have made a hundred paintings at that time. I don't know where they are now. They were big. It was usually house paint. We'd go to the hardware store and they'd have all the rejects. People would come in and mix the wrong colour because the formulation of the house paint was wrong and so we'd take all those paints and paint with them.

I was also learning about printing processes. I learned how to do silkscreen, photogravure, etching, lino cuts, wood cuts and ink transfers. I think what was most memorable about that time was manual making versus industrial making – this collision between the two. When you're on an island, you don't have access to a lot of industrial infrastructure. So having a silkscreen facility was impressive. And it was the only one accessible to young people at then UB. So I think it was an explosion of exploration and looking for things. So much of how artistic practice is represented now is about finding the thing as opposed to looking for the thing. So many of the most iconic artists that we know, in some way, they have the thing. They're not looking for the thing. It's more of a static process than an active process. They've discovered the thing. If you think of Rothko or de Kooning, they found the thing. I think the artists that I look up to – not that I don't look up to those artists – but the artists that I love are the ones that are looking for the thing, and you can tell that they're still looking for the thing. I think I was then looking for the thing and I'm still trying to find it.

ROBECCHI: *That notion of discovering the perfect formula and sticking with it is widespread. Years ago, I worked on a monograph with a famous painter and it was surprising to see how confident he was about his methodology. I'd never met an artist before whose attitude was: 'I figured it all out. This is how you're supposed to do it.'*

STRACHAN: Right. And I think they're very happy with this. But it's never been my approach, because from the first time I figured out what a painting could be, I thought, 'Well, this doesn't make any sense.' And so the idea that it needs to make sense never occurred to me.

During figure-drawing class at UB, I had this teacher named Sue Katz, who just was a nightmare for me. She hovered over me every class. We'd have these nude models and they'd come in and we'd draw them. That was quite unusual because it's a small island: you're going to see the model at the market, so it's kind of risqué. But she just made figure drawing miserable for me. I learned technically how to figure draw at an early age because all of my uncles and aunts drew. I was bored by it by the time I got to university. When you're in Junkanoo, you're just drawing all the time. People like Stanley Burnside were drawing a lot as part of it. I was actually offended by how the academy assumed that everyone coming in lacked technical knowledge about how to render a figure, especially in a culture that's predicated on an independence of making from an early age. The trouble was that those skill sets weren't necessarily valued in the academy. I think the escape from figuration was, for me, more about having had that need already met through Junkanoo and not needing to bring that into the academy.

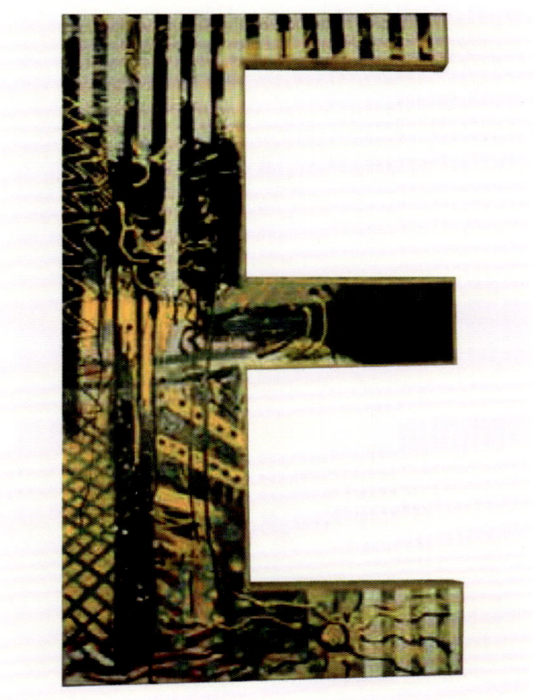

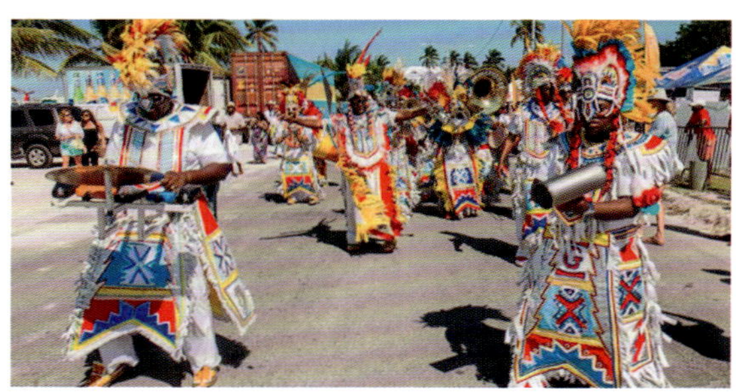

JASON GARDNER
JUNKANOO IN DA CULTURAL VILLAGE, NASSAU, BAHAMAS, 2016
COLOUR PHOTOGRAPH

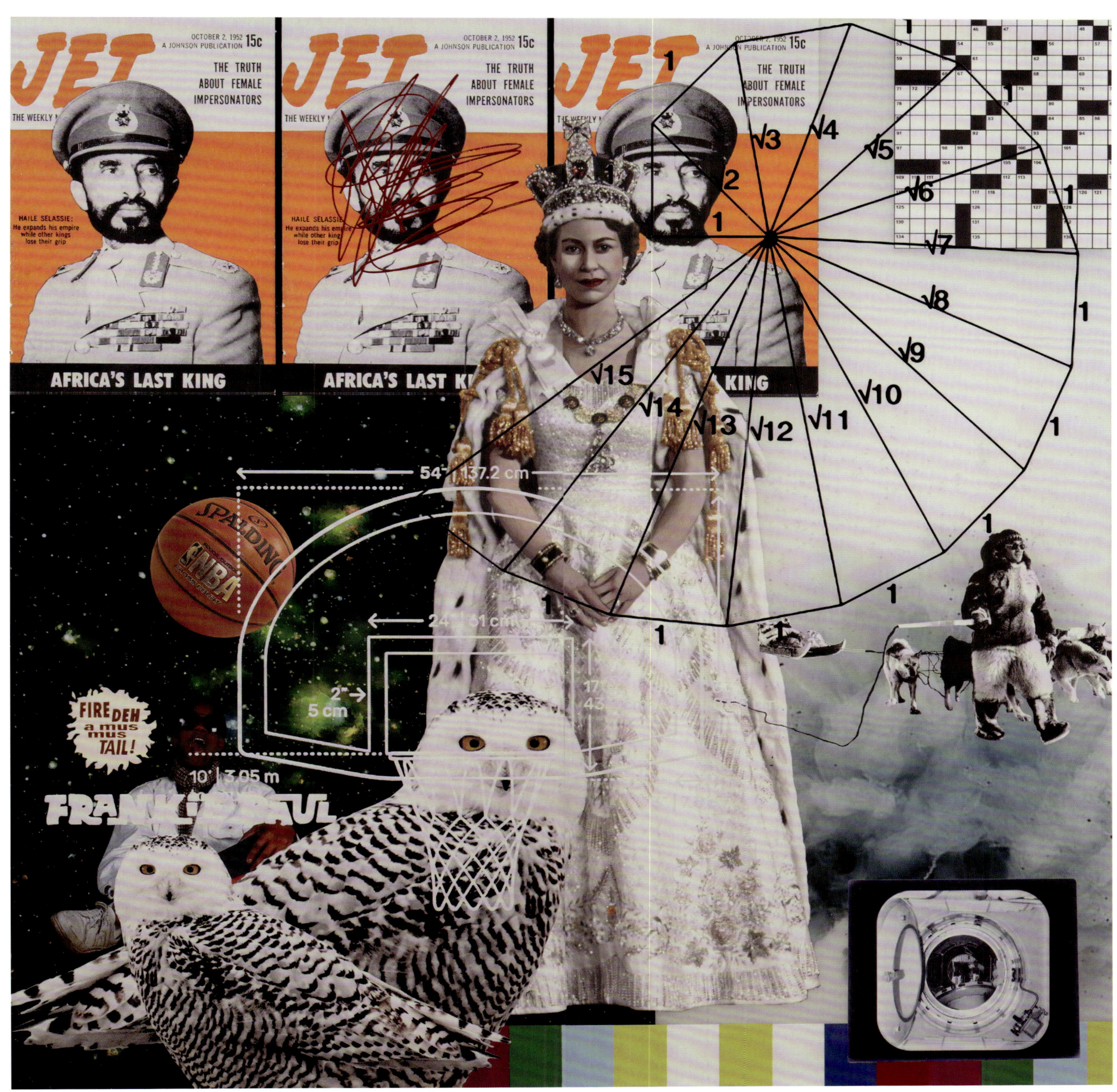
JET
OCTOBER 2, 1952
A JOHNSON PUBLICATION
15c
THE TRUTH ABOUT FEMALE IMPERSONATORS
HAILE SELASSIE:
He expands his empire while other kings lose their grip
AFRICA'S LAST KING
FIRE DEH a mus mus TAIL!
54" | 137.2 cm
24" | 61 cm
2"
5 cm
10' | 3.05 m
SPALDING
NBA

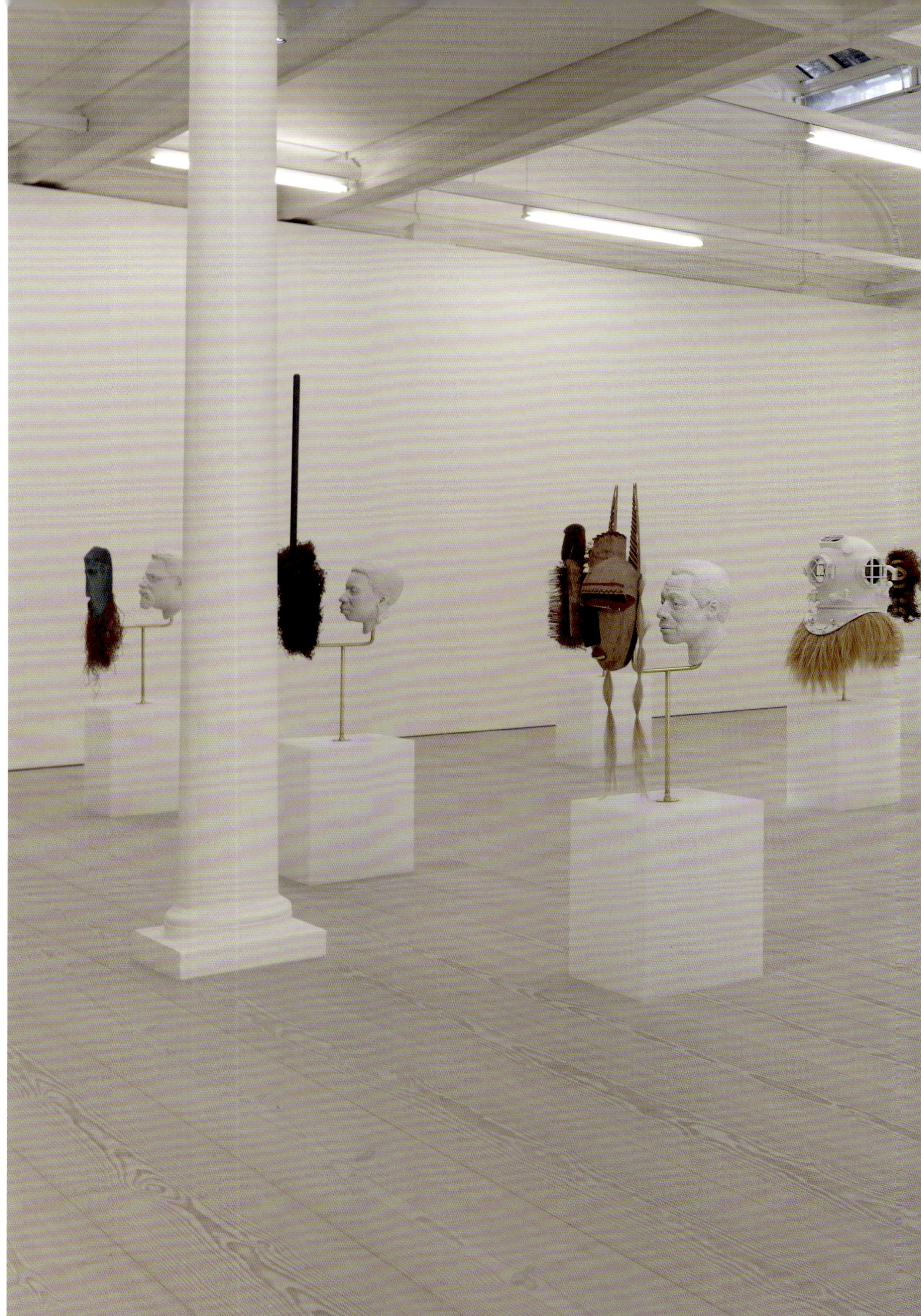

from left,
DISTANT RELATIVES (ROBERT SMALLS), 2020
BEMBE MASK (DEMOCRATIC REPUBLIC OF CONGO), PIGMENT, NATURAL FIBERS, PLASTER, BRASS, ACRYLIC
152 X 56 X 51 CM

DISTANT RELATIVES (SHIRLEY CHISHOLM), 2020
KUBA ELEPHANT MASK (DEMOCRATIC REPUBLIC OF CONGO), PIGMENT, NATURAL FIBERS, COWRIE SHELLS, LEATHER, BEADS, PLASTER, BRASS, ACRYLIC
218 X 130 X 51 CM

DISTANT RELATIVES (VIVIAN ANDERSON), 2020
FANG NGIL MASK (CENTRAL AFRICA), PIGMENT, NATURAL FIBERS, PLASTER, BRASS, ACRYLIC
170 X 61 X 76 CM

DISTANT RELATIVES (JAMES BALDWIN), 2020
BAMBARA MASK (WEST AFRICA), PIGMENT, HORSE-HAIR, GOLD LEAF, PLASTER, BRASS, ACRYLIC
173 X 56 X 47 CM

DISTANT RELATIVES (ANDREA MOTLEY CRABTREE), 2020
PLASTER, NATURAL FIBERS, BRASS, ACRYLIC
158 X 76 X 66 CM

DISTANT RELATIVES (HENRIETTA LACKS), 2020
KIFWEBE SONG MASK (DEMOCRATIC REPUBLIC OF CONGO), PIGMENT NATURAL FIBERS, PLASTER, BRASS, ACRYLIC
155 X 56 X 48 CM

DISTANT RELATIVES (SHIRLEY CHISHOLM), 2020
KUBA ELEPHANT MASK (DEMOCRATIC REPUBLIC OF CONGO), PIGMENT, NATURAL FIBERS, COWRIE SHELLS, LEATHER, BEADS, PLASTER, BRASS, ACRYLIC
218 X 130 X 51 CM

DISTANT RELATIVES (MARY J. SEACOLE), 2020
FANG NGIL MASK (CENTRAL AFRICA), PIGMENT, HORSEHAIR, PLASTER, BRASS,ACRYLIC
150 X 56 X 47 CM

DISTANT RELATIVES (DEREK WALCOTT), 2020
KAVAT MASK (PAPUA NUOVA GUINEA), PIGMENT, NATURAL FIBERS, PLASTER, BRASS, ACRYLIC
183 X 91 X 91 CM

DISTANT RELATIVES (MATTHEW HENSON), 2020
FANG NGIL MASK (CENTRAL AFRICA), PIGMENT, NATURAL FIBERS, PLASTER, BRASS, ACRYLIC
170 X 61 X 76 CM

DISTANT RELATIVES (ROBERT HENRY LAWRENCE JR.), 2020
PLASTER, NATURAL FIBERS, BRASS, ACRYLIC
158 X 76 X 66 CM

INSTALLATION VIEW AT MARIAN GOODMAN GALLERY, LONDON, 2020

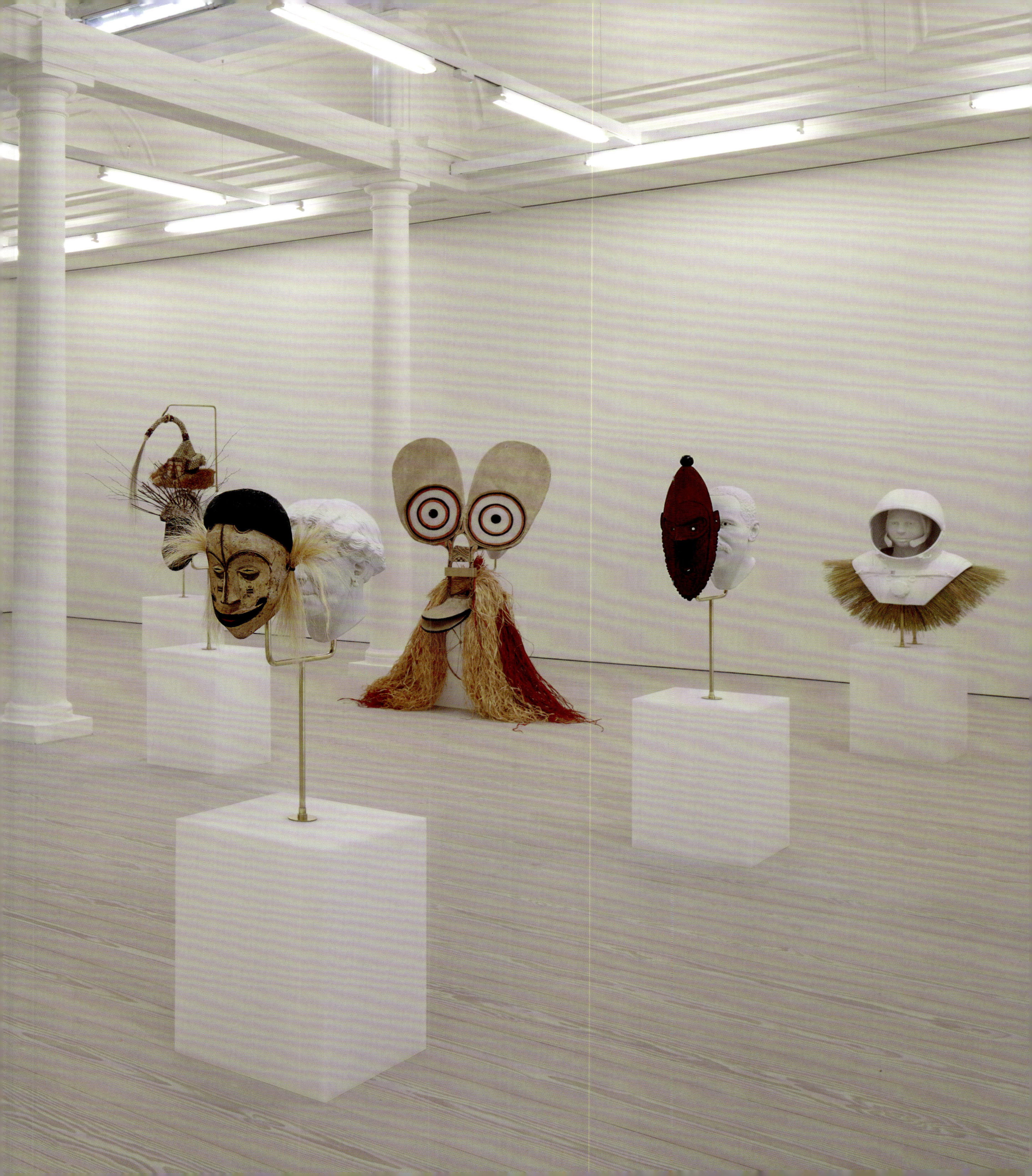

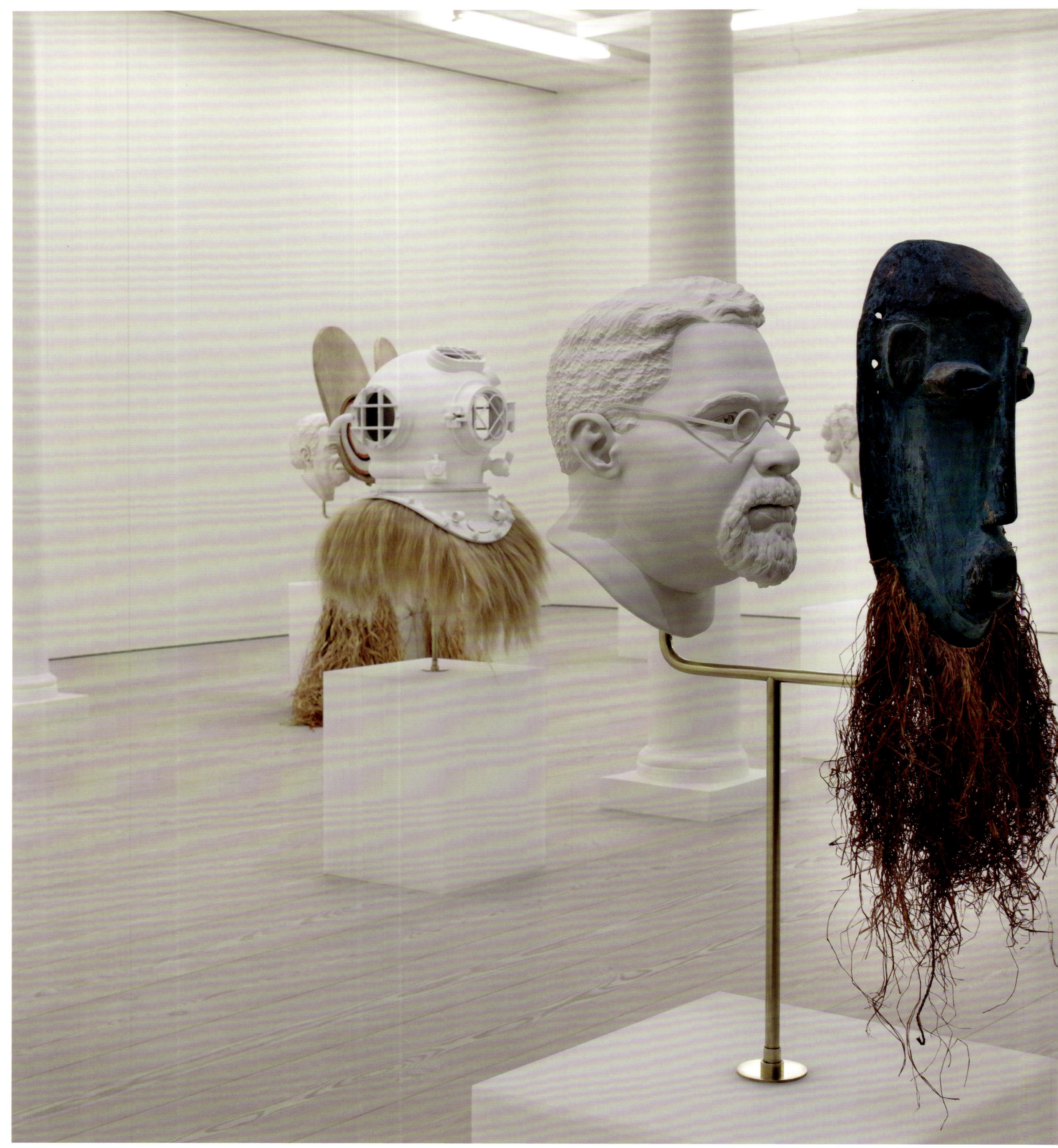

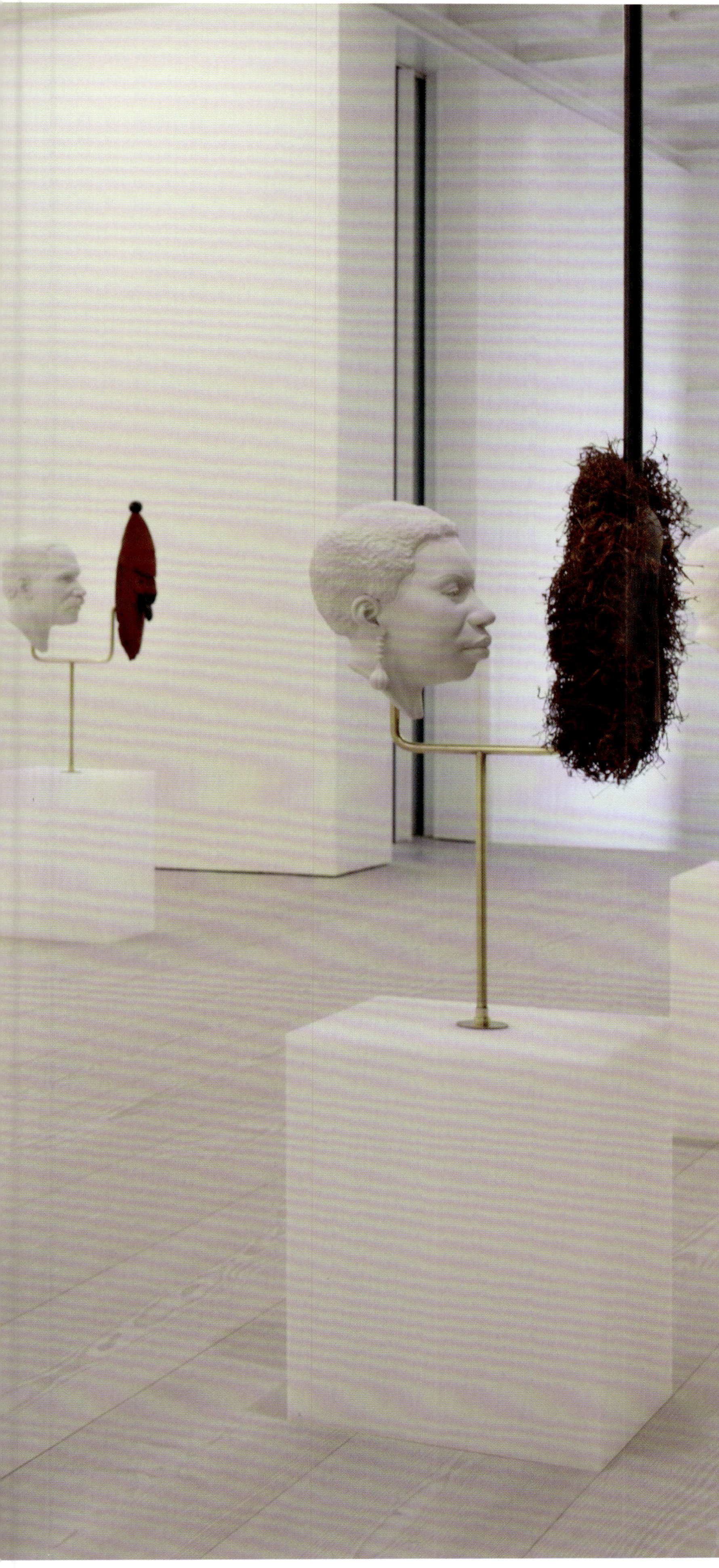

from left,
<u>DISTANT RELATIVES (DEREK WALCOTT)</u>, 2020
KAVAT MASK (PAPUA NUOVA GUINEA), PIGMENT, NATURAL FIBERS, PLASTER, BRASS, ACRYLIC
183 X 91 X 91 CM

<u>DISTANT RELATIVES (ANDREA MOTLEY CRABTREE)</u>, 2020
PLASTER, NATURAL FIBERS, BRASS, ACRYLIC
158 X 76 X 66 CM

<u>DISTANT RELATIVES (ROBERT SMALLS)</u>, 2020
BEMBE MASK (DEMOCRATIC REPUBLIC OF CONGO), PIGMENT, NATURAL FIBERS, PLASTER, BRASS, ACRYLIC
152 X 56 X 51 CM

<u>DISTANT RELATIVES (SISTER ROSETTA THARPE)</u>, 2020
GUERE MASK (LIBERIA), PIGMENT, WOOD, GOLD LEAF, PLASTER, BRASS, ACRYLIC
182 X 81 X 107 CM

<u>DISTANT RELATIVES (MATTHEW HENSON)</u>, 2020
FANG NGIL MASK (CENTRAL AFRICA), PIGMENT, NATURAL FIBERS, PLASTER, BRASS, ACRYLIC
170 X 61 X 76 CM

<u>DISTANT RELATIVES (SHIRLEY CHISHOLM)</u>, 2020
KUBA ELEPHANT MASK (DEMOCRATIC REPUBLIC OF CONGO), PIGMENT, NATURAL FIBERS, COWRIE SHELLS, LEATHER, BEADS, PLASTER, BRASS, ACRYLIC
218 X 130 X 51 CM

INSTALLATION VIEW AT MARIAN GOODMAN GALLERY, LONDON, 2020

ROBECCHI: *Junkanoo gave you a head start. But while learning about art making at the academy, do you feel you were already questioning what its true purpose is – whether art is about coming up with the idea of a glass that can hold water or the skill of making that glass?*

STRACHAN: Yes. I always thought that if it wasn't conceptual in some way, then it couldn't be art, and it was relegated to craft. But at the highest level, obviously, the best craftsmen are conceptual also. I think this is very true for Caribbean art. If you look at Caribbean art, there are a lot of found objects, which is the foundation of Dadaism, as we know. It's in a very different track, but it's the same thing, essentially. It's about taking objects and putting them in a gallery.

ROBECCHI: *And Junkanoo evolves from a combination of different cultures, including some rooted within African tradition. In contemporary African sculpture too there's a large tradition of using found objects. I could see how this approach informed* Distant Relatives, *the series of sculptures you made for your 'In Plain Sight' exhibition in London in 2020, for example.*

STRACHAN: Right. It's all about, we have some grass, we have some fish and lime, we have this old hook, we have this glass bottle, let's make a head. Those traditions already existed. It's easy to get tricked as a youngster into believing that the thing that you have already isn't what you need. And when you go to academia, you get told that the thing that you have isn't enough. Or the methodology is a different methodology. So much of becoming a professional, for me, was just about forgetting everything I'd learned at RISD or Yale because it tries to erode your sense of self for this kind of group way of thinking.

ROBECCHI: *Isn't that true for every artist? You need to transcend your art education if you want to move forward.*

STRACHAN: Totally. I think something interesting happened over the past, call it twenty-five, thirty years, specifically in places like England and America, and even actually in Germany, where the academy has taken over this kind of IP [Intellectual Property] of creativity – as if creativity can only come from the academy. Which is quite clever on their part, right? To create this idea that somehow, if you go to this academy, you're creative and if you didn't, you're lesser than those who did. And so for me, a huge part of my experience over the past twenty years has been unlearning some of the things that I learned in the academy. I think my approach now is radically different from when I was at the academy.

You know, I always lamented that in the Bahamas, we never had a major revolt. Even up to now. In Haiti and in Jamaica and in Cuba, there were all these revolutions that happened. We haven't really had a big revolution. It was particularly peaceful. It upsets me.

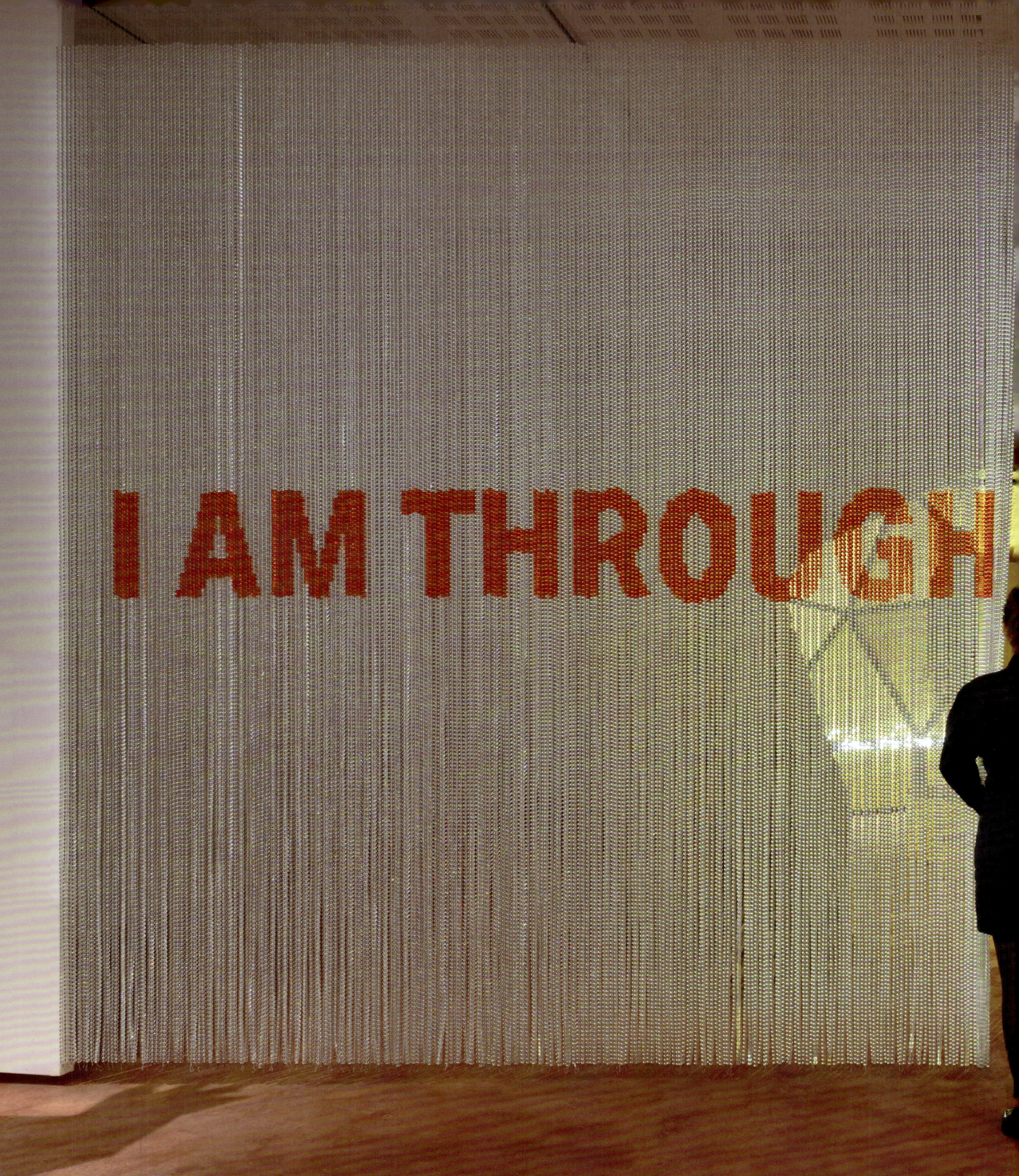
I AM THROUGH

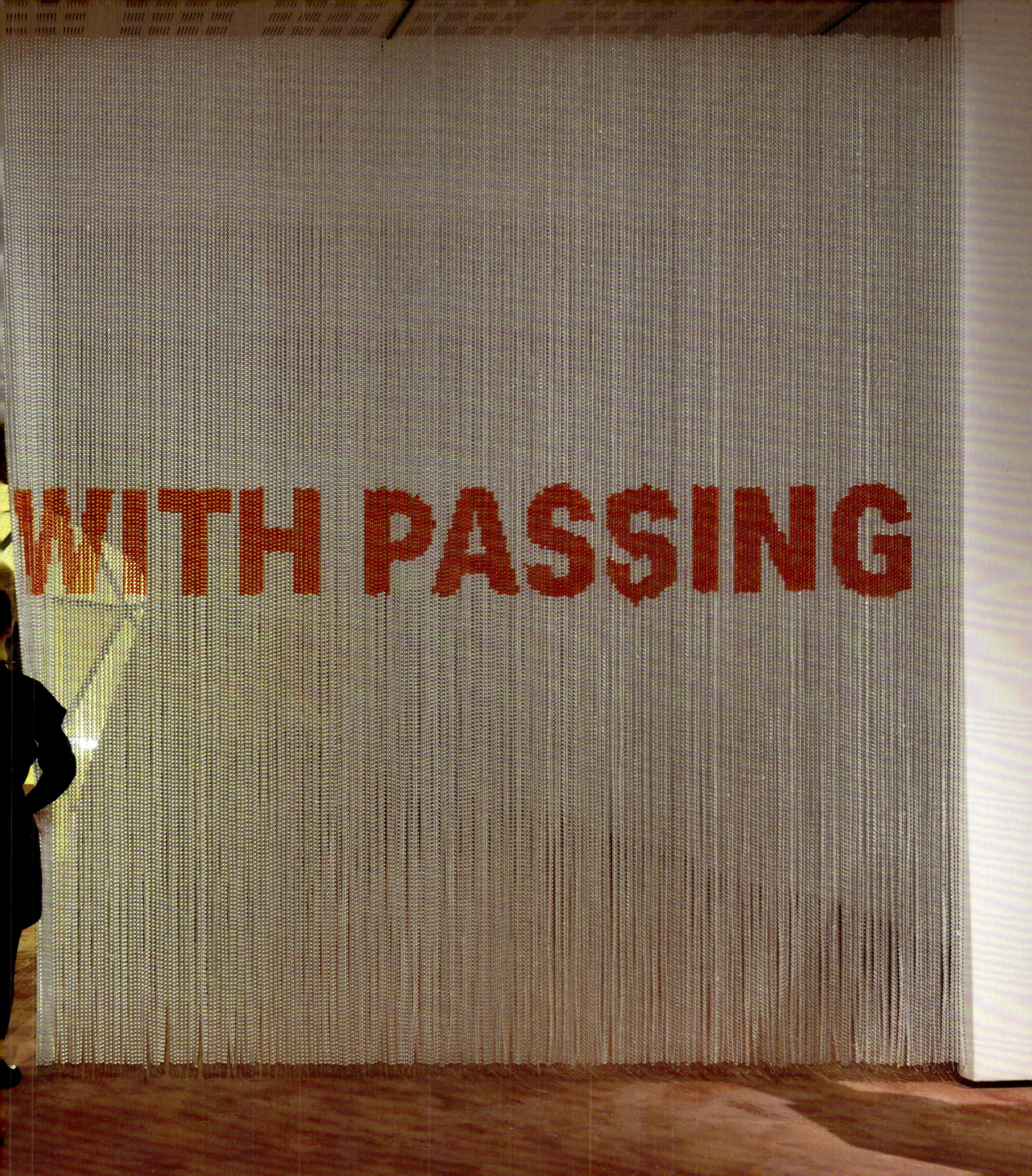
WITH PA$$ING

previous pages,
I AM THROUGH WITH PASSING,
2022
GLASS BEADS AND WIRE WITH
NYLON COATING
378 X 642 CM

opposite, from right,
CORONATION HUT, 2022
THRONE, NEON SIGN, STRAW,
METAL, FRAME, PLYWOOD
SHEET, THATCH ROLLS,
METALLIC POLYESTER FABRIC,
POLYSTYRENE SHEETS,
HESSIAN ROPE
500 X 310 CM

I AM THROUGH WITH PASSING,
2022
GLASS BEADS AND WIRE WITH
NYLON COATING
378 X 642 CM

INSTALLATION VIEW AT MARIAN
GOODMAN GALLERY, PARIS,
2022

ROBECCHI: *This is a problematic issue. If you look at the history of socio-political phenomena of this kind, the rising consciousness in one place invariably ends up affecting neighbouring countries. It almost triggers a domino effect. Why do you think this didn't happen in the Bahamas?*

STRACHAN: I think it's because the Brits that were tasked with taking over the Bahamas were clever. I think they watched as other surrounding countries were becoming independent and they were like, 'Why don't we figure out a way to control the place without violence?' But it ends up being more violent, actually. And so this rebellious spirit you're talking about with the letter 'E' is me, I think, trying to contend with that idea that we're being violated on a subconscious level. And there's no language for it yet, because it's invisible. The British, or the descendants of the British, controlled the shipping lines, all of the banks, the large industries, and they left the civil services to the ex-slaves, which is the illusion of power. So you have your prime minister, you control the fire station, the police station, the hospital, but the economic might was always going to be controlled by those folks. Even from a young age, I just found that odd.

We didn't have this big moment in the Bahamas. If you look through the history, you'll see that it was a very faint moment. Some guy threw a mace out of the window, et voilà, independent Bahamas. I was born in 1979, right around the independence period, so I'm a child of that moment. And I'm sure this is going to be very controversial to anyone Bahamian reading this, but I don't look fondly upon that moment. I think it influences my approach deeply.

ROBECCHI: *You don't look fondly on that moment because you don't feel it was enough?*

STRACHAN: I think there was a trick played. It was a smooth transition. There were no casualties, or very little, which is good. On the other hand, change didn't really happen. And if it did, it happened in a very subtle, nuanced way. That doesn't really serve the big cause. But I get on the surface where that attitude is coming from. Who desires violence? I'm not saying that it needs to be violent. But when it's been enacted on you for hundreds and hundreds of years, it's difficult. Shouldn't we be happy we were spared this violence? Absolutely, but perhaps an even greater form of violence is being enacted today. And again, this is my rationale for critical thinking. No matter what, an artist should be a critical thinker. In order to survive the future, the future human should be a critical thinker. For example, how are you going to determine a computer-generated image from an image generated by another source if you don't have the ability to think critically? And study. And a deep understanding of how things are made. You just can't.

And I think my misbehaving, if you will, had a lot to do with trying to find a language to contend with that. Even conducting this interview in England, I've noticed that there's also this thing about being a good boy. What does it mean to be a good boy? To follow the rules and to queue up? I just hate all of it. I think I'd rather be critical than good. This is Plato, right? This is Socrates. These philosophers are challenging the status quo and they're being deeply scrutinized for it. And I think that's at the core of creativity – being able to ask questions in a way that's inherently uncomfortable to what's going on around it.

ROBECCHI: *Your exhibition 'In Total Darkness' in Paris (2022) dealt with the subject of French colonialism in Haiti. Was it an attempt to address those concerns?*

STRACHAN: In a way. And, to me, this is even harder when we're talking about a context where there was no revolution. It's really hard to identify where you have to go and

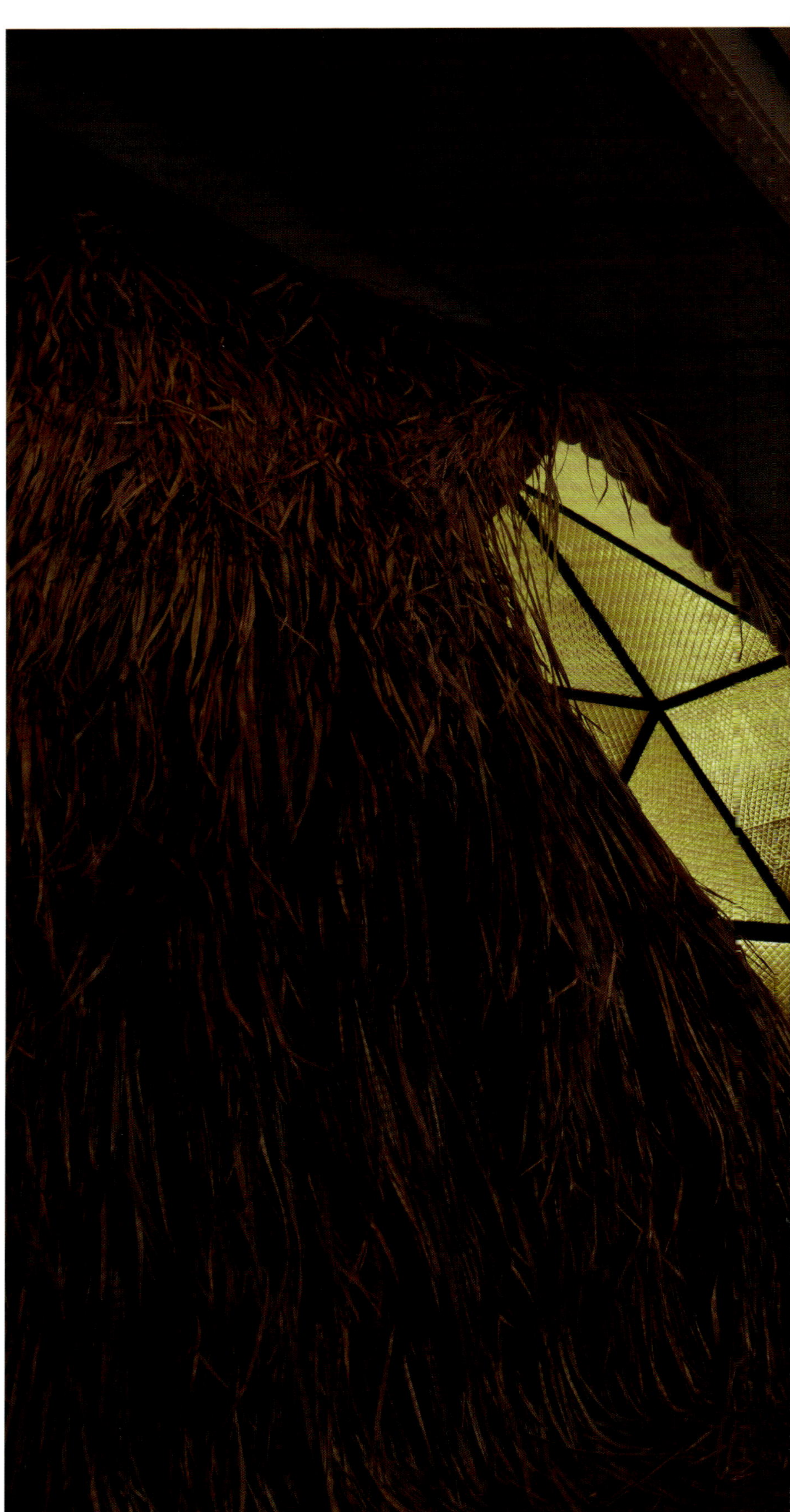

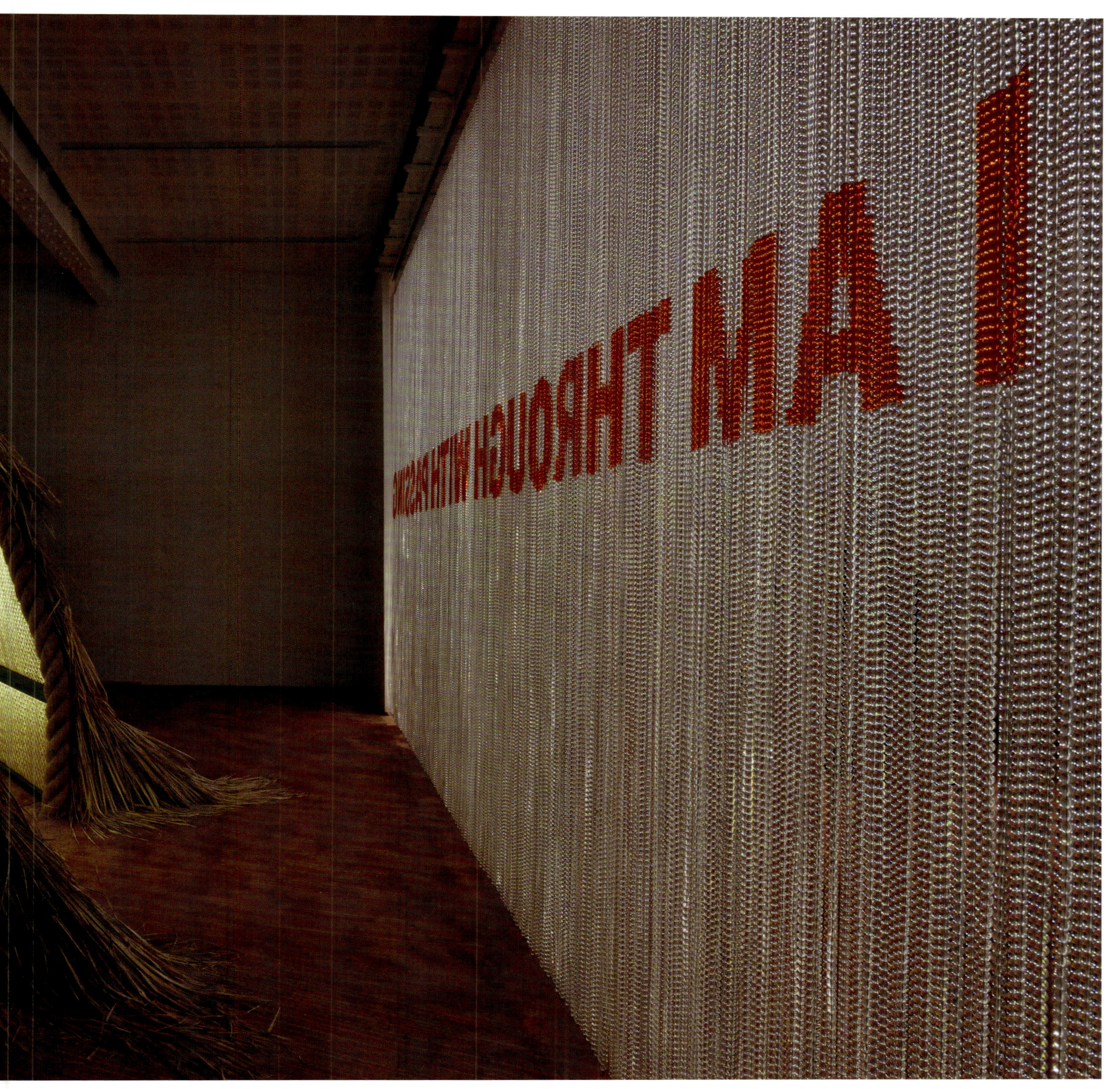
I AM THROUGH WITH

CORONATION HUT, 2022
THRONE, NEON SIGN, STRAW, METAL, FRAME, PLYWOOD SHEET, THATCH ROLLS, METALLIC POLYESTER FABRIC, POLYSTYRENE SHEETS, HESSIAN ROPE
500 X 310 CM

INSTALLATION VIEW AT MARIAN GOODMAN GALLERY, PARIS, 2022

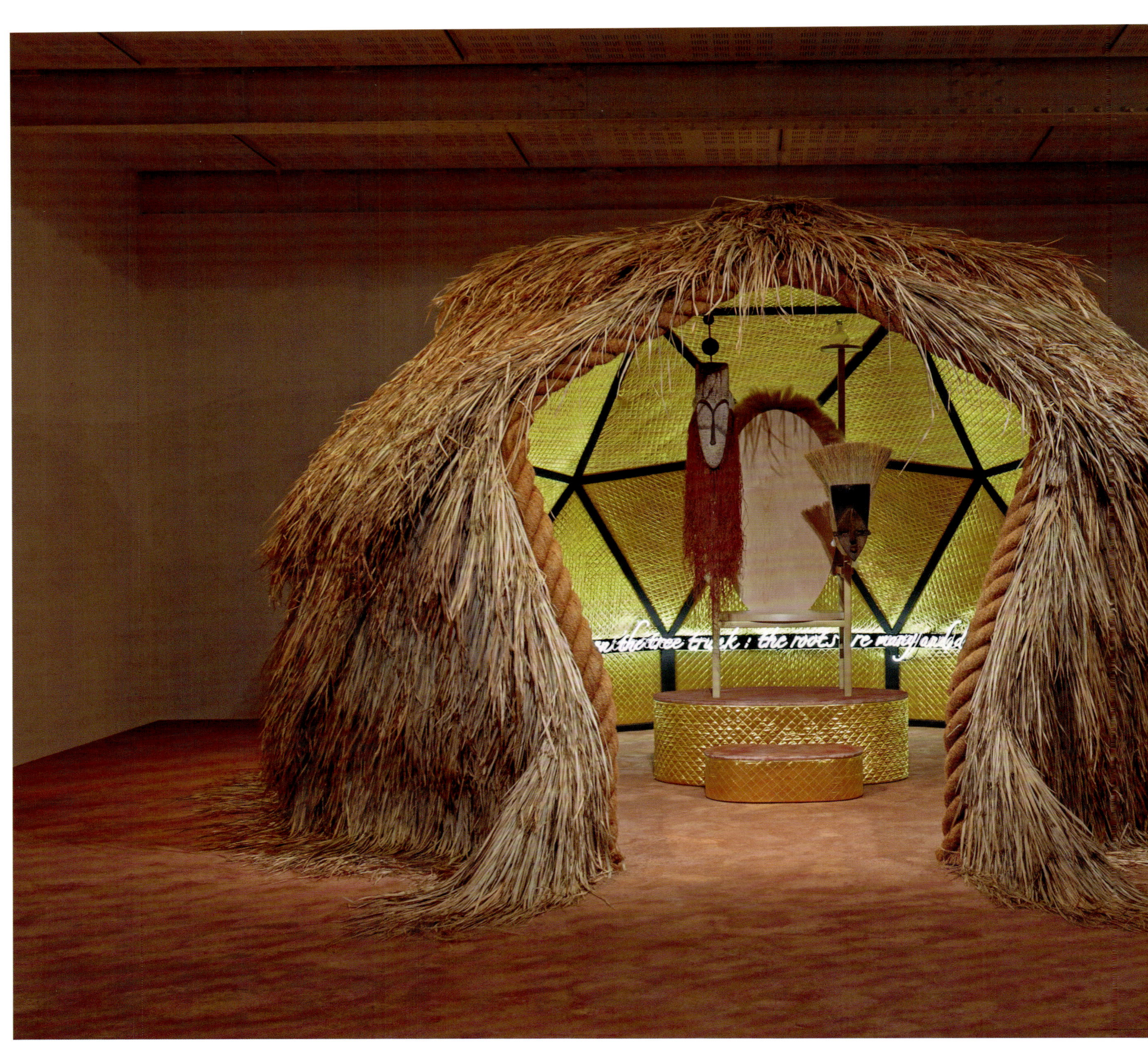

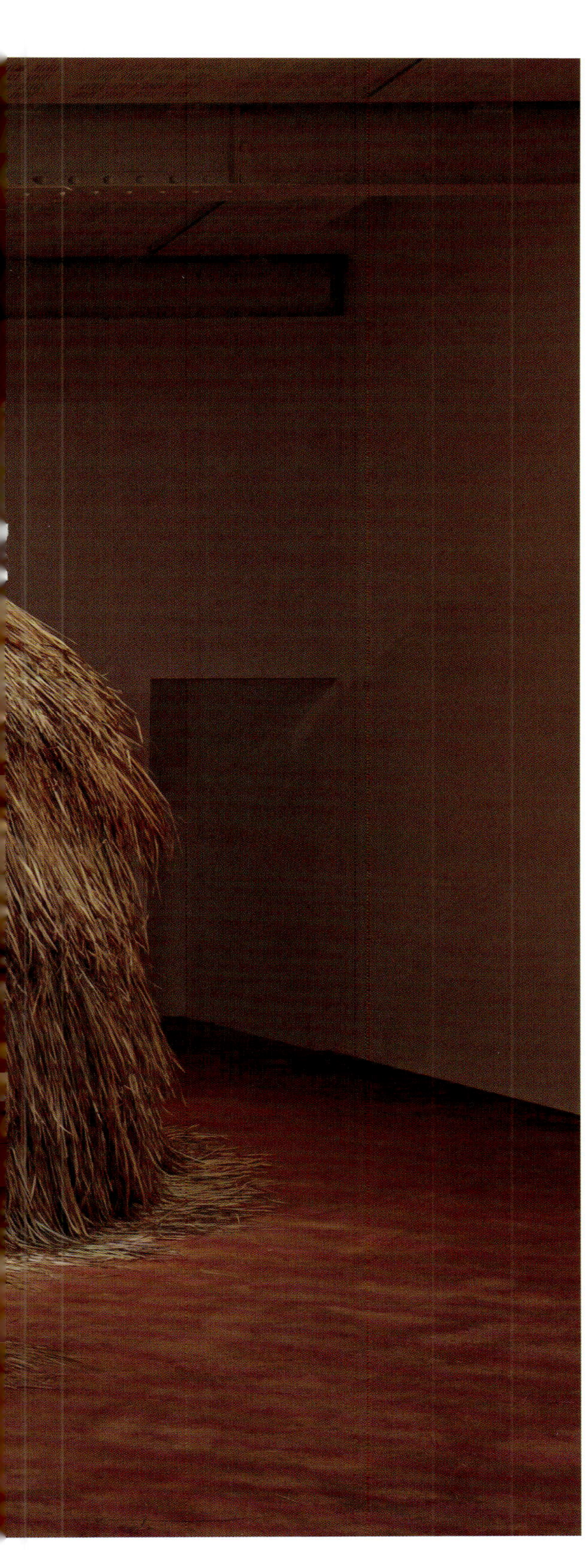

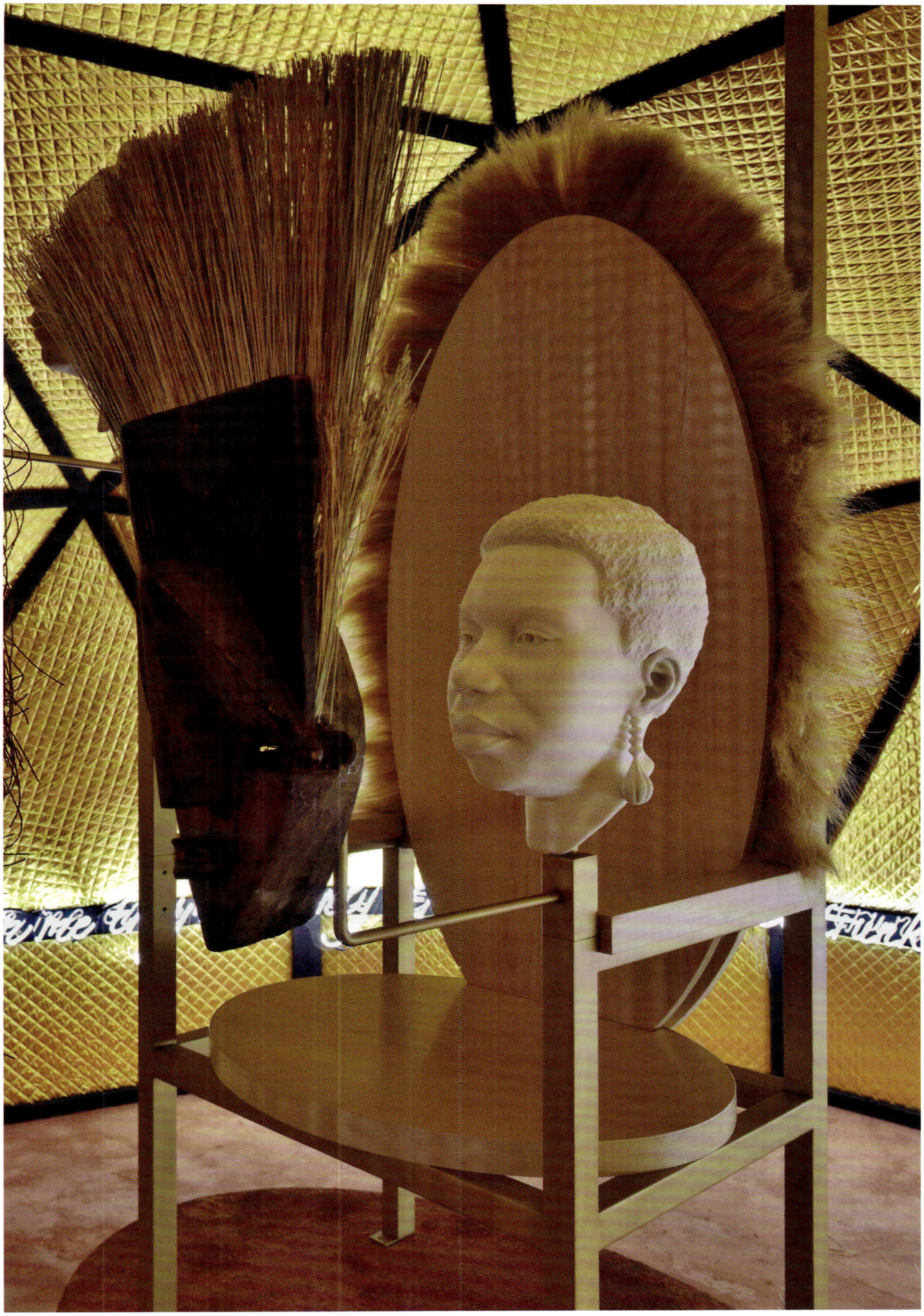

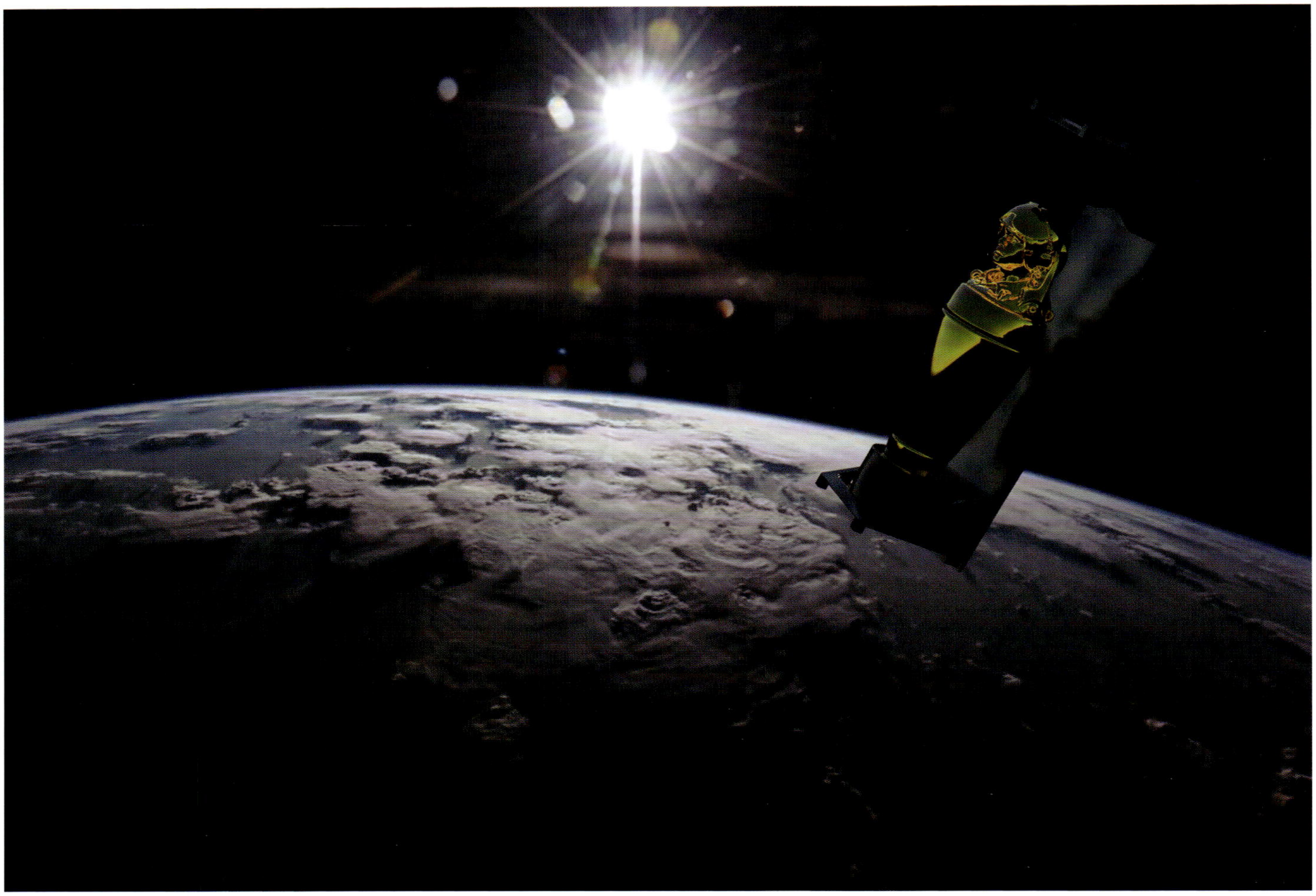

left and opposite,
ENOCH (DISPLAY UNIT),
2015–17
BRONZE, 24K GOLD, STEEL,
SACRED AIR BLESSED BY
SHINTO PRIEST
30 X 30 X 10 CM

change things. I think maybe the way of discussing this may be less threatening if we talked about it through the lens of adaptability and progression and evolution, as opposed to some other thing. Unfortunately, those processes, whether we want to accept it or not, inherently have violence to them. Evolution is a violent process. Adapting is painful. There's a very bad Steven Seagal film from many years ago called *Mark for Death* (1990), where there's a great line from a character called Scarface, this rasta-like bad guy, who says, 'Everybody wants to go to heaven, but nobody wants death.'

ROBECCHI: *You identified quite early on the Space Race as a place where power is implemented. I'm thinking about your experience in cosmonaut training at the Yuri A. Gagarin State Scientific Research-and-Testing Cosmonaut Training Center in Russia in 2006 or the 3U satellite* ENOCH *you launched in space in 2018 to celebrate the forgotten legacy of Robert Henry Lawrence Jr. – the first Afro-American astronaut selected for a national space program When you decided to join that sphere, were you adhering to the traditional sci-fi notion of conveying a message resonating with contemporary life by moving it to outer space, in a future dimension?*

STRACHAN: I think artists are the best indicators of the future, and I don't say that with any bias. I just know from looking at film, that all the films about now, from back then, do actually look like now. And so, if you see a depiction of the future made now, it's probably going to look like that. And I find that fascinating. There's a great deal of research – and by research I mean scientific research, I mean ethnographic research, I mean history, philosophical research – that goes into art making. And this is why I think artists are particularly charged with having this way of understanding the future. So for me, the thing is, the first real places of profound exploration, post 1400s, 1500s, were in these islands. These were the frontiers in a way. So it makes sense that the future of exploration also takes place in these places. Also, when people think about the Space Race, they disconnect, or would like to disconnect, this kind of daisy chain that links

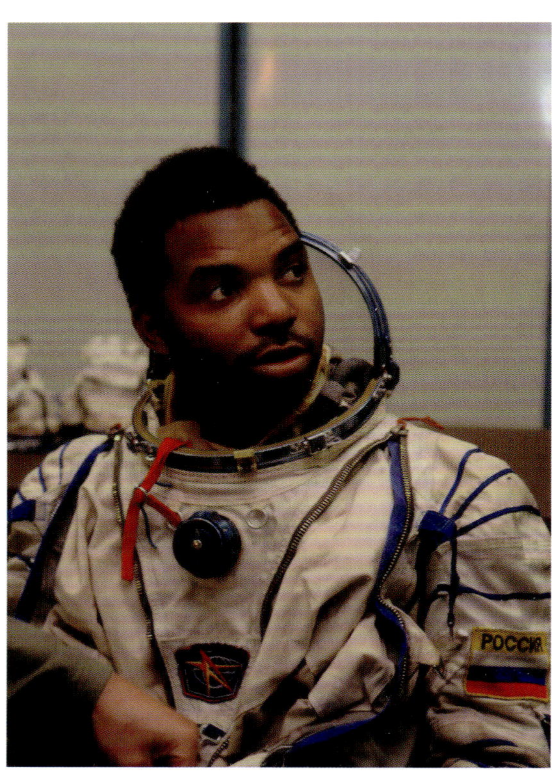

THE ARTIST TRAINING AT THE THE YURI A. GAGARIN RUSSIAN STATE SCIENCE RESEARCH COSMONAUT TRAINING CENTRE, STAR CITY, RUSSIA, 2009–2010. THE PROJECT WAS PART OF THE SERIES BASEC (BAHAMAS AIR AND SEA EXPLORATION CENTER)

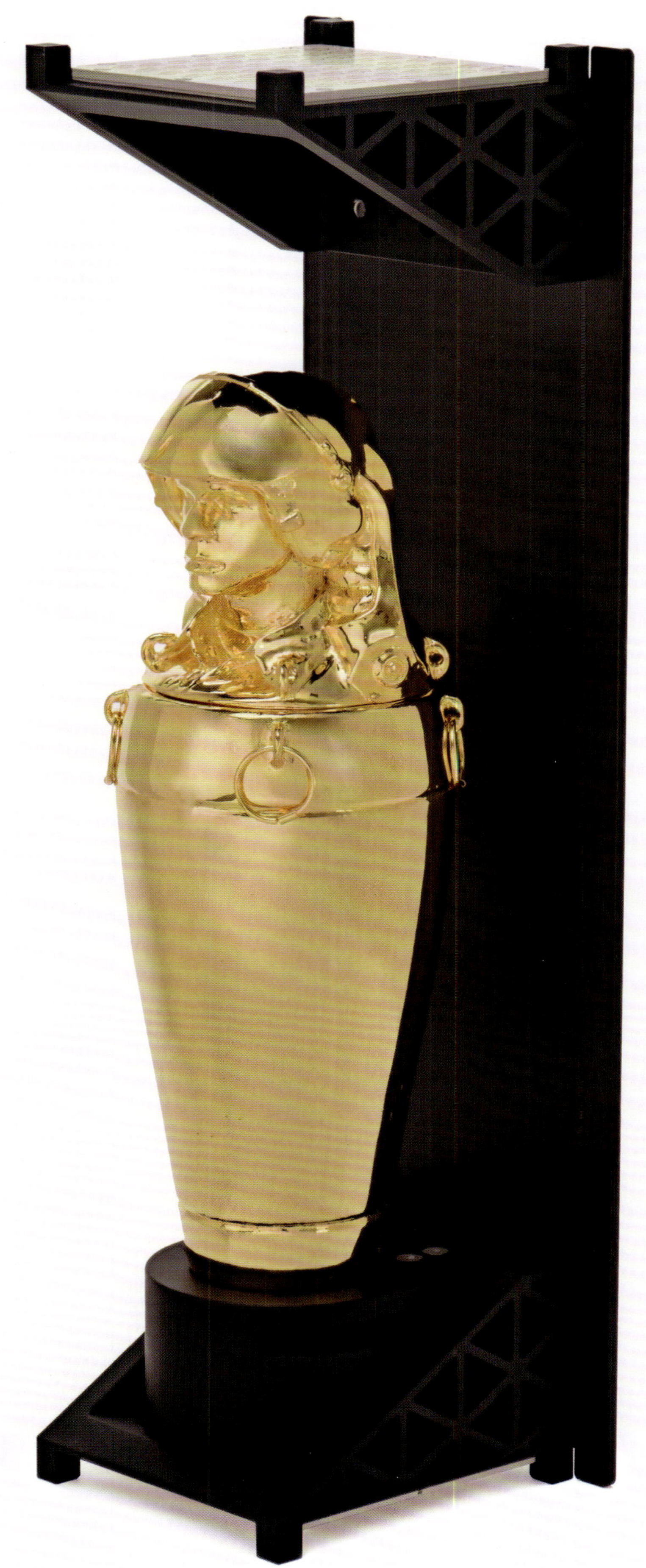

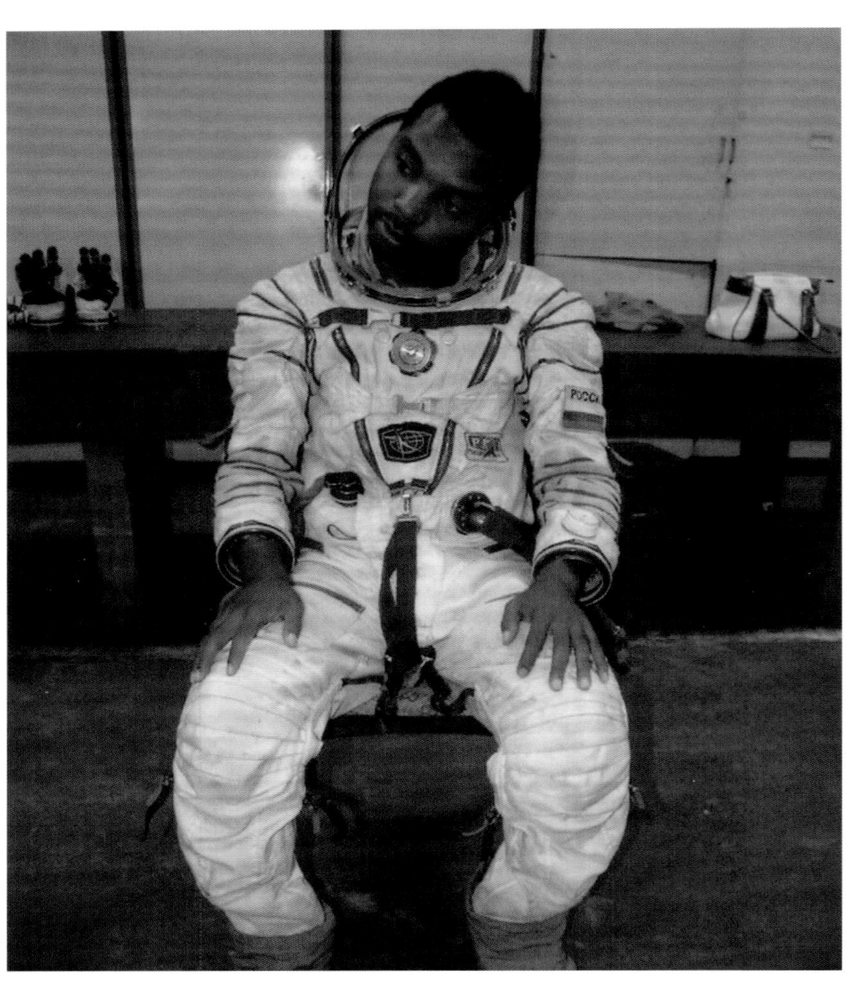

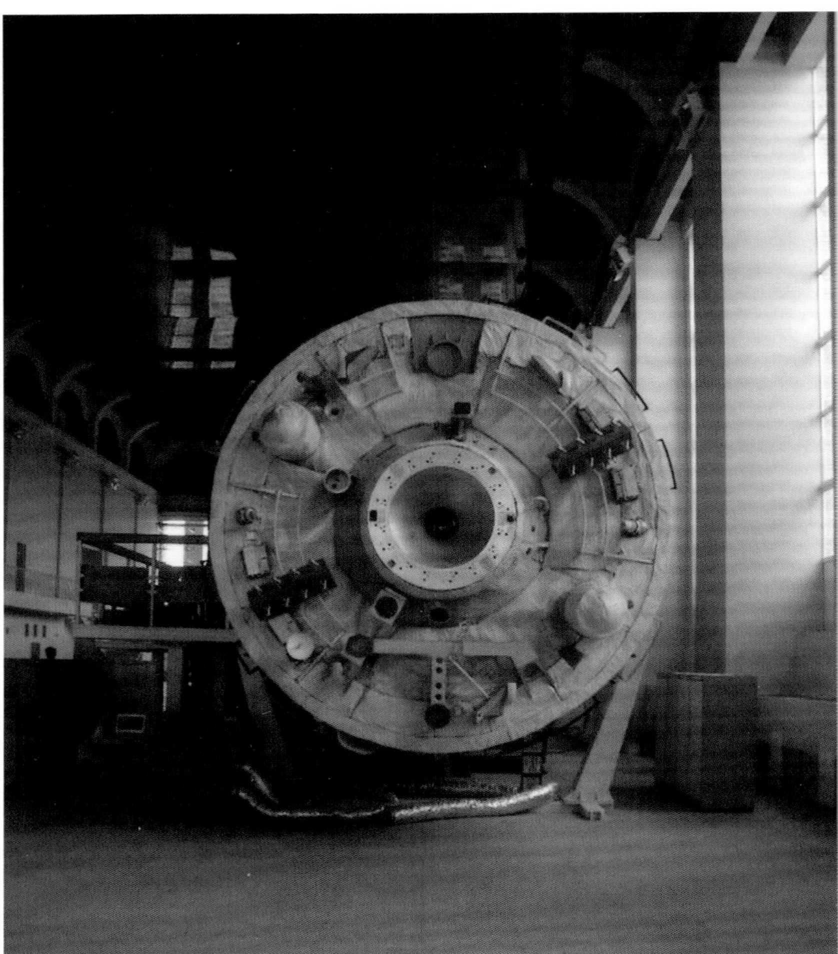

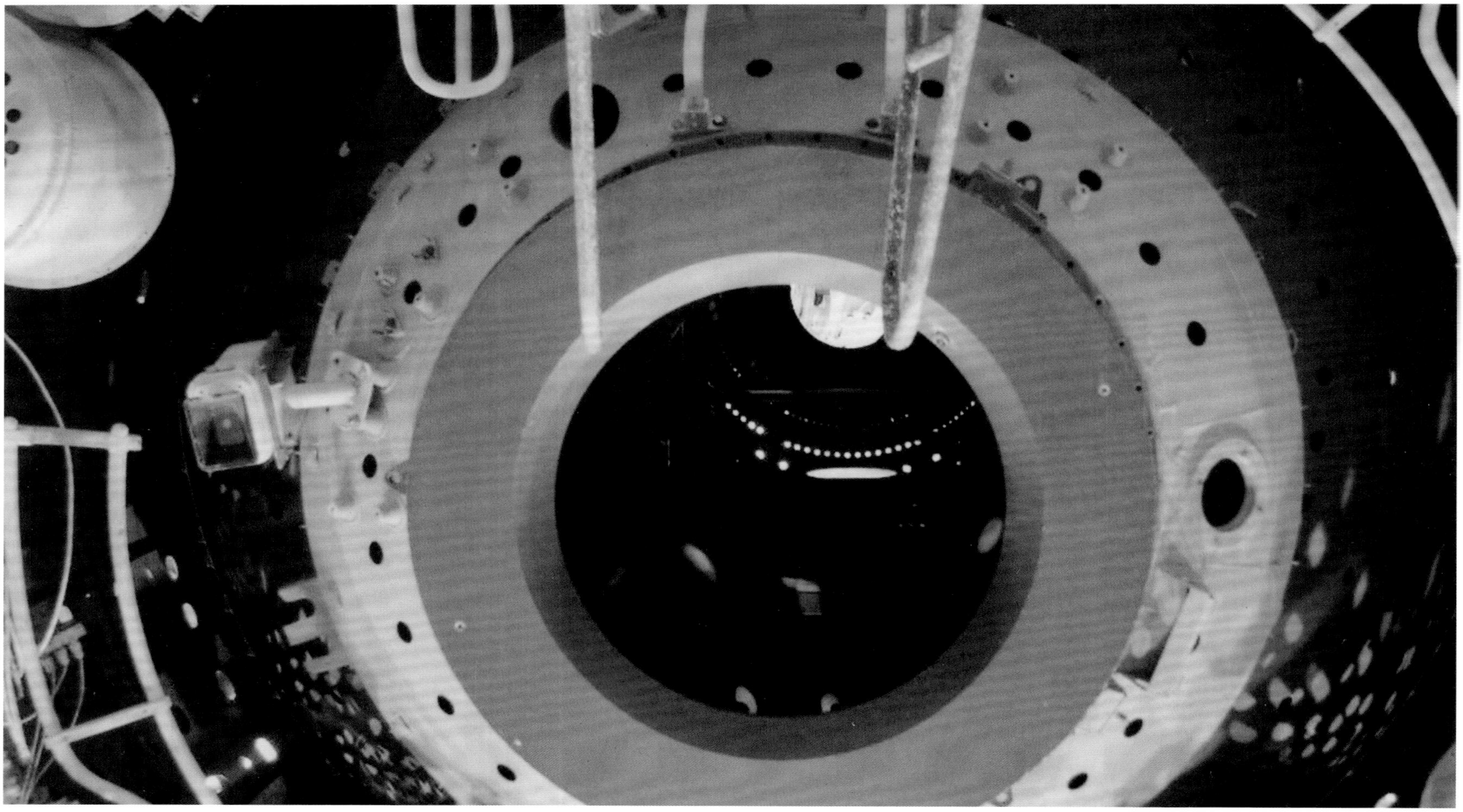

TRAINING IN 6 PARTS: NEUTRAL DIVE, 2009–10
SIX CHANNELS VIDEO
EACH 7 MIN

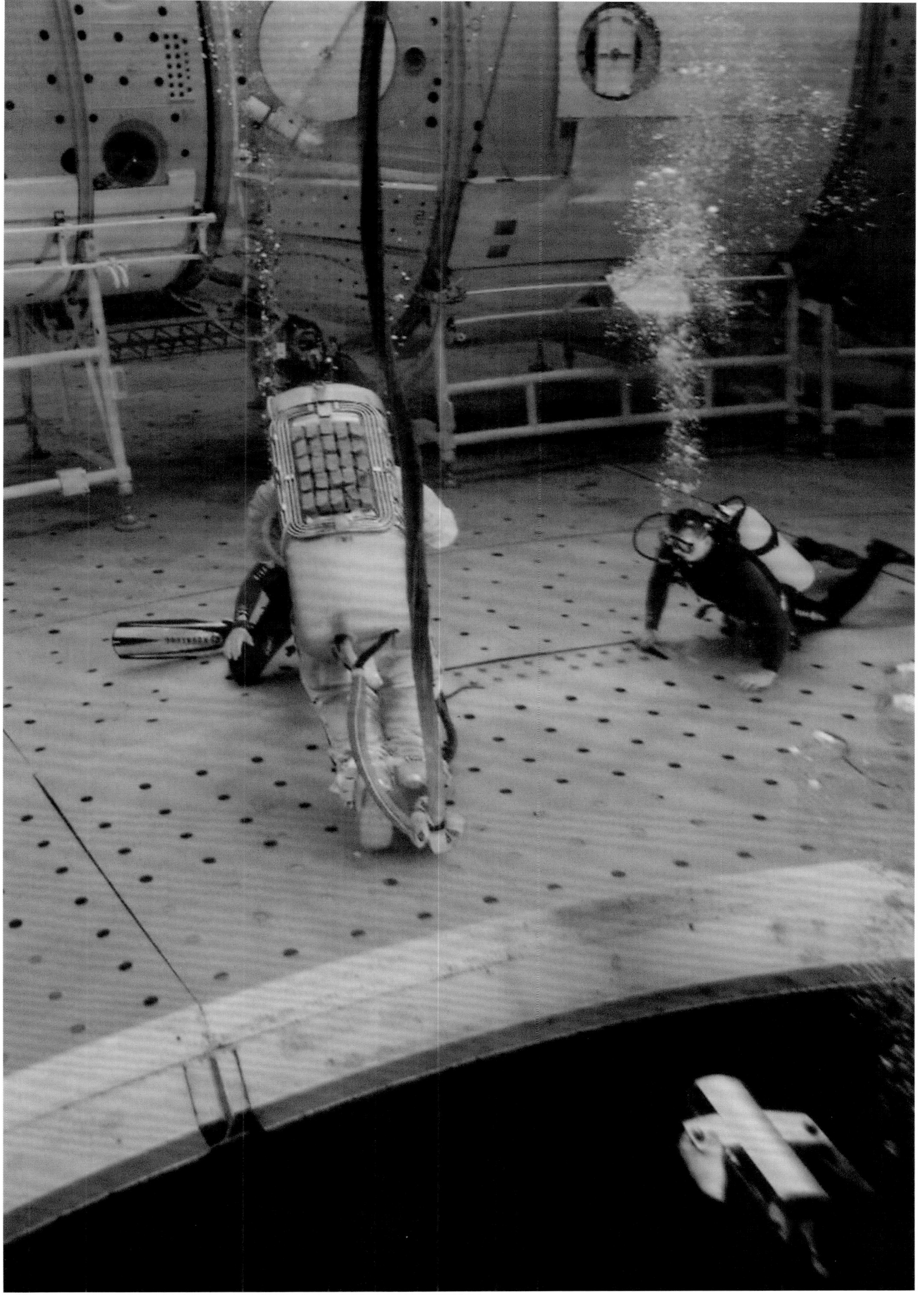

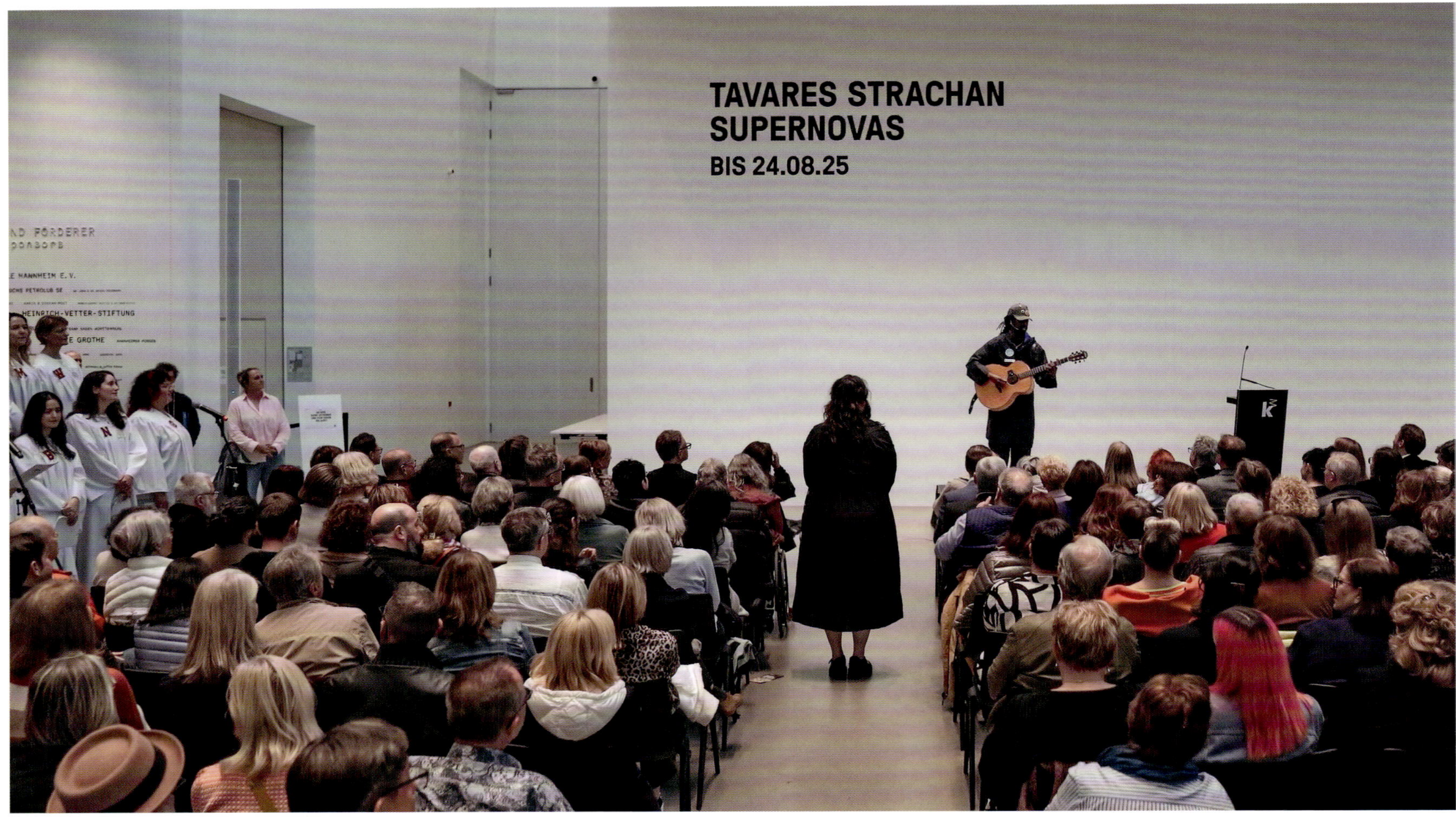

to the power system that's about military might, and using space as a kind of Trojan horse for being able to control and make money and proliferate, to be the most powerful. And it's difficult to talk about art without talking about power. It's difficult to talk about art. I mean, at its essence, even the word 'art' has all these connotations of aristocracy and bourgeois and the elites, etc, etc. That's why it makes sense to talk about space in relation to art, space in relation to exploration, but also exploitation and history and time and space. All those things are deeply reliant on each other. And the way that capital works is, it needs you to segregate things, because it makes shopping easier, and this is the same with the academy.

ROBECCHI: *Right. It's easy to consume if it's separate but it's much harder to consume a more layered piece.*

STRACHAN: Yes. To stay within the sci-fi metaphor, it's a bit like *The Matrix,* right? You don't want to know that you're not in the Matrix, or that you're in the Matrix. You just want to be. You just want to have that piece of steak, and you want to know it's real. In your mind, at least.

ROBECCHI: *There are two distinct trajectories in that film once we learn about the existence of the Matrix. Either you identify with Cypher's position, who cannot deal with this scenario and just wants to be, as you said, on the assumption that ignorance is bliss. Or you go with Neo, who is not afraid of asking all the questions in his quest for the truth regardless of the consequences. Do you remember a particular moment when you realized you were the guy who would take the red pill and not the blue pill?*

STRACHAN: I think it's in you, right? I was just rude from the jump. I was excited to ask the question. I'm still excited to ask the question. I remember I had this classmate

opposite,
RUNKUS PERFORMING AT THE OPENING OF TAVARES STRACHAN: SUPERNOVAS, KUNSTHALLE MANNHEIM, GERMANY, 2025

next pages, foreground,
ENCYCLOPEDIA ROOM: PANEL PAINTING, 2022
INK, PAINT, ACRYLIC MEDIUM, MIXED MEDIA, COLLAGE WORK ON SINTRA PANELS, LEATHER GILDING, ARCHIVAL PAPER, MAPLE, FELT, ACRYLIC
PANELS: EACH 28 X 21 X 5 CM
ENCYCLOPEDIA: 29 X 23 X 10 CM
BOOKSTAND: 76 X 73 X 44 CM

background,
LIVING ROOM, 2022
PERFORMANCE, HIDDEN INSTALLATION
DIMENSIONS VARIABLE

INSTALLATION VIEW AT MARIAN GOODMAN GALLERY, PARIS, 2022

who was making minimal blue paintings, blue squares. And he almost had an existential crisis, because one day he was like, 'I want to make a red one', but this amount of shift was deeply freaking him out. And you couldn't find someone who had the more opposite personality to me. For me, the journey of being an artist is about making trap doors, not traps. I think artists should build trap doors. You shouldn't build a thing that you can't escape from. The whole premise of why I became an artist was that I was sold this idea that you could do whatever you want to do: 'Go be an artist. You can do whatever you want', right? I think it's interesting that you're presented with that premise early on. If you compare it to everything else … you couldn't do whatever you want when you're a doctor, for instance. You have to do what you need to do for the patient to survive. You take an oath.

ROBECCHI: *But I don't think that being an artist is so clear an option to most people. The absence of a practical outlet makes it somehow inaccessible. Did you have a concept of what a contemporary artist was when you were a student?*

STRACHAN: Not at all. Not even remotely. I just had this idea of freedom. I had this idea that somehow being an artist was synonymous with being free. And there was something under the layer of my childhood experience that revealed to me that something was off in a way: it seems like one thing but it's the other. And I think I keep coming back to it because I feel like this is where the conceptual element of my thinking was kind of discovered. I started to understand that when you grow up in a country where everyone is Black but the majority of the people that control the power are not Black, it's weird. I'm not blaming any particular group currently. I'm just saying, if you do the math, that's just weird.

ROBECCHI: *It's not what it seems.*

STRACHAN: Right. And I think that simple idea of it's not what it seems is how I like to string works together that seem like they feel different but they're actually the same. They're actually very much about the same idea. And I find that interesting because the artists who I look up to are the ones who've been able to convince you that the thing that you're looking at isn't the same, when they're actually so the same.

ROBECCHI: *How does music fits into your practice?*

STRACHAN: There are different reasons. I think my appreciation for music has grown more fond over time. If you have an art event in the Caribbean, for example, the first thing people will ask you is if you have to pay. Right? And I think this barrier of entry is built into the psychology of looking at a painting in a space, in a gallery, a museum. I don't think music has that.

ROBECCHI: *Not at a grassroots level. Or at least, not outside the corporate world.*

STRACHAN: Right. And that's one of the beauties of how music gets to manifest itself into the world. There's this immediate breaking down of a barrier. And if you think of every major revolution, there's music. There's sound. Music is at the forefront of every major change that happens in culture. It's difficult to think about trying to infiltrate a system without sound.

ROBECCHI: *How does Runkus's performance on the opening night of your exhibition at the Kunsthalle Mannheim, for example, relate to the work?*

STRACHAN: The performance was in a way thought of as something that would allow the audience to loosen up and to be disarmed a little bit. Music is very disarming. I think a part of it is, every artist wants the audience to be closer to them in some way. I'm constantly working to bring the audience closer and to bring them into my head a little bit. And I think the reason why that's interesting is because when you grow up in a place where there's such a small population, it's very easy to feel like any new idea is a problem. And music helps to soften that. Because it's guttural. It's a part of the human story.

It's the person's voice being projected into space or them making direct sound and that sound is being projected into space. It's sincere.

ROBECCHI: *Live music has an entertainment element attached to it that you can't discount. Aren't you concerned that by offering that kind of distraction, the audience might misread your intentions and end up exoticizing the experience of your art?*

STRACHAN: I think I worry about it just as much as with sculpture.

ROBECCHI: *Yes, but the experience of one of your sculptures is openly filtered through a conceptual lens. There's a tangible twist to pre-existing models that gets recognized and needs to be dealt with. The music performance, conversely, transcends that. It can actually come across as a straight-up music performance.*

STRACHAN: Maybe. But if you think about the big dialogue around figuration, most people would assume that they understand what figuration is and the function of figuration. And I think if you understand the history of dub music or reggae music or samba or merengue, embedded in that music there are all these layers of the story of the people. Yes, it's a gig but it's also abstraction. Take the history of punk music in the UK. It comes from dub. There's no punk without King Tubby. We have to be mindful that when we're interacting with something that seems like one thing, it might be the other thing. And you may be getting the story of, for example, how within the Caribbean people from different countries don't collaborate with each other well. So I'm in Mannheim in Germany with this kid from Jamaica and he's putting on a show. I think that's highly unusual. And you feel like the geographical distance somehow bridges those divisions because if you're in the Caribbean it's one thing, but if you and a Jamaican dude are in Germany, that somehow revises your relationship.

ROBECCHI: *It's about breaking down barriers.*

STRACHAN: Yes. I don't want to have that barrier. You've seen some of the performances that I've constructed. Obviously that language exists. I have that language. But I also think that it's important to have this other language – that's is like, this is a guy on stage singing.

ROBECCHI: *I guess my question is more about the danger of the message getting diluted or misinterpreted when positioned within a specific context. The Blues started in the 1920s as a beautiful cry from the South about what you don't have in life. Now it's mostly music for middle-aged white men. You wrote* We will come for you, we will hunt for you *during your first trip to the African continent – a pivotal moment in your life. How can you make sure that Runkus and a gospel choir singing those powerful lyrics prior to the opening of your exhibition doesn't turn into just a party?*

STRACHAN: But isn't the same true for Duchamp? The Philadelphia Museum has the bicycle wheel and it's worth 20 million dollars.

ROBECCHI: *It's not the actual wheel. It's a reconstruction.*

STRACHAN: But did he make that work for it to become this? Quite the opposite, right? That's exactly it. I think it's very problematic to see the wheel. The question I have for you is, how do you stop the machine from eating everything? Because this artist clearly articulates that this work is actually about the opposite.

ROBECCHI: *I guess it could happen through another cardinal element of your work – the concept of absence. Would absence be an effective strategy to avoid being eaten by the machine?*

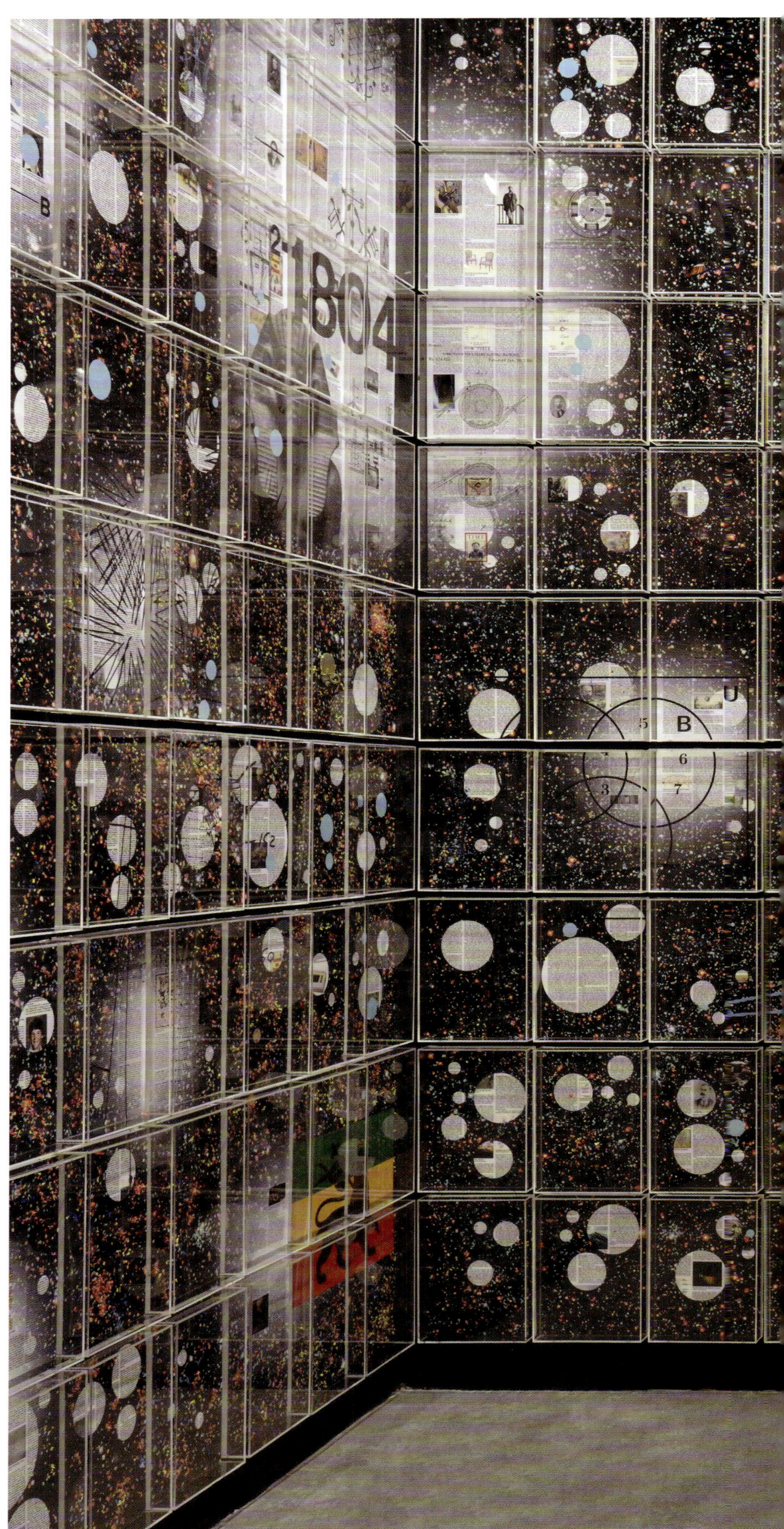

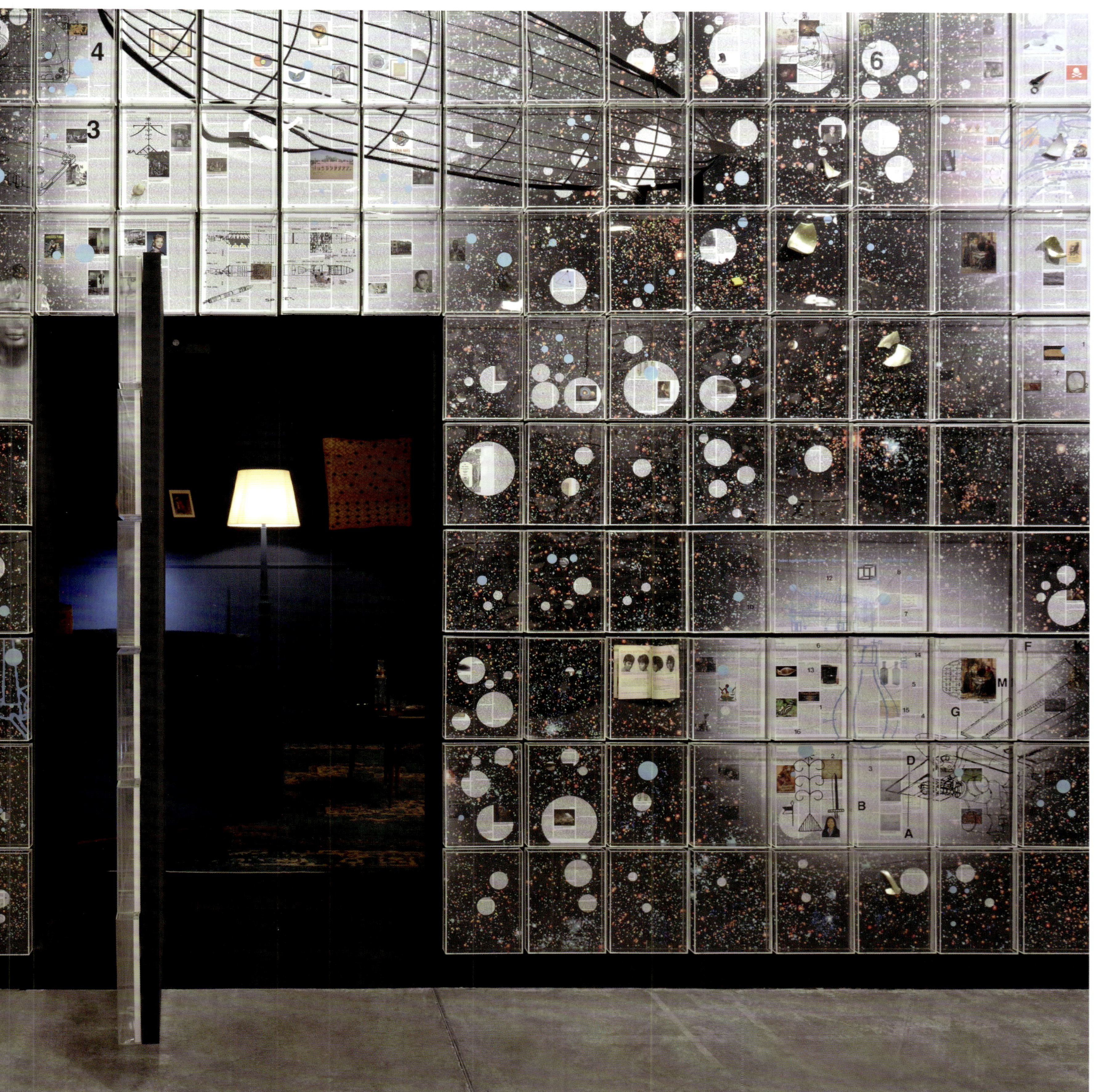

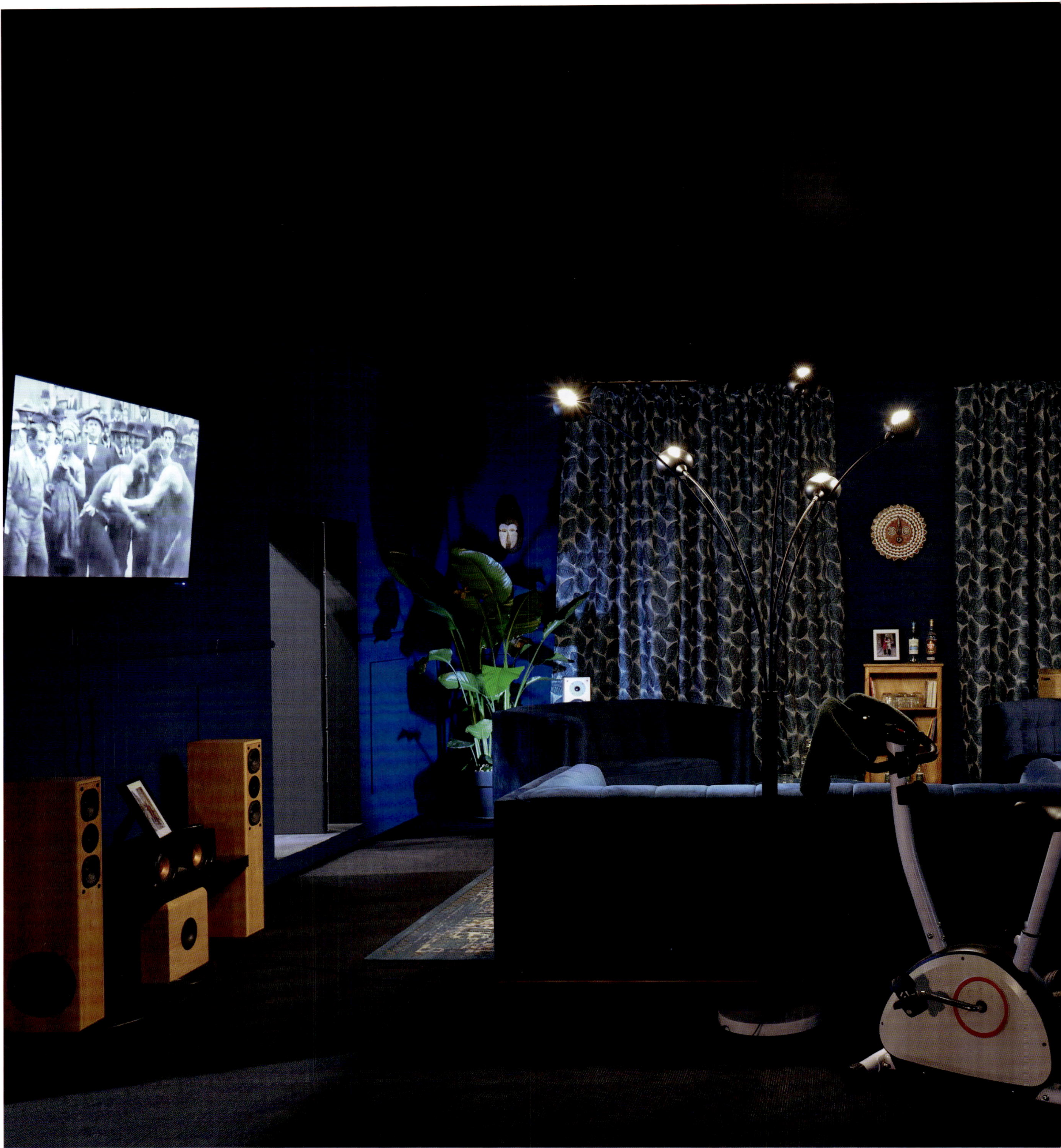

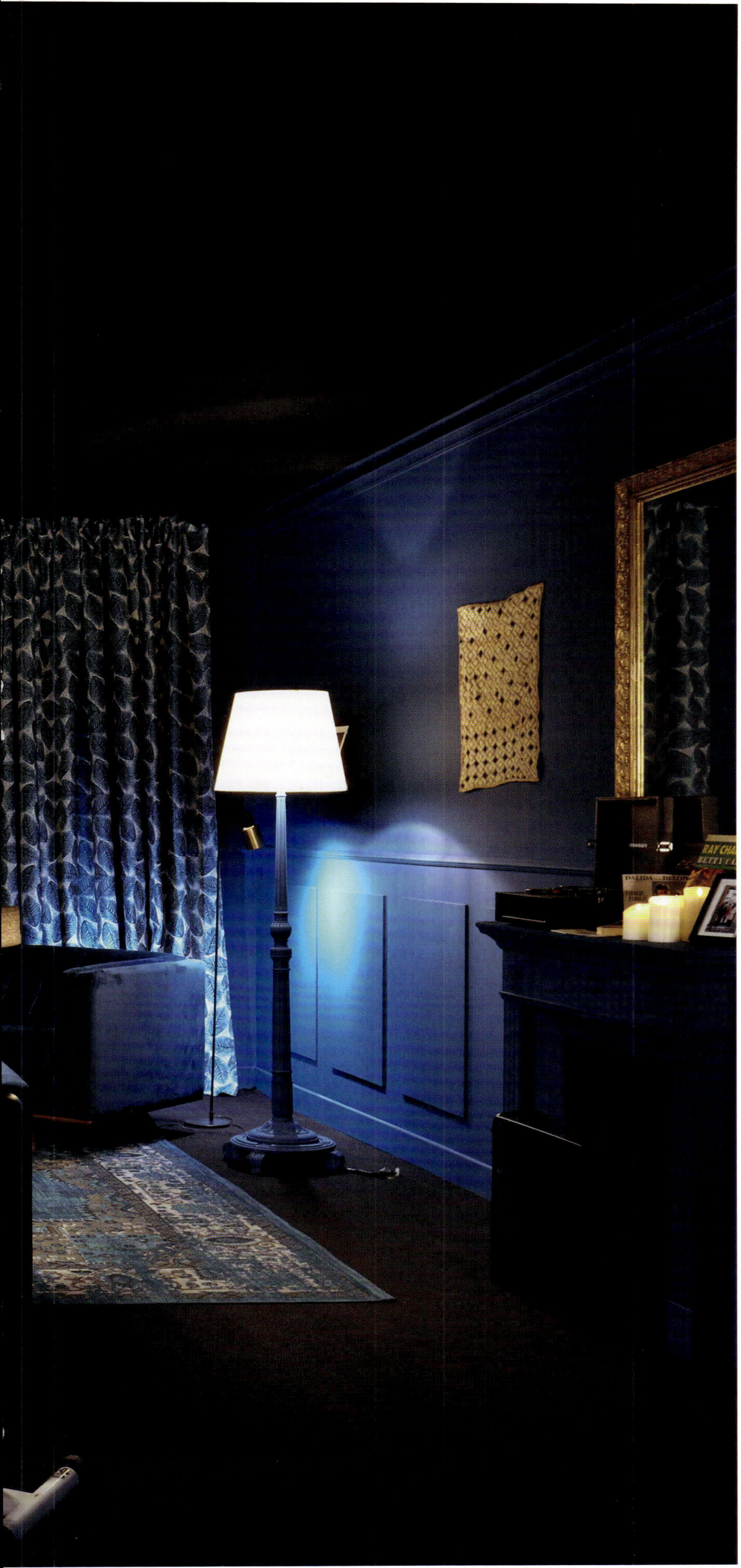

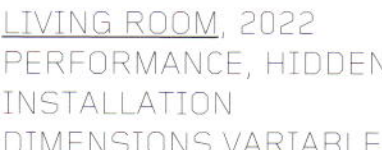

LIVING ROOM, 2022
PERFORMANCE, HIDDEN
INSTALLATION
DIMENSIONS VARIABLE

INSTALLATION VIEW AT MARIAN
GOODMAN GALLERY, PARIS, 2022

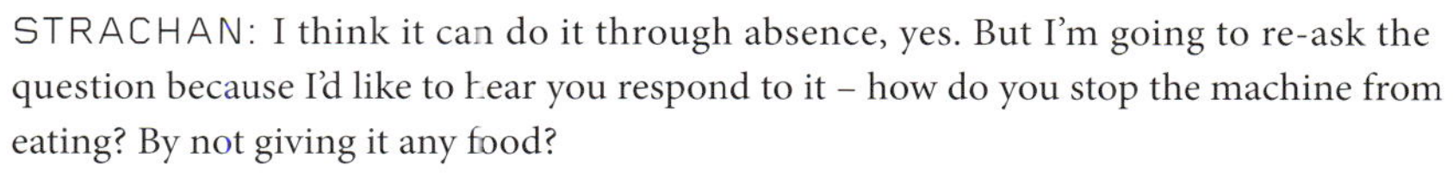

STRACHAN: I think it can do it through absence, yes. But I'm going to re-ask the question because I'd like to hear you respond to it – how do you stop the machine from eating? By not giving it any food?

ROBECCHI: *Possibly. I think Duchamp was successful in trying not to give the machine any food until people like Arturo Schwarz came along later and converted what Duchamp did – with Duchamp's permission, I agree – into food for the machine.*

STRACHAN: Right. And I think the reason why I'm rehashing this is because I think the machine will want to eat absence also. It will find a way to eat absence. It'll say, 'Hmm, absence is trending.' I mean, could a street vendor win a Michelin star? There's a guy in Mexico City right now making bomb tacos on the side of the street probably better than any big chef anywhere in the world. You eat it. It makes you cry. But if you want to fight that, shouldn't you question the Michelin star instead of what I'm doing? The question I'm asking is, how are we creating value? Who's creating value? Who's deciding to create value? And who's deciding that a dancehall show, a traditional straight-up reggae show shouldn't be right next to a conceptual art exhibition? Who's making that rule? I think the onus is on us to imbue a spirit of dialogue and criticism and conversation around how we're organizing hierarchy in our heads. And I think this is why I asked the Michelin star question. Does it need a Michelin star to be the best, the most delicious thing? I mean the thing about food is, it has to taste good. Right? And I think that's true about any other art form. It has to somehow talk to you on a visceral level. It has to say something to you. You have to taste it and you have to be like, 'No words necessary. I ate it and I want more of that.' So that's the way I think about it. I think categories are a distraction. I once had a visiting critic come in when I was at Yale and he said to me that I couldn't put a photo next to a sculpture.

ROBECCHI: *What?! Why?*

STRACHAN: Because I'm not a photographer and only real photographers take real photos. That's a scary piece of advice to give to an art student. I make clothes, right? I think making clothes as a contemporary visual artist is a dangerous thing to do. It's incredibly risky. Yet everyone I know wears clothes. Why is it so? Why is that a problem for some people who represent or occupy a certain place in culture? Especially in the art world. Why would that be threatening?

ROBECCHI: *Perhaps it's because they fear that you're slipping into museum-shop logic – mugs, calendars, watches and t-shirts, which they feel somehow diminish the impact of the original art.*

STRACHAN: Right. But isn't that so? Or is it a conceptual project?

ROBECCHI: *Doesn't that depend on how you present it?*

STRACHAN: On how you frame it. Right. But going back again to the Michelin-star analogy – is the guy on the side of the street a Michelin-star chef? Could he be rated on that level? I think the reason why I go back there in relation to the museum-shop logic is, I think that's one approach – that's one way to read it. It's just like, pre-1960, a Jack Whitten painting wasn't considered art. Because at the time Black artists just weren't artists. That was the popular view. It's not just what the artist is doing – it's the framework. The same painting that wasn't a painting in 1960 is now in a retrospective at the MoMA. Why is it a painting now? Why is all of a sudden the street chef on the street corner of Mexico City a Michelin-star chef? What happened?

LIVING ROOM, 2022
PERFORMANCE, HIDDEN INSTALLATION
DIMENSIONS VARIABLE

INSTALLATION VIEW AT MARIAN GOODMAN GALLERY, PARIS, 2022

ROBECCHI: *What happened isn't pretty. I feel that although there's an initial consciousness, there's an initial recognition of value and that's a good thing, once it goes through the machine, as you said, it begins to be perceived as a trend, and the question becomes how long is this going to last?*

STRACHAN: Right. Sometimes the thing that needs to change isn't the practitioner – 99% of the time it's the cultural condition. Going back to the question 'Could a contemporary visual artist be involved in music and apparel making and graphic design and filmmaking?' You know, there are loads of examples of that happening. So maybe it's the framework. I mean, I think if I was born in the Renaissance, I'd be called a Renaissance man, no?

ROBECCHI: *Do you see this deliberate attempt to challenge the cultural context in which you operate as an inherent part of your work?*

STRACHAN: I don't think so. I learn all these different languages and I like to speak them. I learned the language of food from my grandmother and I worked on my craft like any other person who likes food. I cook regularly. I try new things. I take classes. I try to eat at interesting places to inspire my palate. Am I trying to make some comment about the context of being a contemporary visual artist? I think that viewpoint is perhaps a part of the problem of narcissism that exists within the framework of contemporary visual art as the centre of creativity. This goes back again to the question of academia. It's like, well that's one way to look at it. When I go home to do the Junkanoo, I'm not thinking about being a contemporary visual artist at all – not for one millisecond. It's important for us as practitioners to help the culture reimagine what it means to practise critical thinking across all languages, because if we're talking about the future, I'm very concerned about our inability to think critically about the layers of existence that we're faced with today: the layers of meaning, the overlapping of media, how things are produced, why things are produced a certain way. It's so easy to misunderstand artistic creative production. I guess that's why we're having this conversation.

ROBECCHI: *Food is another facet of your practice. How did a project like the dinner you've co-organized at the Christ Church Spitalfields in London come about?*

STRACHAN: What happened was, the curator Beth Greenacre reached out to me and asked me if I'd do something. And I thought, I've been cooking a lot lately. I cooked in New York for forty-five people. And it became this layer to my practice that I wasn't even aware of. We basically had thirteen courses broken into four. It was a taste of all these flavours that I grew up with. Guests were welcome to put together the whole pudding part themselves. I spent two days in the kitchen just cooking. I really love to eat, but I think the way that Caribbean people eat is a weird combination of the story of the slave trade and the influence of the slave trade on the diet, portion size, quality of ingredients, or lack thereof. And we weren't eating the best ingredients. This survival became a part of the culinary story. Cut to 500 years later – what do we think of this? Do we like it? Do we not like it? Do we want to tweak it? Can we modify it? Can we reimagine it? The dinner was my interpretation of what it would be like if we had the best quality ingredients, as opposed to pig intestines and all the other things that allowed slaves to survive. But the culinary is always a journey. It's never steady. It evolves all the time.

ROBECCHI: *Totally. Some of the world's most celebrated cuisine's foundational elements actually come from other places or cultures.*

STRACHAN: Exactly. It's one of the most contaminated forms of expression that I know. It's interesting. Society is a very dug in on the dogma of how they understand their culinary tradition. They're like, 'This is ours, that's not yours.' And this is true particularly in the Caribbean. Why? Because our histories are so recent in terms of one's relationship to your DNA and geography. In the Caribbean, people are striving for something. They want to latch on to some identity. It's almost like the early days of modernism: you're a painter, you're a sculptor, you're a graphic designer, you're a filmmaker. It goes back

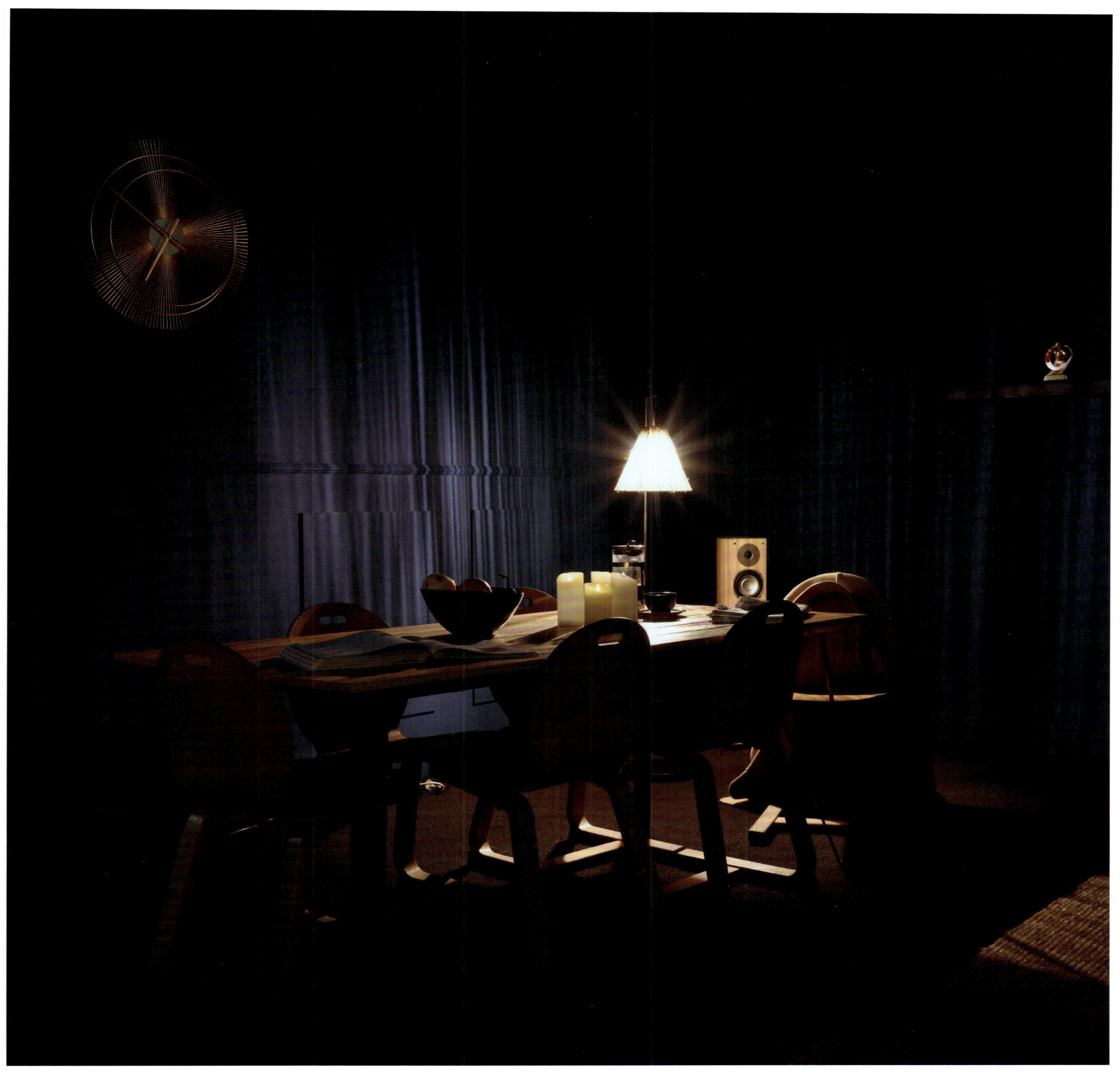

right and opposite,
THE LAST SUPPER (A FAREWELL TO THE FLAVOURS WE MIGHT LOSE), 2025
SUPPER DEVISED AND CURATED BY THE ARTIST

THE CRYPT, CHRISTCHURCH SPITALFIELDS, LONDON, 5 JUNE 2025

next pages,
THE WASH HOUSE, 2025
PERFORMANCE, INSTALLATION
DIMENSIONS VARIABLE

THE WASH HOUSE (LARGE), 2025
NEON
50 X 425 CM

THE WASH HOUSE (SMALL), 2025
NEON
17 X 137 CM

SOME LOADS ARE TOO HEAVY TO CARRY ALONE, 2025
NEON
38 X 337 CM

INSTALLATION VIEW AT THE LOS ANGELES COUNTY MUSEUM OF ART, 2025

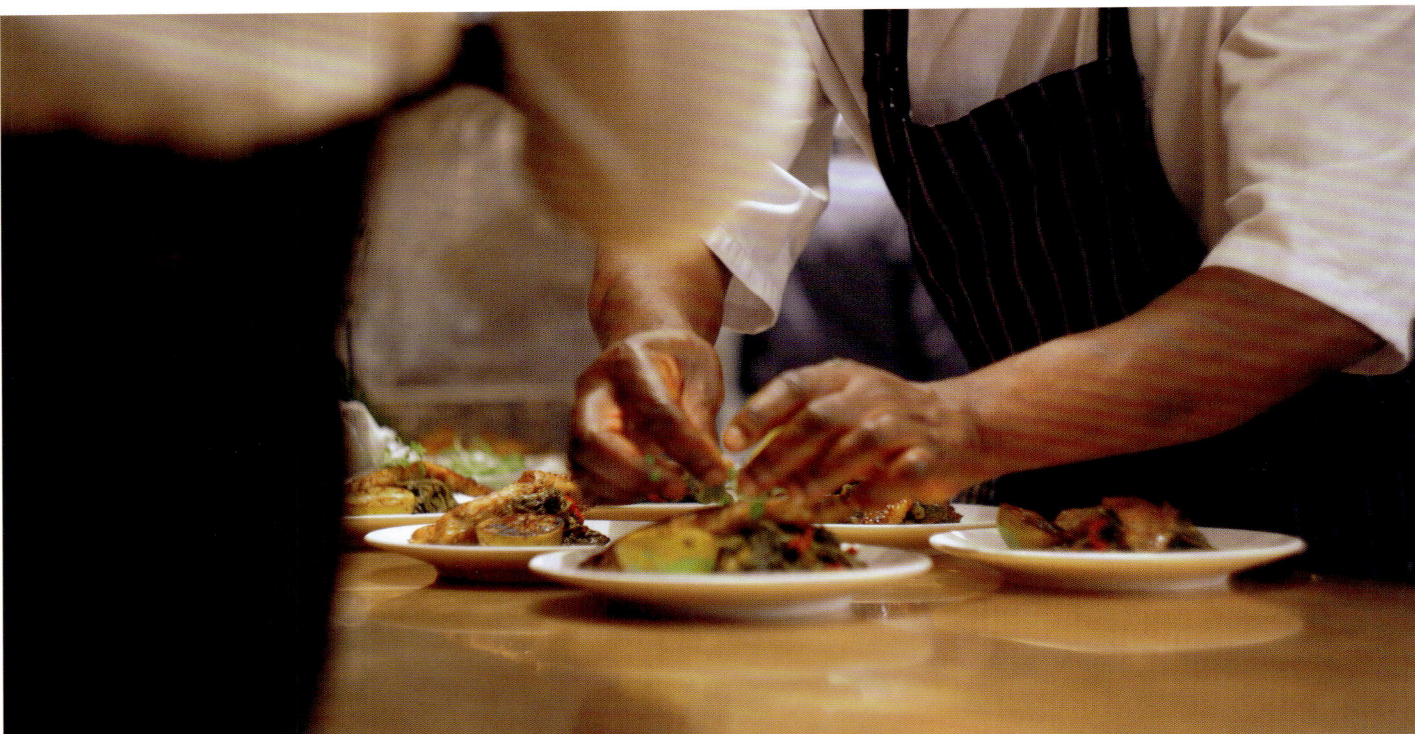

to the dialogue we were having about music. You're attached to these traditions that are, on the one hand, as old as time, and on the other hand, as recent as 100 years ago. So why are we not more flexible about these things? Why is the language not adapting and evolving?

Anyway, I find all these stories about how we've come from what we were to now inherently fascinating. With food, you surpass knowledge in a very personal way. I'm very fond of my grandmother's recipes now.

ROBECCHI: *Grandmother's recipes are the best!*

STRACHAN: Yeah! Actually, I have a story. And in a way, I realize, going into this conversation with you, how much my grandparents influenced everything that I've done and the way that I think about making. I just remember this one holiday. My grandmother and I didn't really share recipes as much as we should. Because most people, I think, were in the mood of survival. Grandma was just trying to feed the family – she didn't have time to sit down and explain to you how to make the thing. She's just like, I have ten other things to do. So how do I have time to articulate how to make this? Anyway, I go home. We're in the kitchen. And I'm like, 'Hey, I need you to show me how to make this pie.' And I'm not as meticulous as she is at making it. So I'm being scolded continually. And I'm constantly doing the wrong thing. And I realize, she's actually furious at me. She's like, 'You don't do it like that. You do it like this.' She wasn't critical. She was more technical. It was just like, 'You have to beat the eggs this way because you want to add air to the eggs. That's the whole point of beating them. If you don't beat them this way, you're not adding air. And the pie won't lift.' And she was just a stickler for it. You know there's a little eye in the egg? She wants you to take that out. I never took that out. But when I was with her, she was like, 'You better take that out.' And there were all these nuances to that exchange that made me realize she was a very technical cook. And she taught my mom how to sew. And so all the clothing things that I do come from that line also, because I grew up around making clothes since I was a kid. I think I told you this already: my mother made my brother and me our first tuxedos when we were three and four. So we grew up around a lot of making.

ROBECCHI: *I can see why your grandmother is so technical and specific about her cooking. She wants you to learn properly because she's aware that she's passing on something to you.*

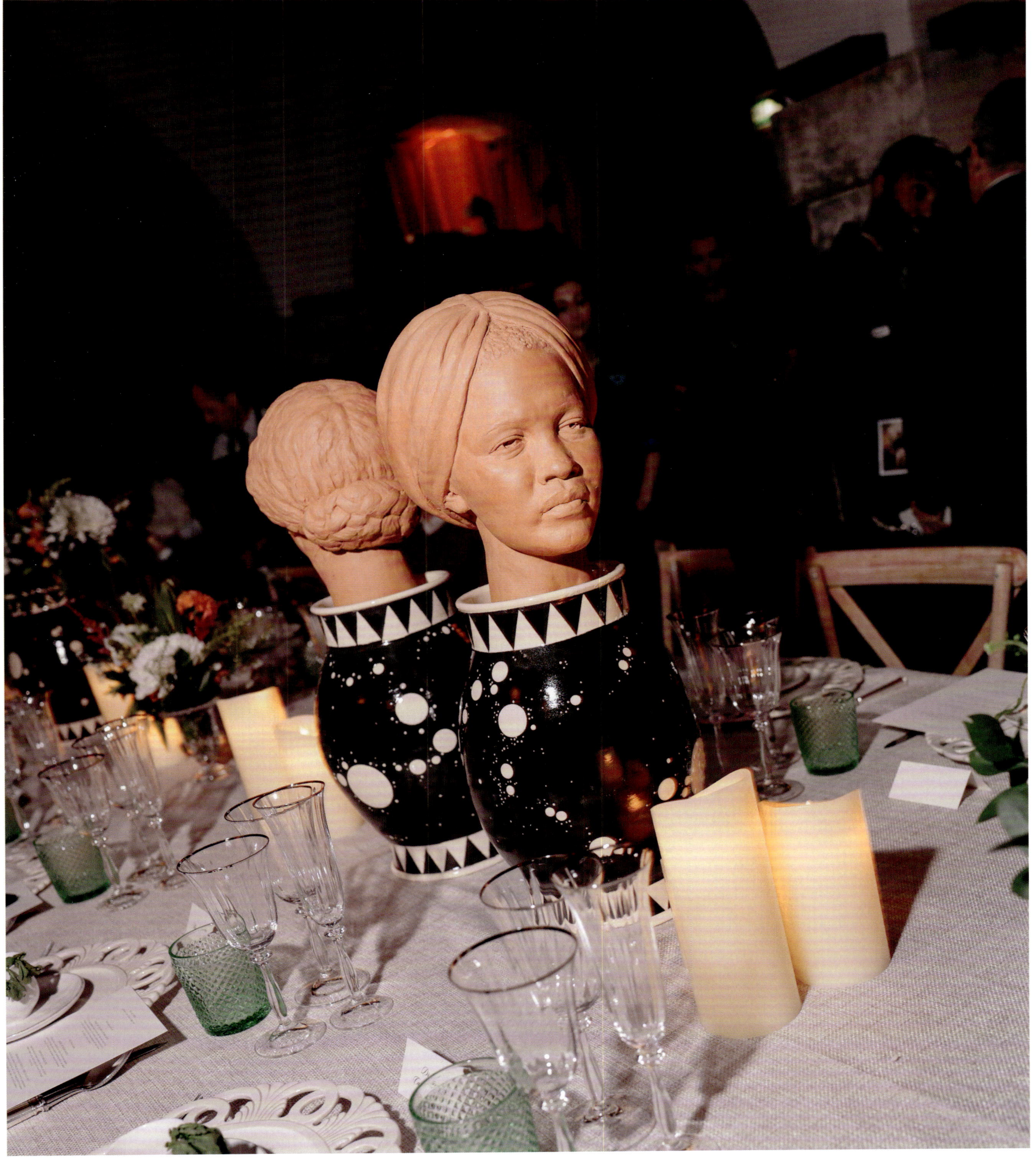

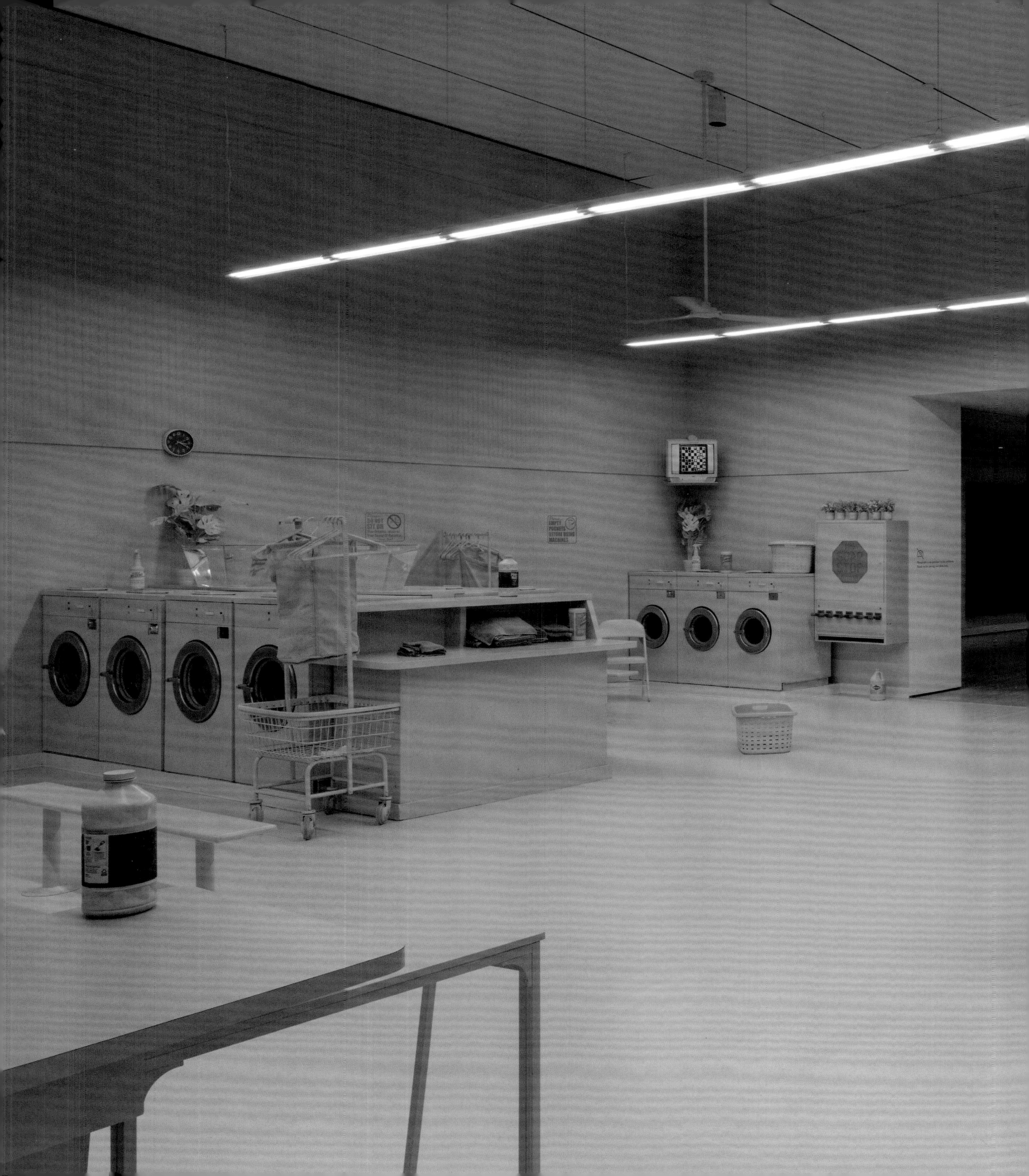
EMPTY
POCKETS
BEFORE USING
MACHINES

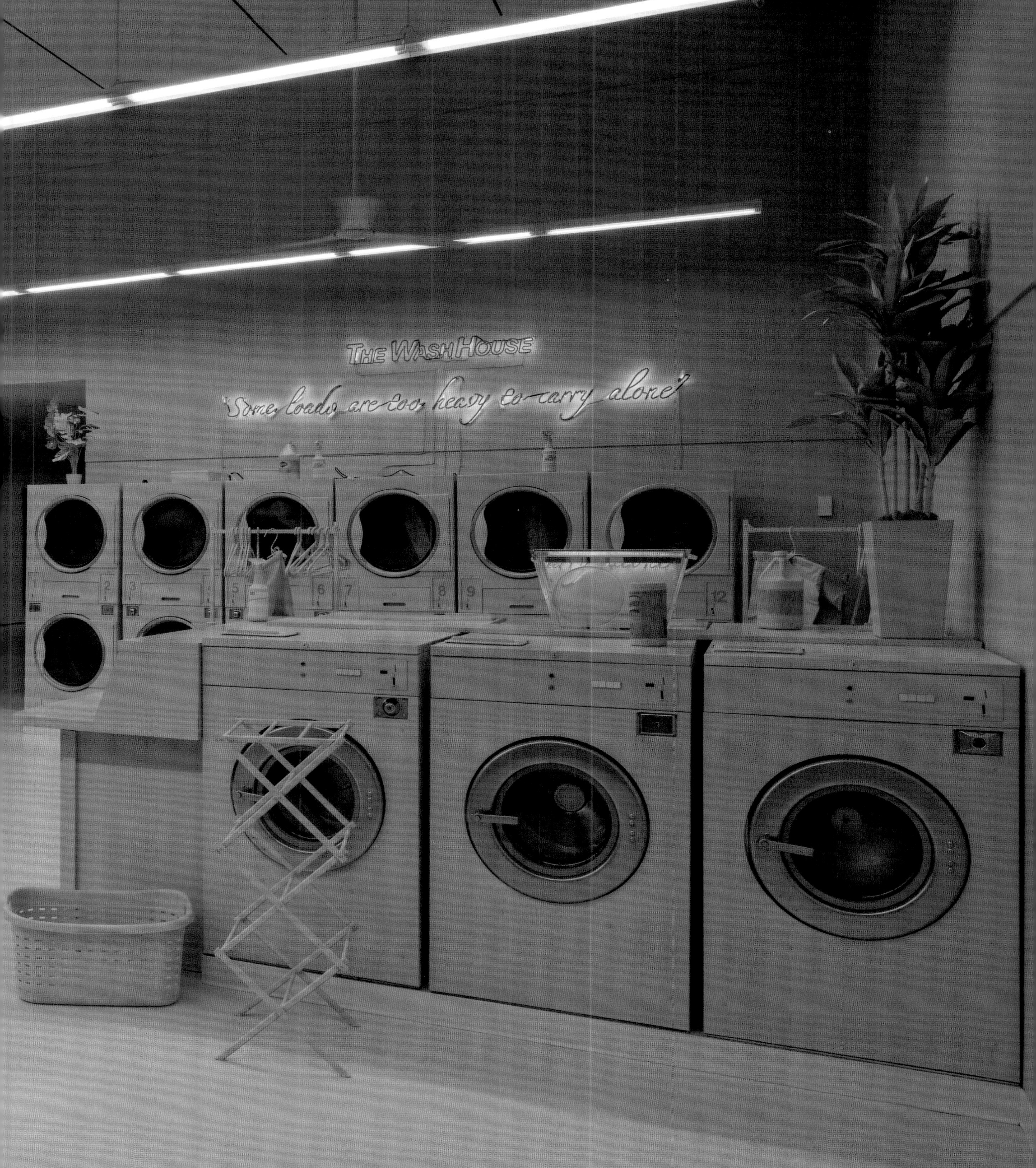
THE WASHHOUSE
'Some loads are too heavy to carry alone'

So it has to be right. But it's interesting to see how the culinary has entered the art world in recent years. Just like fashion designers in the 1980s, most chefs today see themselves as artists. And of course, there are procedural analogies, if you like. The kitchen is an experimental space, like a studio.

STRACHAN: Right. You create a lot. You invent things.

ROBECCHI: *There are a couple of projects you started, like the* Bahamas Aerospace and Sea Exploration Center *or* The Encyclopedia of Invisibility, *that have been growing bigger over the years. Do you know what the end game is?*

STRACHAN: No, I don't. And that's part of what I was saying initially: I'm here because I'm interested not so much in knowing what I'm doing, but figuring it out along the way. I often say this thing that irritates my mates in the studio – I say 'The answer is always the question.' I think it's a very irritating statement for a reason: because it's easy for us to just accept that it looks like that so that's what it is. I think I'm interested in misunderstandings. It's like when my grandma would say 'Put your phone down.' You're holding up the phone most of the time, but when you put the phone down, then maybe something else can be discovered. Maybe it turns out that Jack Whitten is an artist after all because we put our phone down and now we can see actually that this is a long line of making that's irrespective of place, race, background story, gender and all these things. There's a story of picture making that goes from the beginning of picture making to now and all those people fit in that kaleidoscope of picture making. That's more interesting to me.

ROBECCHI: *What about collaborating, which is another big part of your work?*

STRACHAN: There's no-one in the Junkanoo parade who doesn't collaborate or doesn't understand collaboration. I think this is why it's a collective effort. It's also why I loved making glass. I'm sure you've seen glass fabrication happen. There's no such thing as making glass without a team. When I left the Junkanoo and went to RISD, I learned how to make glass. It just made sense. It was just a perfect marriage of one way of collaborating with another way of collaborating. And then after that, I discovered conceptualism, which is like the quintessential deconstruction of the processes of making. And it comes down not just to the idea, but how the idea is related to the making, which is a kind of collaboration in and of itself. It's the history of someone like Rebecca Horn or Richard Serra, or David Hammons selling snowballs on the side of the street. The process of making and the kind of infrastructure, whether it's found infrastructure or by-products of the Industrial Revolution, that history of making things with complex arrangements of people and ideas is part of what drives me, because I come from that. That's how I think about collaboration.

And I keep going back to AI, because I think there's a beautiful relationship between Marcel Duchamp and AI. Duchamp in a way is talking about intelligence, he's forcing us to ask the questions, he's asking about the future of making, like how are we going to contend with the lexicon of production? What is actually important about the cultural construct of presenting an art object? I think that question is at the centre of artificial intelligence. So it's finally coming full circle. But do we want that, and who's determining that? It's sometimes too much.

ROBECCHI: *Is this the reason why you, as a conceptual artist, elected to use a visual vocabulary so ingrained within the traditional art-making process?*

STRACHAN: Yes, because I'm actually trying to talk to you. There are all these ideas in my head and at the end of the day I don't want to walk into a room with you and start talking to you without asking you how you're doing and saying good morning and would you like something to drink. And so the making piece of it is that: it's like me saying good morning to you and then eventually, hopefully, after you've had your coffee, we can get into it. That's how I think about exhibition making. The objects that you see on the surface are like the welcome. I want to share some things with you and as we get into it, as you start to move around the space, hopefully we sink into it a little heavier, but you have to have manners.

I BELONG HERE, 2011
NEON AND GLASS TUBES
210 X 320 CM

INSTALLATION VIEW AT AN UNDISCLOSED LOCATION IN NEW YORK CITY, 2011

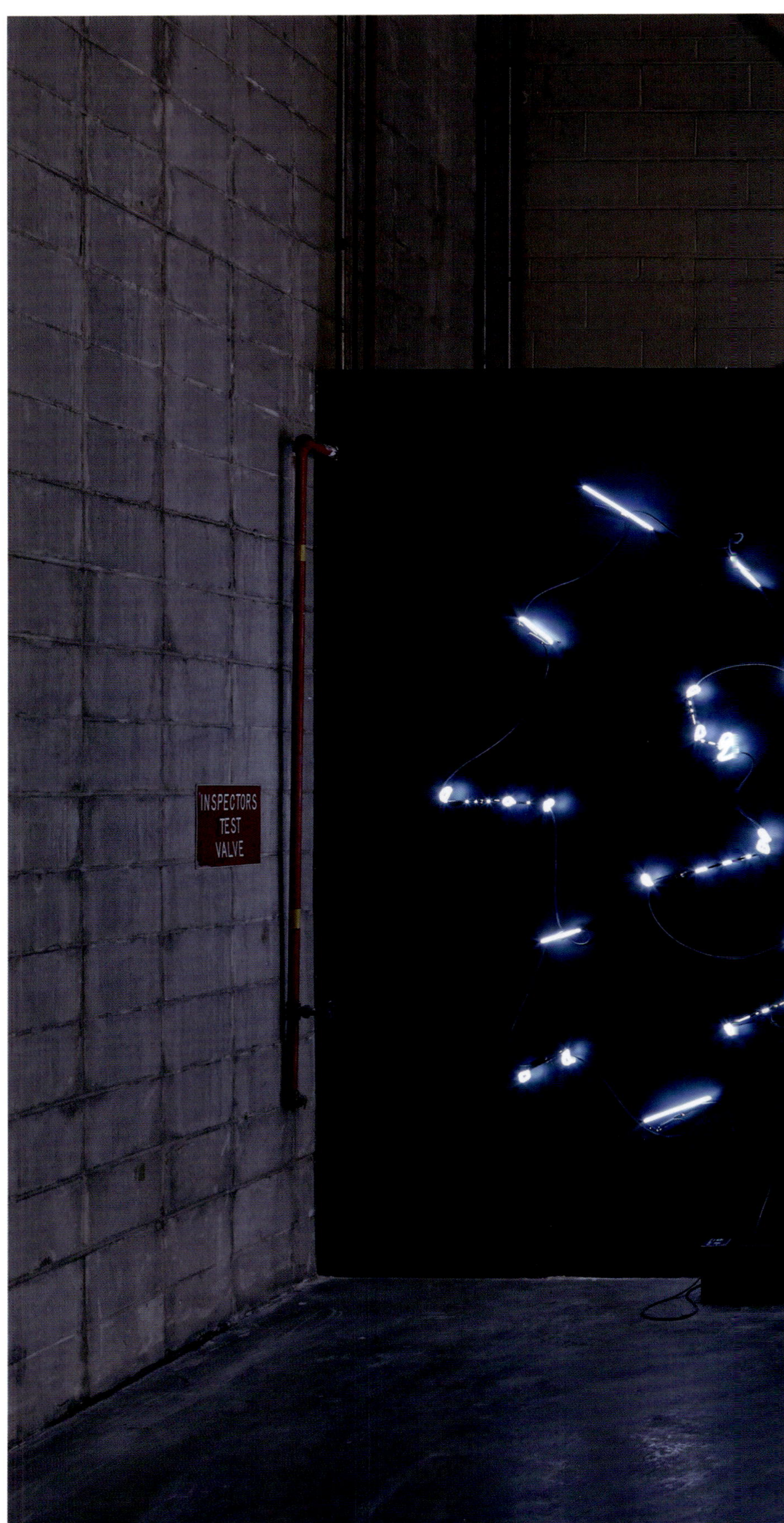

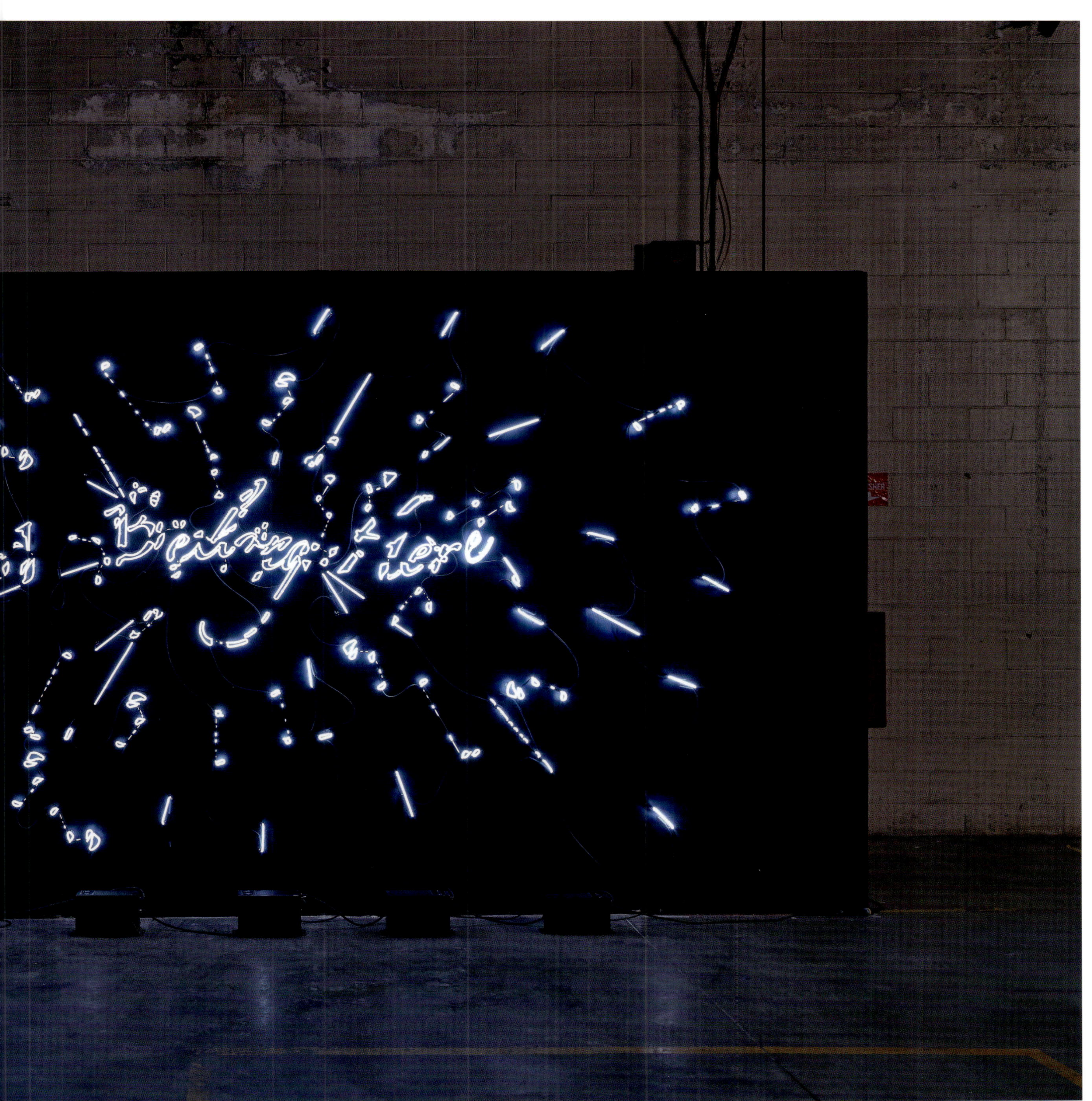

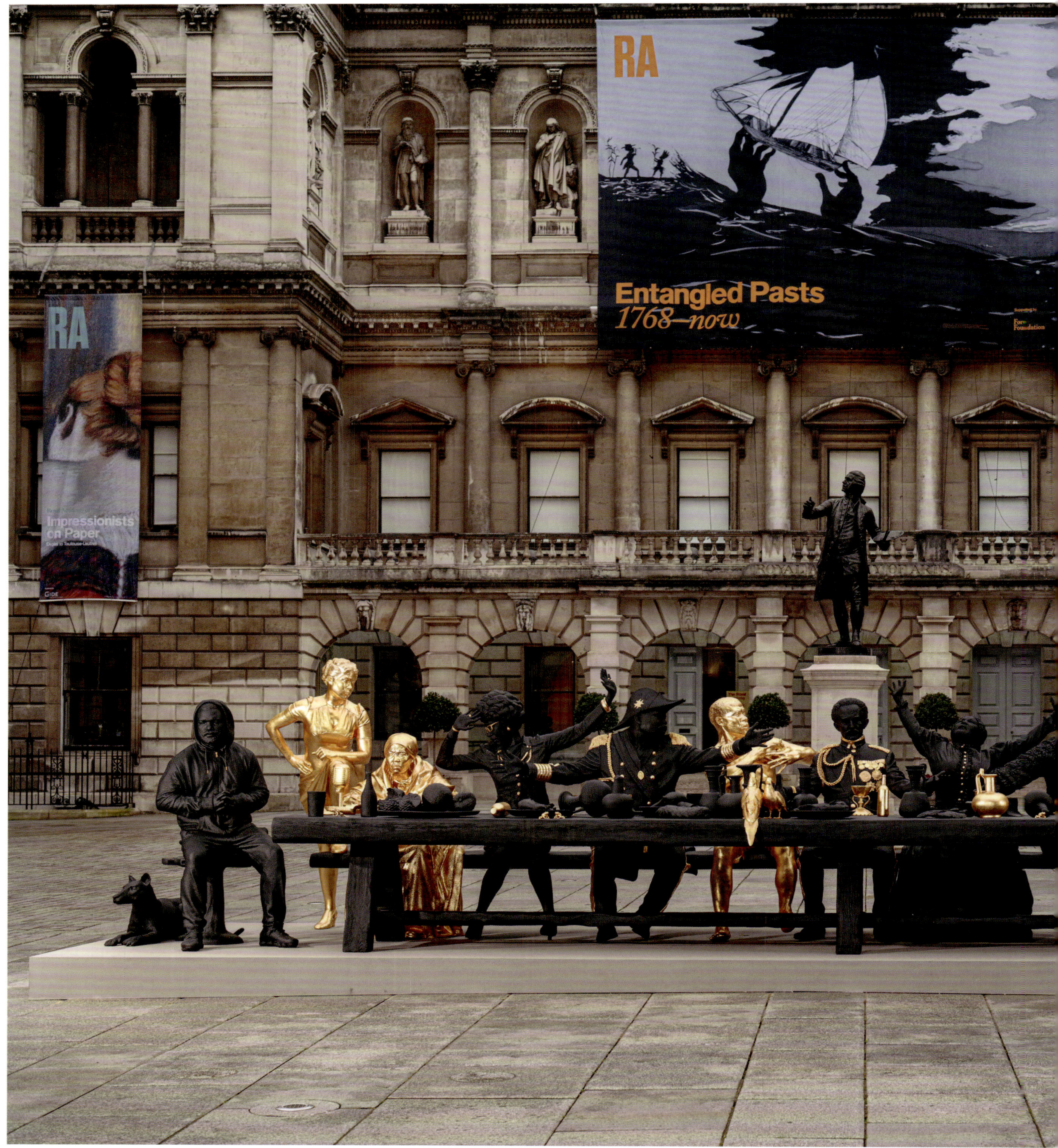
RA
Entangled Pasts
1768–now
RA
Impressionists on Paper

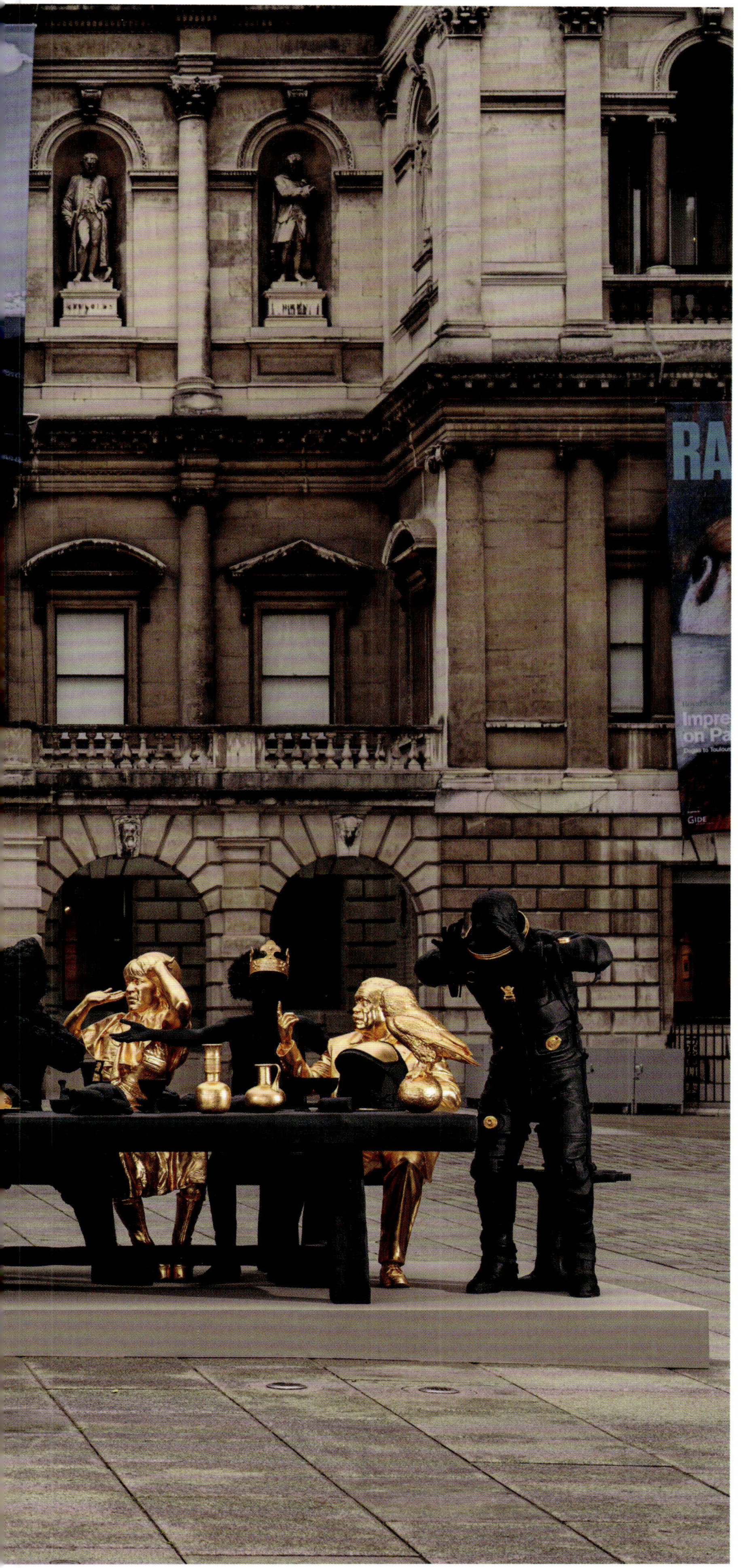

THE FIRST SUPPER (GALAXY BLACK), 2023
BRONZE, BLACK PATINA, GOLD LEAF
217 X 929 X 268 CM

INSTALLATION VIEW AT THE ROYAL ACADEMY, LONDON, 2023

The full list of figures from left to right is as follows:
Tavares Strachan (b. 1979)
Sister Rosetta Tharpe (1915–1973)
Harriet Tubman (1822–1913)
Shirley Chisholm (1924–2005)
Marcus Garvey (1887–1940)
Zumbi dos Palmares (1655–1695)
Haile Selassie (1892–1975)
Mary Seacole (1805–1881)
Matthew Henson (1866–1955)
Marsha P. Johnson (1945–1992)
King Tubby (1941–1989)
Derek Walcott (1930–2017)
Robert Henry Lawrence (1935–1967)

ROBECCHI: *It goes back to what you were saying about building trap doors. The performance in 'Total Darkness' was almost literally built that way.*

STRACHAN: I think it's my decorum. I've been to exhibitions where everything is just super smart, super challenging but just so rough. I come from that rough tradition too, but I also want to make you a nice meal and I want it to taste good and I do have this desire for you to at least understand.

ROBECCHI: *One of the most distinctive traits in the work of conceptual artists from the 1990s – Pierre Huyghe's early films, Pipilotti Rist's installations or Rirkrit Tiravanija's gatherings – is that they felt somehow compelled to introduce an element of comfort or entertainment to make their art more relatable. I wonder if the formative years you spent with Junkanoo and your decision to put the spirit of Junkanoo at the core of your practice is ultimately the source of the decorum you just described.*

STRACHAN: I think it's part of it. Junkanoo isn't one thing or the other. It's not art, it's not West African tradition, it's not music, it's not performance, it's all of those things at once. On the one hand, people in my community are sometimes able to dissect quite complicated concepts. Take, for example, the concept of Trinity within Christianity. They're able to get that the Father, the Son and the Spirit are the same but they're different, and honestly when you slow down and think about it, it doesn't really make any sense. But the humans who are Christian and live in large and small communities all over the world, they get it somehow. How is that not art?

ROBECCHI: *I think one of the reasons why Christianity was so successful was because they were able to co-opt the most mundane aspects of life and elevate them to a symbol. Case in point – having dinner. It means that every time you have a meal, whether you like it or not, there's a gestural connection to the Last Supper. Ultimately this is perhaps one of the reasons why your grandmother had a picture of the Last Supper at home, and how your seeing it within that context resulted in your seminal piece* The First Supper (Galaxy Black).

STRACHAN: I think there's a long line of world-making that we haven't really touched on that's actually more important to me than anything else. Junkanoo was a kind of world-making. I think every successful artist is a world maker: they make a world that you inhabit and the more rigorous the world is, the more flexibility there is within the world. There are more crude examples of this, like the Bible and Walt Disney and then there are more complex examples of this, like Richard Serra and Matthew Barney.

ROBECCHI: *Barney and Serra definitely fall into the world-making category. And, at least in Serra's case, there is a strong spiritual element attached to it. Do you feel like you're building your own cathedral?*

STRACHAN: No. I think I'm trying to build more like a set of ideals. If you're able to understand the Father the Son and the Holy Spirit – they're separate but they're one and they all have different jobs but they somehow have the same job, and the Son is sent to die for the people and the Spirit existed before time and space – if you can understand that then I think, I hope, that one can understand the idea that you can move tonnes of ice from the Arctic and you can make a rendition of an African meal based on the Last Supper or you can paint or make instruments that play autonomously or you could send light particles from one part of the world to the other and celebrate within the same tradition as Pierre Huyghe, Roman Signer, David Hammons and Bruce Nauman and all those artists who build trap doors and not traps.

ROBECCHI: *I think there's been a formal evolution in your work, in the sense that you're making more organic statements. I see your work as an oeuvre. It's no longer about taking a block of ice from the Arctic and bringing it to a gallery, which is a somewhat confrontational statement. Your recent work draws simultaneously from different sources and ties them together. It's a more immersing, multi-layered experience.*

STRACHAN: I think it's probably easier to make a love song after you've made love. One of the things that the younger version of me didn't understand and that I think this version of me understands is that the grace of being an artist is allowing space for other voices within the framework of what you're doing and not being so sensitive about other people's views. I think that violates the premise of being an artist in the first place, because you're in the business of free expression. If someone says something about your work that you don't particularly jive with, I think the grace in practice is to find the space in you to acknowledge and accept it and appreciate it as a part of the process, if that makes sense. What makes the next piece better is me being able to say 'I do make clothing with my mom as a conceptual work but I could understand how that could be misconstrued as a part of this merchandising arm of what I'm doing.' In my mind it's not, but I could understand that, and I think it makes me go back to the drawing board and rethink that a little bit. If I'm in the business of making freely, how can I then chastise somebody else who's making freely and creatively even if they're commenting about what I'm doing? That's their expression, right? If I'm in the business of expression I feel like it's incumbent upon me to be open to the fact that every single hour of the day has inherent miscommunication built into it. The guy taking your order at the restaurant, the person working on the farm, the rug maker – at some point during their day, there's miscommunication. Why as artists should we be immune from that? It's a part of language. We're trying to find each other and while we're trying to find each other sometimes we miss a part of it. We should accept that. I think what has allowed me to exist up to this point is that there's this moment where we know that we could be misinterpreted or misunderstood, but we go back and we make again. I liken it to being in a small town somewhere and you need directions. You're trying to find the place and one guy writes the instructions down word by word, and another guy draws it, and another guy describes the big tree next to the church down the road. These are all ways to get you to the same place, but maybe only one of those would be translatable to you.

ENCYCLOPEDIA ROOM: PANEL PAINTING, 2022
INK, PAINT, ACRYLIC MEDIUM, MIXED MEDIA, COLLAGE WORK ON SINTRA PANELS, LEATHER GILDING, ARCHIVAL PAPER, MAPLE, FELT, ACRYLIC
PANELS: EACH 28 X 21 X 5 CM
ENCYCLOPEDIA: 29 X 23 X 10 CM
BOOKSTAND: 76 X 73 X 44 CM
INSTALLATION VIEW AT THE LOS ANGELES COUNTY MUSEUM OF ART, 2025

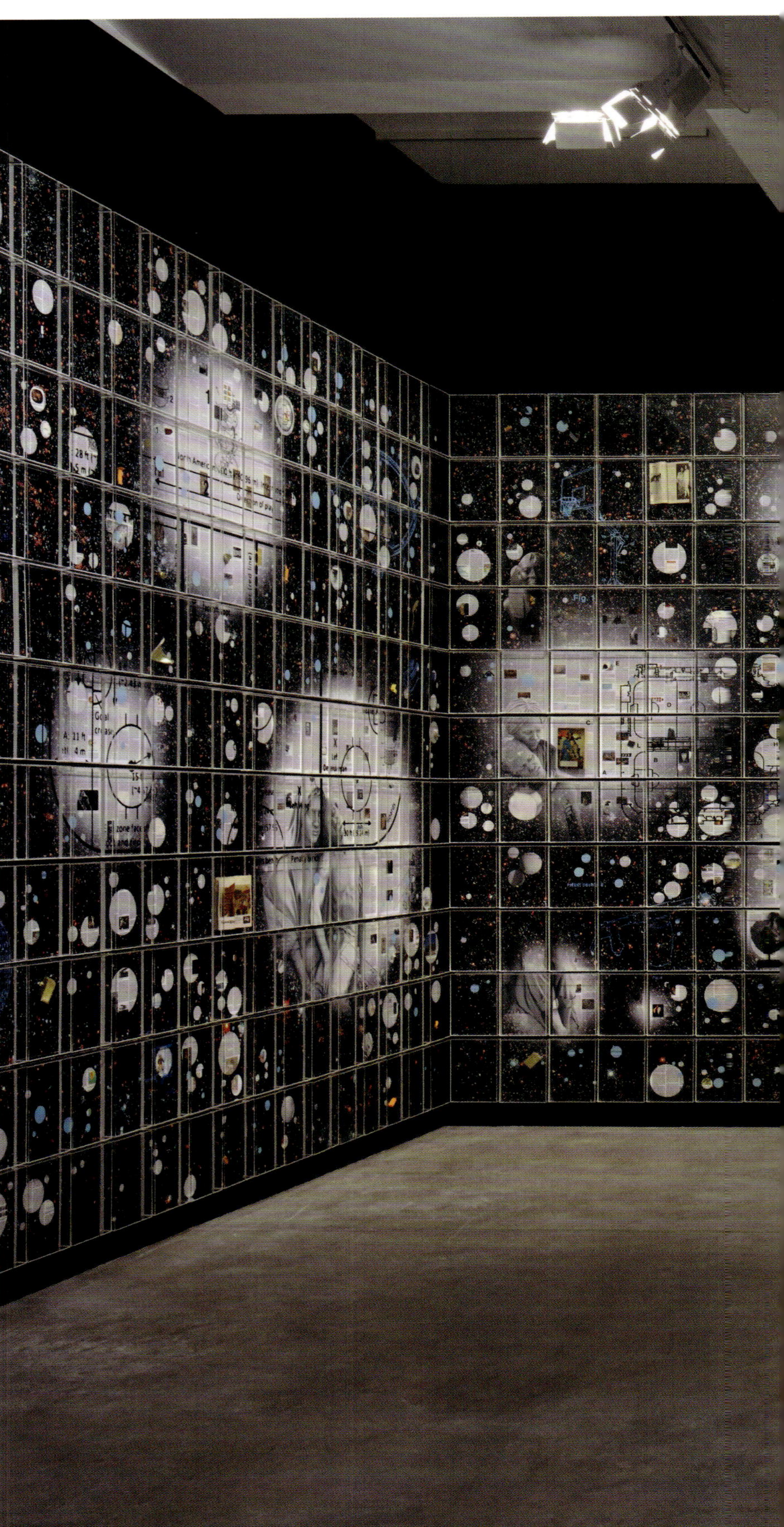

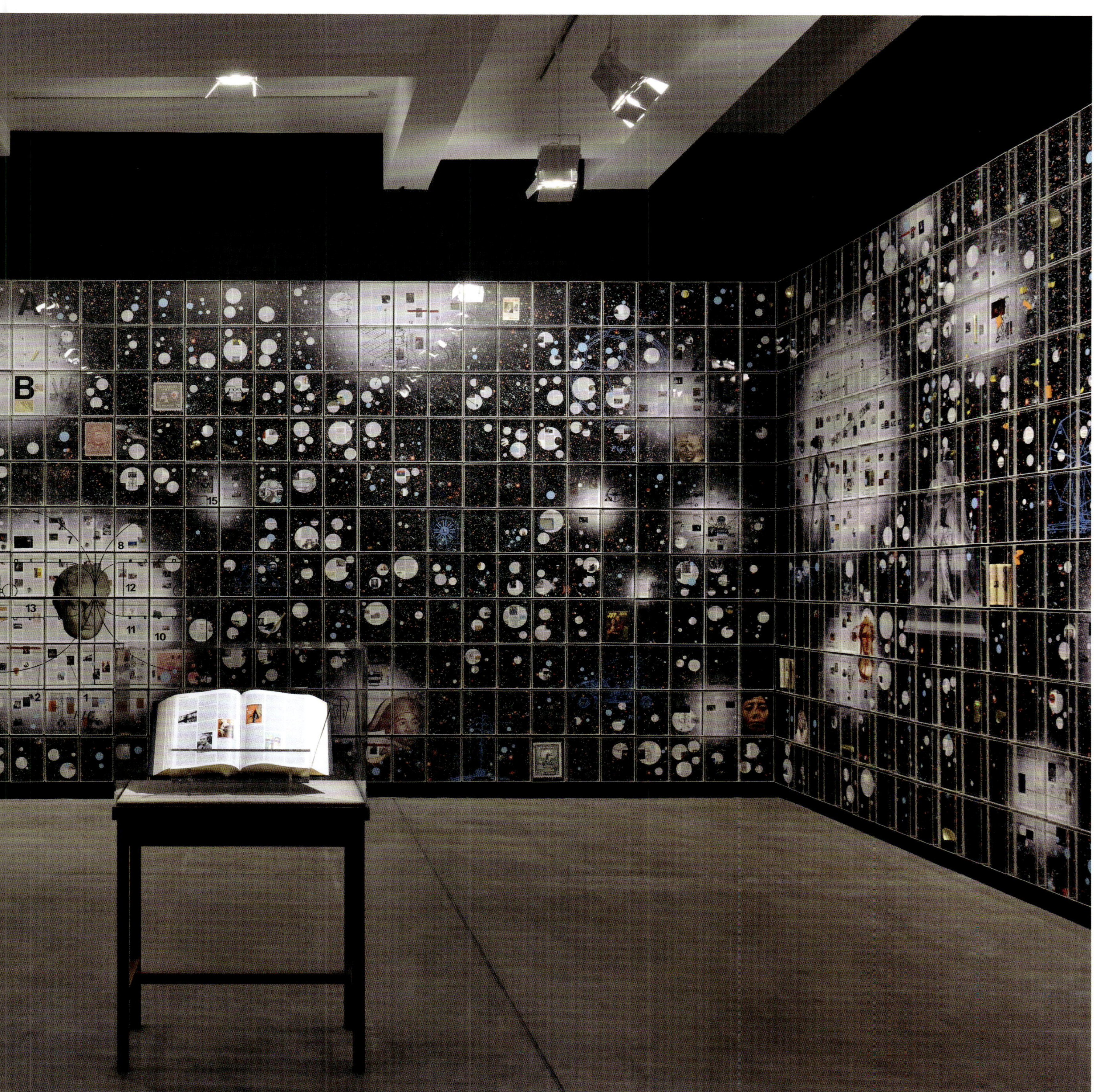

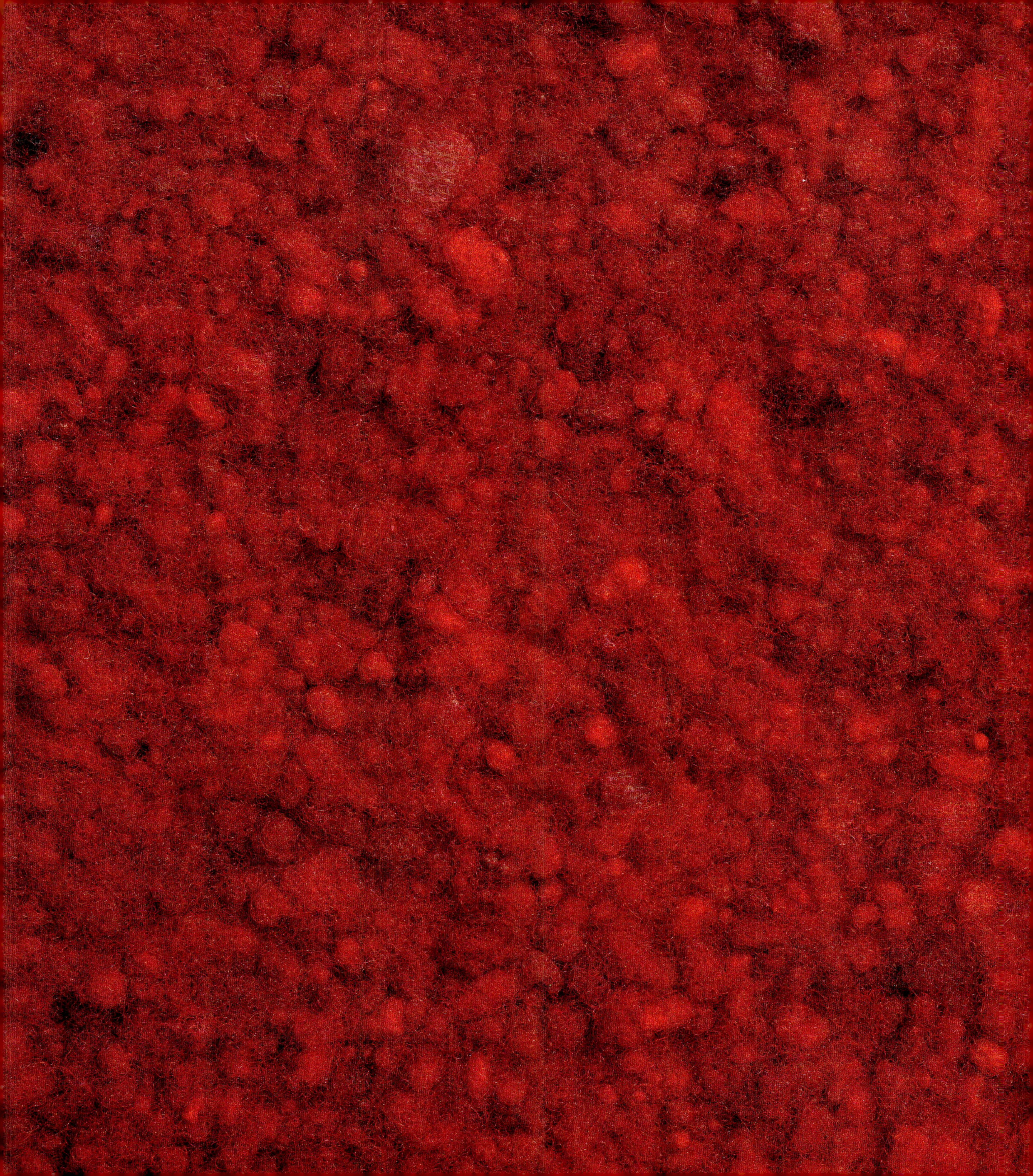

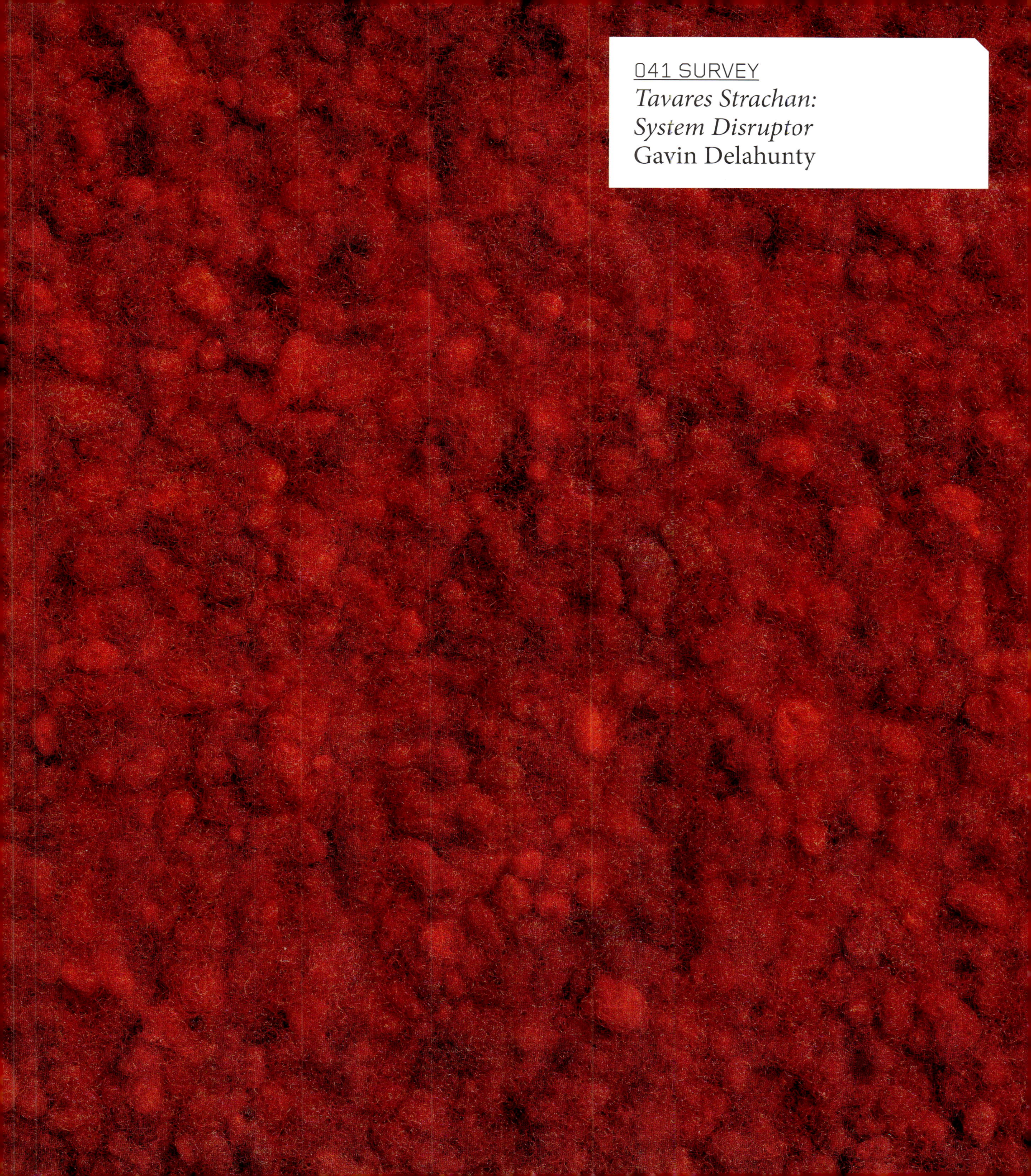
041 SURVEY
Tavares Strachan:
System Disruptor
Gavin Delahunty

previous pages,
OSHUN (RED STAR) (DETAIL),
2025
FLOCKED HAIR ON CANVAS
184 X 184 X 6 CM

right,
THE DISTANCE BETWEEN WHAT WE HAVE AND WHAT WE WANT,
2005–06
4.5-TON ICE BLOCK

ALASKAN NORTH POLE, 2005, AND ALBURY SAYLE PRIMARY SCHOOL, NASSAU, 2006

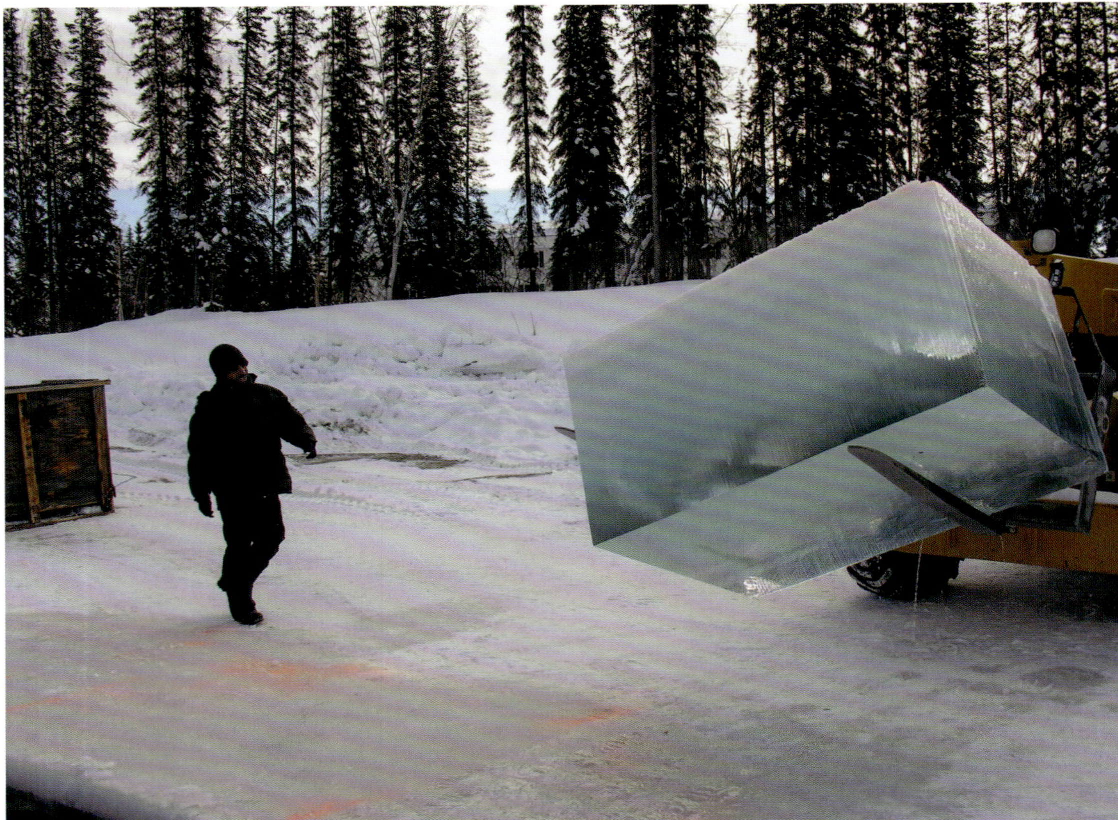

I think being an artist, to me, always had to do with disrupting some system or another.
— Tavares Strachan[1]

For over twenty years, Bahamian artist Tavares Strachan has pursued a visual and informational critique of Western systems of knowledge. Understanding a system as a complex of interacting components, Strachan has explored the environmental, mechanical, organ, semiotic, and epistemological systems that became central to scientific, philosophical, and artistic inquiry in the second half of the twentieth century.[2] He researches these systems, analyzing their components and operations, while remaining attentive to their blind-spots and exclusions. In collaboration with communities and organizations, Strachan then constructs machines, companies, archives, and images that offer alternative ways of thinking and seeing.

Strachan's engagement with systems has something in common with Conceptual art as it emerged in the 1960s, but with a new attention to the biased and exclusionary ways in which history is written and knowledge evaluated and disseminated. In 1968, Jack Burnham's seminal essay 'Systems Esthetics' argued that contemporary art was shifting towards a 'systems approach', where artists are no longer concerned with creating isolated objects, but instead engage with complex networks that encompass social, technological and environmental factors. It was a shift that required artists to consider the aesthetic implications of systems beyond traditional art boundaries, integrating scientific and technological knowledge into their practice to address larger societal issues.[3] Artists like Hans Haacke utilized the term 'system' to describe 'certain non-static "sculptures"', writing that 'a "sculpture" that physically reacts to its environment can no longer be regarded as an object. The range of outside factors affecting it, as well as its own radius of action, reach beyond the space it materially occupies. It thus merges with the environment in a relationship that is better understood as a "system" of interdependent processes. These processes evolve without the viewer's empathy. They become a witness.'[4]

Curator Kynaston McShine embraced system-based approaches when thinking about art, and he articulated this in his landmark exhibition 'Information' held at The Museum of Modern Art, New York, in 1970. 'Information' was the first exhibition of its kind to explore how an increasing number of younger artists were becoming preoccupied with the implications of systems – whether computational, physical, economic or social – and 'those represented are part of a culture that has been considerably altered by communication systems'.[5] In his essay McShine challenged audiences to 'extend the idea of art, to renew [its] definition, and to think beyond the traditional categories – painting, sculpture, drawing, printmaking, photography, films, theatre, music, dance, and poetry [since] such distinctions have become increasingly blurred'.[6] Strachan's work exemplifies this extension of art practice, incorporating traditional media but moving well beyond them. Yet while an earlier generation of Conceptual artists treated these interconnected structures as neutral and objective, Strachan shows how prejudice can also operate systemically via structures, laws and institutionalism, rather than the actions of individuals.[7] By disrupting these ingrained beliefs and practices, Strachan offers a fresh perspective that is prescient, enlightening and paradigm shifting.

Environmental Systems

A 4.5-ton rectangular block of ice sits in a purpose-built refrigerated vitrine. A mobile generator powering the display unit and maintaining the environmental conditions can be seen in the background. One can imagine its mechanical hum, together with the buzzing of the electrical current in the overhead fluorescent tubes that cautiously light this mysterious underground warehouse and the ghostly machines it protects. More than any other installation image of *The Distance Between What We Have and What We Want (Arctic Ice Project)*, 2004–08 this one stirs imaginings of a not-too-distant dystopian future in which global warming has caused polar

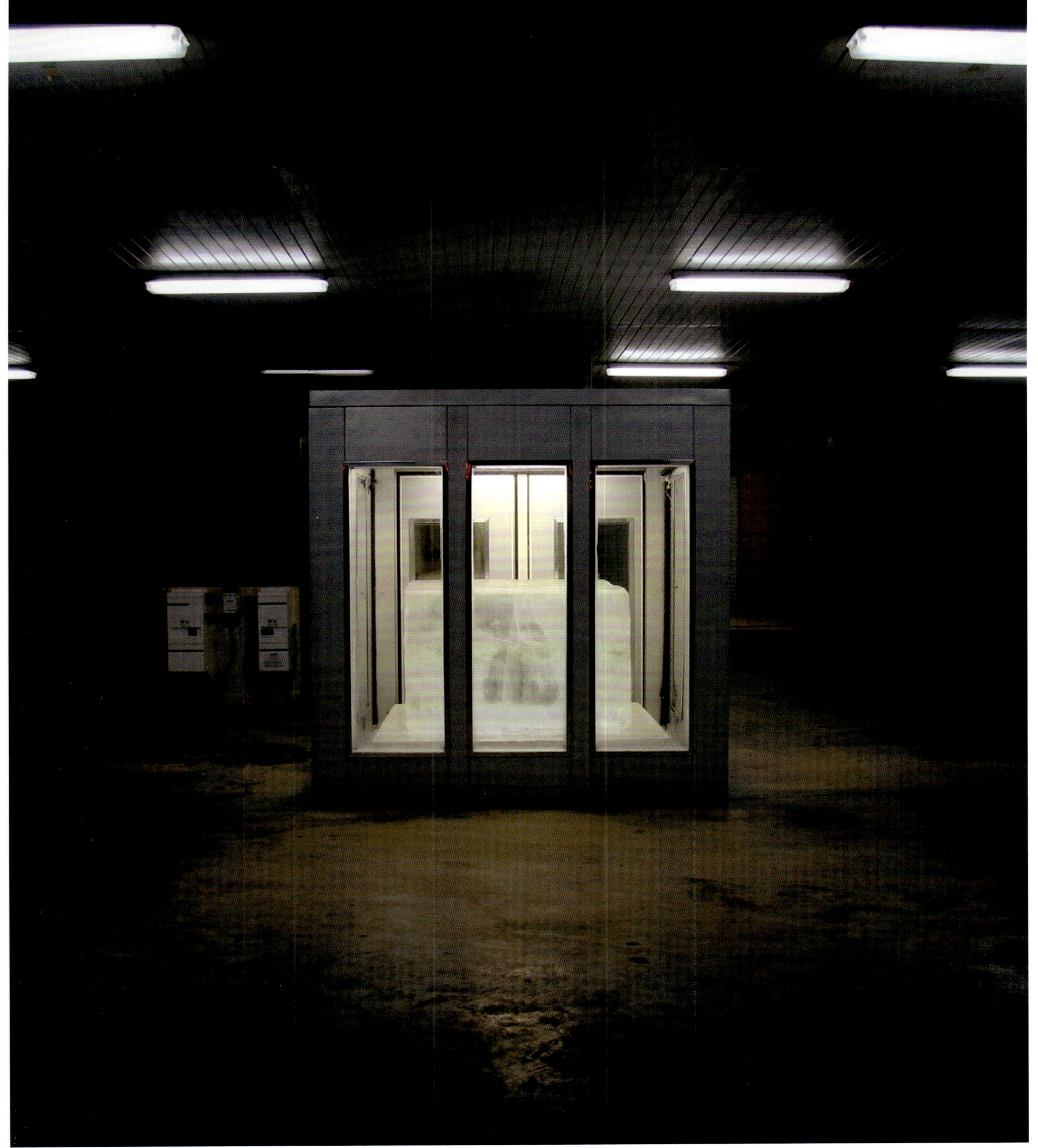

BLAST OFF, 2008–09
GLASS, BAHAMAS SUGAR FUEL
CELL
38 X 187 X 60 CM

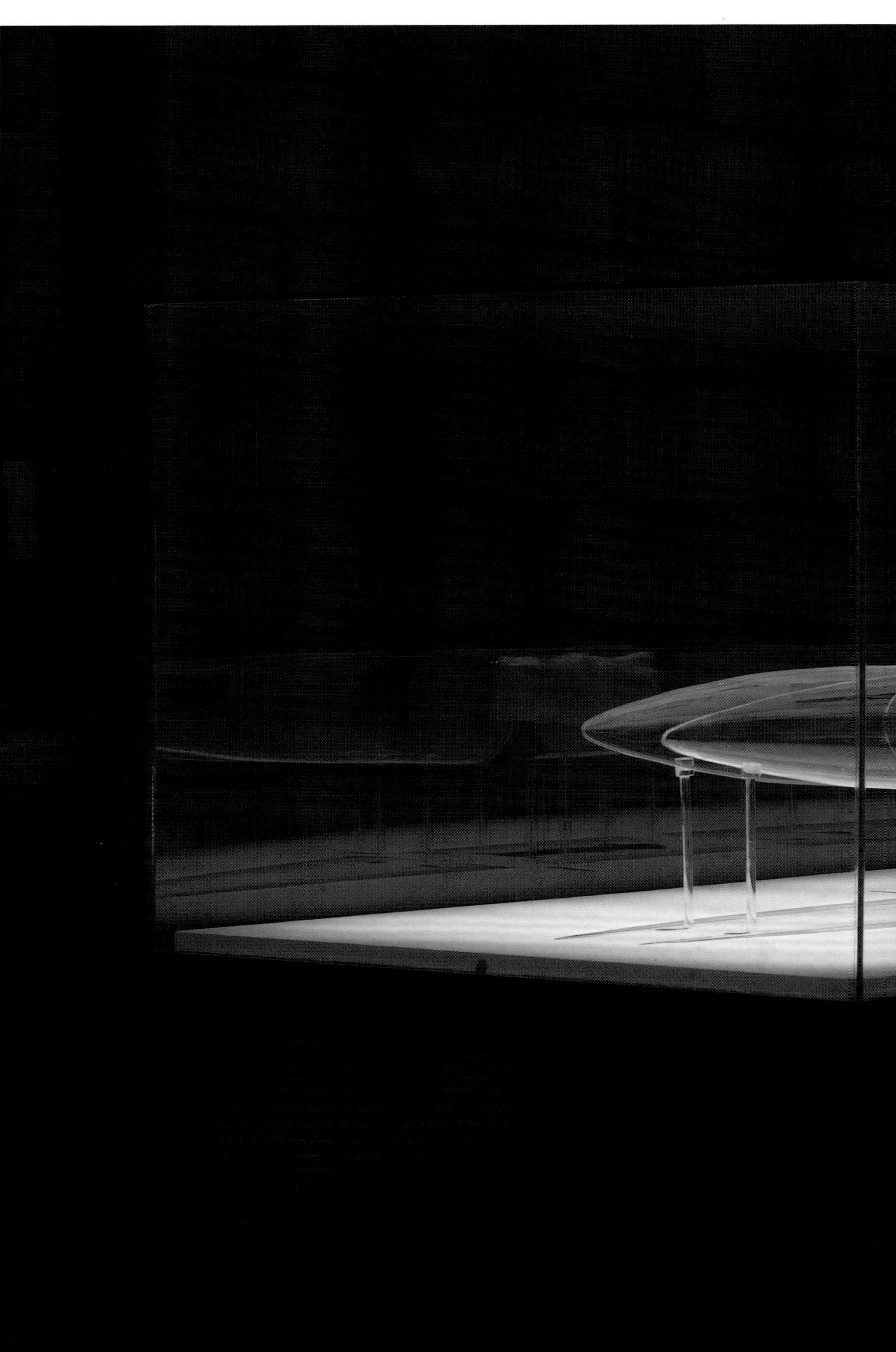

ice-caps, sea ice and glaciers to melt and shrink at such a rapid rate that they have disappeared from the Earth, leaving behind this single frozen relic. It is a striking image that eerily communicates the urgent need to face the realities of climate change and the fact that it is a rapidly progressing threat, causing rising sea levels and biodiversity loss, with catastrophic consequences for human health, food security and global stability.

A crucial part of the work not communicated by this image is that Strachan transported the ice, its cold storage unit, and its solar-powered energy management system for display in Nassau, The Bahamas. The work was subsequently shown in Miami, Florida, and Brooklyn, New York. Its first relocation from Arctic Alaska to the Aubrey Sayle Primary School in the Bahamas – which the artist attended as a child – was its most consequential.[8] This ostensibly absurd, even comical gesture of excavating a solid mass of ice from one geographic location where it naturally occurs and transporting it to another site where it can only survive artificially, contained a very serious message about the interconnectivity of ecosystems despite the vast oceans between them. As Strachan has said: 'people don't necessarily think how closely the global north and the global south are linked together'.[9] For example, melting polar ice caps can affect trade winds by disrupting global atmospheric circulation patterns, potentially leading to changes in wind strength and direction, particularly in the tropical regions.[10] This audacious recontextualization raises awareness about the vital importance of protecting ice in a region that rarely, if ever, sees it or has had the opportunity to marvel at its raw beauty. On the other hand, the survival of the icy artifact is now contingent on solar radiation – energy that The Bahamas has in abundance – to power the technically complex apparatus required for its existence – the very same energy that could destroy it if it were exposed to it directly.

Embedded in *The Distance Between What We Have and What We Want (Arctic Ice Project)* –like the microorganisms in the ice – are the very foundations of Strachan's research-driven artistic practice. It is an early and hugely important work that links to all his subsequent output and anticipates his interest in the sociological nature of the art world by revealing his engagement with form, function and the reliance of the work on its physical and social contexts. It hinges on the creation of a stable system to avoid the threat of physical transformation, and references the disappearance of large masses of ice that cover the North and South Poles via the deliberate protection of a glacial specimen to preserve its material integrity from destructive outside forces. It reminds us that we are all responsible for the conservation of natural resources and affected by the increasing instability of our climate.

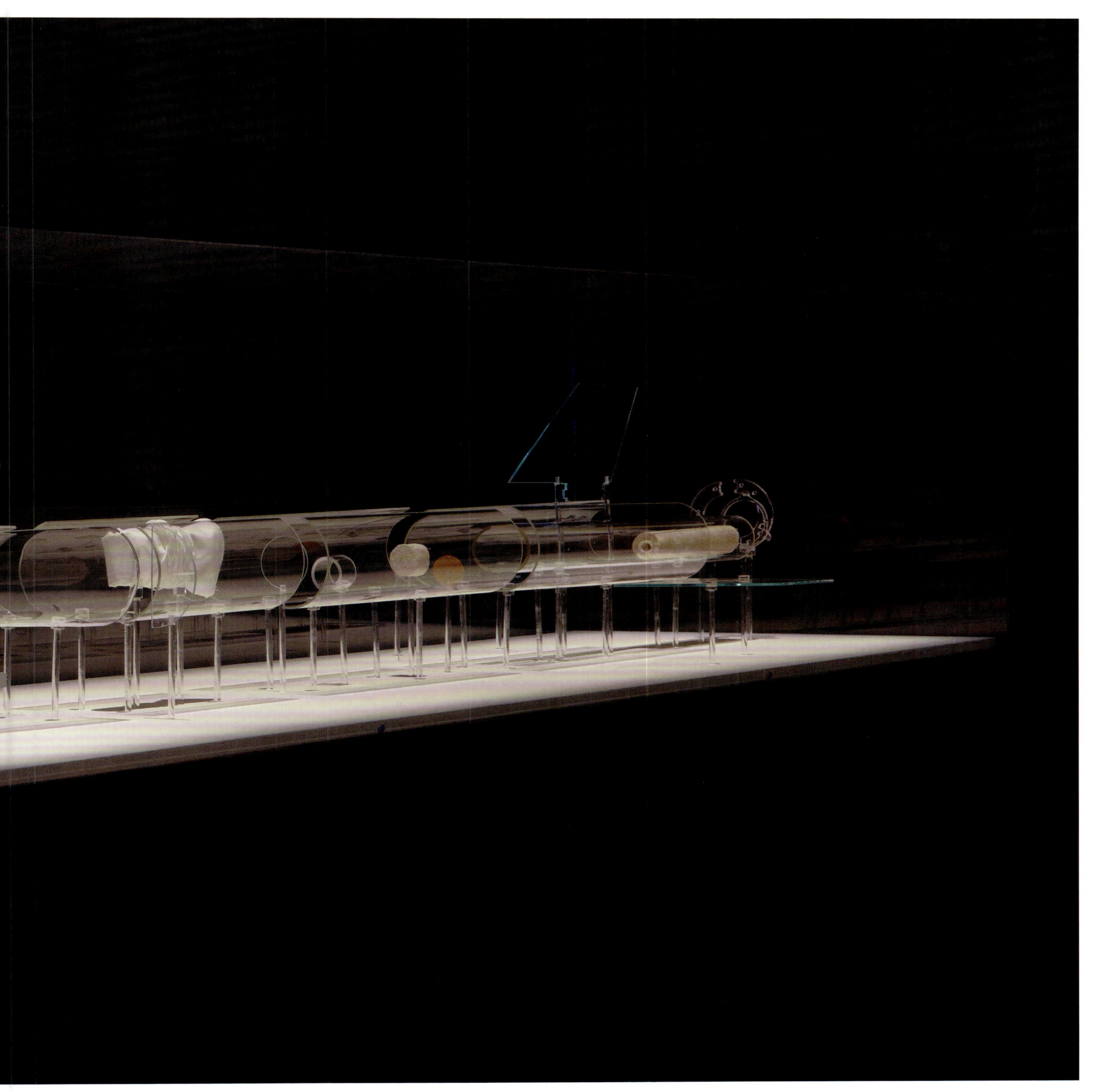

from left,
ROCKET LAUNCH ABACO 1,
2010–11
BLACK AND WHITE
PHOTOGRAPH
102 X 66 CM

ROCKET LAUNCH ABACO 2,
2010–11
BLACK AND WHITE
PHOTOGRAPH
102 X 66 CM

ROCKET LAUNCH ABACO 6,
2010–11
BLACK AND WHITE
PHOTOGRAPH
102 X 66 CM

ROCKET LAUNCH ABACO 7,
2010–11
BLACK AND WHITE
PHOTOGRAPH
102 X 66 CM

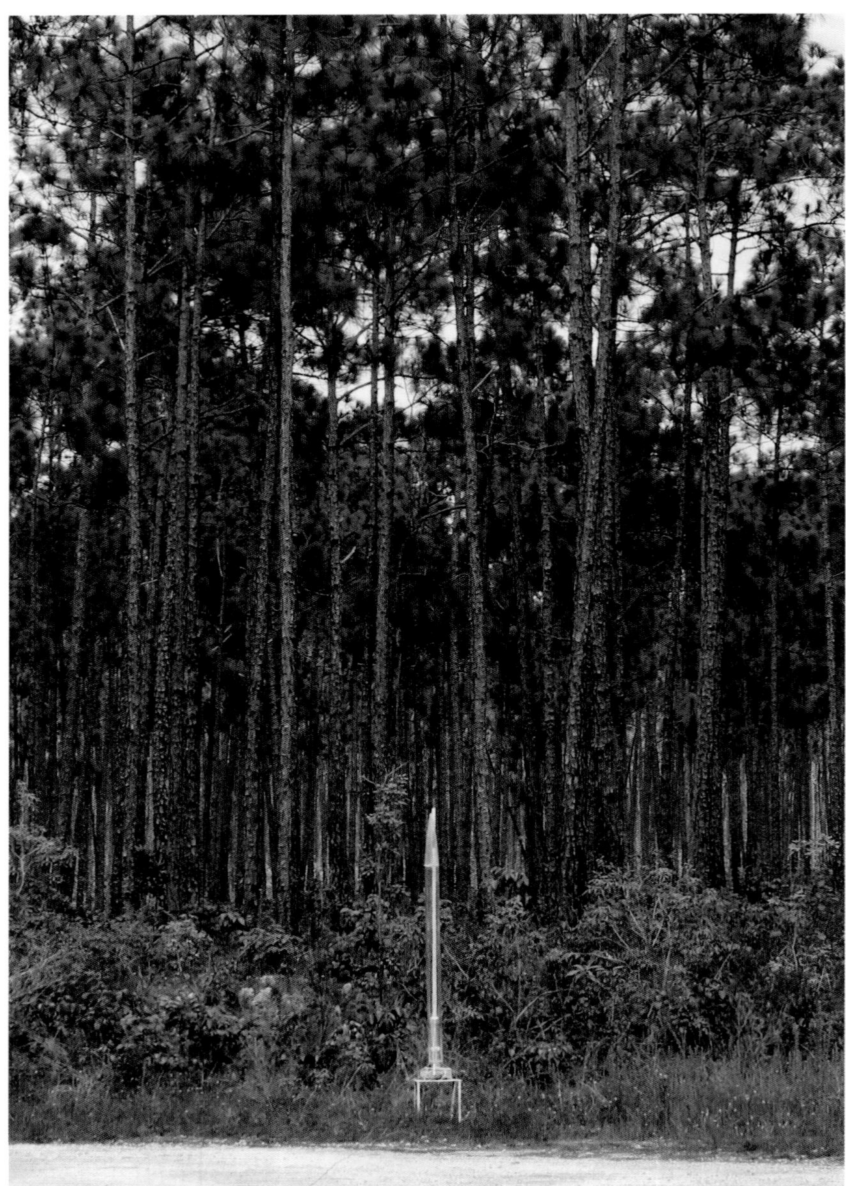

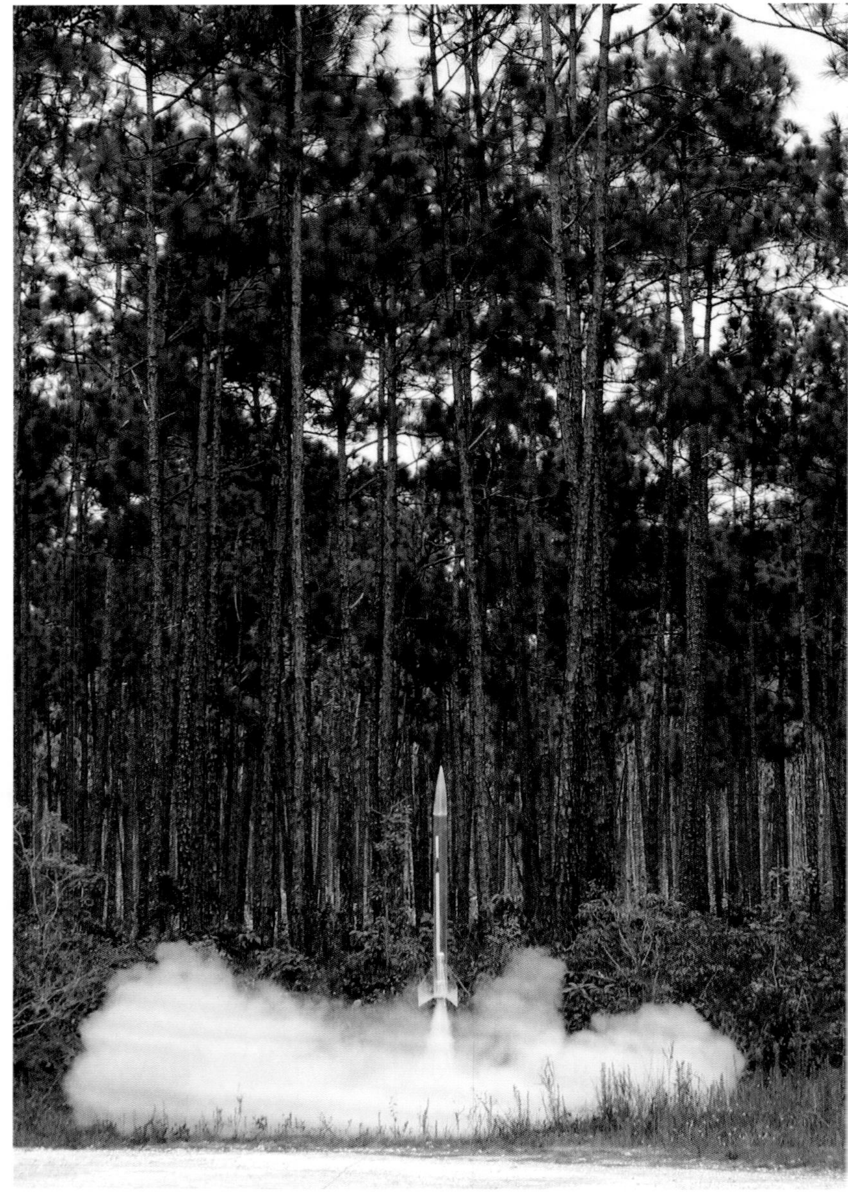

Mechanical Systems

Four years later, Strachan turned his attention to aeronautical engineering in the design and production of his dynamic sculpture *Blast Off*, 2008–09, a glass rocket that could be propelled into the air using sugar cane as its fuel. It is a work that sits at the intersection of various artistic movements such as Auto-destructive art, Minimalism, post-Minimalism and Process art, while also engaging in scientific conversations around renewable biological energy sources. The display of the work consists of two long museological vitrines, one containing a transparent to-scale replica of the rocket used by the artist during test-flights, and the other presenting the residual pieces of a prototype shattered during testing. The unbroken model has been separated into its constituent parts for the easy viewing of its anatomy, revealing a pointed nose cone at the front, a long cylindrical body tube and fins. Overall, its shape resembles that of a bullet.

Complimenting the two vitrines is a dramatic documentary photograph of the rocket at the precise moment of liftoff, thrusting itself forcefully into the air from its launch pad and leaving behind a voluminous exhaust plume composed of gas and smoke. Launched on a beach in Nassau and set against a backdrop of Bahamian pineyard trees, the photographic image is a potent symbol of Strachan's self-determination, his interest in exploration, devotion to his home country, and his constant pursuit of reaching beyond boundaries. In *Blast Off*, conventional rules about materials and fuels are upended. The rocket is made from

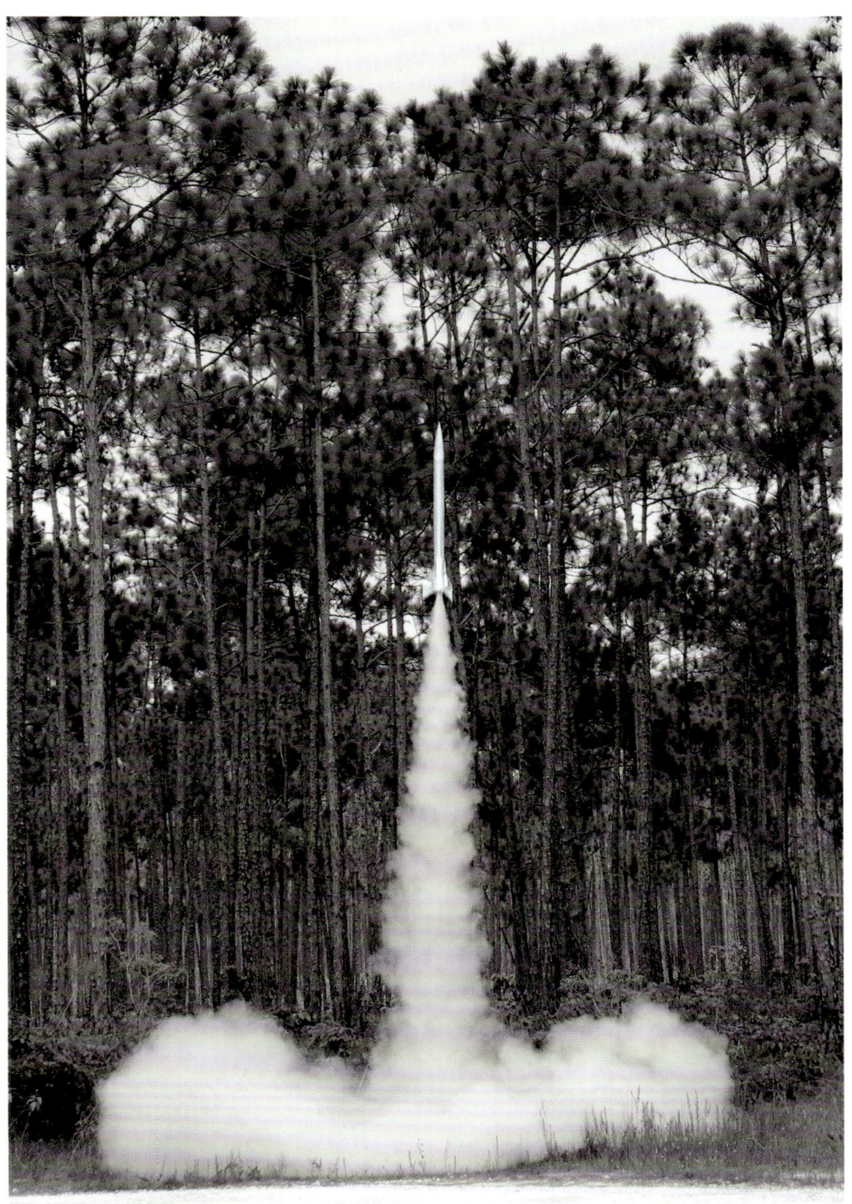

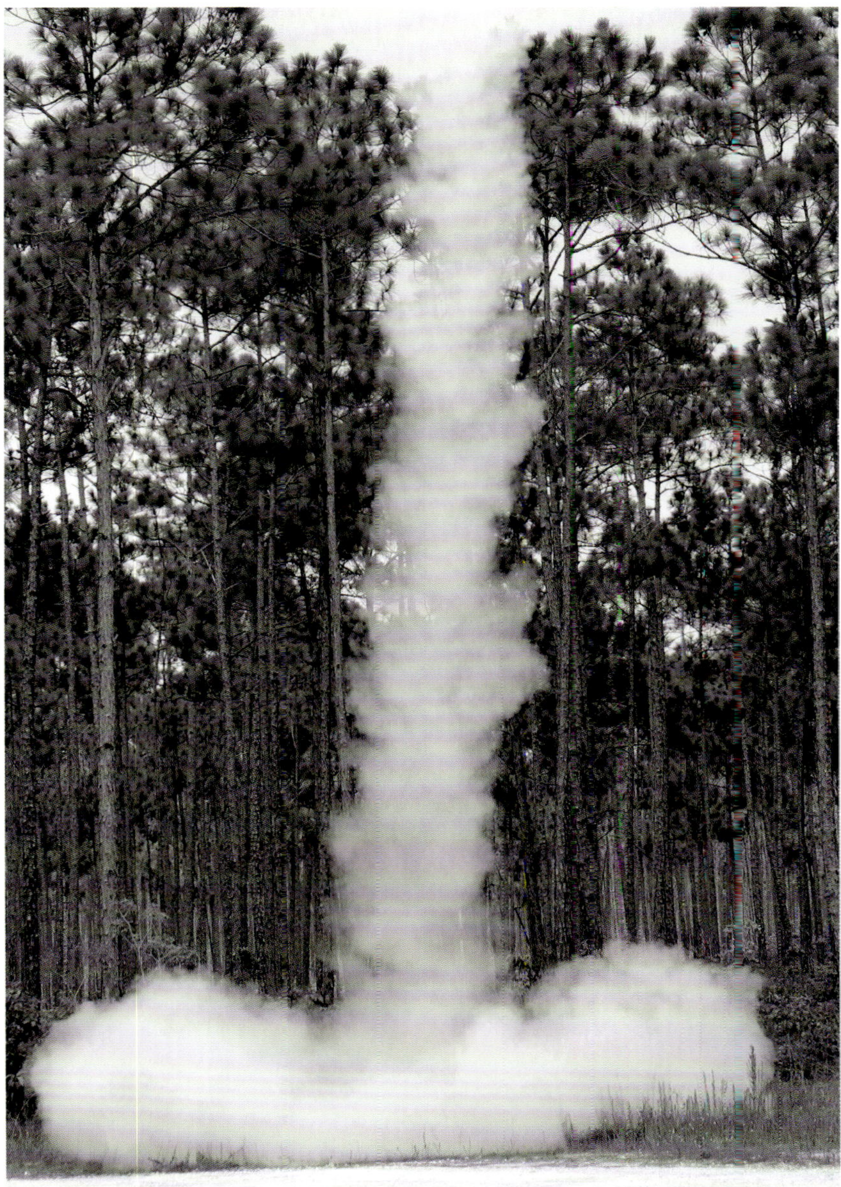

glass, a non-lethal material ineffectual as a weapon and not strong enough to withstand the stress of the energy produced at launch or the impact it would face on landing, making it a highly unusual choice of material. Powering the engine with locally sourced sugar cane by processing it to create a type of syrupy propellent, while scientifically sound, is equally unorthodox. While Strachan's surprising use of biofuels like sugar and materials like glass suspend any threatening or militaristic connotations of the rocket as a missile, the work does give expression to his ideological views, orbiting questions of Black power.

In 2008, concurrent with *Blast Off*, Strachan established B.A.S.E.C., the Bahamas Aerospace and Sea Exploration Center, a company where he develops conceptual projects that pertain to his belief that 'art can be a powerful driver of opportunity and a medium to reclaim a mantle of knowledge and share lost narratives'.[11] *Blast Off*'s first 'mission' was literally an exercise in salvaging shards of glass created during the exercise, and metaphorically piecing together poignant narratives, especially those that relate to space travel. For example, the Space Race (1955–75) between the United States and the Soviet Union coincided with the Civil Rights Movement in the US, where the national focus on achieving dominance in space exploration ran parallel to the fight for racial equality. This led to discussions about representation within the space programme and criticism from some civil rights activists regarding the allocation of resources towards space travel while domestic issues remained unresolved. On the day before the Apollo 11 launch, 15 July 1969, Reverend Ralph Abernathy – who had succeeded the Rev.

SEATED PANCHEN LAMA, 2011
HAND-BLOWN GLASS, MINERAL OIL, PLEXIGLASS TANK, WOOD BASE
90 X 90 X 58 CM

Dr Martin Luther King Jr as the head of the Southern Christian Leadership Conference (SCLC) after King's assassination in 1968 – led civil-rights activists in protest. Abernathy and others objected to the government prioritizing the space programme over the earthly problems of inequality and poverty, asserting, 'I am here to demonstrate with poor people in a symbolic way against the tragic and inexcusable gulf that exists between America's technological abilities and our social injustices.'[12] The Apollo 11 mission went on to be hailed as humankind's greatest technological achievement and a moment of national and international unity. And while Strachan's *Blast Off* doesn't dispute this – in many ways it is inspired by it – the symbolism of the materials, the side-by-side presentation of one whole and one broken rocket, and its launch from a Caribbean island, disturbs this singular narrative of achievement. Strachan puts the pieces of the story back together in a slightly different way, orientating our attention towards several hidden histories embedded in the familiar mythology. It is a work that skillfully balances unity and fragmentation, the personal and the collective, the static and the dynamic, reduction and expansion.

The Space Race also demonstrated to the world that rocket technology is an excellent display of national strength and global influence. Strachan's establishment of B.A.S.E.C. in 2008 was a wonderfully grandiose move that consciously attempted to insert his home country into a global conversation about space travel. As of 2024, There are over seventy countries with space programs across the world. Still, only sixteen space agencies boast launch capabilities of their own, and only three have managed to send humans into space. An increasing number of private space agencies continue to spring into existence, such as SpaceX and Blue Origin, typically based around space tourism.[13] On 19 February 2025, history was made in The Bahamas when SpaceX's Falcon 9 booster successfully landed on a drone ship off the coast of The Exuma Islands, making The Bahamas the first ever international location to welcome a SpaceX rocket landing. It marked the beginning of a new collaboration between The Bahamas and SpaceX, with nineteen more landings planned for the future. The Bahamian Prime Minister, Phillip E. Davis was quoted as saying 'This historic feat positions our nation as a global hub for space tourism and technological advancement … The Bahamas is not only a destination of beauty, but also of innovation and limitless possibilities in the future of exploration and discovery.'[14] Strachan uncannily prefigured these events seventeen years earlier by launching his rocket into the air and declaring his visionary belief in the immense potential of the Bahamas as a site for the growing space industry.

Organ Systems

Combining certain formal elements from *The Distance Between What We Have and What We Want (Arctic Ice Project)* and the interplay between art and technology in *Blast Off*, the semi-transparent geometric sculpture *Seated Panchen Lama*, 2011, recalls any number of Minimalist cubes produced in the mid-1960s from synthetic polymers such as acrylic or Plexiglas. However, unlike its stoic historical predecessors that were all too often self-referential and devoid of emotional or narrative content, Strachan's captivating sculpture engages with the science and symbolism of light, as well as eliciting a deep concern for the suffering of others. Measuring 35 x 35 x 23 inches, the scale, materials, transparency and optical play of *Seated Panchen Lama*'s highly polished surfaces create a hypnotic, even bewildering effect. It seems to exhibit properties of both a solid and a liquid simultaneously by bending and distorting the environment in which it is situated. On closer inspection, and depending on the light and the angle of vision, a mysterious disembodied figure materializes inside – a liminal form that hovers somewhere between visibility and invisibility. More precisely, this is a ghostly representation of the cardiovascular system of the Panchen Lama, the second most important figure in Tibetan Buddhism after the Dalai Lama who has been missing since 1995 when he was taken captive by the Chinese authorities at the age of six.[15]

Strachan achieves the uncanny effect of this sculpture by first constructing the body out of Borosilicate glass, before submerging it in mineral oil. Because Borosilicate glass and mineral oil have a similar refractive index, and wavelengths of light pass through both materials at equivalent speeds, the glass can seem to disappear when suspended in the oil. This renders the Panchen Lama visible from certain angles and invisible from others. Strachan's decision to only represent the Panchen Lama by way of his cardiovascular system is notable for several reasons. In Tibetan Buddhism, the cardiovascular system, particularly the heart, is considered highly important because it is seen as the seat of consciousness and compassion, essentially representing the 'mind-heart' connection,

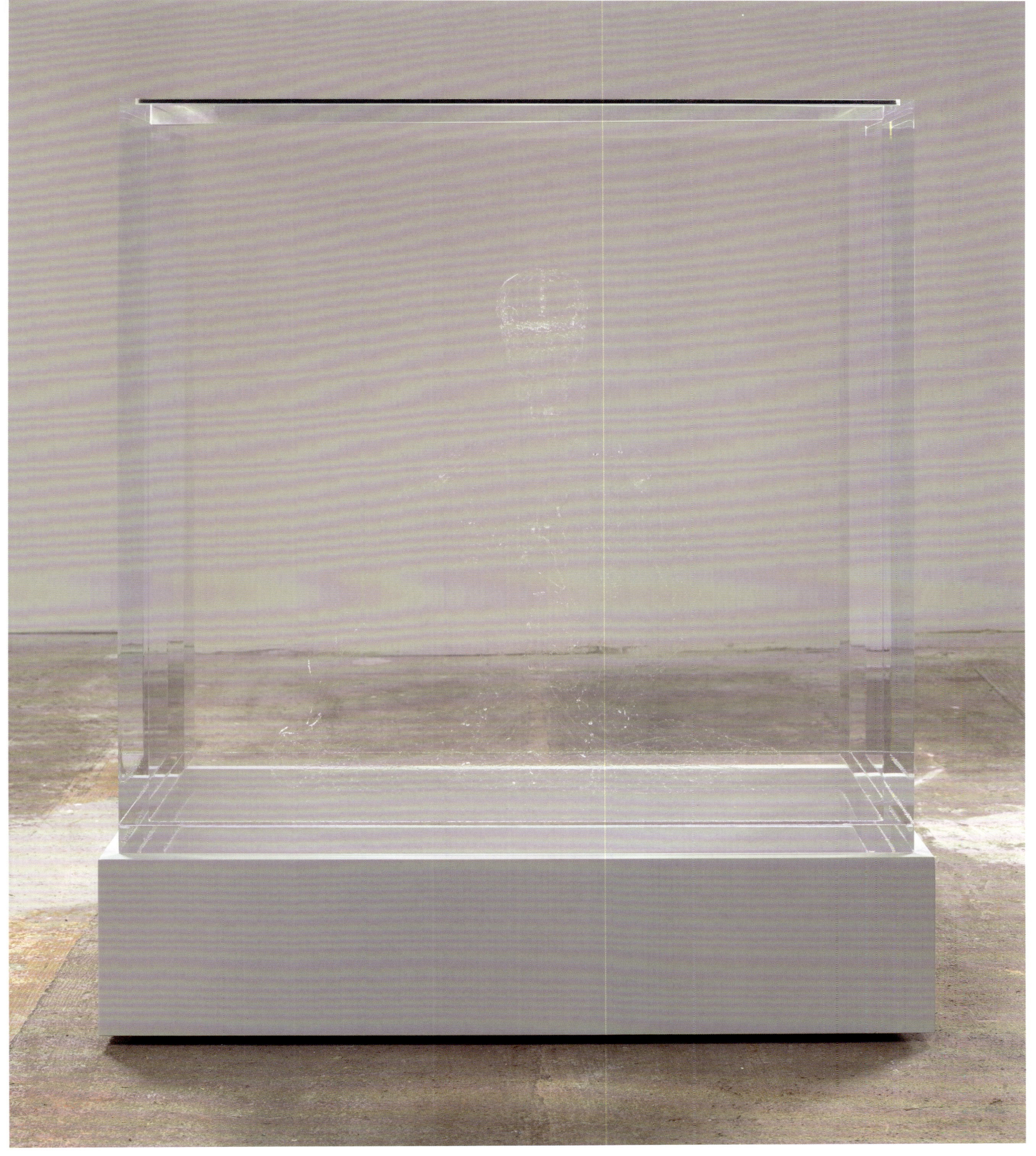

SEATED PANCHEN LAMA
(DETAIL), 2011
HAND-BLOWN GLASS,
MINERAL OIL, PLEXIGLASS
TANK, WOOD BASE
90 X 90 X 58 CM

WHAT WILL BE REMEMBERED IN THE FACE OF ALL THAT IS FORGOTTEN, 2014–15
NEON, STAINLESS STEEL, SEVEN TRANSFORMERS, 22AWG CABLES
163 X 43 X 46 CM

where thoughts, emotions and spiritual development are deeply intertwined. What's more, since no one has officially seen the Panchen Lama since 1995, his physical appearance can only be estimated, but the core power of what he represents for Buddhists can be symbolized by this complex network of vessels.

While extremely subtle and almost invisible, *Seated Panchen Lama* encompasses many of the essential elements of Strachan's interdisciplinary practice, which has been described as marking 'the passage of time, light, and darkness, intelligence and ignorance, memory and amnesia, success and failure, stardom and anonymity, distance, displacement, disorientation and home'.[16] In a video about the work produced to accompany the artist's 2024 exhibition in London's Hayward Gallery, Strachan explained: 'what is important for me about this particular story is how fragile culture can be'.[17] And while fragility is certainly evoked by the thin hand-blown glass and the double membrane that protects the treasured subject inside, this sculpture is also a work that in some way manages to transcend the forceful imprisonment of this spiritual icon. It asserts that despite his abduction, the spirit of the Panchen Lama – the reincarnation of Amithaba, the Buddha of infinite light and the symbol of compassion and rebirth – continues to sit peacefully, meditatively waiting for the appropriate time to return.

Similar themes of exclusion and perseverance pulse throughout Strachan's neon sculptures *What Will Be Remembered in the Face of All That is Forgotten, (Rosalind Franklin)*, 2014–15, *Robert*, 2018, *Alicia Alonso*, 2020, and most recently *Daughter of Ra (Mary Jackson)*, 2025. Each depicts the cardiovascular system of an individual who until recently had been omitted from history, missing from the stories of technological and creative innovation in which they played pivotal roles. Rosalind Franklin made a critical contribution to the discovery of the structure of DNA.[18] Aviator and astronaut Robert Henry Lawrence Jr had only been informally recognized as the first African American astronaut from the time of his selection for the 1967 Manned Orbiting Laboratory (MOL) programme – a precursor to the International Space Station programme – before officially being designated an astronaut by the air force in January 1997.[19] Alicia Alonso overcame the loss of her peripheral vision to become a star ballerina and choreographer.[20] In the 1950s, NASA Mathematician and Engineer Mary W. Jackson 'very well may have been the only Black female aeronautical engineer in the field'.[21]

In each sculpture, the subject is elevated in such a way that they appear to float, as if they have achieved a state of microgravity or neutral buoyancy – conditions that simulate the feeling of weightlessness in space or water. The electrified glass tubes in each sculpture fluctuate with an irregular pattern, mimicking each body's specialized system that generates and conducts electrical signals to produce power. Each figure has a distinct pose that communicates a particular disposition. Franklin's arms are outstretched in an open and receptive posture, Lawrence Jr is distinguishable by a deep bend in the back and a curved leg line. Alonso is captured mid-execution of a *brisé volé* but claps her hands neatly below the belt line in a gesture of confidence that perhaps camouflages certain vulnerabilities. Mary Jackson's exceptional abilities in life allow her to defy gravity. While both Franklin and Lawrence Jr died tragically in their thirties, Alonso lived well into her nineties and Jackson into her eighties. Strachan's decision to portray all four in a state of levitation suggests that despite attempts to stifle the impact of these highly influential figures, they have ultimately transcended active resistance in their professions to posthumously reach a higher state of awareness in our collective consciousness.

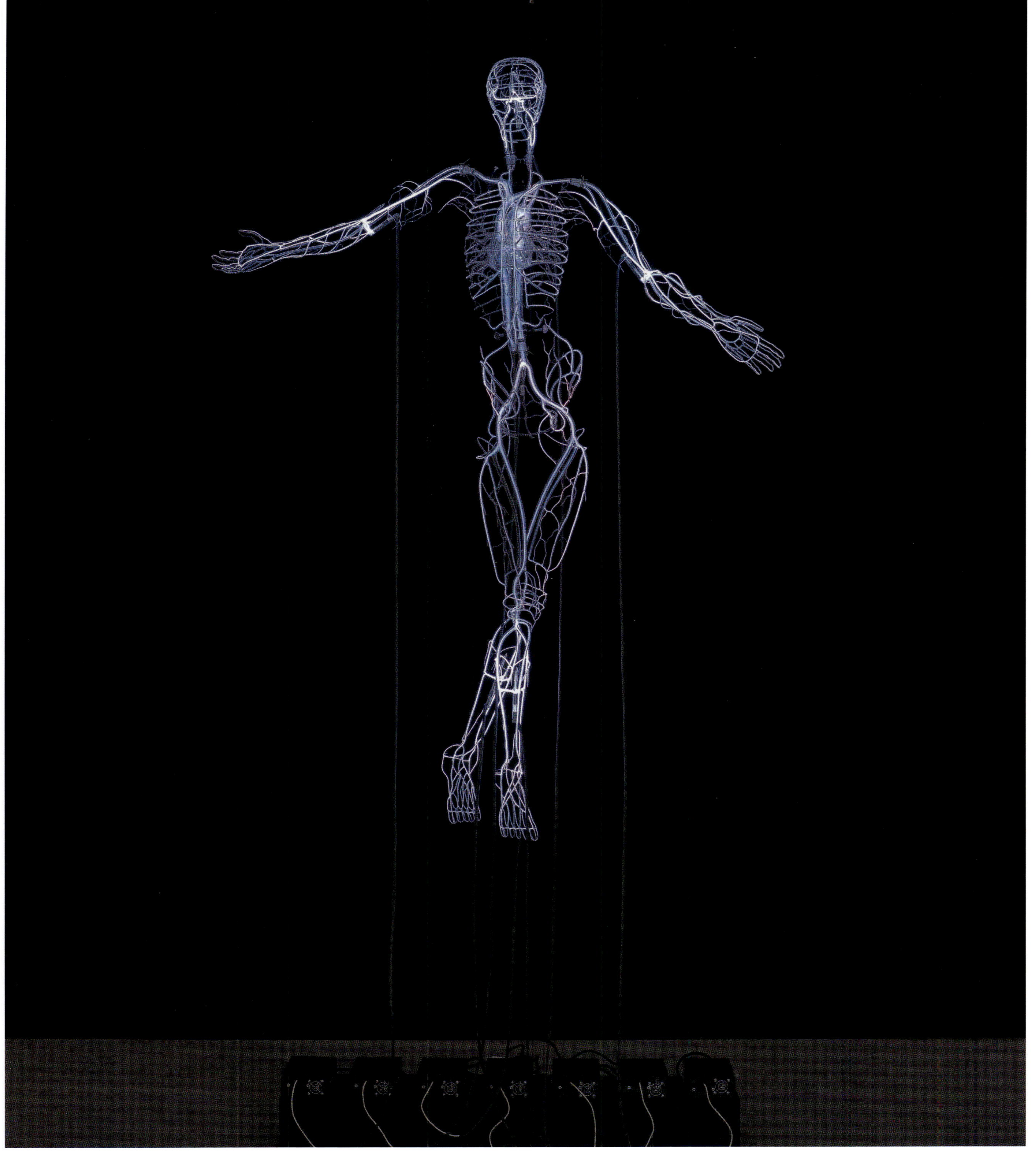

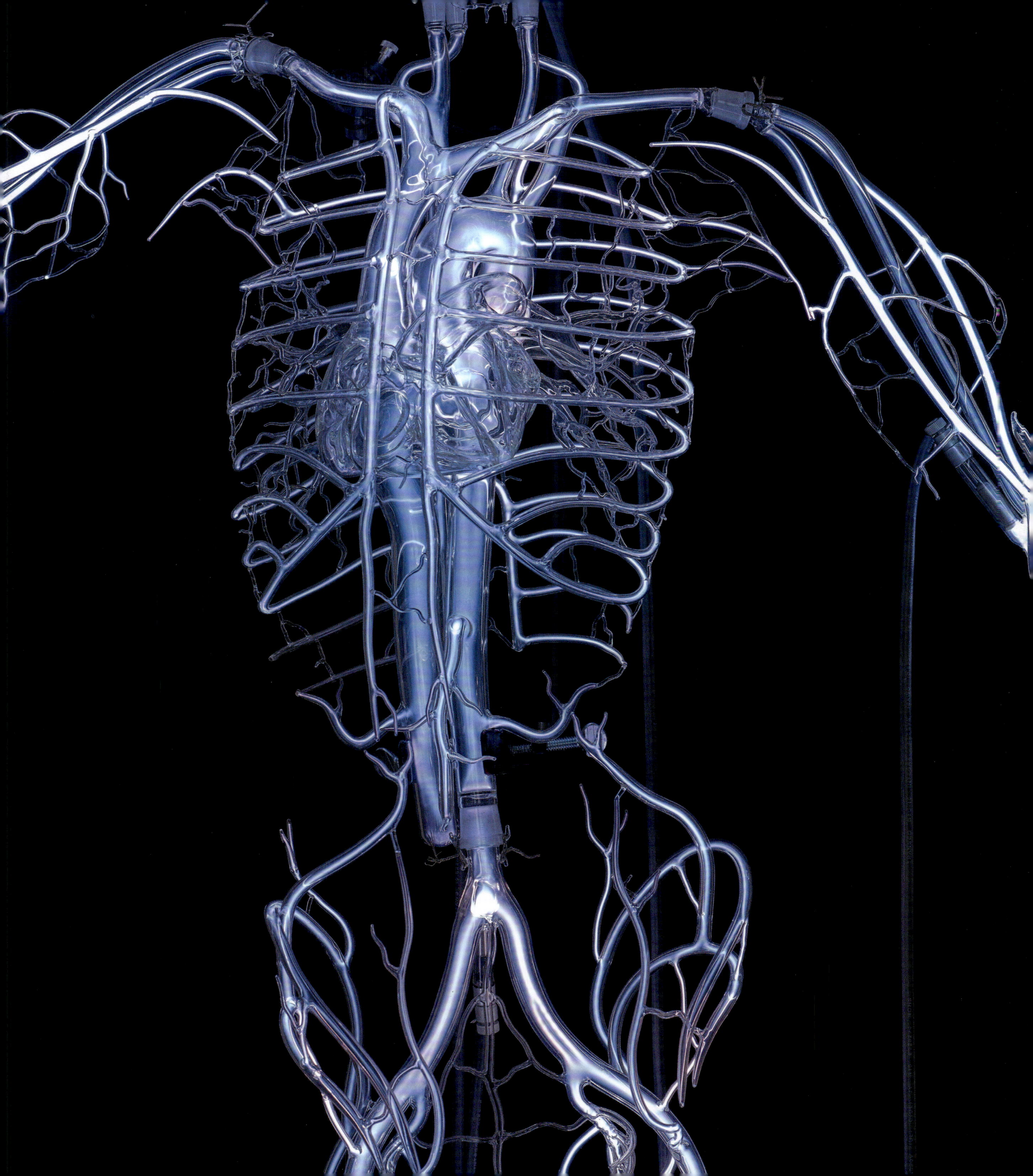

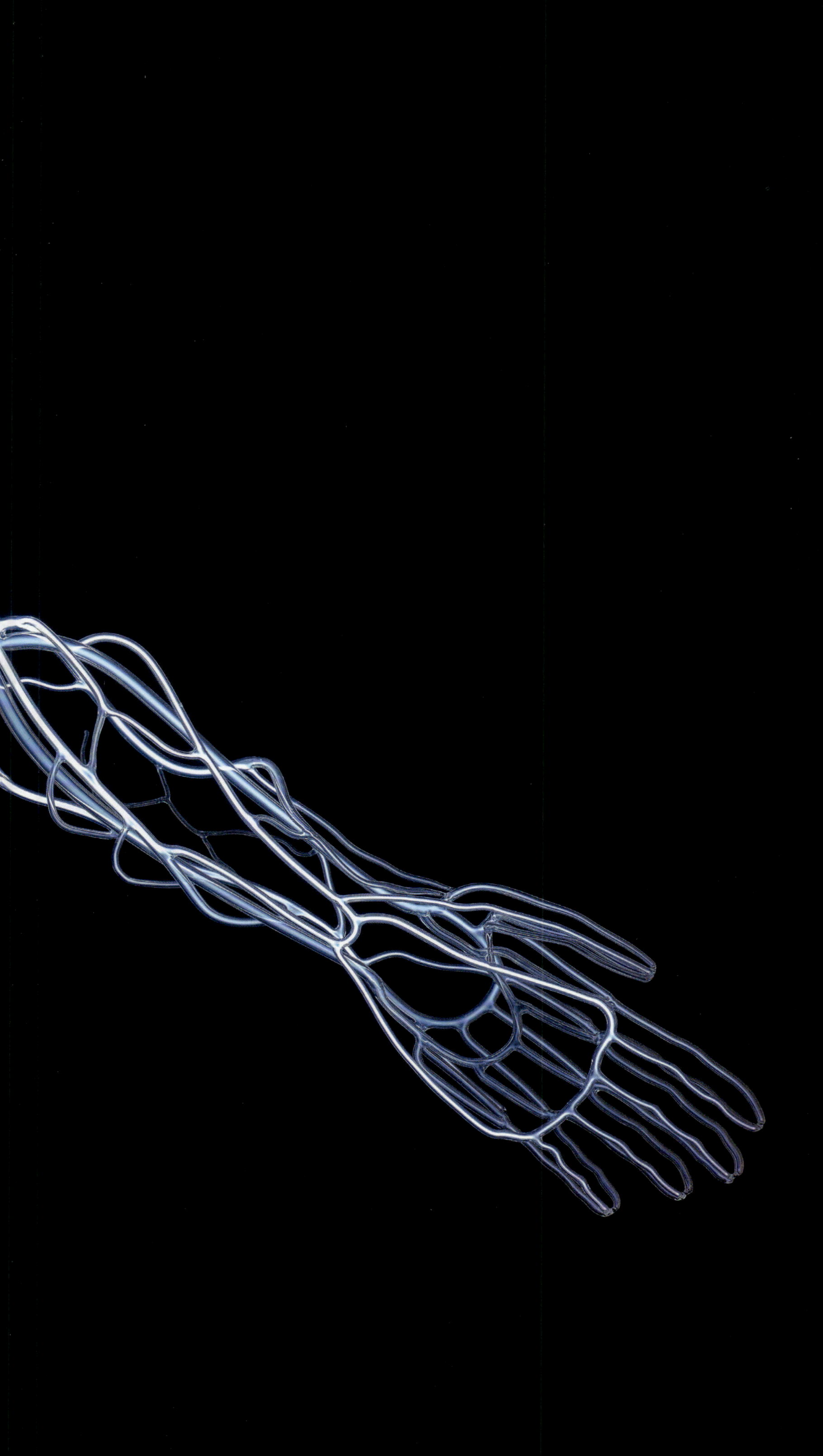

WHAT WILL BE REMEMBERED IN THE FACE OF ALL THAT IS FORGOTTEN (DETAIL), 2014–15
NEON, STAINLESS STEEL, SEVEN TRANSFORMERS, 22AWG CABLES
163 X 43 X 46 CM

MIND FIELD NO 7, 2023
FLOCKED HAIR ON CANVAS
213 X 213 CM

The relationship between permanence and impermanence central to many philosophical and spiritual traditions is further explored in Strachan's *Mind Field* series started in 2023 and made using 'flocked hair' on canvas. Flocking refers to a technique where tiny fibres are applied to a surface, creating subtle, fuzzy textures. However, these psychologically loaded and densely layered works are neither sentimental nor fragile. As a series they entangle organic matter with twentieth-century traditions of monochromatic painting in works that resonate between body and space. These voluminous paintings focus on form, texture and composition, and have three distinct colours: black, red and blonde. Hundreds of tightly curled balls of hair are secured to vary each surface in texture and pattern. for example, *Mind Field No. 1*, 2023, has a striking geometric design following a concentric circle pattern. Its sister work *Mind Field No. 7* follows a more irregular pattern akin to an archipelago of tiny islands across its surface. These initial works suggest landforms such as mountains, valleys and plains depicted on maps, but also aerial landscapes like rainbands or cosmic structures including spiral galaxies.

More overt references to the body start to appear in *Mind Field No. 5*, where a series of almond and round shapes conspire to suggest a human eye. Later works such as *Mind Field No. 14*, 2024, are more tightly constructed to create a thick uniform field that functions like an insulating layer protecting and camouflaging the imagined body beneath. It is important to note that 'the hair for Strachan's paintings is collected as clippings from the artist's personal network of geographically dispersed family and friends.'[22] This information underscores the works' corporeal quality. In recent years, the artist shifted to giving them titles such as *Oshun (Red Star)*, 2025 – a reference to a goddess in the West African religion of the Yoruba people. *Oshun (Red Star)* hints at rufous albinism, a genetic condition that can affect the colour or pigmentation of the skin, hair, and eyes resulting in unusual combinations of colour. Once we have made this conceptual leap, we start to question if blond-coloured works like *Mind Field No. 8*, 2023, have been created to draw our attention to people or cultures such as the Melanesian people of the Solomon Islands in the South Pacific, where it is common for the dark-skinned islanders to have bright blond hair. Unquestionably the series title, 'Mind Field', is a deliberate play on 'minefield' – a subject or situation fraught with unseen hazards. It provokes a certain discomfort when analyzing these works and reinforces their association with the body, death and decay. It also emphasizes the transgressive and abject qualities of hair – that it is both dead and alive at the same time. While Strachan has washed and processed the hair for his artistic use, it remains an indexical trace of the body or bodies from which it came.

Semiotic Systems

Created as part of the inaugural Desert X exhibition held in the Coachella Valley in Southern California, *I AM*, 2017, involved Strachan digging 290 depressions into a surface area measuring almost three acres. Each carefully plotted hole was executed in a dizzying array of shapes including triangles, ovals, rhombuses, parallelograms and trapezoids. Interior walls were reinforced and installed with acrylic mounts, after which florescent tubing was carefully inserted to follow the perimeter of each shape. By day, the work functions like a strange grouping of geoglyphs etched into the desert sands. At dawn, dusk or by night – once illuminated and viewed from some high vantage point – the diffuse fragments of subterranean neon coalesce to spell out the phrase 'I AM' in cursive script, around which a shockwave of light radiates

opposite,
MIND FIELD NO. 1 (DETAIL),
2023
FLOCKED HAIR ON CANVAS
152 X 152 X 5 CM

below,
MIND FIELD NO. 1, 2023
FLOCKED HAIR ON CANVAS
152 X 152 X 5 CM

below,
MIND FIELD NO. 8, 2023
FLOCKED HAIR ON CANVAS
213 X 213 X 5 CM

opposite,
MIND FIELD NO. 8 (DETAIL),
2023
FLOCKED HAIR ON CANVAS
213 X 213 X 5 CM

opposite,
OSHUN (RED STAR), 2025
FLOCKED HAIR ON CANVAS
184 X 184 X 6 CM

next pages,
I AM, 2017
TWO HUNDRED AND NINETY CRATERS, NEON TUBES
111 X 90 X 1 M

INSTALLATION VIEW IN THE PALM SPRINGS DESERT, CALIFORNIA

outwards. Deceptively simple, the combination of the two words 'I AM' emit a wealth of meaning across a millennium of knowledge.

Displayed for two months between 25 February 25 and 30 April 2017, the work was both fragmentary and temporary in nature, which could be interpreted as extending the artist's interest in Buddhist thought, in which the concept of 'I am', or a fixed, permanent 'self' is rejected. Instead, the 'self' is understood as a dynamic, impermanent, ever-changing process of interconnected elements. In his posthumously published *The Search for Truth by Natural Light,* c. 1647, French philosopher and scientist René Descartes expressed his famous philosophical dictum 'I doubt, therefore I am – or what is the same – I think, therefore I am.' The introduction of doubt here seems particularly relevant to Strachan, whose work often displays something of a recalcitrant spirit in pursuit of freedom and autonomy. Often, he seeks 'to deconstruct hierarchy: hierarchy in viewing, hierarchy in learning, the hierarchies of audiences'.[23] For Descartes, only curiosity, reason, creativity and performing good actions could raise knowledge to the highest level that it can possibly attain – sentiments frequently and often effusively echoed by Strachan who has commented 'when I was at primary school, I just learned a bunch of s**t I didn't need to learn'.[24]

In 1968, the phrase 'I Am A Man' was worn as a placard by workers struggling for dignity and recognition as part of the Memphis sanitation workers strike.[25] It has been said that the source for the now infamous slogan was a rousing speech delivered in the days leading up to the strike by Billy Lucy, who was at that time the highest-ranking Black official in the national office of the American Federation of State, County, and Municipal Employees (AFSCME). Lucy observed with barbed anger: 'He's treating you like children, and this day is over because you are men and must stand together as men and demand what you want.'[26] The strikers summarized Lucy's sentiment into a clear-cut slogan of pride and defiance. 'The strikers and their allies questioned what had been a monolithic (and monochromatic) model of masculinity … [they were interested in] creating new possibilities for working-class Black men, Black youth, and others to define their own identities.'[27] By abbreviating I AM A MAN, Strachan's I AM further refines the ways in which gender and race might shape assumptions about this work, opening it up to a more gender-neutral call for recognition. In this sense, amongst these patterns of thought in the fields of art, philosophy and politics, Strachan's I AM is an open-ended inquiry into the nature, capacity and potential of the human.

Strachan continues to explore these linguistic systems in his recent work. Measuring eighty-five inches square, *Gemini I (Woman King),* 2025, is a commanding abstract work. It is a tessellation of several large square typographic panels subdivided into smaller sections attached to a structural support. Each individual panel is filled with a selection of coloured letters that collectively amount to thousands of individual characters; when viewed together, they create a strong optical effect. From a distance

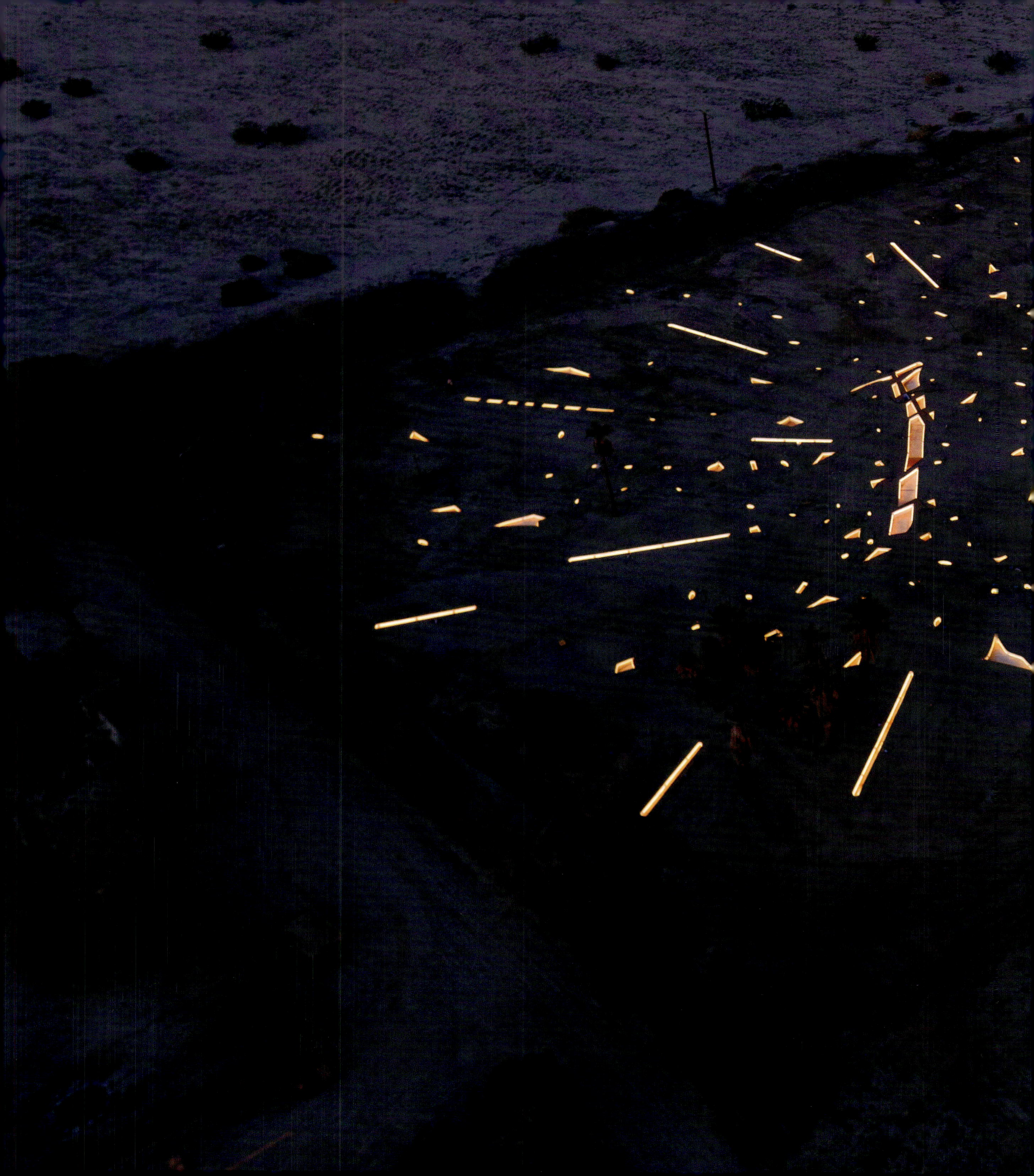

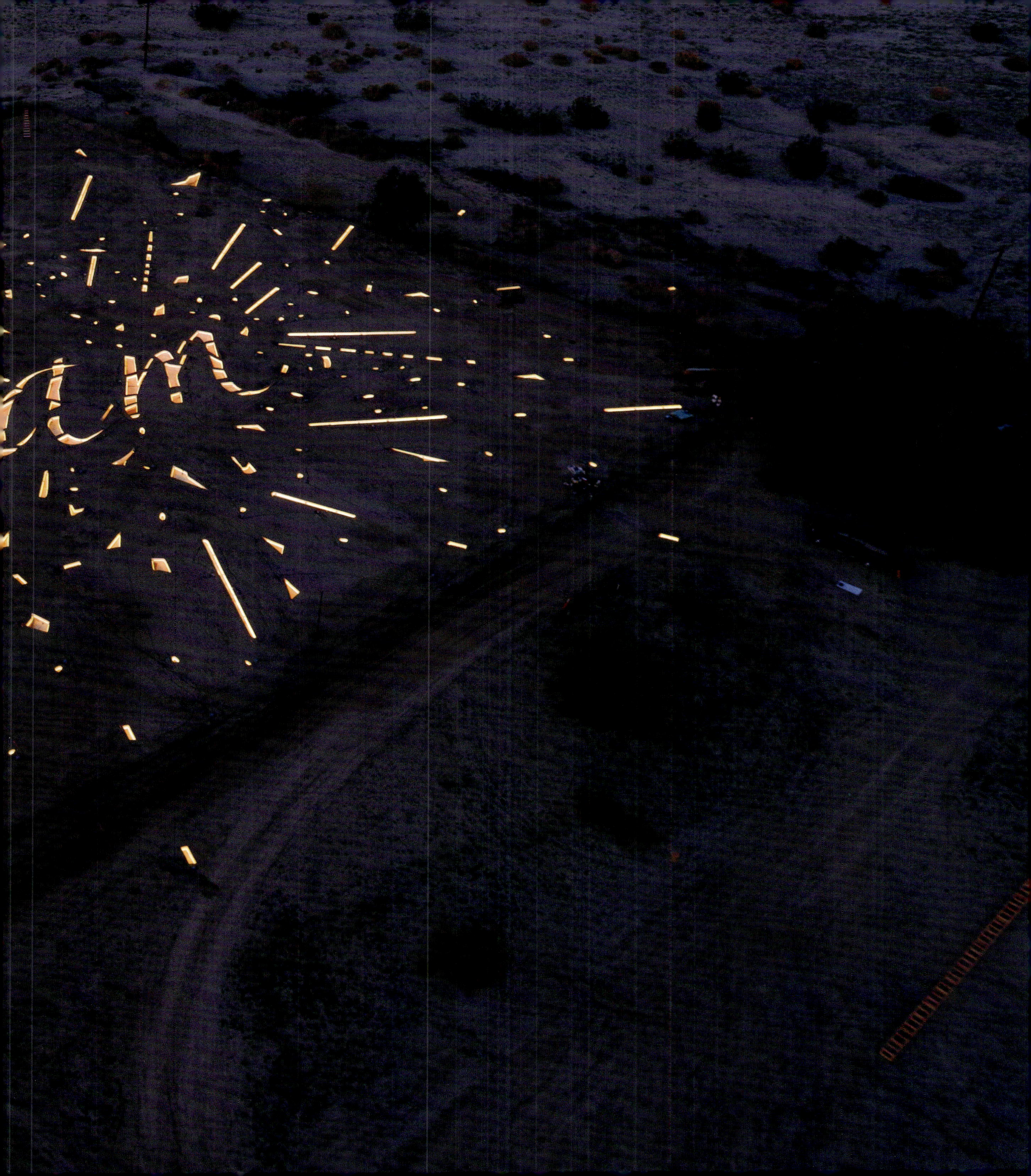

right,
GEMINI 1 (WOMAN KING), 2025
PIGMENT, ACRYLIC, PAPER ON PANEL
213 X 213 X 5 CM

next pages,
GEMINI 1 (WOMAN KING) (DETAIL), 2025
PIGMENT, ACRYLIC, PAPER ON PANEL
213 X 213 X 5 CM

the hand-painted letters mingle with one another to produce a visual instability. The polychromatic visual field forces a complex interplay between light and the brain's processing mechanism, which can't quite distinguish each letter separately so instead translates the hazy mix into a unified visual tapestry that pulsates and shimmers as the eye constantly readjusts and reinterprets what it sees. On a closer inspection of the work's surface, each embossed letter recalls certain primitive technologies, such as a typewriter key or a letter used for block printing, types of machines that have largely been replaced by modern digital technologies. This suggestion of an antiquated writing system implies that there may be some underlying structure, pattern or code embedded in the work, a language to be deciphered, half visible and half invisible.[28]

Epistemological Systems

On more than one occasion, Strachan has been described – or has described himself – as a storyteller, a narrator of history. He began his 2023 Technology, Entertainment, Design (TED) talk titled 'The Encyclopedia of Invisibility – A Home for Lost Stories' with the statement 'I really love lost stories.'[29] His exploration of historical truth originates from an early encounter with a general encyclopedia as a child. It was an experience that sparked a lifelong interest in history as a discipline and an inquiry into its theoretical and methodological agendas, ultimately leading to the publication of his conceptual artwork and magnum opus the *The Encyclopedia of Invisibility*, 2018. With 2,400 pages and measuring 15 x 13 x 5 inches, this goat-skin bound, denim-coloured, gilt-edged reference book is a formidable object. Conceived as an unfinished or continuous project, part of its allure as an idea lies in its incompleteness and potential for infinite expansion. As an object, it references both Collier's *Encyclopedia* and the *Encyclopedia Britannica*, the latter being the world's oldest English-language encyclopedia, which in recent years has been reassessed as 'an ambitious attempt to democratize knowledge. But by virtue of its biases and exclusions, it reinforced a Eurocentric view of the world which was then circulated to distant reaches of the globe.'[30] Strachan first encountered an example of these well-known reference books of knowledge aged twelve, in the Bahamas.

Instead of the inspiration he was anticipating, he discovered a problematic document that did not represent life as he knew it or wished to imagine it – an outdated worldview that was finely ordered, with everything, and everyone, in their place. As a Black boy hunting for heroes with whom he could identify, the *everyone* represented was frustratingly lacking in diversity, particularly regarding non-Western cultures and women. Addressing his frustration, Strachan undertook a twelve-year research project involving 'library sourcing, note collecting, interviews, bar conversations, and Google searches' to collate what he felt would be a more 'accurate' record of human ingenuity and accomplishment.[31] And while externally *The Encyclopedia of Invisibility* looks like a facsimile of a single volume of the encyclopedia that disappointed him as a child, its interior operates as so much more

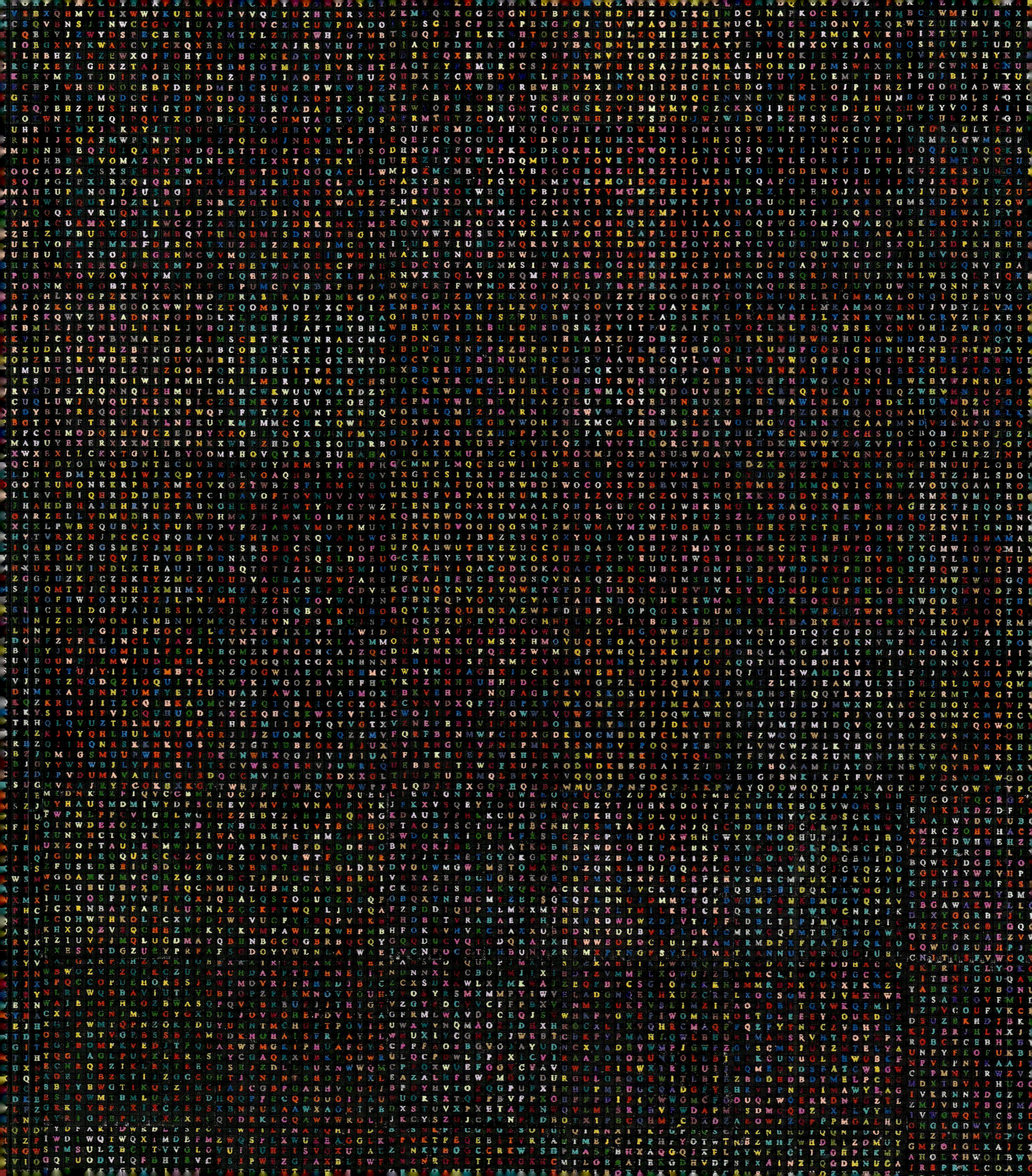

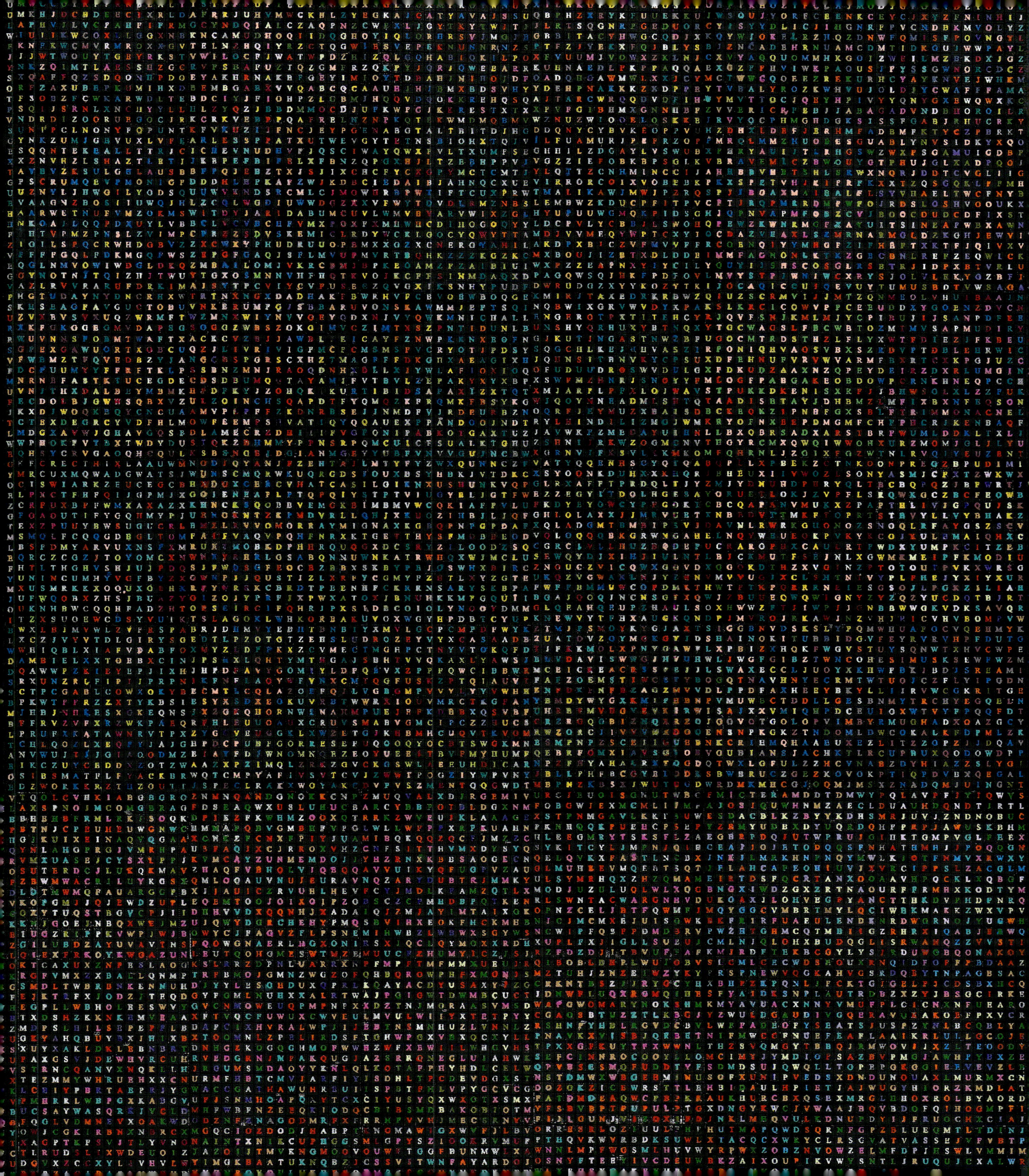

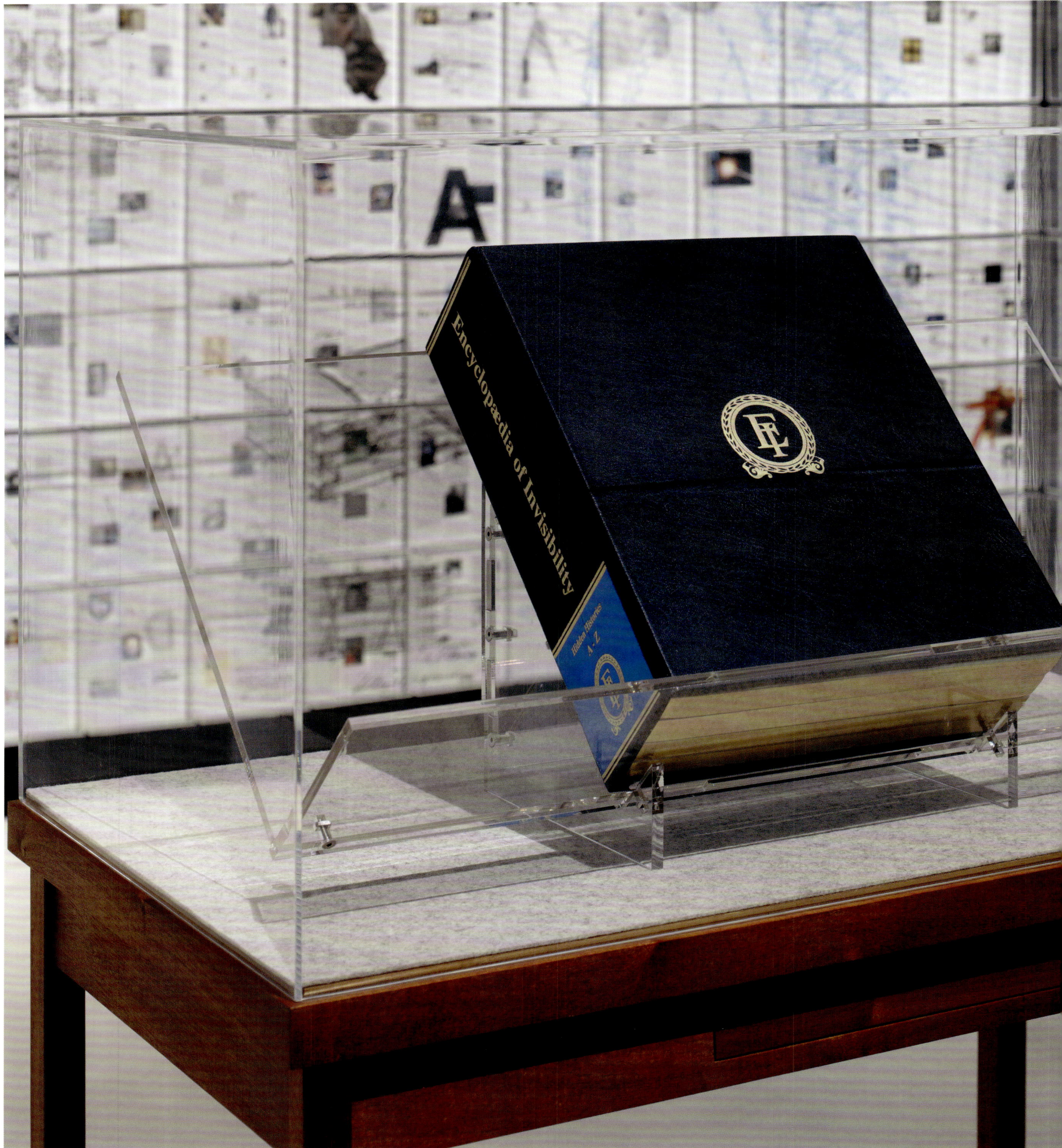
Encyclopædia of Invisibility
Hidden Histories
A–Z

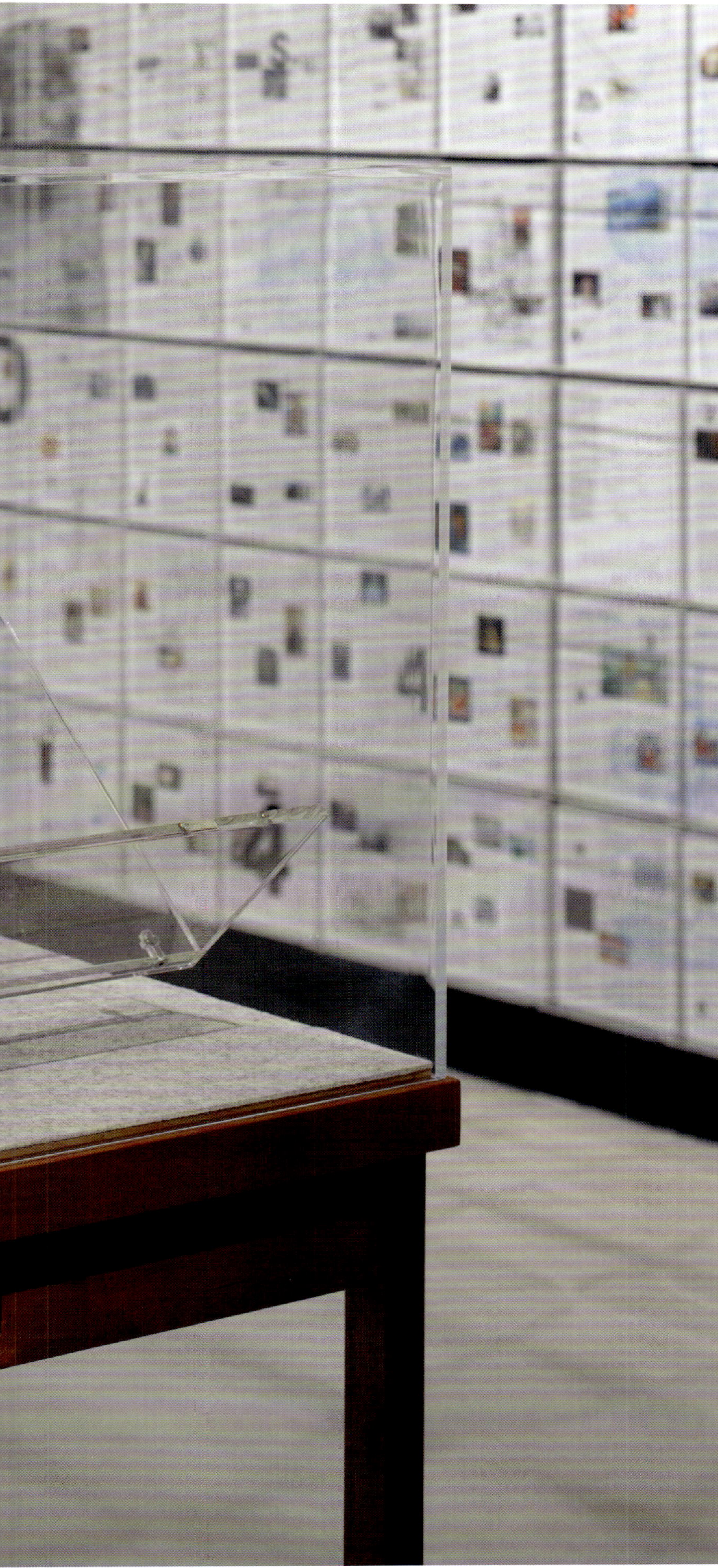

ENCYCLOPEDIA ROOM: PANEL PAINTING, 2022
INK, PAINT, ACRYLIC MEDIUM, MIXED MEDIA, COLLAGE WORK ON SINTRA PANELS, LEATHER GILDING, ARCHIVAL PAPER, MAPLE, FELT, ACRYLIC

PANELS: EACH 28 X 21 X 5 CM
ENCYCLOPEDIA: 29 X 23 X 10 CM
BOOKSTAND: 76 X 73 X 44 CM

INSTALLATION VIEW AT MARIAN GOODMAN GALLERY, LONDON, 2020

– challenging its predecessor, a symbol of old-world erudition and gravitas, in several important ways.

Structurally, *The Encyclopedia of Invisibility* follows the core design principles and format of an encyclopedia: alphabetical organization, short, specific entries, with some longer detailed articles, cross-referencing to connect related topics, and images, maps, and other visual aids to enhance understanding and viewer engagement.[32] Strachan's tome of knowledge, with its subtitle *Hidden Histories: A – Z*, currently features 17,000 entries that are by turns astonishing and fantastical. At its core the work is a compendium of historically significant individuals, places, things and events that have been either unintentionally or intentionally overlooked by the more established interpreters of the past, or as the artist has said, information and individuals that have been 'hidden or erased from history'.

More broadly, however, the work addresses questions of bias and editorial subjectivity in the creation of a canon of knowledge. It also relates to more recent debates on the quality and accuracy of historically 'trusted sources' contrasted with the rise of digital technologies in the twenty-first century that have revolutionized research by democratizing access to information and facilitating new methods of data collection and analysis, transforming research in the process. These ideas go right to heart of Strachan's project, which can be summarized as a deeply held scepticism toward master narratives of all types. 'I like the idea of interrogating systems of power because they are, in a way, how we define ourselves. Can we as individuals create systems of our own? Can we investigate where knowledge is coming from, on an individual level? That used to be a huge part of scholarship, and *The Encyclopedia of Invisibility* is a kind of interrogation of these kinds of power systems.'[33]

Strachan is acutely aware that history is inherently subjective and reflects the perspective of the historian, the sources used and the time-period in which it's being interpreted. Since their founding, encyclopedias relied upon outside experts as well as internal editors to write the entries. Each entry was then fact-checked, edited and copyedited. But with such expert knowledge and vast resources at their disposal, the question remained for Strachan 'How can there be so many glaring omissions?'[34] His *The Encyclopedia of Invisibility* proposes that no one can claim the omniscience needed to organize the whole field of human knowledge. His is more an open-ended question: 'What happens when you take all the things that weren't included and put them in one spot? It's not necessarily a solution to a problem,

ENCYCLOPEDIA ROOM: PANEL PAINTING, 2022
INK, PAINT, ACRYLIC MEDIUM, MIXED MEDIA, COLLAGE WORK ON SINTRA PANELS, LEATHER GILDING, ARCHIVAL PAPER, MAPLE, FELT, ACRYLIC
PANELS: EACH 28 X 21 X 5 CM
ENCYCLOPEDIA: 29 X 23 X 10 CM
BOOKSTAND: 76 X 73 X 44 CM

INSTALLATION VIEW AT THE LOS ANGELES COUNTY MUSEUM OF ART, 2025

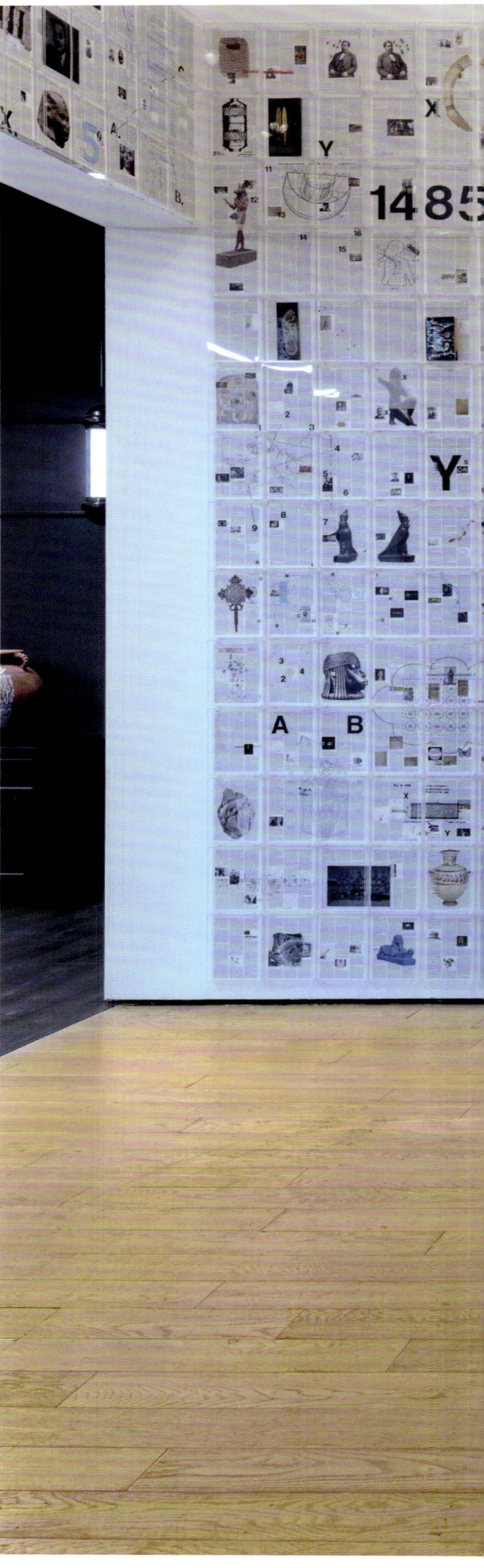

but more a series of curiosities that were inspired by a problem.'[35] But as a counterpoint to centuries of exclusion, *The Encyclopedia of Invisibility* does raise important questions about how our understanding of the past and present could be shaped if a book existed that only recorded and remembered those overlooked or minimized.

An alternative version for the display of the work exists as the room-sized installation *Six Thousand Years*, 2018.[36] In this immersive environment the encyclopedia is displayed in a hooded vitrine in what could be described as a 'museum-like' presentation, implying that this is an important document of age and significance. It sits in the centre of a room, the walls of which have been lined floor-to-ceiling with individual panels that incorporate modified pages from the encyclopedia. Each page has been altered using UV ink, vinyl, graphite, oil stick and collage, and encased in an acrylic box. The vertiginous graphic vocabulary consists of printed and collaged images of African sculpture, classical sculpture and archival photographs, together with drawn notations, schematics, illustrations, visualizations, graphs, charts and other symbols. While the fragmentary information superimposed over the text obscures our ability to fully read each page, the diversity of mark-making and illustrations suggest that *The Encyclopedia of Invisibility* is being used as a tool to work through complex thought, utilizing statistical analysis and numerical data to study history, focusing on patterns and relationships within large datasets to understand social, economic and political phenomena. These altered sheets represent only a small selection from the book and as an installation must be carefully planned and reconfigured for each new iteration. In conceiving of the work in this way, Strachan animates the book and grants audiences permission to physically step inside and explore it. It is a visceral viewing experience that is unique to everyone who encounters it, in that according to the person's height, certain entries are viewable up to their eye level, but even for the tallest of visitors much of the room remains beyond reach. This limited legibility echoes in the space and is amplified by the book itself, which sits there, stoically confident in the knowledge that it contains many, many more entries than we may ever have opportunity to discover.

The Encyclopedia of Invisibility has been enormously generative for the artist, with a steady stream of elements from it showing up in his sculptures, performances, videos and paintings.[37] Tumbling out of its pages are a foundational group of works: *The Alchemist, The Explorer, The Stranger,* and *The Student,* 2018 – titles that hint at how Strachan might self-reflexively consider his role in relation to the information, concepts and ideas contained in *The Encyclopedia of Invisibility*, or interpret his relationship to the creation and communication of new visual knowledge with which he is engaged. Take *The Alchemist*, for example. The background of the image is divided in two, one half a pre-print layout of multiple pages from *The Encyclopedia of Invisibility* before cutting and binding, juxtaposed with a reproduction of Strachan's earlier work about exploration *Blast Off*. On top of these the artist has overlaid images of an airship, a crossword puzzle, the Hindu goddess Shakti, a diagram of an American football and a cricket ball and a Native American beaded bracelet. As the title suggests, the meaning for each individual element has been transformed by their compositional relationship to one another, creating a new narrative that mixes engineering, design, religion and geometric abstraction. As hinted at by the crossword puzzle, *The Alchemist* is a problem-solving exercise that requires both direct observation and speculative knowledge to solve. For example, is there a relationship between the spheroid shape of the modern American football and the airship, the numbered squares of the word game and the gridded design of the bracelet, the divine power of Shakti versus the finite man-made power of an engine?

The same decoding challenge is required when analyzing *The Student*. Once again, Strachan integrates *The Encyclopedia of Invisibility*'s signature with an image: a gyrfalcon, a spacecraft launch, a diagram of the brain pointing out the lobes of the cerebrum, a television test pattern or colour bar, an iceberg, and an archival image of arctic explorer Robert Peary, who is usually credited with leading the first expedition to reach the North Pole in 1909. Centrally positioned in this elaborate composition is a glossy whiteboard with a variety of handwritten notes, presumably the artist's, beneath an underlined title 'How Can Someone be Made Invisible?' They include

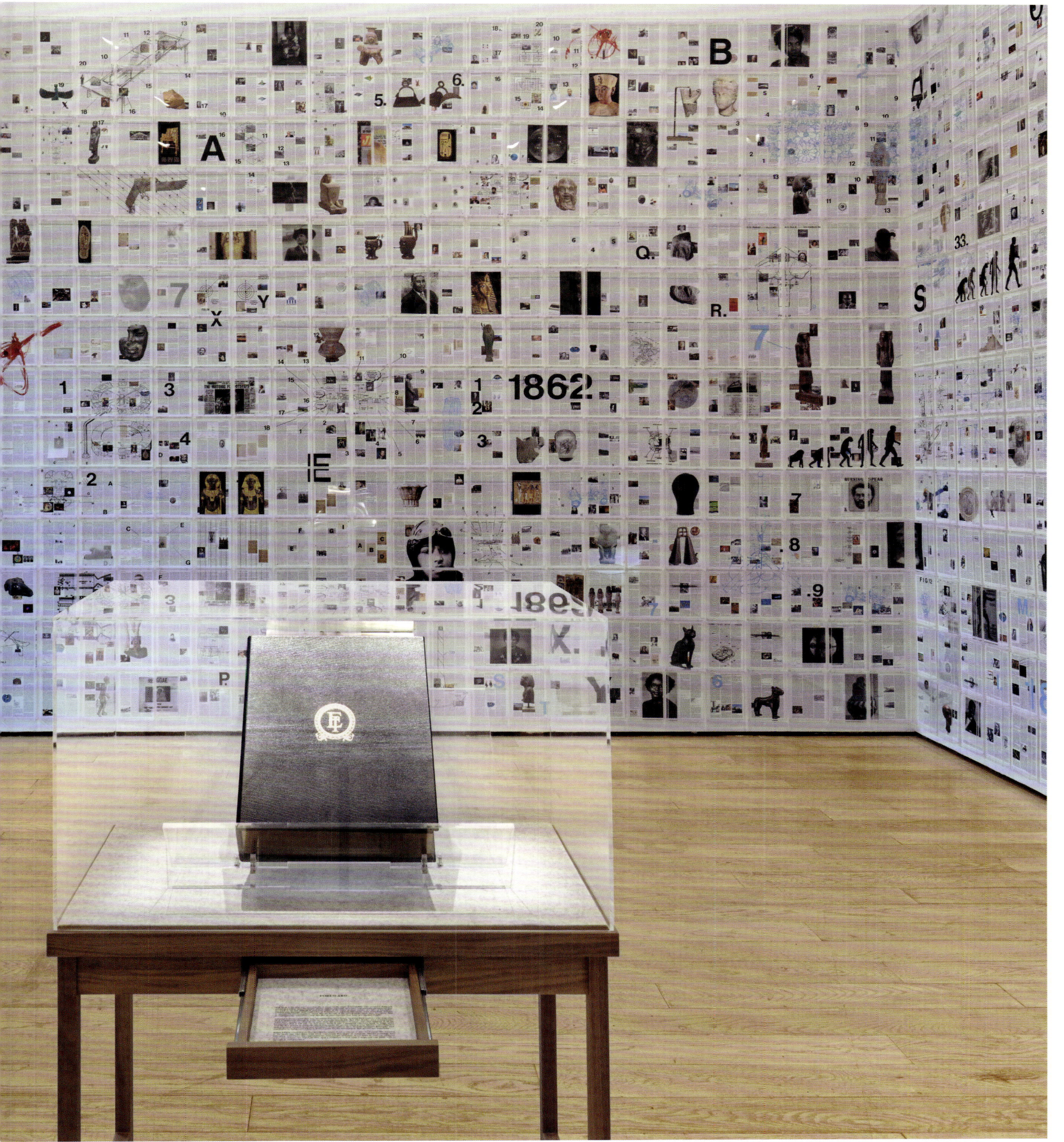

plush, and coarse woolen hose—the complete costume of the peasant from Nassau. For a moment I felt stunned; then flames passed before my eyes. I recollected those precipices which entice with an irresistible power; those wells or pits, which the police have been compelled to close, because men threw themselves into them; those trees which had been cut down because they inspired men with the idea of hanging themselves; that contagion of suicides, of robberies, of murders, at certain epochs, by desperate means; that strange and subtile enticement of example which makes you yawn because another yawns, suffer because you see another suffer, kill yourself because you see others kill themselves—and my hair stood up with horror.

How could this Fledermausse, this base, sordid creature, have derived so profound a law of human nature? how had she found the means to use this law to the profit or indulgence of her sanguinary instincts? This I could not comprehend; it surpassed my wildest imaginations. But reflecting longer upon this inexplicable mystery, I resolved to turn the fatal law against her, and to draw the old murderess into her own net. So many innocent victims called out for vengeance! I felt myself to be on the right path. I went to all the old-clothes sellers in Nuremberg, and returned in the afternoon to the Inn Boeuf-Gras, with an enormous packet under my arm. Nichel Schmidt had known me for a long time; his wife was fat and good-looking; I had painted her portrait. "Ah, Master Christian," said he, squeezing my hand, "what happy circumstance brings you here? What procures me the pleasure of seeing you?" "My dear Monsieur Schmidt, I feel a violent, insatiable desire to sleep in the Green Room."

We were standing on the threshold of the inn, and I pointed to the room. The good man looked at me distrustfully. "Fear nothing," I said; "I have no desire to hang myself." "À

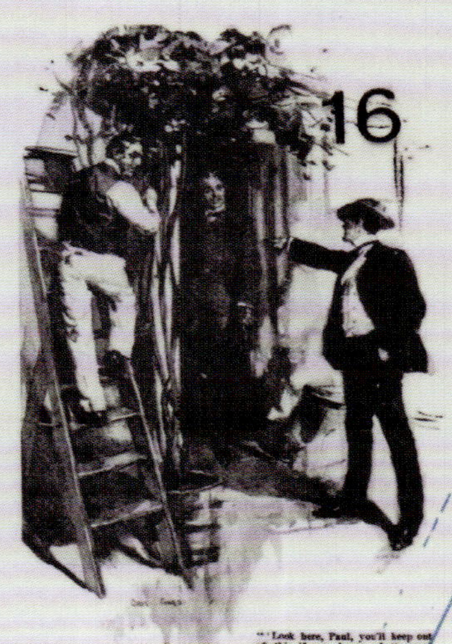

Illustration from Hawthorne's compendium
Courtesy of sffaudio.com

la bonne heure! à la bonne heure! For frankly that would give me pain; an artist of such merit! When do you wish the room, Master Christian?" "This evening." "Impossible! it is occupied!" "Monsieur can enter immediately," said a voice just behind me, "I will not be in the way." We turned around in great surprise; the peasant of Nassau stood before us, with his three-cornered hat, and his packet at the end of his walking stick. He had just learned the history of his three predecessors in the Green Room, and was trembling with rage. "Rooms like yours!" cried he, stuttering; "but it is murderous to put people there—it is assassination! You deserve to be sent to the galleys immediately!" "Go—go—calm yourself," said the innkeeper; "that did not prevent you from sleeping well." "Happily, I said my prayers at night," said the peasant; "without that, where would I be?" and he withdrew, with his hands raised to heaven.

"Well," said Nichel Schmidt, stupefied, "the room is vacant, but I entreat you, do not serve me a bad trick." "It would be a worse trick for myself than for you, monsieur." I gave my packet to the servants, and installed myself for the time with the drinkers. For a long time I

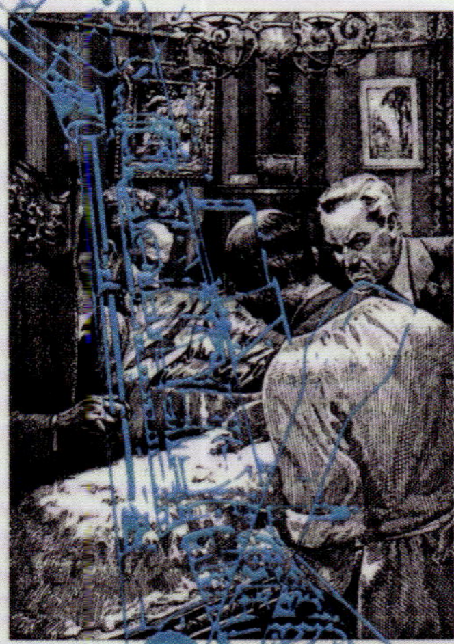

Illustration from Hawthorne's compendium
Courtesy of sffaudio.com

had not felt so calm and happy. After so many doubts and disquietudes, I touched the goal. The horizon seemed to clear up, and it appeared that some invisible power gave me the hand. I lighted my pipe, placed my elbow on the table, my wine before me, and listened to the chorus in "Freischütz," played by a troupe of gypsies from the Black Forest. The trumpets, the hue and cry of the chase, the hautboys, …
into a vague reverie, and, at ti…
look at the hour, I asked …
which had happened …
But the wa… I have
the *salle*, a… se…
thoughts were … soul, and in deep
meditation I … Charlotte, who preceded me w… to my room. We mounted the sta… story. Charlotte gave
me the ca… nted to the door. "There,"
said she … ded rapidly. I opened the
door. Th… m was like any other inn
room. … was very low, the … ery
high. … nce I explored the exterior,
and the … the window. No house was to
be seen … se of Flederma… only, in
some … , an obscure light was burning. So… on the watch. "That is well,"
said I, … curtain. "I have all necessary
time." … packet, I put on a woman's
bonnet … g lace; then, placing myself
before a … k a brush and painted wrinkles in m… s took me nearly an hour.
Then I pu… s and a large shawl, and I
was actual… myself.

Flederm… d to me to look at me
from the mi… moment the watchman cried out, … k!" I seized the
manikin which … my packet,
and muffled it in a … imilar
to that worn by the ol…
the curtain. Certainly, after …
the Fledermausse, of her inferna…

prudence, her adroitness, she could not in any way surprise me; and yet I was afraid. The light which I had remarked in the chamber was still immovable, and now cast its yellow rays on the manikin of the peasant of Nassau, which was crouched on the corner of the bed, with the head hanging on the breast, the three-cornered hat pulled down over the face, the arms suspended, and the whole aspect that of absolute despair.

The shadows, managed with diabolical art, allowed nothing to be seen but the general effect of the face. The red vest, and six round buttons alone, seemed top shine out in the darkness. But the silence of the night, the complete immobility of the figure, the exhausted, mournful air, were well calculated to take possession of a spectator with a strange power. For myself, although forewarned, I was chilled even to my bones. How would it, then, have fared with the poor simple peasant, if he had been surprised unawares? He would have been utterly cast down. Despairing, he would have lost all power of self-control, and the spirit of imitation would have done the rest. Scarcely had I moved the curtain, when I saw Fledermausse on the watch behind her window. She could not see me.

I opened my window softly; the window opposite was opened! Then her manikin appeared to rise slowly and advance before me. I, also, advanced my manikin, and seizing my torch with one hand, with the other I quickly opened the shutters. And now the old woman and myself were face to face. Struck with sudden terror, she had let her manikin fall! We gazed at each other with almost equal horror. *She* extended her finger—I advanced *mine*. *She* moved her … —I agitated *mine*. She breathed a profound sigh, and leaned upon her elbow. I imitated her. To describe all the terrors of this scene would be impossible. It bordered upon confusion, madness, delirium. It was a death struggle between two wills, between two intelligences; between two souls—each one wishing to destroy the other; and, in this struggle, I had the advantage—her victims struggled with me.
… g imitated for some seconds
… Fledermausse, I pulled a
… and attached it to the
… gazed at me with
gaping mouth … ope around my
neck; her pup… ened; her face
was convulsed. No, … , in a whistling voice. I pursued … impassability of an executio… ed to take
possession of her. … exclaimed,
straightening herself up, … hands contracted on the crossbeam. "Old fool!" I gave
her no time to go on, blowing out my lamp. I
stooped, like a man going to make a vigorous
spring, and, seizing my manikin, I passed the
rope around its neck, … precipitated it below.
A terrible cry resounded through the street, and
…
… listened
… an hour
… voice of
the watchman, crying, "In… Nuremberg, midnight, midnight s… Now justice … satisfied!" I cried, … victims
are avenged. Pardon me, … bout five
minutes after the cry of th… n, I saw
Fledermausse attracted, al… y manikin (her exact image), spri… window,
with a rope around her n… suspended
from the crossbea… of death
undulating … the moon,
… the summit of
… rays reposed upon
… ideous head. Just as I had

left, opposite and next pages,
THE ENCYCLOPEDIA OF INVISIBILITY (DETAILS),
2014–18
LEATHER, GILDING, ARCHIVAL PAPER, MAPLE, FELT, ACRYLIC
38 X 34 X 12 CM

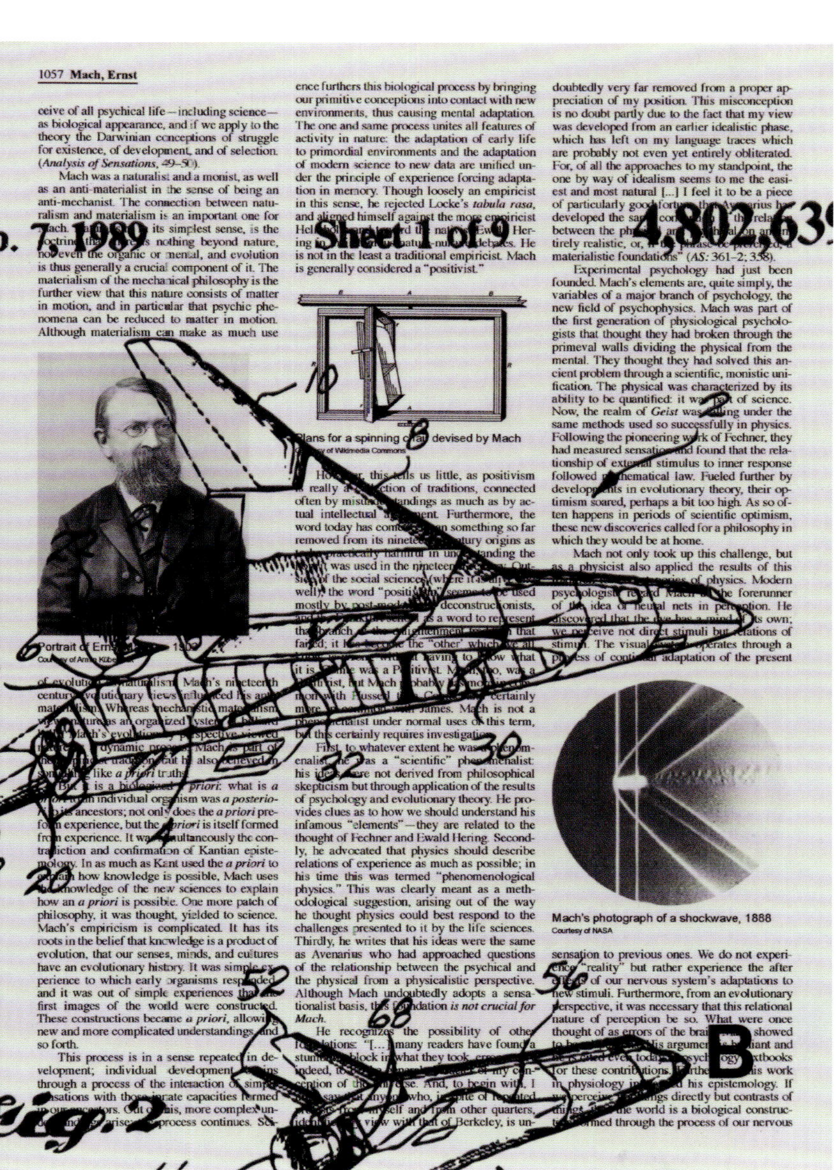

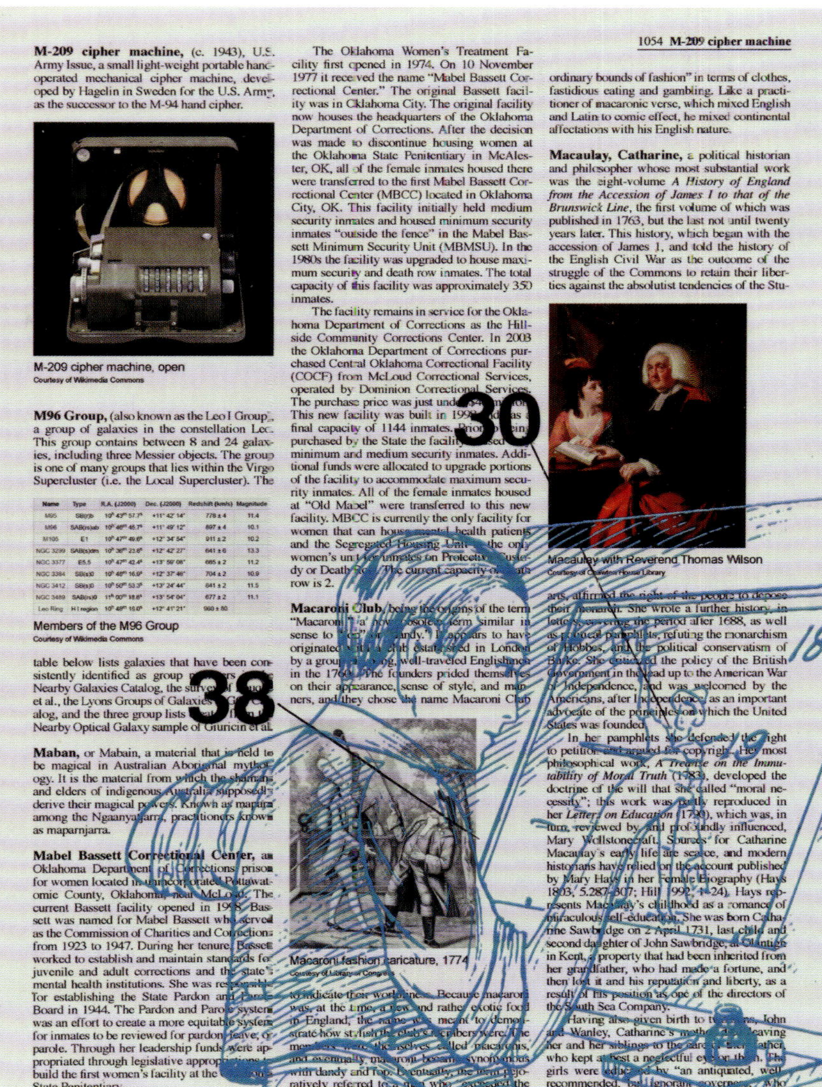

musings on emission theory, which proposes that objects are perceived because light is emitted from the eyes, rather than entering them. Other notes contain various hypotheses on how to make someone or something invisible by means of camouflage and cloaking devices that bend light.

The message embedded in *The Student* is perhaps less hidden. The problem of concealment and invisibility being worked out by Strachan on the whiteboard is presumably an attempt to understand the initial erasure of Matthew Henson, an African American explorer who accompanied Robert Peary to the North Pole in 1909 and who is now considered to be the first man to have reached the North Pole.[38] On their return from their pathbreaking expedition, Peary had accepted the accolade, despite Henson's revelatory 1912 memoir *A Negro Explorer at the North Pole*, which included an effusive foreword by Peary and an introduction by Booker T. Washington. However, despite these endorsements, the book's oft-cited statement 'and as in the past, from the beginning of history, wherever the world's work was done by a white man, he had been accompanied by a colored man', sums up the 'color bar' that Henson encountered at that time.[39]

If the question at the centre of The Student is how can someone be made "invisible?" the central question of *The First Supper (Galaxy Black)*, 2023 might be how to make a commemorative sculpture to honour individuals, events and ideas that makes them 'visible'? Put another way, Strachan highlights a single person, place, object, or event and uses it to open a window onto broader historical questions. This may seem like a straightforward question for a visual artist, yet the conceptual complexity and semiotic orientation of Strachan's sculpture has more-or-less been overlooked in favour of a more cursory or convenient analysis since its inaugural presentation in 2024.[40] To the casual eye, *The First Supper* is a figurative sculpture representing a gathering of historically significant Black figures, accompanied by a Tasmanian tiger and a self-portrait of the artist. It includes sculptural

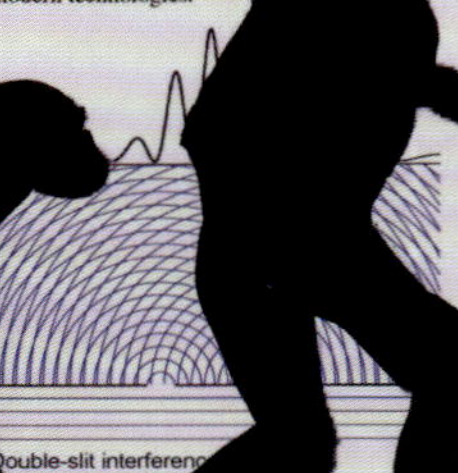

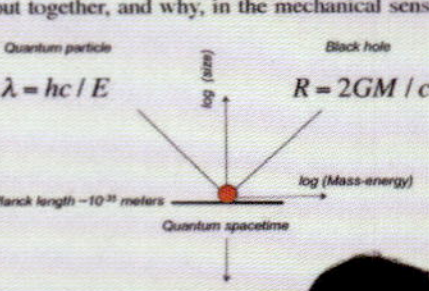

Planck scale between a particle

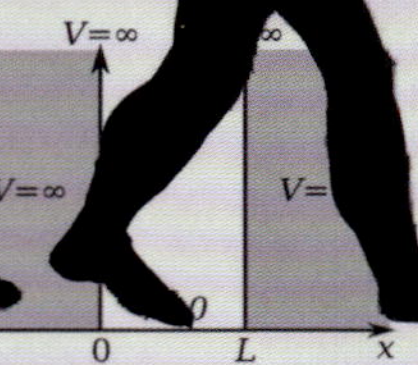

Double-slit interference

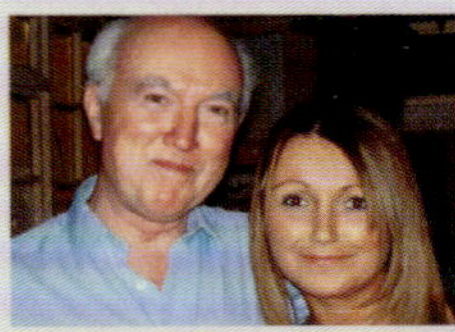

Particle potential in an infinite potential well

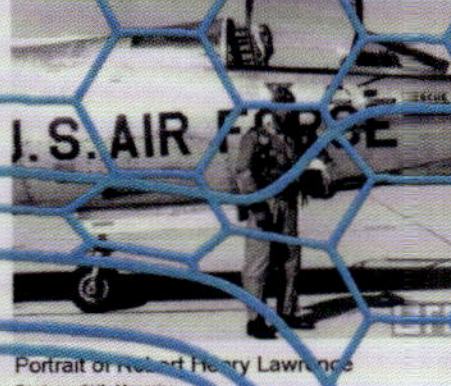

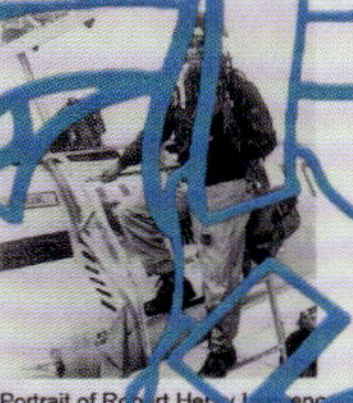

Portrait of Robert Henry Lawrence

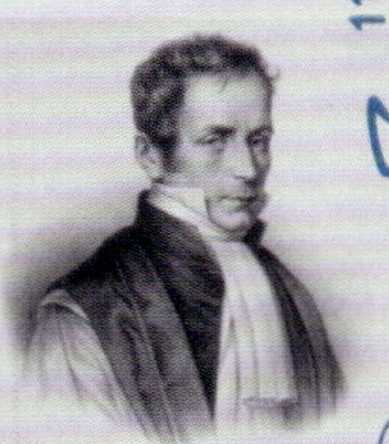

Portrait of René Laennec

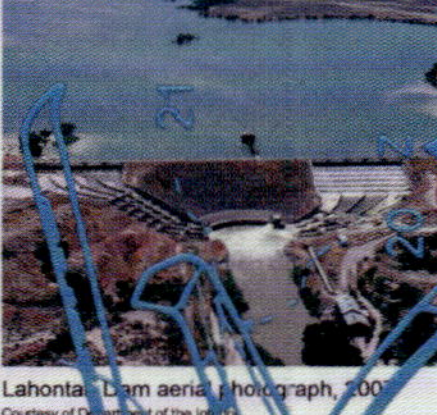

Lahontan Dam aerial photograph, 2007

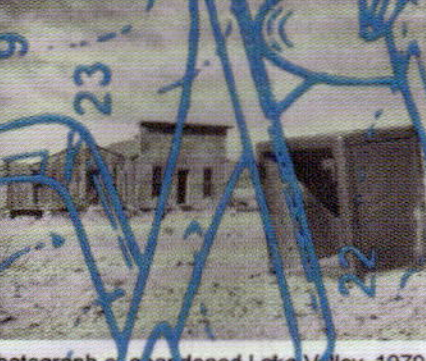

Photograph of abandoned Lake Valley, 1970

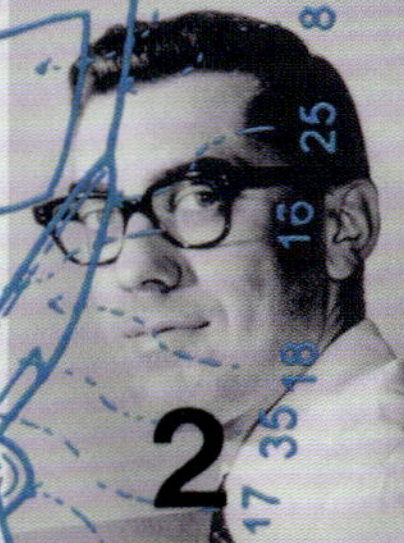

Portrait of John Lake, c. 1965

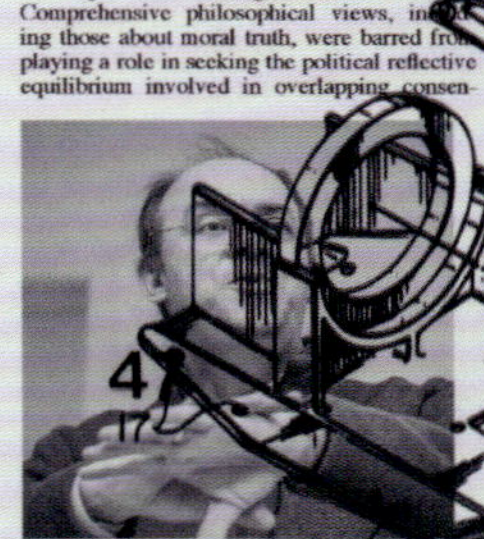

Realism philosopher Graham Oddie

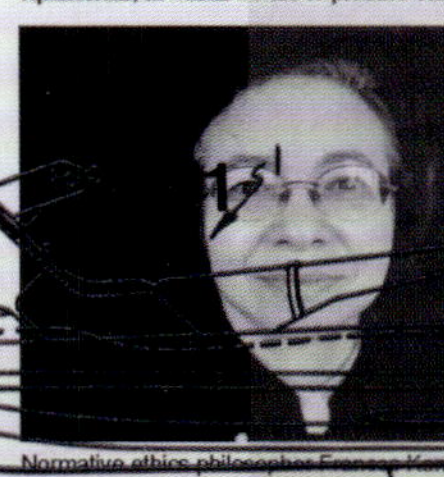

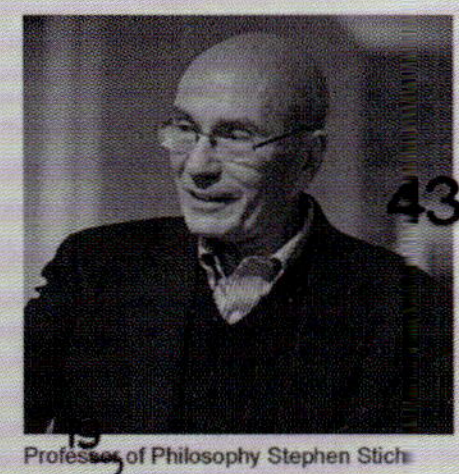

Professor of Philosophy Stephen Stich

pear to have been exempted. Zulju, who [illegible] probably a Mongol from Turkistan, wrea[illegible] devastation in 1320, when he commanded a force that conquered [illegible] regions of the Kashmir Valley. However, [illegible] probably not a Muslim. The actions of Sultan [illegible] shikan (1389–1413), the seventh Muslim ruler in Kashmir were also significant to the [illegible]. The Sultan has been referred to as an iconoclast because of his destruction of many non-Muslim religious symbols and the manner in which forced the population to convert or flee.

Many followers of the traditional religion who did not convert to Islam instead migrated to other parts of India. The migrants included some Pandits, although it is possible that some of this community relocated for economic reasons as much as to escape the new rulers. Brahmins were at that time [illegible] offered

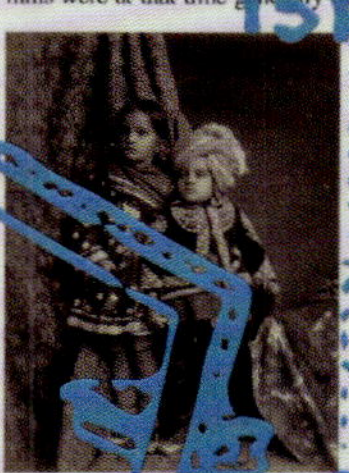

Kashmiri children, c. 1895
Courtesy of British Library

grants of land in [illegible] areas by rulers seeking [illegible] the traditionally high literacy and general [illegible] of the community, as well as the legitimacy [illegible] by association. The outcome of this [illegible] population and in religion was that the Kashmir Valley became a predominantly Muslim region. Butshikan's heir, the devout Muslim Zain-ul-Abidin (1423–74), was tolerant of Hindus to the extent of sanctioning [illegible] return to Hinduism of those who had been forcibly converted to the Muslim faith, as well as becoming [illegible] the restoration of temples. He respected the learning of these Pandits, to whom he gave land as well as encouraging those who had left to return.

He operated a meritocracy and both Brahmins and Buddhists were among his closest advisors. Akbar conquered Kashmir in 1587 CE. During his mughal rule the Hindus enjoyed security of person and property and were allotted high government posts. It was he, who, pleased with their intelligence, gave them the surname Pandit. The Mughals rule was followed by that of Afghans. Gradually, many Kashmiris converted to Islam, leaving smaller population of Kashmiri Pandits who still practiced the Shaivite religion. Not much was done to win back the converts to Hinduism. The majority, though still remained Hindus in Jammu and Kashmir. The Brahmin Pandits of Kashmir established themselves in the Northern area of India, first in the Rajput and Mughal courts and then in the service of the Dogra rulers of Kashmir. This cohesive community, highly literate and socially elite, were one of the first to discuss and implement social reforms. There are zones set up with offices for relief. Many Orders, Circulars and recommendations have been issued [illegible] Jammu And Kashmir Migrant Immovable Property (Preservation, Protection And Restraint On Distress Sales) Act, 1997, provides [illegible] any person who is an unauthorized occupant or recipient of any usufruct of any immovable property of the migrant shall pay to the migrant such compensation for the period of unauthorized occupation and in such a manner as

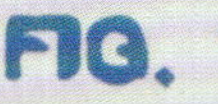

Kashmiri priests, c. 1895
Courtesy of British Library

may be determined by the District Magistrate." Following the migration of the Kashmiri Pandit community, various socio-political organizations have sprung up to represent the cause of the displaced community. The most prominent among these are the All India Kashmiri Samaj or AIKS, All India Kashmiri Pandit conference, Panun Kashmir & Kashmiri Samiti. These organizations are involved in rehabilitation of the community in the valley through peace negotiations, mobilization of human rights groups and [illegible] for the Pandits. Panun Kashmir has

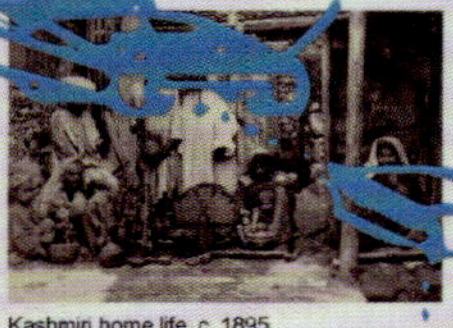

Kashmir home life, c. 1895
Courtesy of British Library

made demands for a separate homeland for [illegible] community in the southern part of Kashmir. According to Aljazeera, the estimated population of Kashmiri Pandits in the Kashmir Valley in 2011 was around 2,700–3,400. Others who left the Valley are now scattered throughout India, particularly in Jammu and the National Capital Region. Some emigrated to other countries entirely.

Katha, (unit), (variously spelled kattha or cottah), a unit of area in Bangladesh and India approximately equal to 1/20 of a bigha. This unit is still in use in much of Bangladesh and India, but the size varies significantly from place to place. In the Indian state of Bihar, one katha may vary from 750 ft. to [illegible]. Also this can be 32 by 30 feet in length and breadth respectively. In Bangladesh, one katha is standardized to 720 sq ft area, and 20 katha equals to 1 bigha. The Katha is still in use in Nepal, where it is equivalent to 338.57 m. (3,644.3 ft.).

dance and drama. It originated in present day Kerala in the 17th century. Stories from indian epics are told only with facial expressions, hand signals and body motions.

Kathlamet, a Chinookan language that was spoken around the border of Washington and Oregon by the Kathlamet people. The most extensive records of the language were made by Franz Boas, and a grammar was documented in the dissertation of Dell Hymes. It became extinct in the 1930s and there is little text left of it. Kathlamet was spoken in northwestern Oregon along the south bank of the lower Columbia River. It has been classified as a dialect of Upper Chinook, or as Lower Chinook, but was mutually intelligible with neither.

Katsurao, Fukushima, a village located in Futaba District, Fukushima Prefecture, Japan. As of December 2014, the village had an nominal registered population of [illegible] and a population density of 17.2 persons per km2, although the current actual population is zero, as the village has been evacuated in the wake of the Fukushima Daiichi nuclear disaster. The total area was 84.3 square kilometers (32.79 sq mi). Katsurao is located in the Abukuma Plateau of central Fukushima with a mean altitude of over 500 meters. The area of present-day Katsurao was part of Mutsu Province, and was included in the territory holdings of the Tokugawa shogunate during Edo period Japan. After the Meiji restoration, on April 1, 1889, the village of Katsurao was created within Futaba District, Fukushima. Although Katsurao escaped significant damage from the 2011 Tōhoku earthquake and tsunami, it was located downwind of the Fukushima Daiichi Nuclear Power Plant.

Although outside the nominal 20 kilometer exclusion zone, as a result of wind patterns following the Fukushima Daiichi nuclear disaster the entire population of the village was evacuated by government order by May 2011. In March 2013, the government divided the village into three zones, with the majority of the village area

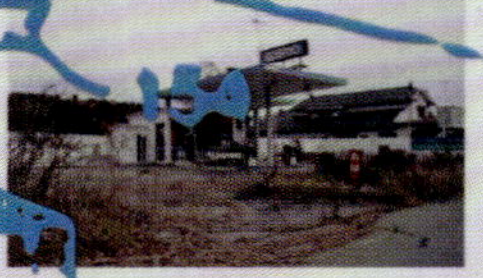

Abandoned gas station in Katsurao
Courtesy of [illegible]

cleared for unrestricted return of its inhabitants by spring of 2014, a smaller area cleared for daylight return only, and a larger area in which the existing restrictions against entry would be maintained until at least 2017. However, in March 2014, the government postponed lifting of the restrictions on return for a year due to remaining high levels of radiation. The economy of Katsuro was formerly heavily dependent on agriculture. Katsurao had one middle school and one elementary school in March 2011. Katsurao is not served by any train stations.

Katz, Jonathan Ned, (b. 1938), an American historian of human sexuality who has focused on same-sex attraction and changes in the social

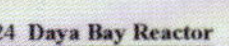

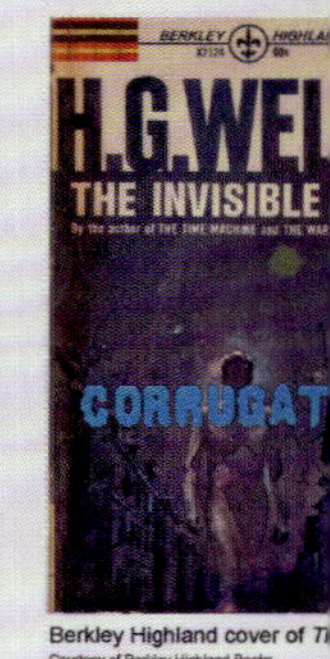

Berkley Highland cover of Ti[illegible]
Courtesy of Berkley Highland Books

the east a davoch would be a portion of land that could support 60 cattle or oxen. MacBain reckoned the davoch to be "either one or four ploughgates, according to locality and land."

A ploughgate contains about 100 Scots acres (5.3 km2). Watson, in *The Place-names of Ross & Cromarty* says, "usually four ploughgates." Skene in *Celtic Scotland* says: "In the eastern district there is a uniform system of land denomination consisting of 'dabhachs', 'ploughgates,' and 'oxgangs,' each 'dabhach' consisting of four 'ploughgates' and each 'ploughgate' containing eight 'oxgangs.' As soon as we cross the great chain of mountains separating the eastern from the western waters, we find a different system equally uniform. The 'ploughgates' and 'oxgangs' disappear, and in their place we find 'dabhachs' and 'pennylands.' The portion of land termed a 'dabhach' is here also called a 'tirung' or 'ounceland,' and each 'dabhach' contains 20 'pennylands.'"

The "pennyland" is thought to be of Norse origin, so it is possible that Norse and native systems were conflated in the west. Prof. MacKinnon in *Place and Personal Names of Argyll* says, "In Pictland the unit of land measure was the 'dabhach,' a unit which properly denotes a liquid measure. An old farmer in Western Gaeldom frequently speaks of his fields, not as containing so many acres of land, but as the sowing of so many bolls of oats,' 'the bed of so many barrels of potatoes.' Accordingly, from a measure of capacity, 'dabhach' came early to be used as a measure of land surface. In Gaeldom, where arable land is scant and scattered, the variations in the acreage [illegible] 'dabhachs' or 'ounces' must have been very great, still the extent of land [illegible] by these terms seems to have been, as a rule, about 104 Scots acres, or 120 English acres" (547,000 m).

The lexicographer Jamieson claimed that a daugh was enough to produce about 48 bolls, and averaged an area of approximately 1 1/2 square miles (3.9 km2). Daughs are referred to in the Book of Deer, and were recorded as being in use in the late 18th century in Inverness-shire. In some areas, a quarter of a davoch was a "ploughgate," and an eighth an "ochdamh."

Daya Bay Reactor Neutrino Experiment, a China-based multinational particle physics project studying neutrinos. The multinational collaboration includes researchers

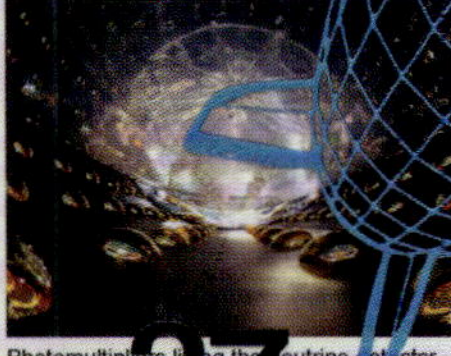

Photomultipliers lining the neutrino detector
Courtesy of Lawrence Berkeley National Laboratory

from China, the United States, Taiwan, Russia, and the Czech Republic. The U.S. side of the project is funded by the U.S. Department of Energy's Office of High Energy Physics. It is situated at Daya Bay, approximately 52 kilometers northeast of Hong Kong and 45 kilometers east of Shenzhen. There is an affiliated project in the Aberdeen Tunnel Underground Laboratory in Hong Kong. It measures the neutrons produced by cosmic muons, which may affect the Daya Bay Reactor Neutrino Experiment. The experiment consists of eight antineutrino detectors, clustered in three locations within 1.9 km (1.2 mi) of six nuclear reactors. Each detector consists of 20 t of liquid scintillator (linear alkylbenzene doped with gadolinium) surrounded by photomultiplier tubes and shielding. A much larger follow-up is in development in the form of the Jiangmen Underground Neutrino Observatory (JUNO) in Kaiping, which will use an acrylic sphere filled with 20,000 t of liquid scintillator to detect reactor antineutrinos. Groundbreaking began 10 January 2015, with operation expected in 2020.

Dazzle camouflage, (also known as Razzle Dazzle or Dazzle painting), a military camouflage paint scheme used on ships, extensively during World War I and to a lesser extent in World War II. The idea is credited to the art-

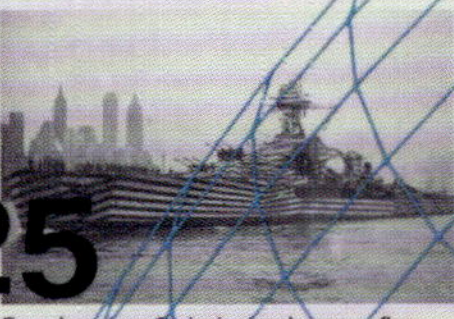

French cruiser *Gloire* in dazzle camouflage
Courtesy of imgur.com

ist Norman Wilkinson who was serving in the Royal Naval Volunteer Reserve when he had the idea in 1917. After the Allied Navies failed to develop effective means to disguise ships in all weathers, the dazzle technique was employed, not in order to conceal the ship, but rather to make it difficult for the enemy to estimate its type, size, speed and direction of travel. After seeing a canon painted in dazzle camouflage trundling through the streets of Paris, Picasso is reported to have taken credit for the innovation which seemed to him a quintessentially Cubist technique.

DC-3 (DST) disappearance, [illegible] disappearance of a *Douglas* DST [illegible] NC16002 occurring on the [illegible] 28 December 1948 near the end of a [illegible] from San Juan, Puerto Rico [illegible]. The aircraft carried 29 [illegible] crew members. [illegible] was determined [illegible] and it remains unsolved. [illegible] Robert Linquist, assisted by [illegible] and stewardess Mary Burkes, the aircraft ended its Miami–San Juan leg at 19:40 EST on 27 December. Linquist informed local repair crewmen that a landing gear warning light was not functioning and that the aircraft batteries were discharged [illegible] on water. Unwilling to delay the [illegible] scheduled takeoff for Miami for [illegible] Linquist said the batteries would be recharged by the aircraft's generators en route. Linquist taxied NC16002 to the end of runway 27 for takeoff, but stopped at the end of the apron due to lack of two-way radio communication.

Though capable of receiving, Linquist reported to the head of Puerto Rican Transport, who had driven out to the aircraft, that the radio could not transmit because of the low batteries. After agreeing to stay close to San Juan until they were recharged enough to allow two-way contact, NC16002 finally lifted off at 22:03. After circling the city for 11 minutes, Linquist

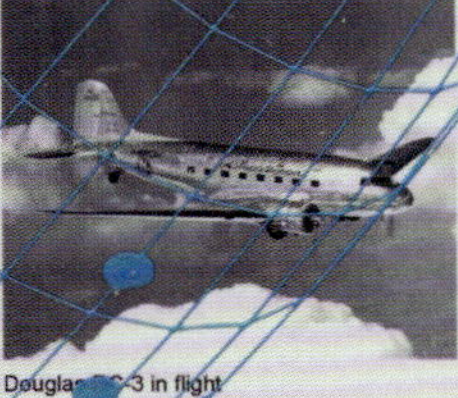

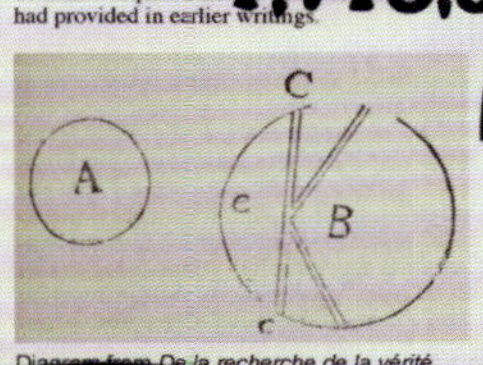

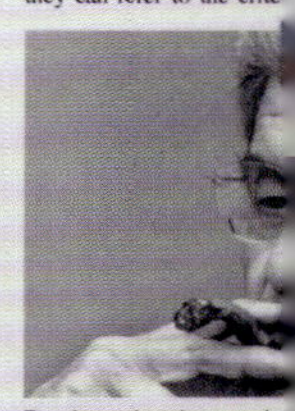

opposite and next pages,
THE FIRST SUPPER (GALAXY BLACK) (DETAILS), 2023
BRONZE, BLACK PATINA, GOLD LEAF
217 X 929 X 268 CM

INSTALLATION VIEW AT THE ROYAL ACADEMY, LONDON, 2023

opposite, clockwise from top left,
Haile Selassie (1892–1975)
Marcus Garvey (1887–1940)
Robert Henry Lawrence (1935–1967)
Sister Rosetta Tharpe (1915–1973)
Harriet Tubman (1822–1913)
Shirley Chisholm (1924–2005)

next pages, from top left,
Marsha P. Johnson (1945–1992)
King Tubby (1941–1989)
Derek Walcott (1930–2017)

representations of resistance fighter Zumbi Dos Palmares; nurse Mary Seacole; activists Harriet Tubman, Marcus Garvey and Marsha P. Johnson; explorer Matthew Henson; astronaut Robert Henry Lawrence; politician Shirley Chisholm; emperor Haile Selassie; musicians Sister Rosetta Tharpe and King Tubby; and poet Sir Derek Alton Walcott. But following a career of working on large scale multi-year conceptual projects, why the about-turn to the language of art history?

On 25 May 2020, the murder of George Floyd, captured on video, sparked worldwide protests and awakened a renewed focus on racial injustice that ultimately led to the reassessment, removal or destruction of historical monuments and memorials in many cities, as well as other symbols of racism and oppression. By the end of 2020, the Southern Poverty Law Center (SPLC) released its *Whose Heritage?* report, which found that 168 Confederate symbols were renamed or removed from public spaces in 2020.[41] Since it is from within this context, this vacancy, that Strachan makes a sculpture, it is important to approach *The First Supper* not only using formal analysis but also to think of it as a signifying structure, a system of signs and strategies that critique representation and 'an attempt to use representation against itself to challenge its authority, its claim to possess some truth or epistemological value.'[42] You might even describe it as a trojan horse, intended to subvert its outward expression from within, a call for discursivity within the structure of sculpture, an attempt to stimulate a conversation on the ways in which figurative sculpture has been historically used to construct, maintain and legitimize social inequalities.

For example, Strachan's use of cast bronze embellished with a gold patina references material cultures and trade networks in Africa. Some of the earliest and most accomplished bronze works found in Africa date to the tenth century and are among the first examples of lost-wax casting techniques in the production of bronze sculpture. Certain figures and details are embellished with gold leaf, a material that is also culturally loaded. Gold is one of Africa's most abundant natural resources and has indisputably shaped its history and its people throughout time. As early as the seventh century, the trans-Saharan trade linked the sub-Saharan region to Mediterranean economies through the business of gold. West Africa was one of the world's leading exporters of gold during the Middle Ages, but the material also drew Europeans to the 'Gold Coast' in the fifteenth century, contributing to the development of the transatlantic slave trade.

In *The First Supper,* the artist's selection of crops and foods connect the work to broader spiritual, philosophical and ideological perspectives guiding the sculpture. Spread out across the table are items such as African rice, breadfruit, catfish, chicken, cocoa, custard apple and soursop. These foods consumed in the Caribbean have been traced to Indigenous and African influences, along with the histories of enslavement and indentured servitude. For example, enslaved people carrying African rice played a crucial role in the expansion of rice cultivation in the Americas during the Atlantic slave trade. These subtle but critical quotations enrich the sculpture, allowing it to engage with broader issues of technology transfer, Indigenous knowledge and the agency of enslaved people.

Following a long tradition of representation of the *Last Supper*, one of the most striking aspects of *The First Supper* is the linear seating arrangement of the dinner guests. Typically, dinner guests face one another to encourage conversation. In *The First Supper* the attendees face outward toward an imagined individual or audience. We normally only encounter this type of seating at a wedding reception or in an interview, an audition, or a trial. In each of these contexts the individuals seated in this configuration represent positions of importance, power or judgement. The work therefore presents a hypothetical meeting of influential minds, without determining the events that follow. As the viewer reflects on the evolution and interaction of intellectual ideas being discussed at the table by the figures portrayed, numerous possibilities emerge.

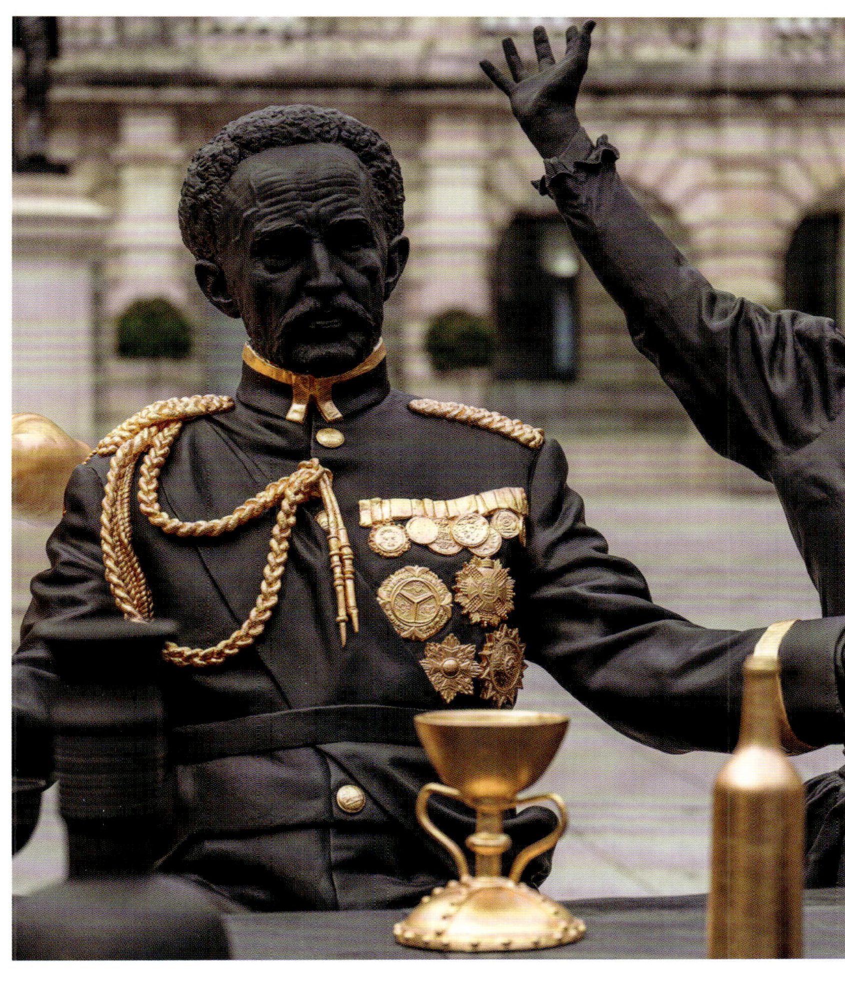

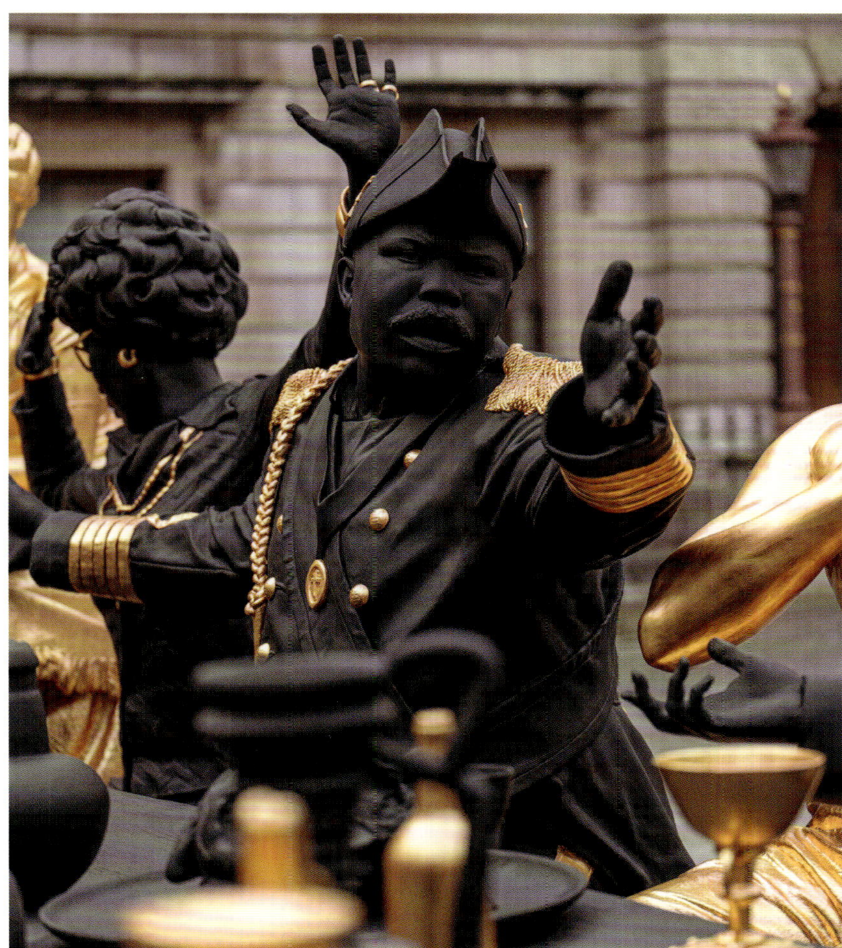

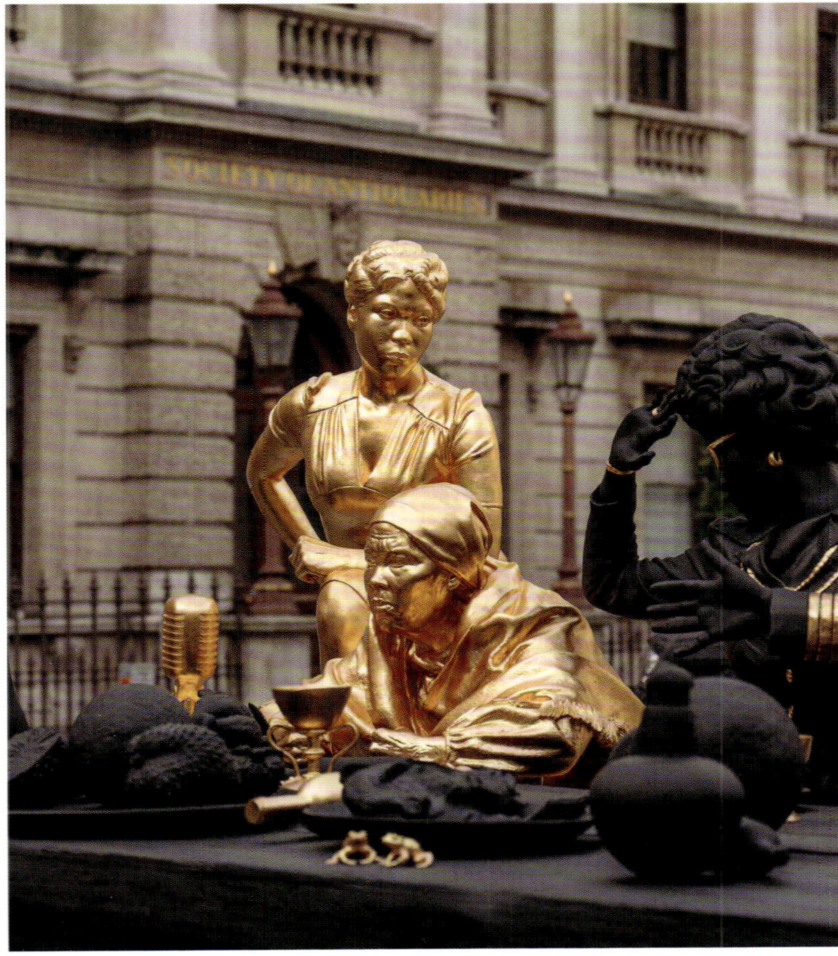

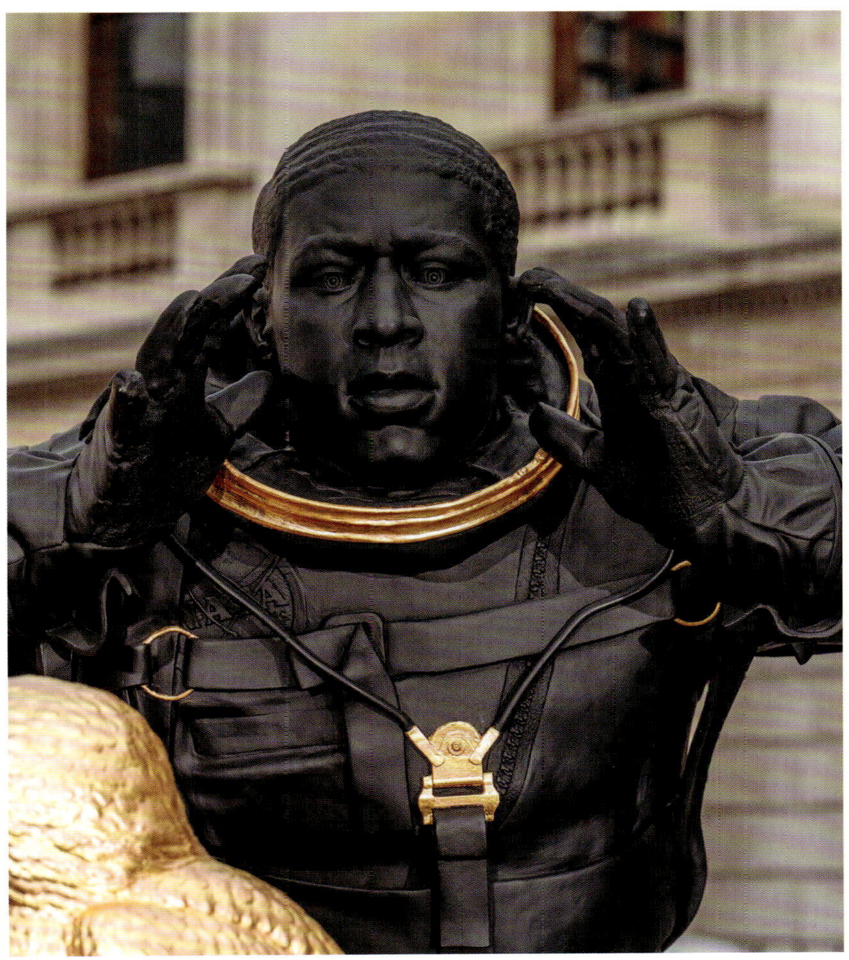

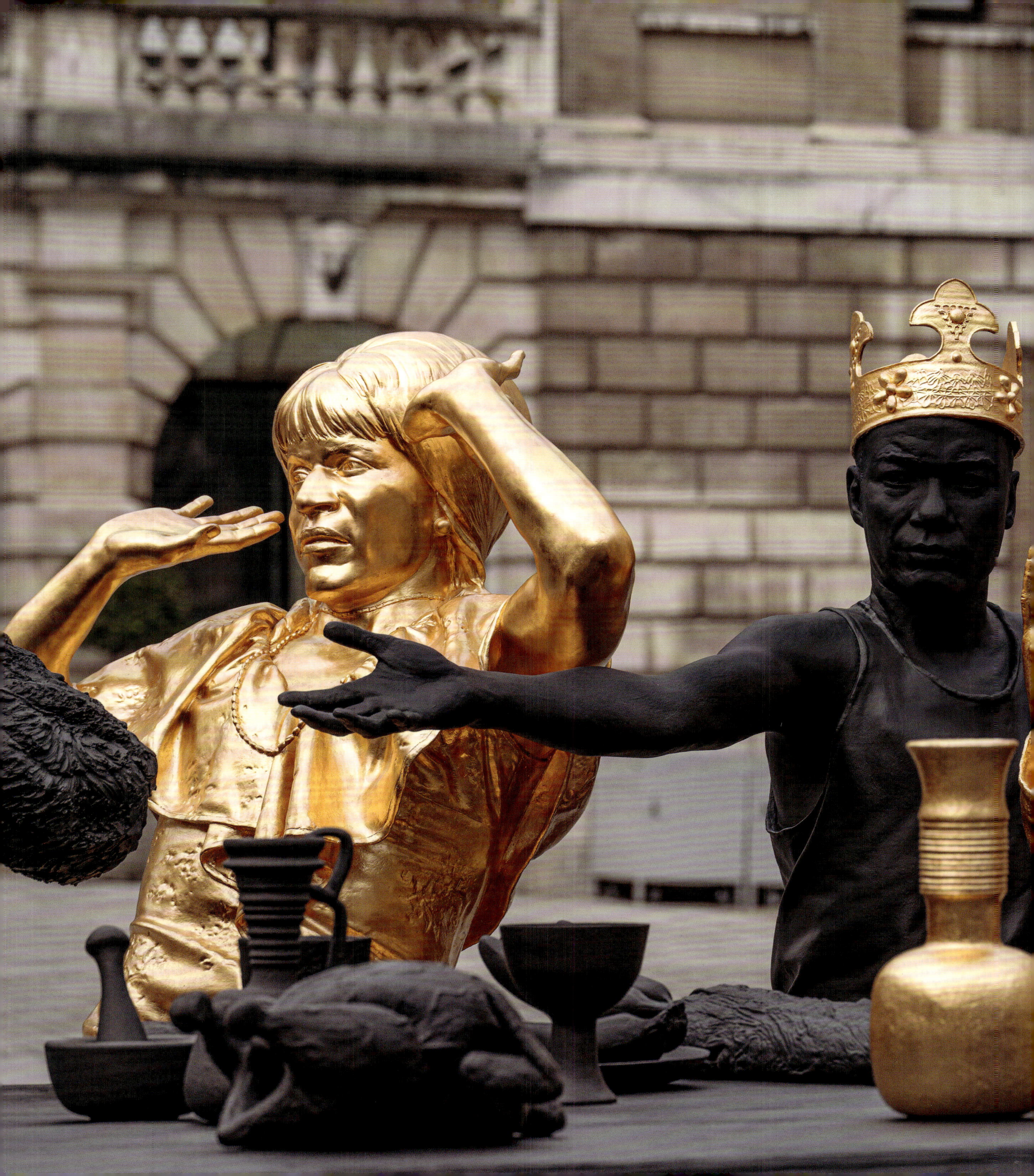

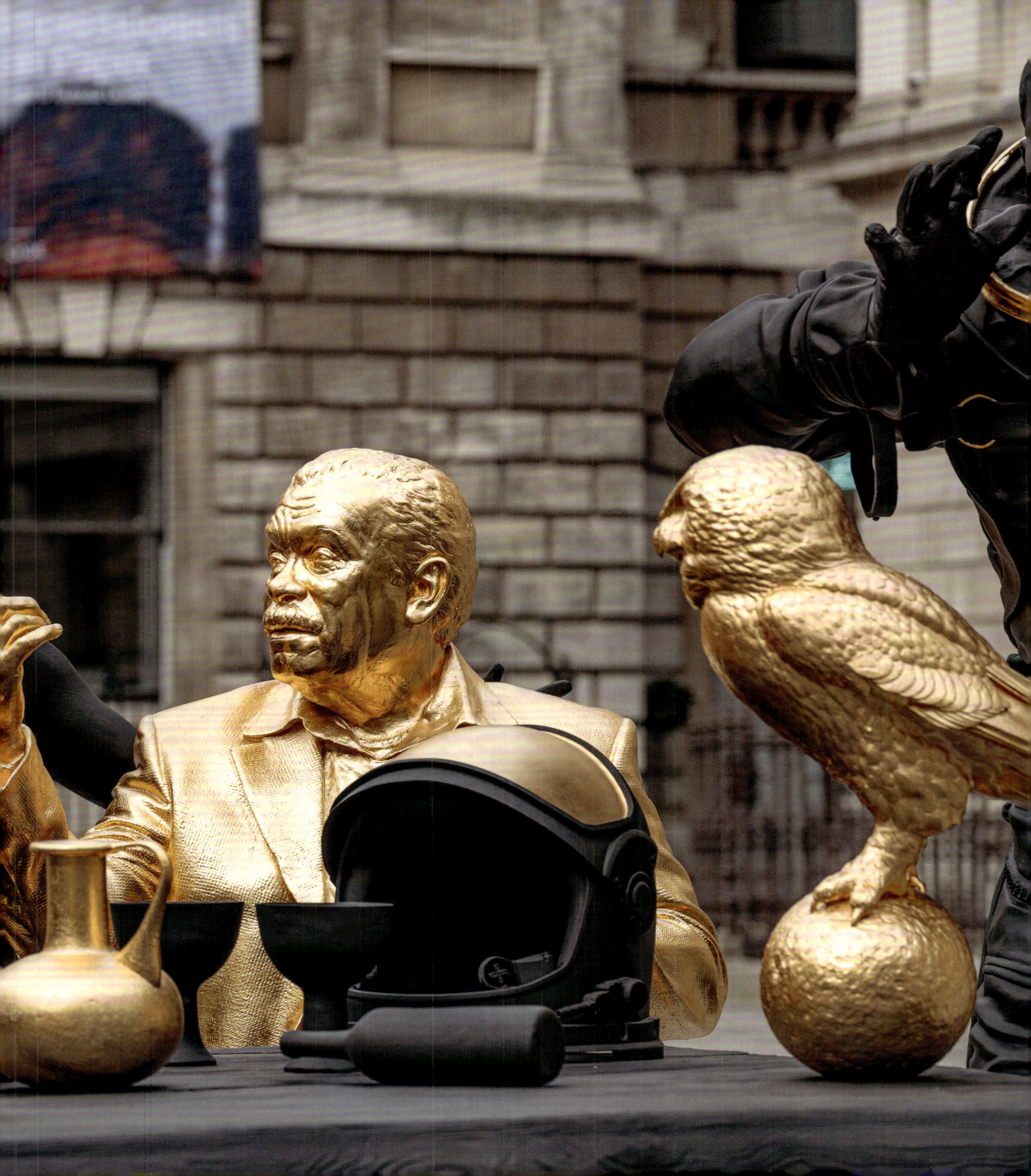

DISTANT RELATIVES (ANDREA MOTLEY CRABTREE) (DETAIL), 2020
PLASTER, NATURAL FIBERS, BRASS, ACRYLIC
158 X 76 X 66 CM

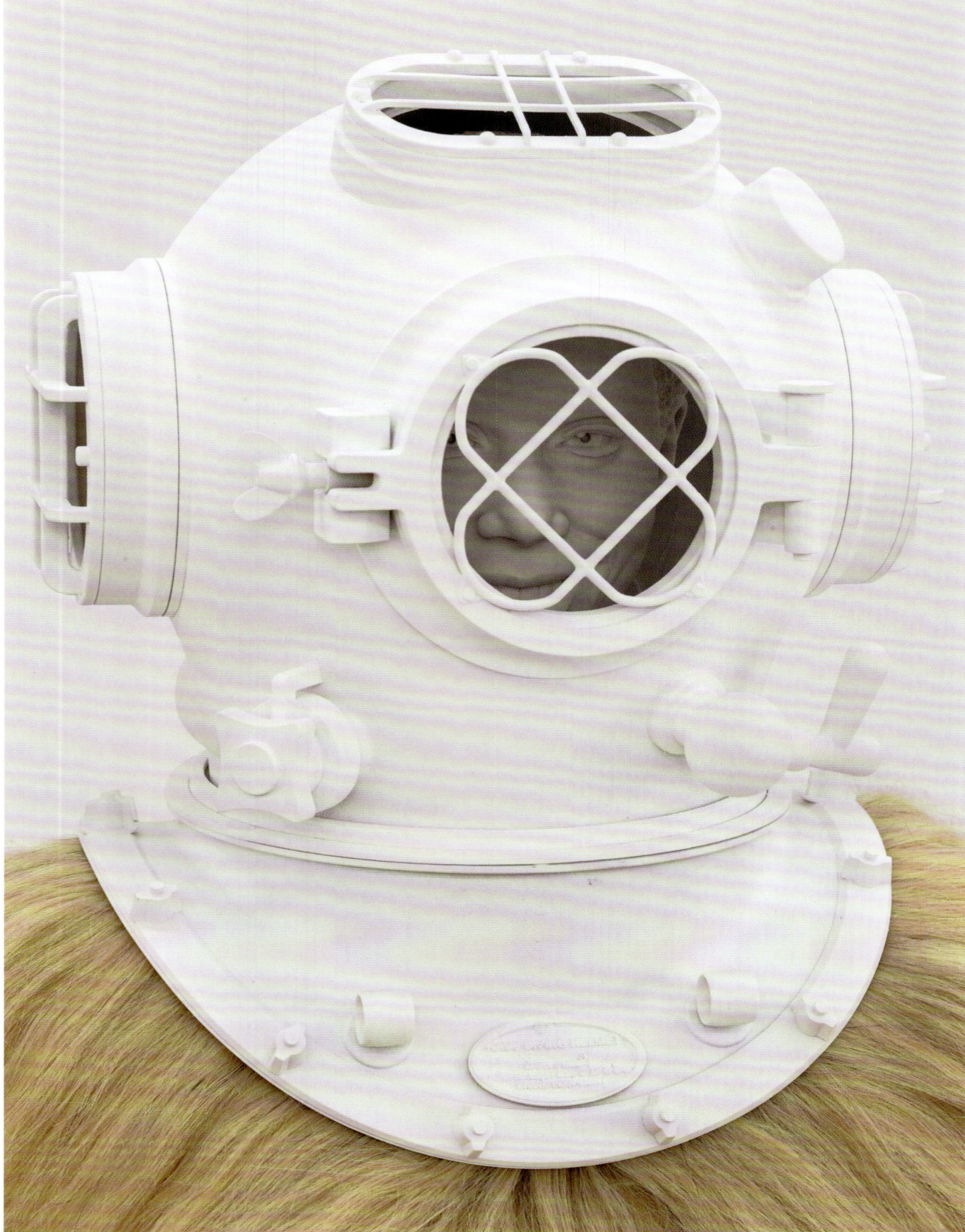

Strachan's decision to use sculptural traditions from which he had felt estranged all his life to rescue from historical oblivion people and ideas that might otherwise have disappeared may seem paradoxical, contradictory even.[43] Yet perhaps the power of *The First Supper* is its allegorical attitude. Throughout history, allegory has been used 'in the gap between a present and a past which, without allegorical reinterpretation, might have remained foreclosed. A conviction of the remoteness of the past, and a desire to redeem it for the present.'[44] It occurs whenever one thing is doubled by another; *The Last Supper* by Leonardo da Vinci, for example becomes allegorical when it is read as a prefiguration to *The First Supper*. Strachan's work is a critical reinterpretation of Leonardo's, not only referencing its antecedent but exposing the ways in which representational systems of the West have historically worked to exclude, dominate and subjugate.

Understood in this way, allegory becomes one way to interpret Strachan's subsequent sculptures that blend elements to create a richer and more complex narrative experience. These works include his sculptural assemblage *Distant Relatives* series 2020, bronze *Ruin of a Giant* series 2023, and singular ceramic works such as *Heart on Head*, 2022 and *Inner Elder (Nina Simone as Queen of Sheba)*, 2023, insofar as they are involved in reusing or confiscating figurative imagery but also suggest a blatant disregard for 'aesthetic' categories. They both solicit and frustrate our desire for the image to be directly transparent to its signification. As a result, they appear strangely incomplete – fragments or runes that need to be deciphered. Allegory can also be used to explore Strachan's site-specific installations, whereby his sculpture appears to have physically merged with its settings. In *Jah Rastafari with Rice Field (Stacked with Pineapple, Shield, and Football)*, 2023 and *The Birth of Exuma (Eagle Talon)*, 2024, for instance, the ceramic sculptural elements emerge from a field of rice plants. Strachan uses the dried rice plant, and its distinctive fragrance, not only for its topographical specificity but also for its psychological resonances. The sculpture (permanent) and rice (impermanent) stand in dialectical relationship to one another.

right,
DISTANT RELATIVES (ANDREA MOTLEY CRABTREE), 2020
PLASTER, NATURAL FIBERS, BRASS, ACRYLIC
158 X 76 X 66 CM

next pages, clockwise from left,
DISTANT RELATIVES (DEREK WALCOTT), 2020
KAVAT MASK (PAPUA NUOVA GUINEA), PIGMENT, NATURAL FIBERS, PLASTER, BRASS ACRYLIC
183 X 91 X 91 CM

DISTANT RELATIVES (SISTER ROSETTA THARPE), 2020
GUERE MASK (LIBERIA), PIGMENT, WOOD, GOLD LEAF, PLASTER, BRASS, ACRYLIC
182 X 81 X 107 CM

DISTANT RELATIVES (VIVIAN ANDERSON), 2020
FANG NGIL MASK (CENTRAL AFRICA), PIGMENT, NATURAL FIBERS, PLASTER, BRASS ACRYLIC
170 X 61 X 76 CM

DISTANT RELATIVES (JAMES BALDWIN), 2020
BAMBARA MASK (WEST AFRICA), PIGMENT, HORSE-HAIR, GOLD LEAF, PLASTER, BRASS, ACRYLIC
173 X 56 X 47 CM

DISTANT RELATIVES (ROBERT SMALLS), 2020
BEMBE MASK (DEMOCRATIC REPUBLIC OF CONGO), PIGMENT, NATURAL FIBERS, PLASTER, BRASS, ACRYLIC
152 X 56 X 51 CM

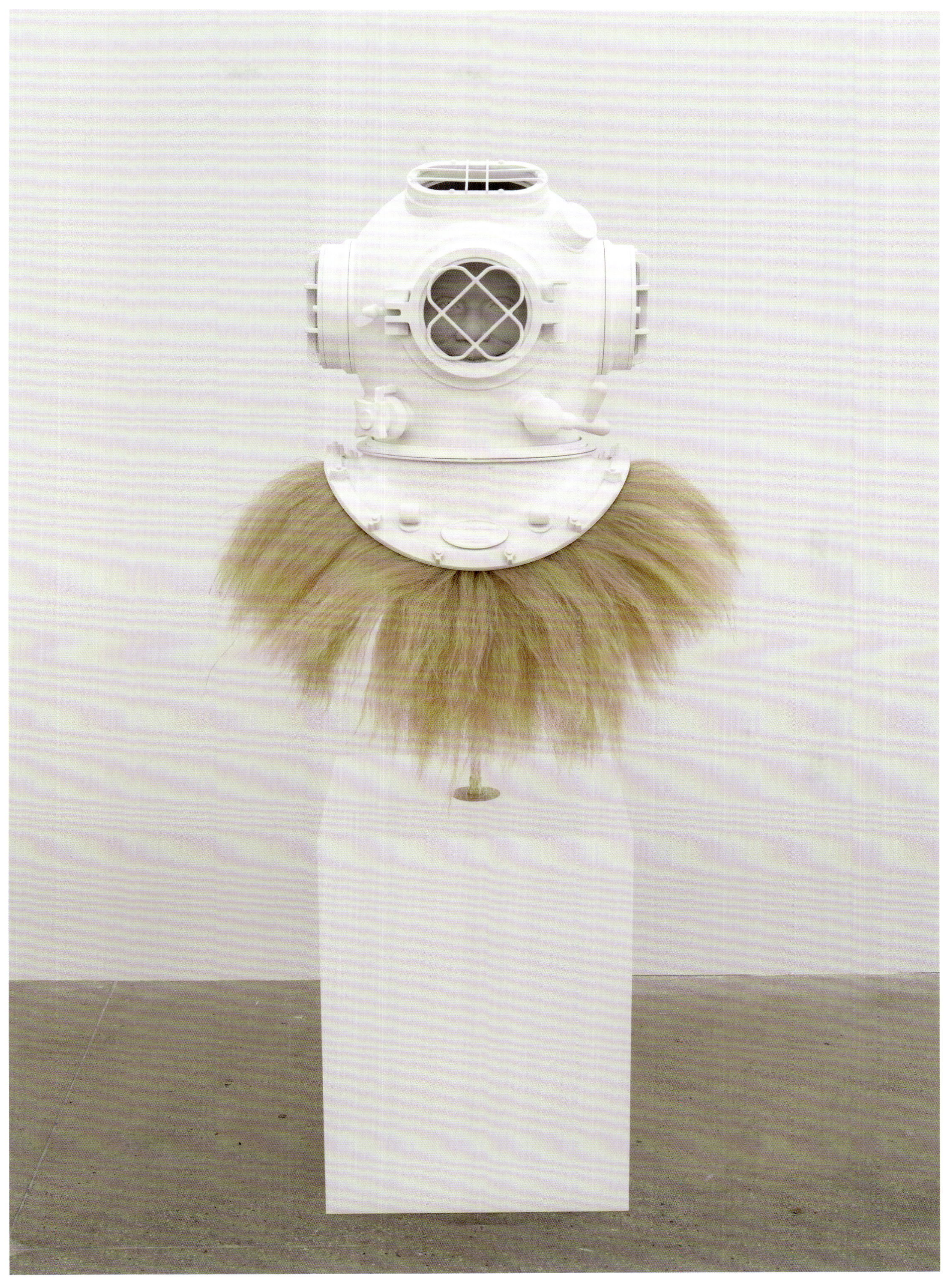

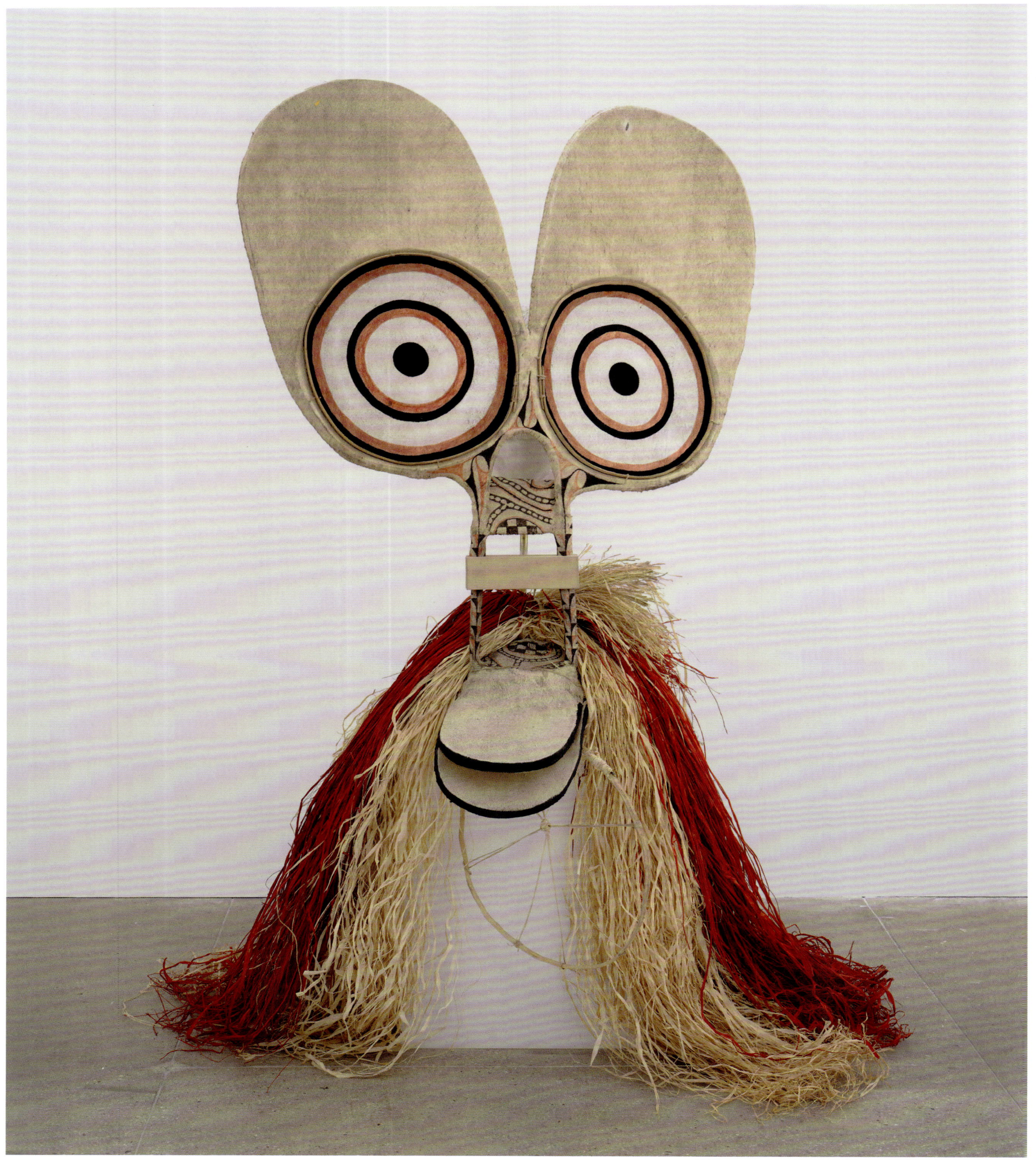

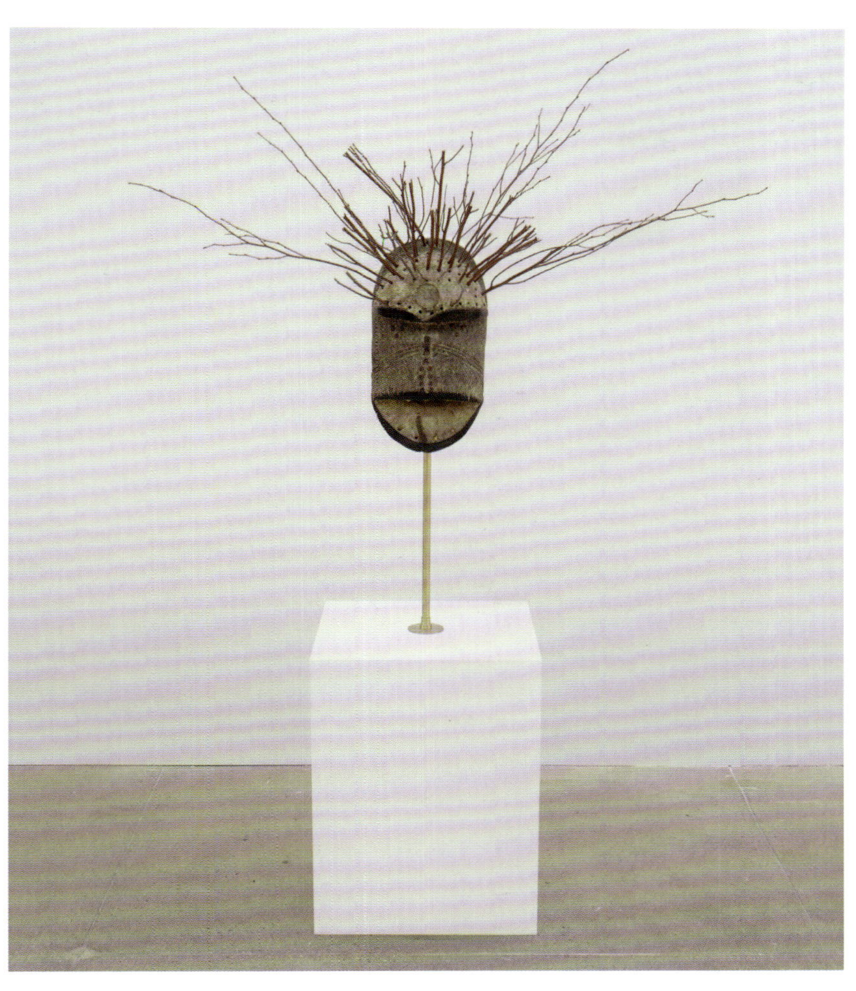
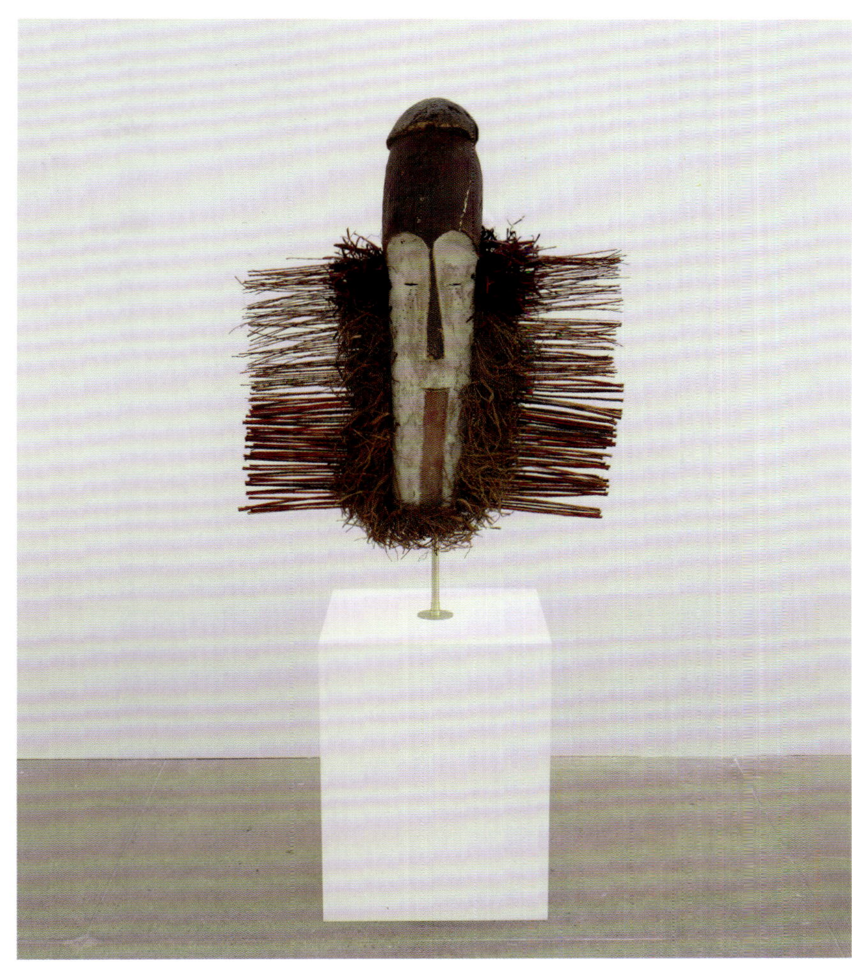
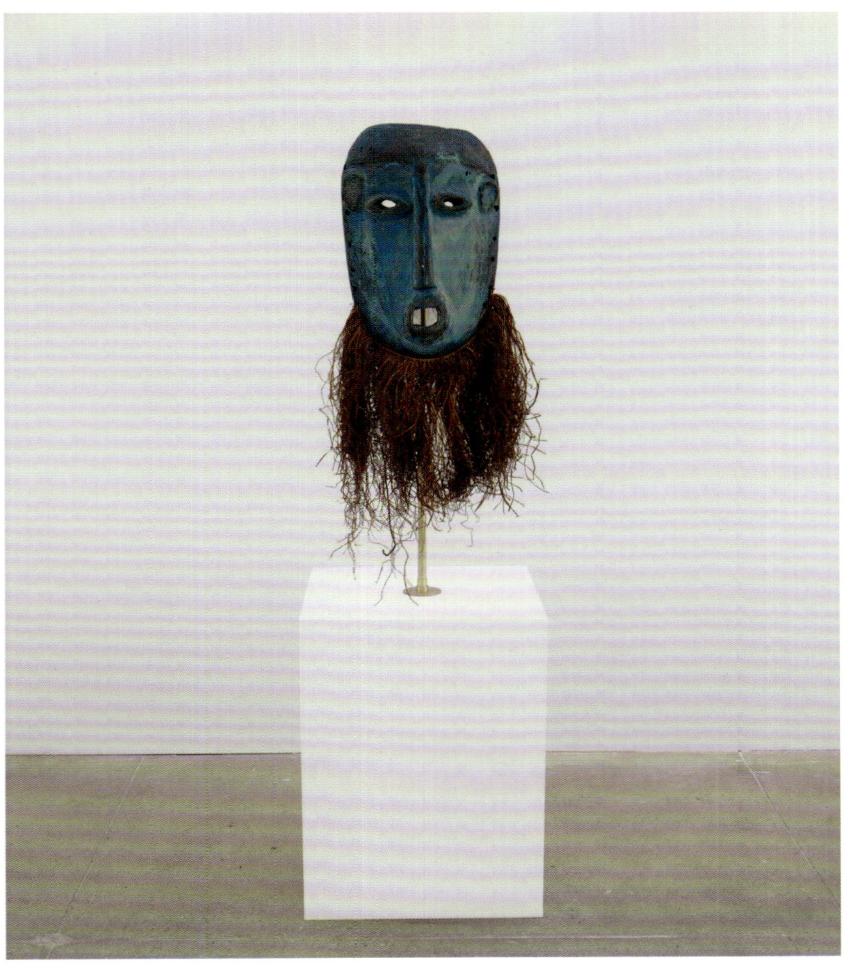
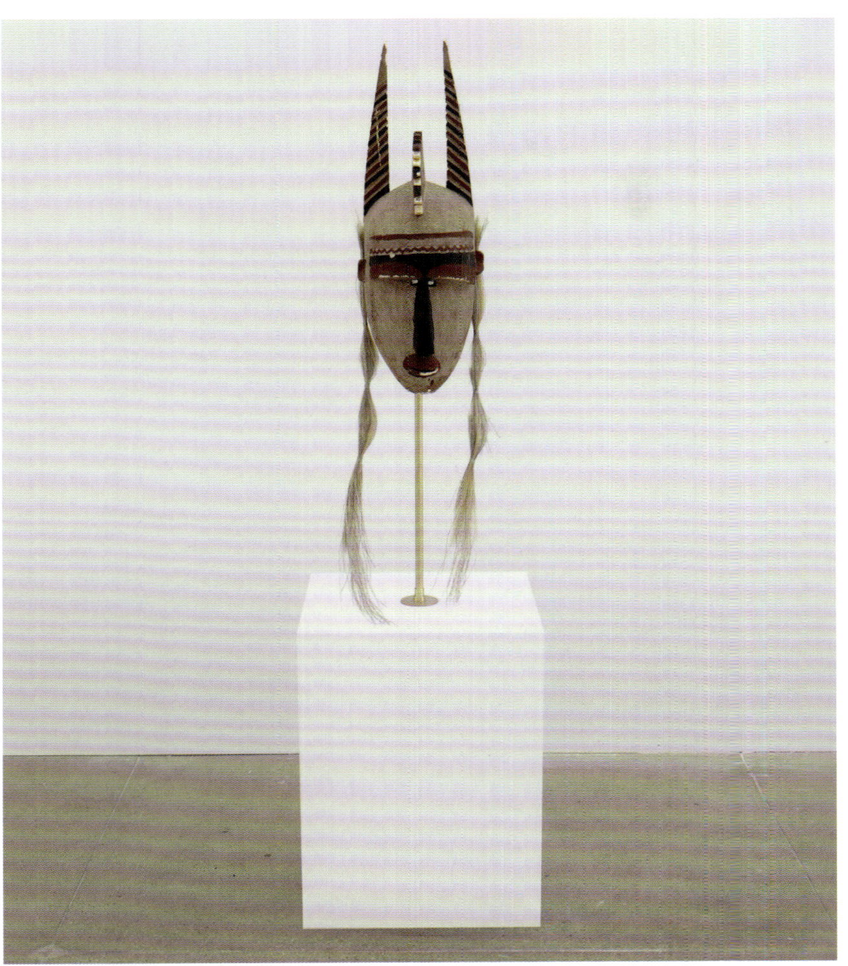

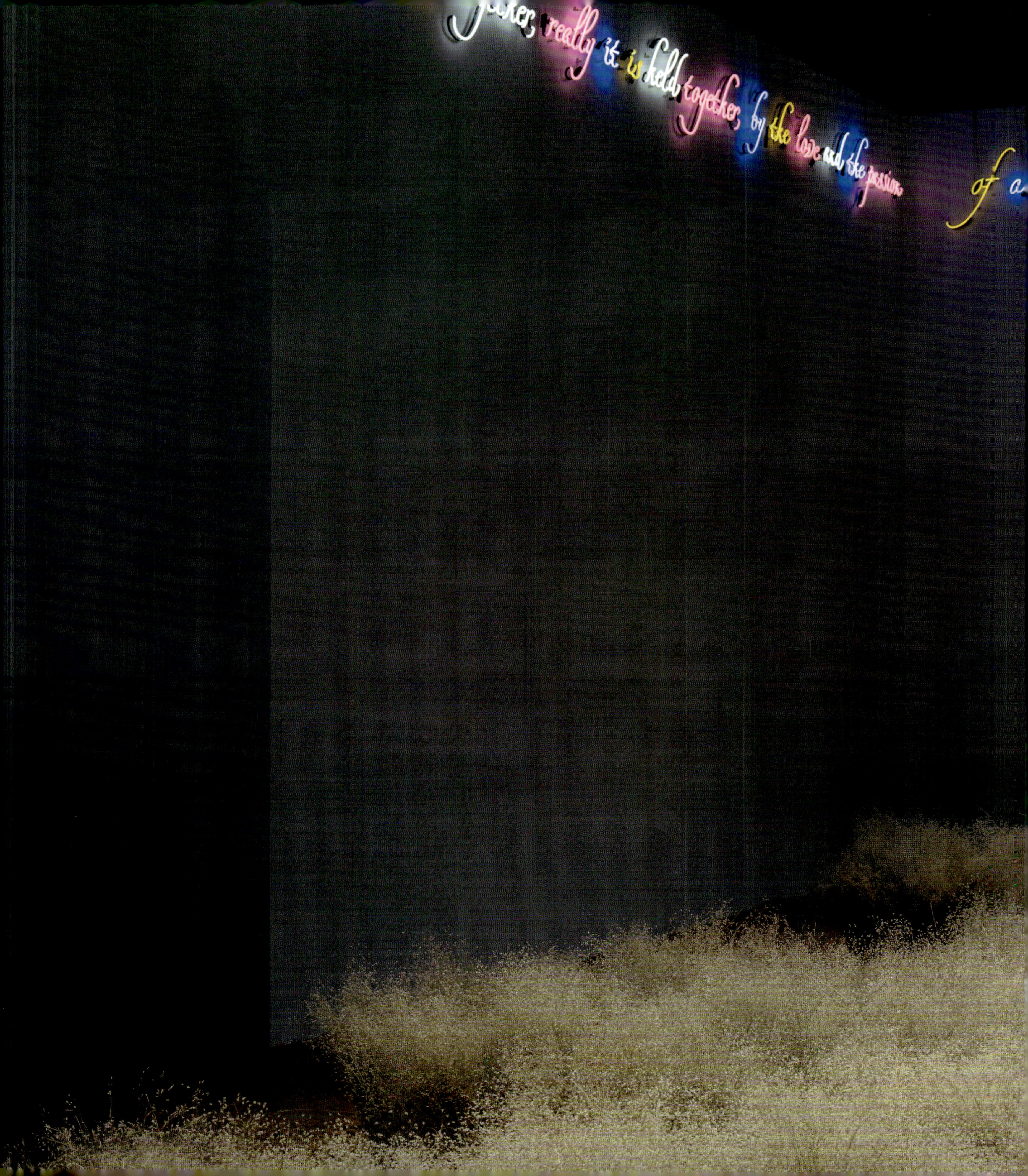
really it is held together, by the love and the passion of a

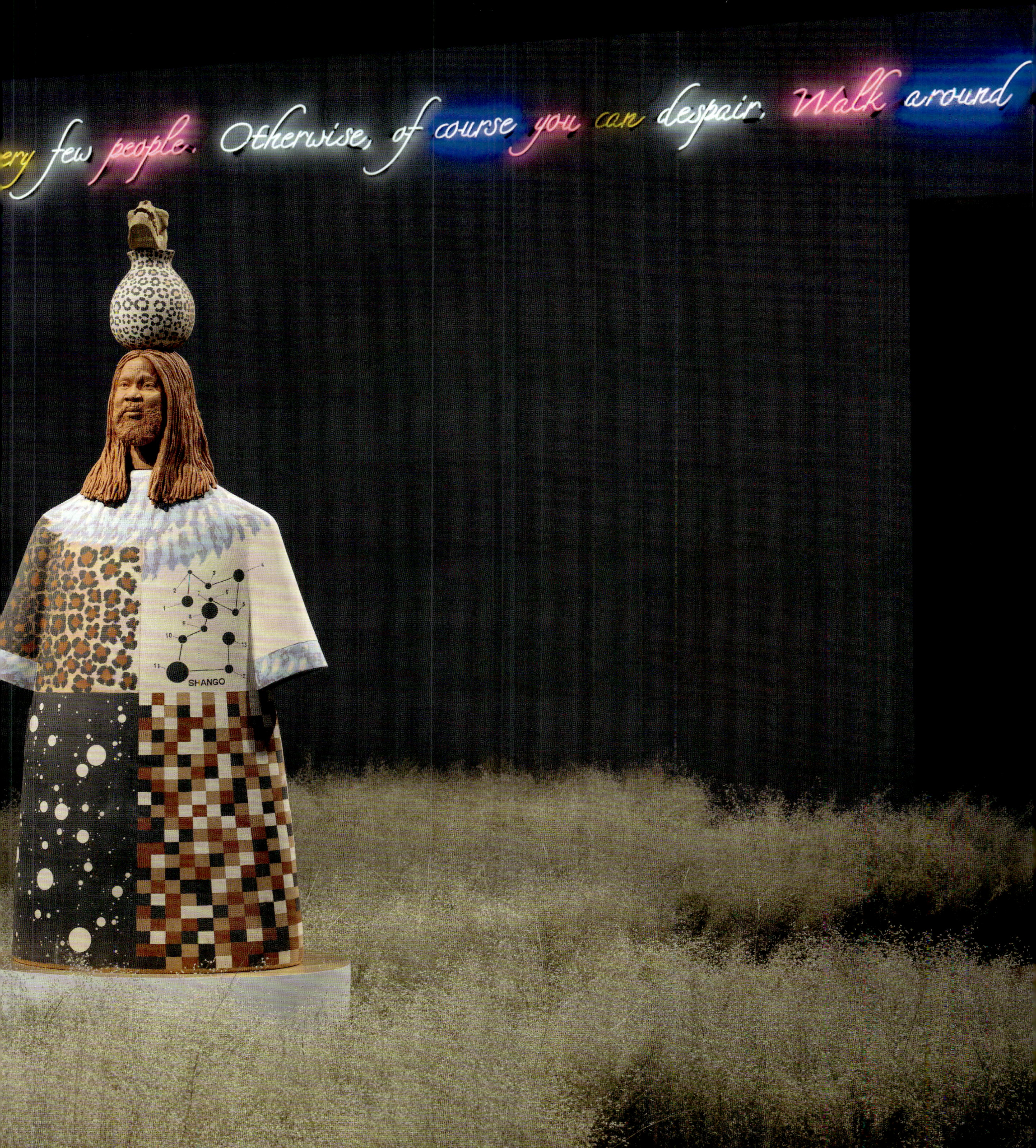

few people. Otherwise, of course you can despair. Walk around
SHANGO

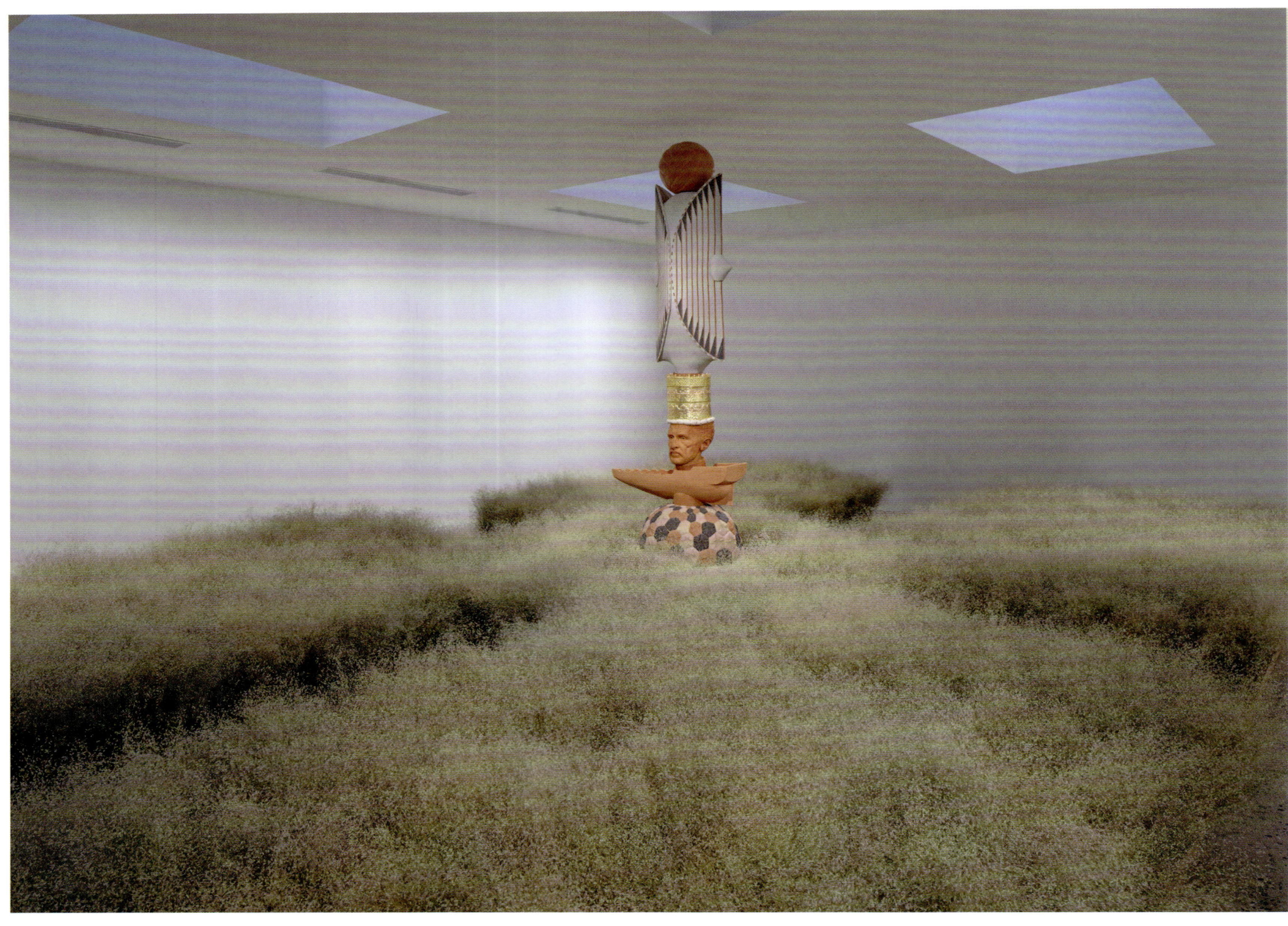

Conclusion

Produced almost twenty years apart, Strachan's *The Distance Between What We Have and What We Want (Arctic Ice Project)* and *The First Supper* are strikingly divergent in form and in process – a block of ice excavated and transported from Alaska to the Bahamas, versus a monumental figurative sculpture shown for the first time in the courtyard of London's Royal Academy. Yet these works highlight Strachan's longstanding interests in complex, interconnected systems including global ecology, networks of exchange and cultures of knowledge. Moreover, both works demonstrate the revelatory potential of geographical and historical recontextualization. Relocating the block of ice from one climate to another prompted viewers to see it anew, just as Strachan's reworking of Leonardo's *The Last Supper* turns a familiar image into startling meditation on the still overlooked histories of Black activism, innovation and material culture. In these works, existing systems are not simply analyzed or co-opted but actively *disrupted,* challenging received knowledge and offering alternative ways of narrating history and envisaging the future.

right and opposite
JAH RASTAFARI WITH RICE FIELD (STACKED WITH PINEAPPLE, SHIELD, AND FOOTBALL), 2023
CERAMIC, RICE FIELD
230 X 150 X 150 CM

INSTALLATION VIEW AT MARIAN GOODMAN GALLERY, LOS ANGELES, 2024

previous pages
THE BIRTH OF EXUMA (EAGLE TALON), 2024
CERAMIC, RICE FIELD
CERAMIC: 165 X 68 X 38 CM
RICE FIELD: 1355 X 480 CM

THAT PERSON (JAMES BALDWIN), 2025
NEON
DIMENSIONS VARIABLE

INSTALLATION VIEW AT MARIAN GOODMAN GALLERY, LOS ANGELES, 2024

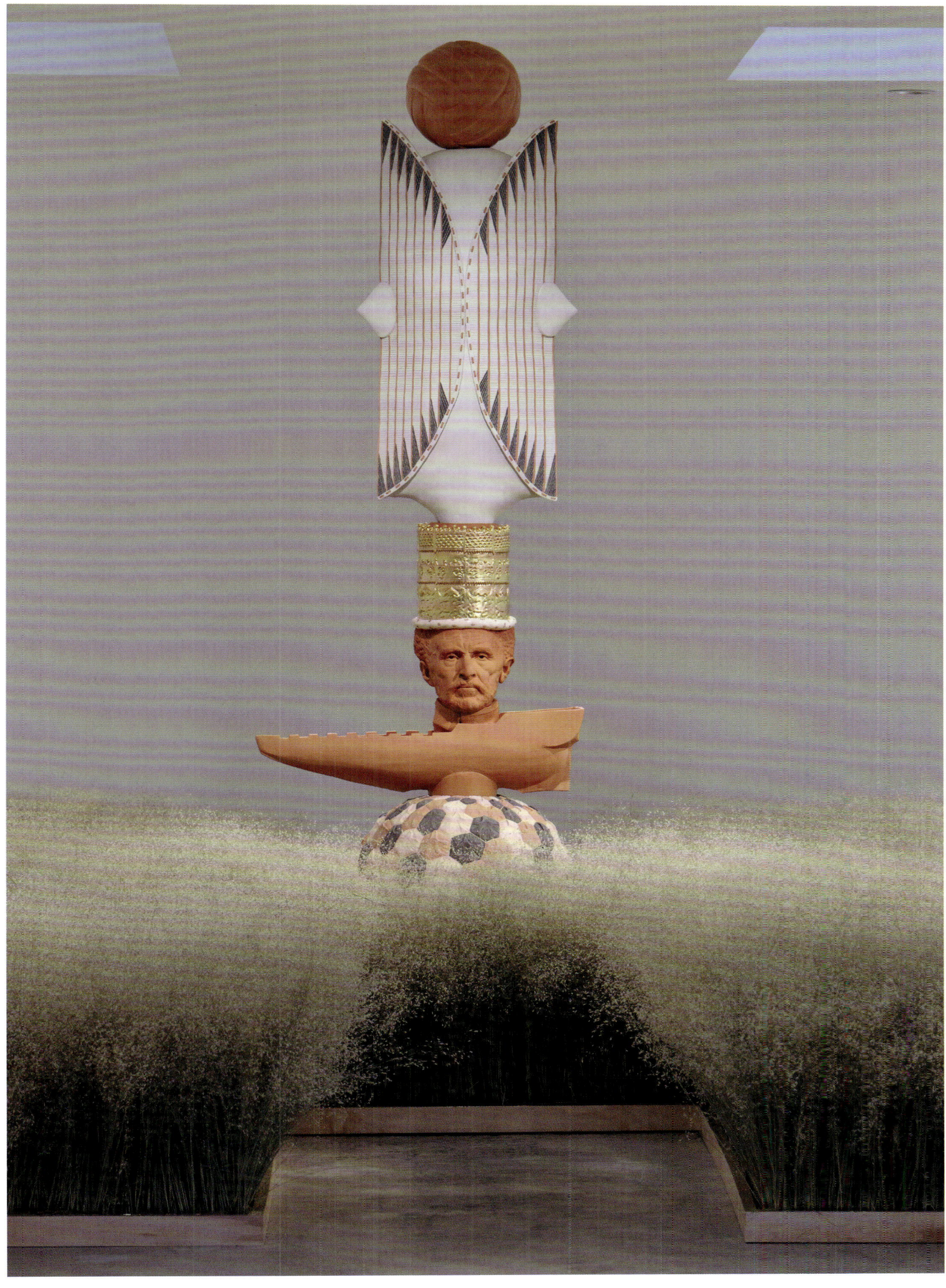

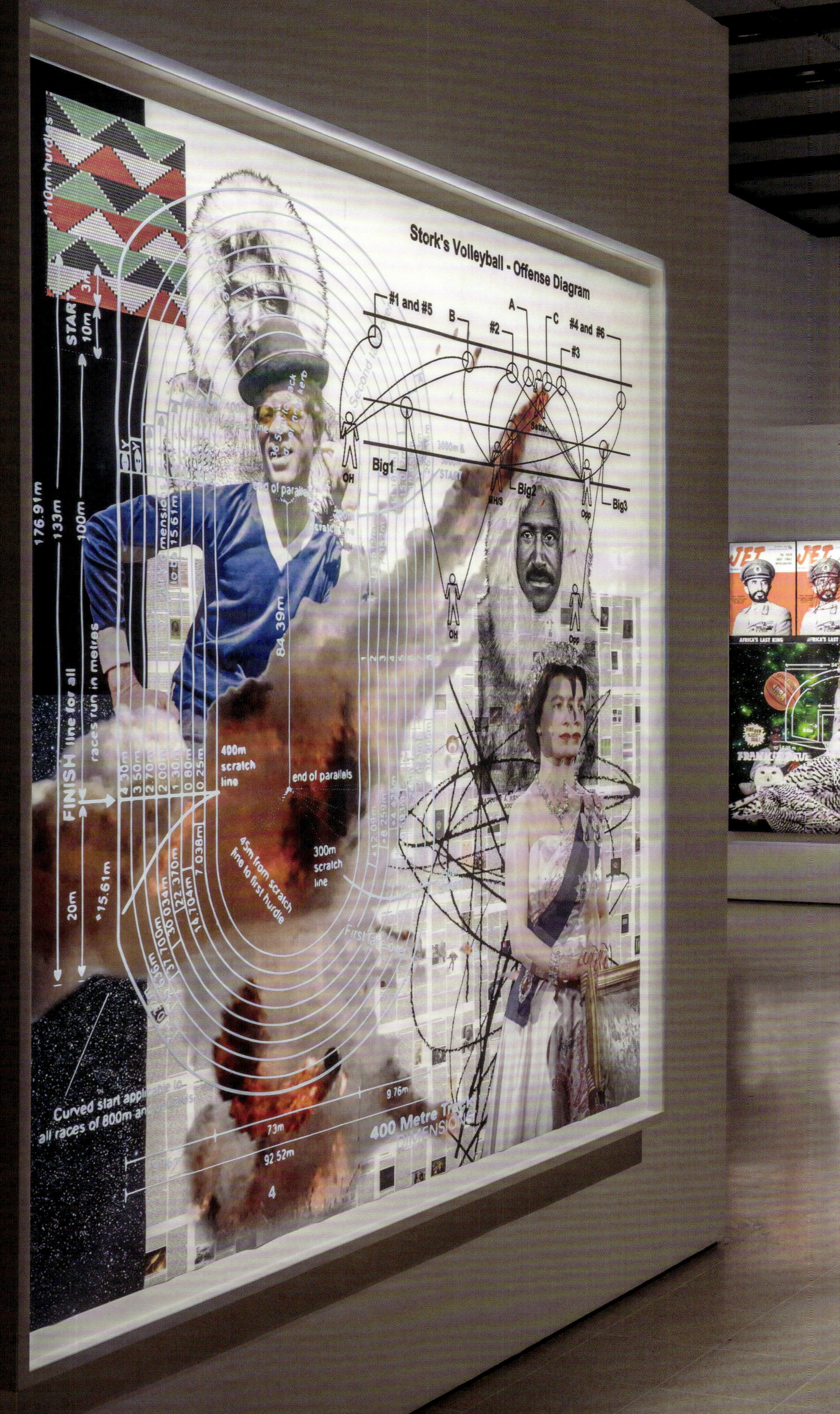
Stork's Volleyball - Offense Diagram
#1 and #5
B
#2
A
C
#4 and #6
#3
Big1
Big2
Big3
Opp
OH
110m hurdles
START
176.91m
133m
100m
84.39m
FINISH line for all races run in metres
400m scratch line
end of parallels
300m scratch line
45m from scratch line to first hurdle
20m
Curved start applies in all races of 800m and upwards
9.76m
73m
92.52m
400 Metre Track
4
JET
AFRICA'S LAST KING

They Shall Not Die

Emma Dabiri

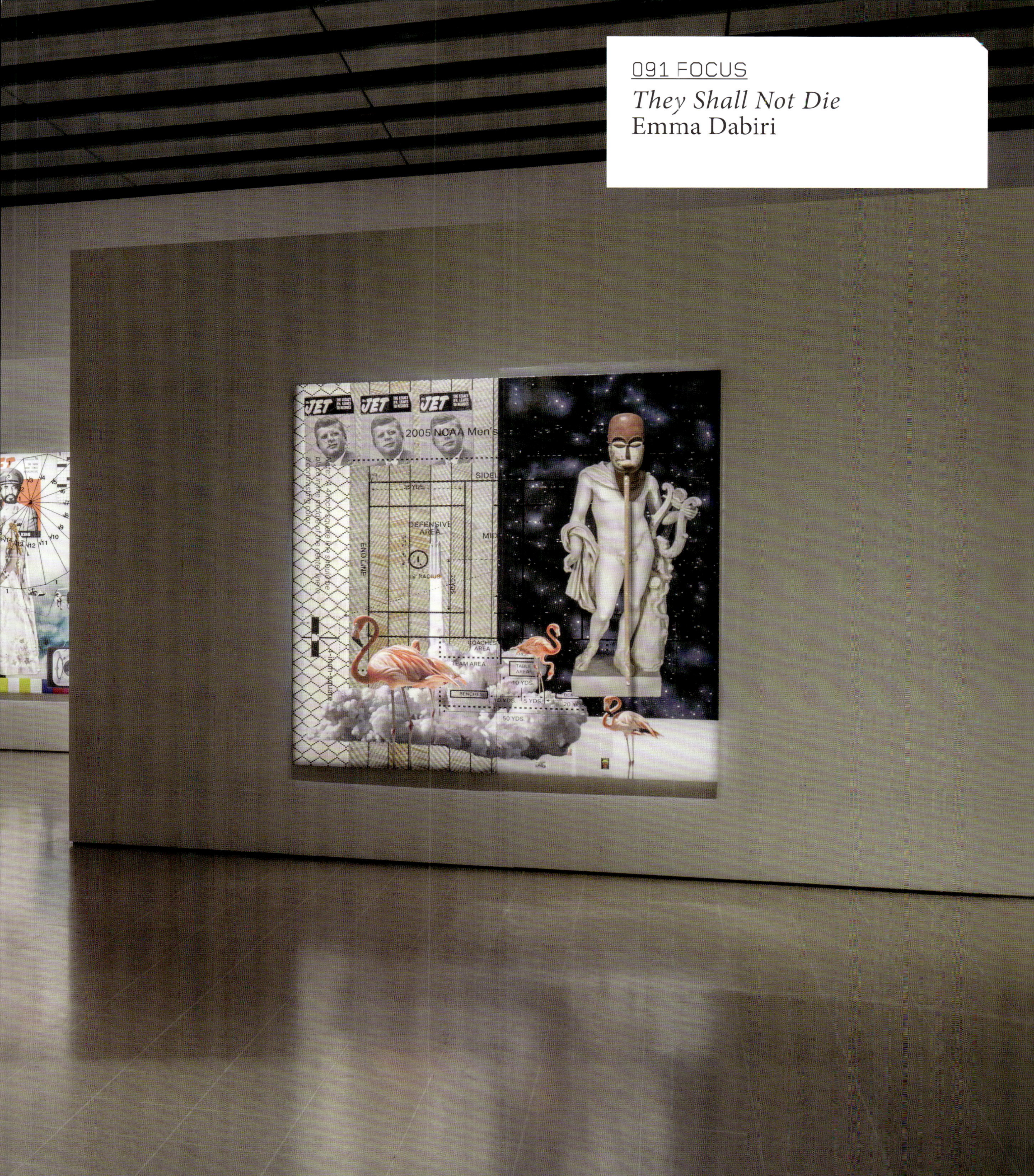

previous pages, from left,
FOUR-HUNDRED METER DASH, 2018
MYLAR, MATTE PAPER, PIGMENT, SPRAY PAINT, ACRYLIC, OIL STICK, ENAMEL, VINYL, GRAPHITE
213 X 213 CM

EVERY TONGUE SHALL CONFESS, 2023
OIL, ENAMEL, PIGMENT, ACRYLIC
TWO PANELS
OVERALL DIMENSIONS: 213 X 213 X 5 CM

THE LEGACY, 2023
OIL, ENAMEL, PIGMENT, ACRYLIC, MATBOARD, MASK, WOO
TWO PANELS
OVERALL DIMENSIONS: 213 X 213 X 5 CM

opposite,
MATTHEW HENSON (HUNTER'S SHIRT STACKED WITH FOOT-BALL AND SPEAR), 2023
CERAMIC
200 X 90 X 40 CM

INSTALLATION VIEW AT HAYWARD GALLERY, LONDON, 2024

To walk into There is Light Somewhere is to enter the world as re-imagined by Tavares Strachan – a parallel universe of immersive installations, where the properties of space and time are reoriented to pre- and post-colonial settings, and we can experience a reality full of immeasurable possibility liberated from the constraints of imperial logic.

Much of Strachan's work is a direct intervention into epistemic history and traditions. One of his most renowned pieces The Encyclopedia of Invisibility is a forensically detailed collection of important but marginalized figures from the past, individuals excluded from the historical record because the dishonest fiction of white supremacy demands the denial of non-white people's contributions to scientific, technological and cultural advances, in order to elevate its own achievements.

The Encyclopedia of Invisibility is a sculpture but also a book of 2,400+ pages featuring people such as Matthew Henson, the Black American arctic explorer, Henrietta Lacks, a Black American woman whose cancer cells were used without her or her family's knowledge after her death, becoming the first immortalized human cell line, one of the most important in medical research, and Kojo Tavalou Houénou, an activist from present day Benin described as the 'most devastating African critic of the French colonial order'.[1] Many of the individuals included within the encyclopedia re-emerge from its pages to reappear in other forms throughout the exhibition. Ruin of a Giant features a massive sculpture of King Tubby, the Jamaican sound engineer Osbourne Ruddock, and a key figure in the invention of dub music in the 1960s. Legendary Jamaican reggae producers such as King Tubby and Lee 'Scratch' Perry stripped back instrumental versions of reggae tracks and added elements such

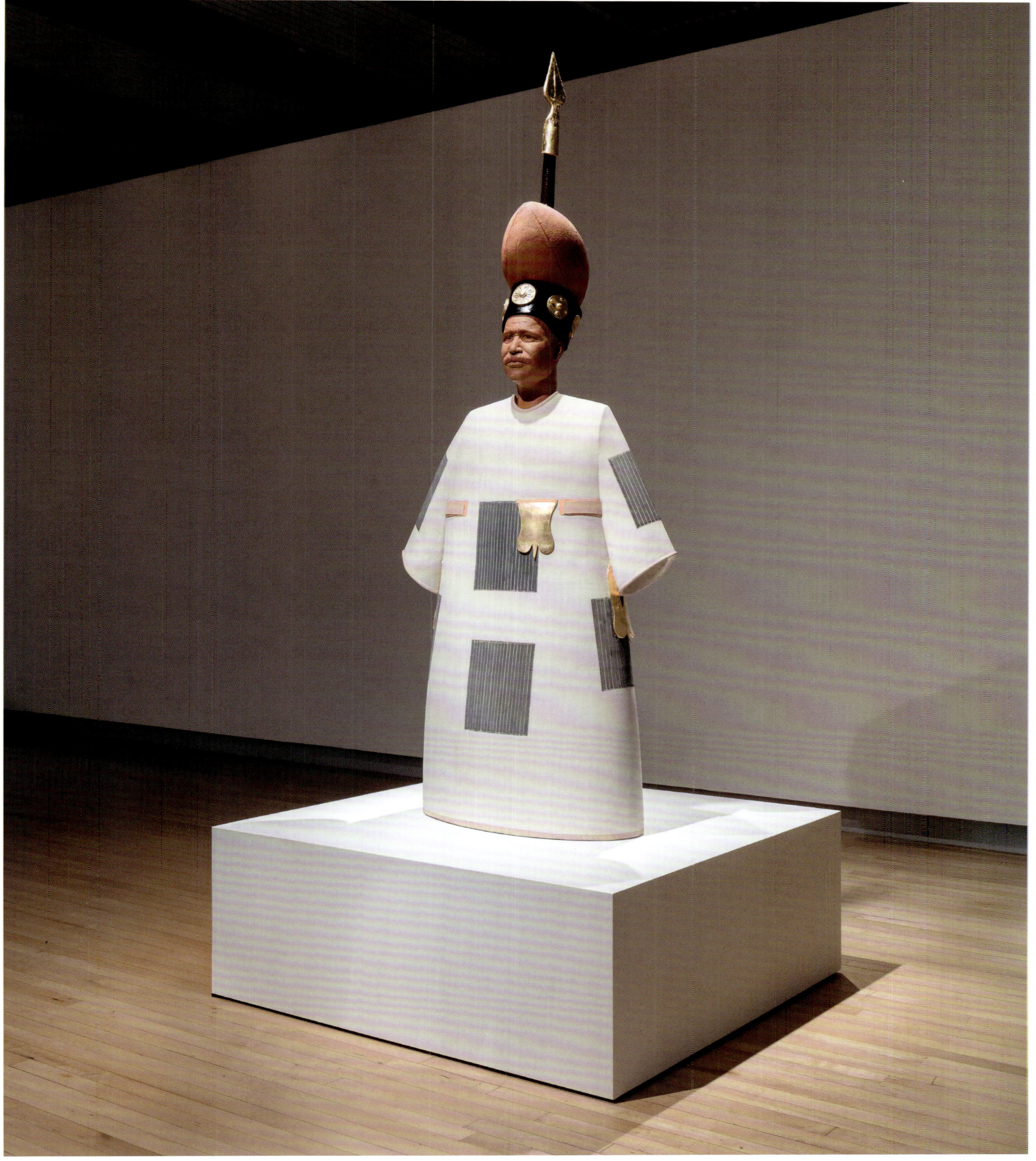

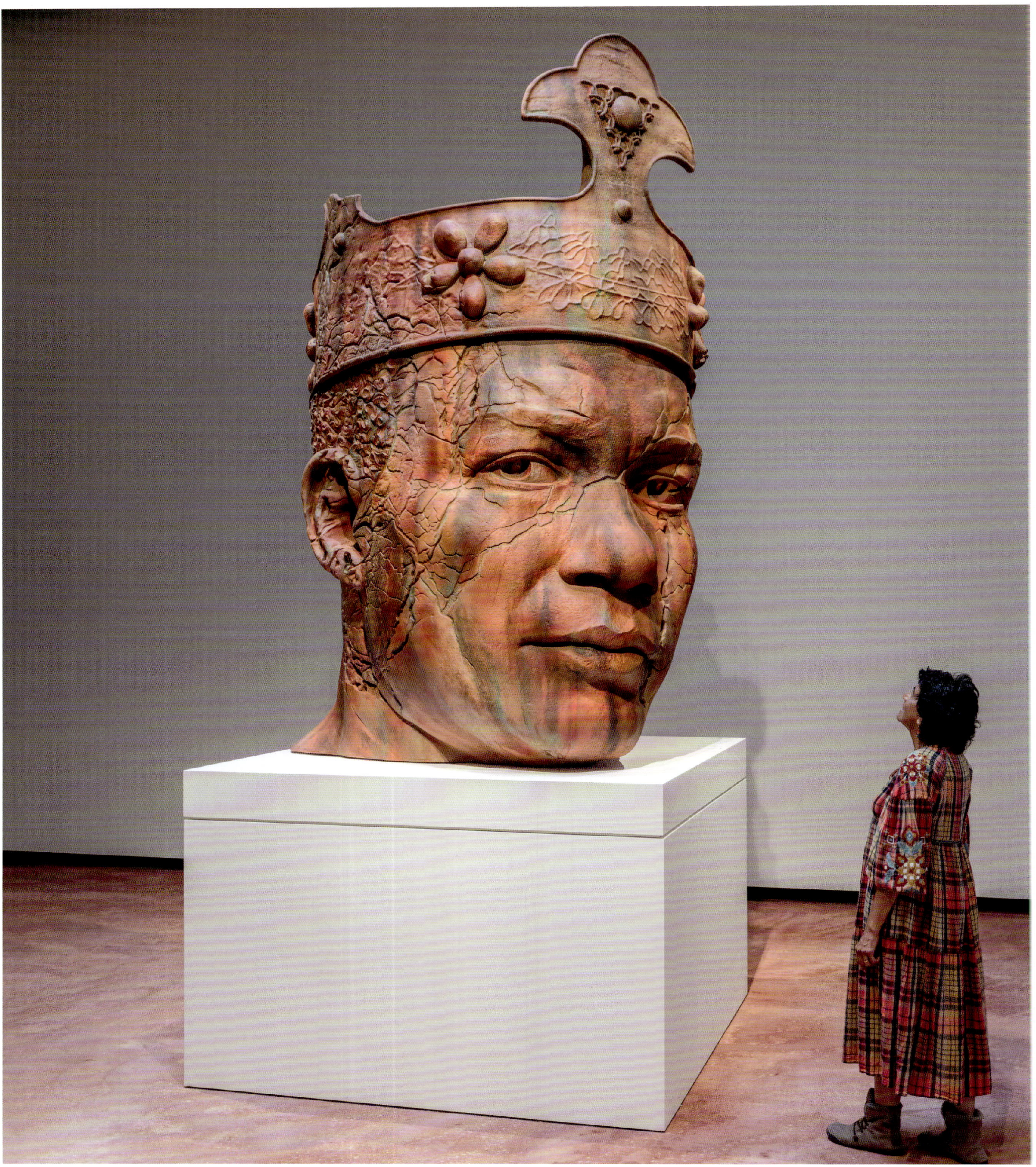

opposite,
RUIN OF A GIANT (KING TUBBY),
2024
MODELLING CLAY, STEEL, FOAM
265 X 150 X 188 CM

next pages, from left,
INTERGALACTIC PALACE, 2024
WOOD, THATCH, NATURAL FIBERS, ALUMINIUM, NEON, ACRYLIC, AUDIO COMPONENTS, ACRYLIC PAINT, STOLIT
450 X 610 CM

RUIN OF A GIANT (KING TUBBY),
2024
MODELLING CLAY, STEEL, FOAM
265 X 150 X 188 CM

INSTALLATION VIEW AT HAYWARD GALLERY, LONDON, 2024

as echo, reverberation and delay, to create an avant-garde, experimental sonic landscape. As reggae singer Mikey Dread explains 'King Tubby truly understood sound in a scientific sense. He knew how the circuits worked and what the electrons did. That's why he could do what he did.'[2]

Constructed from carved sandstone, Ruin of a Giant could be a prehistoric sculpture, a relic unearthed on a recent architectural dig – the remnants of an ancient lost civilization just re-discovered. The sculpture resembles a historic wonder of the world – preserved as an object of reverence, outliving generations of observers over the centuries. Yet although the carving is indeed a tribute to a dead legendary figure, Ruddock only passed away in 1989 – not 89 BC. These historical interventions, interruptions of chronological timelines, are characteristic of Strachan's work. Many of the pieces redress the intentional absence of Black people's innovations and contributions to Western scientific knowledge, not to mention popular culture. Because of the way Black people (and other historically oppressed groups) have been treated for the past few centuries, their (our) ambitions and achievements have not often been recognized or memorialized in the way that the products of the white male imagination have. Through the creation of monumental structures like Ruins of a Giant Strachan offers us a way to think through the idea that there is hope … that you can create and manifest in the world stories that actually kind of override the linear timeline … [I]n a few thousand years one could stumble upon these sculptures and they would fit into a lineage of our society's way of understanding, articulating and honouring individuals who had done magnificent things … It's very thrilling for me to think through the idea that time is a very conceptual bit of reality.[3]

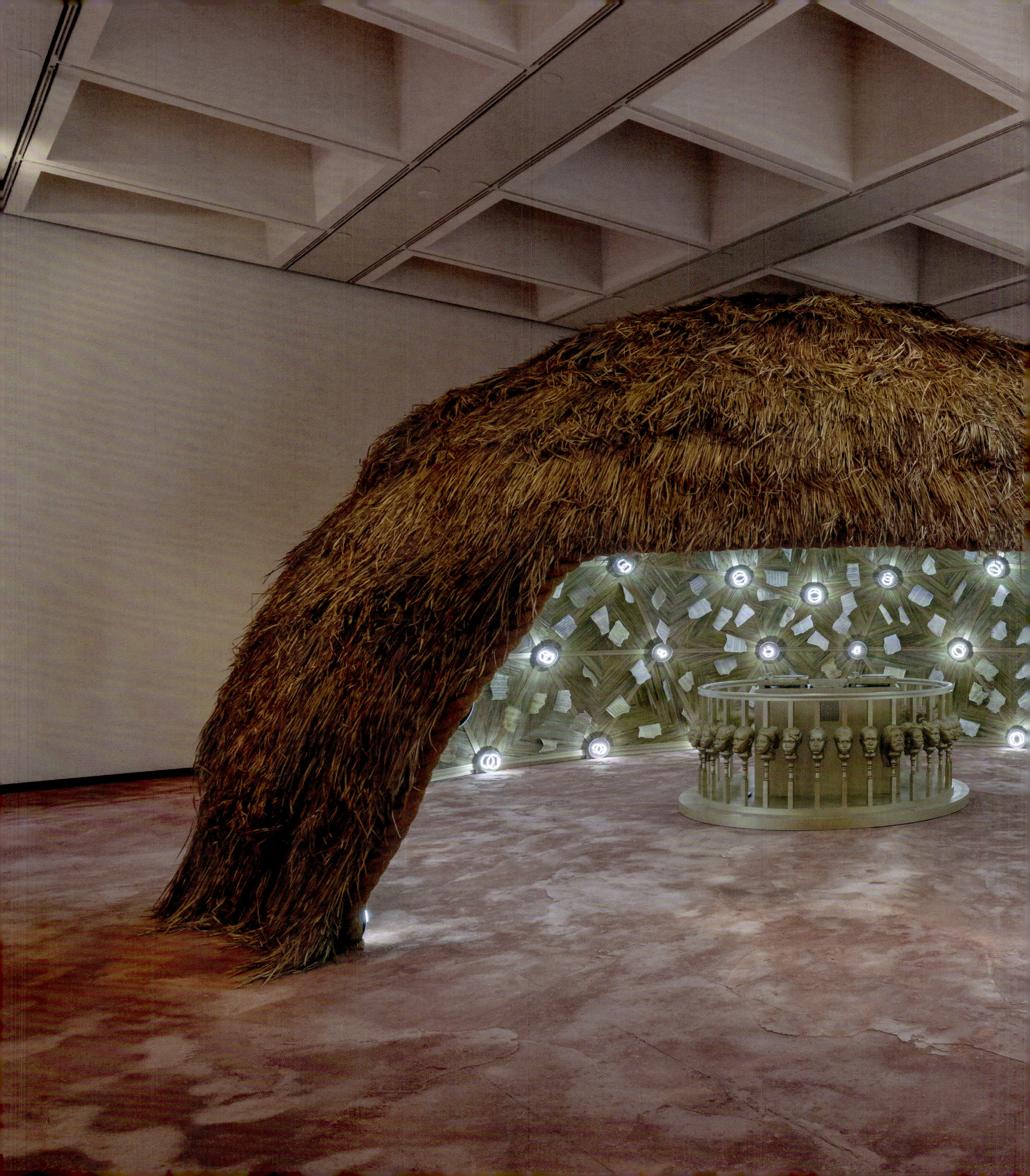

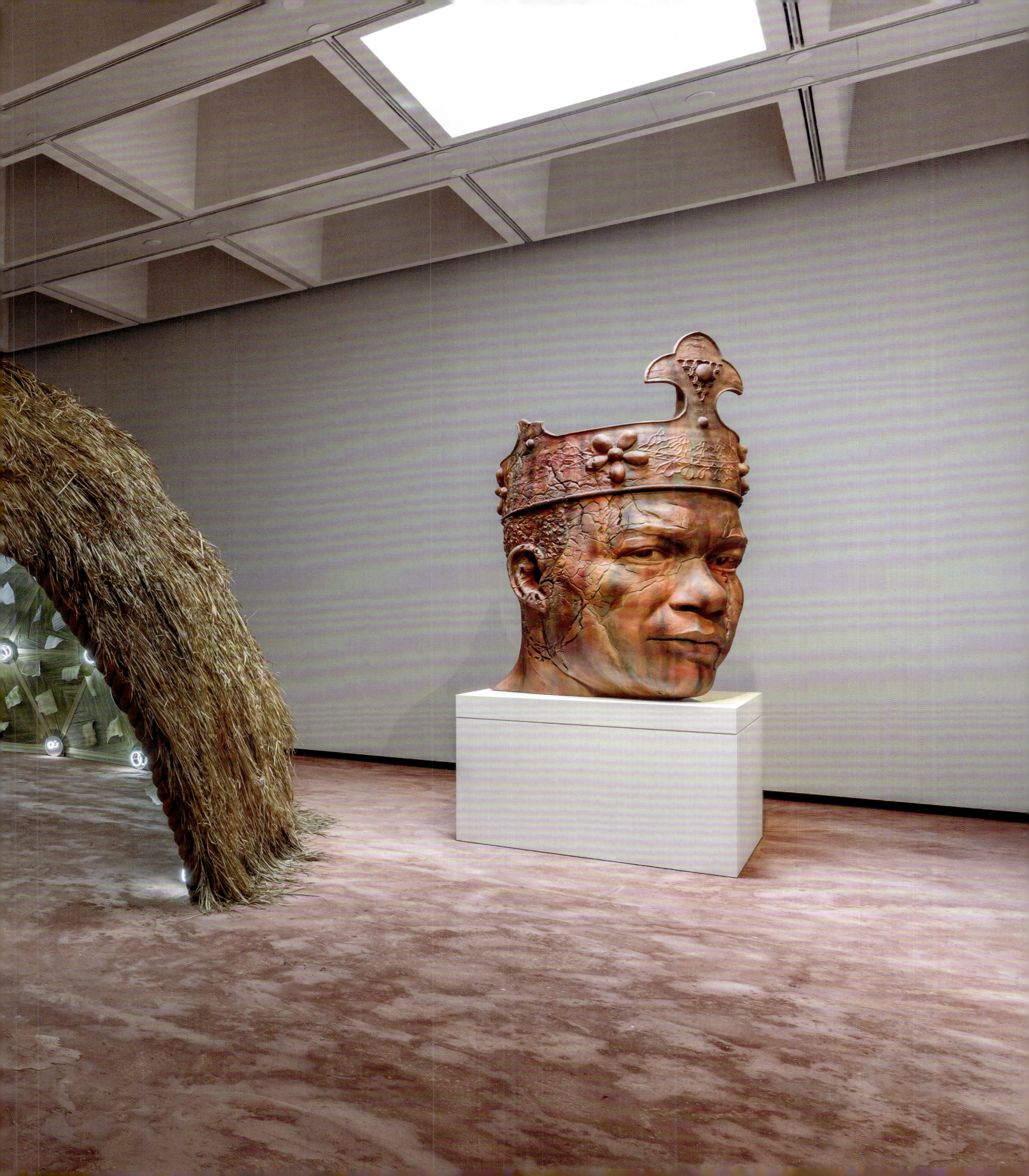

INTERGALACTIC PALACE, 2024
WOOD, THATCH, NATURAL FIBERS, ALUMINIUM, NEON, ACRYLIC, AUDIO COMPONENTS, ACRYLIC PAINT, STOLIT
450 X 610 CM

Ruin of a Giant stands guard over the Intergalactic Palace – a thatched structure, reminiscent of traditional African dwellings. Its interior glows with light and its walls are lined with sheet music. In the centre, a golden mixing desk is resplendent, encircled by a protective guard of golden busts of Black people. Once more, the centrality of music to Strachan's world building as well as to Black ontologies is apparent.

I've long been fascinated by the continuities that exist across West African and African-Caribbean metaphysics. Not only does Strachan provide the audience with new information, sharing knowledge that has been wilfully obscured or disregarded by hegemonic systems, but he creates alternative epistemic frameworks drawing on the characteristics of African and African-diaspora knowledge systems, elements such as non-sequential and non-chronological temporality, as well as the rejection of discretely bounded, limiting and reductive categories, offering other frameworks to approach, organize, assess and make sense of this knowledge.

As Strachan reminds us, Einstein proved that time is not linear. This understanding is central to African and African-diasporic approaches to time. Ironically dismissed by colonizers as 'primitive', such approaches bear far closer relation to the workings of quantum physics than Western fantasies, which imagine time as unfolding according to a linear chronological order.

In quantum physics, the Many Worlds Theory proposes the existence of multiverses – the idea that all realities exist simultaneously. When American physicist Hugh Everett introduced this concept at a conference in Dublin in 1952, it was, like many groundbreaking scientific, mathematical and philosophical propositions before it – the formula for proving infinity for instance – dismissed as rubbish, essentially too much of a headmelt to contend with. But the continued research of physicists like David Deutsch has brought us to the present day, where the concept has moved from fringe theory to the centre stage of debates on the most pioneering developments in quantum mathematics.

Deutsch argued that the unprecedented – one might say unparalleled – efficiency of quantum algorithms could only be fully understood if quantum computers were understood as working across parallel universes. In December 2024, Google's new Willow chip solved a computational problem – one that would have taken the world's fastest supercomputer approximately ten septillion years to calculate (this is longer than the Earth has actually been in existence) – in under five minutes.

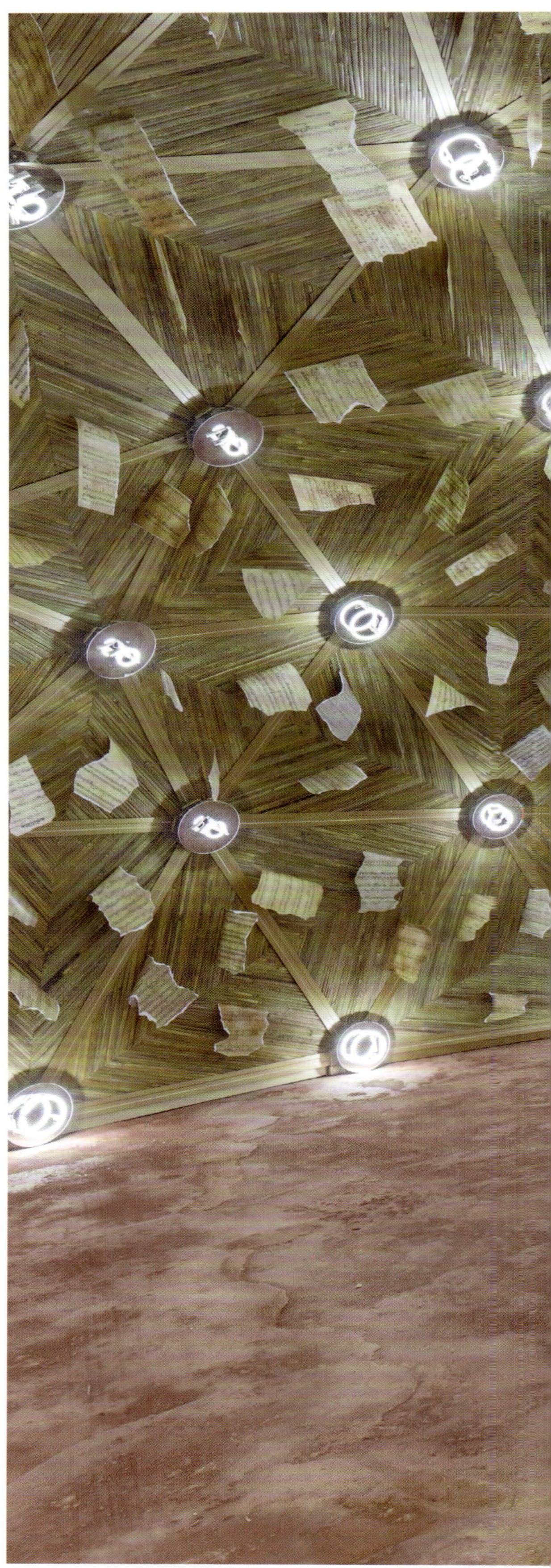

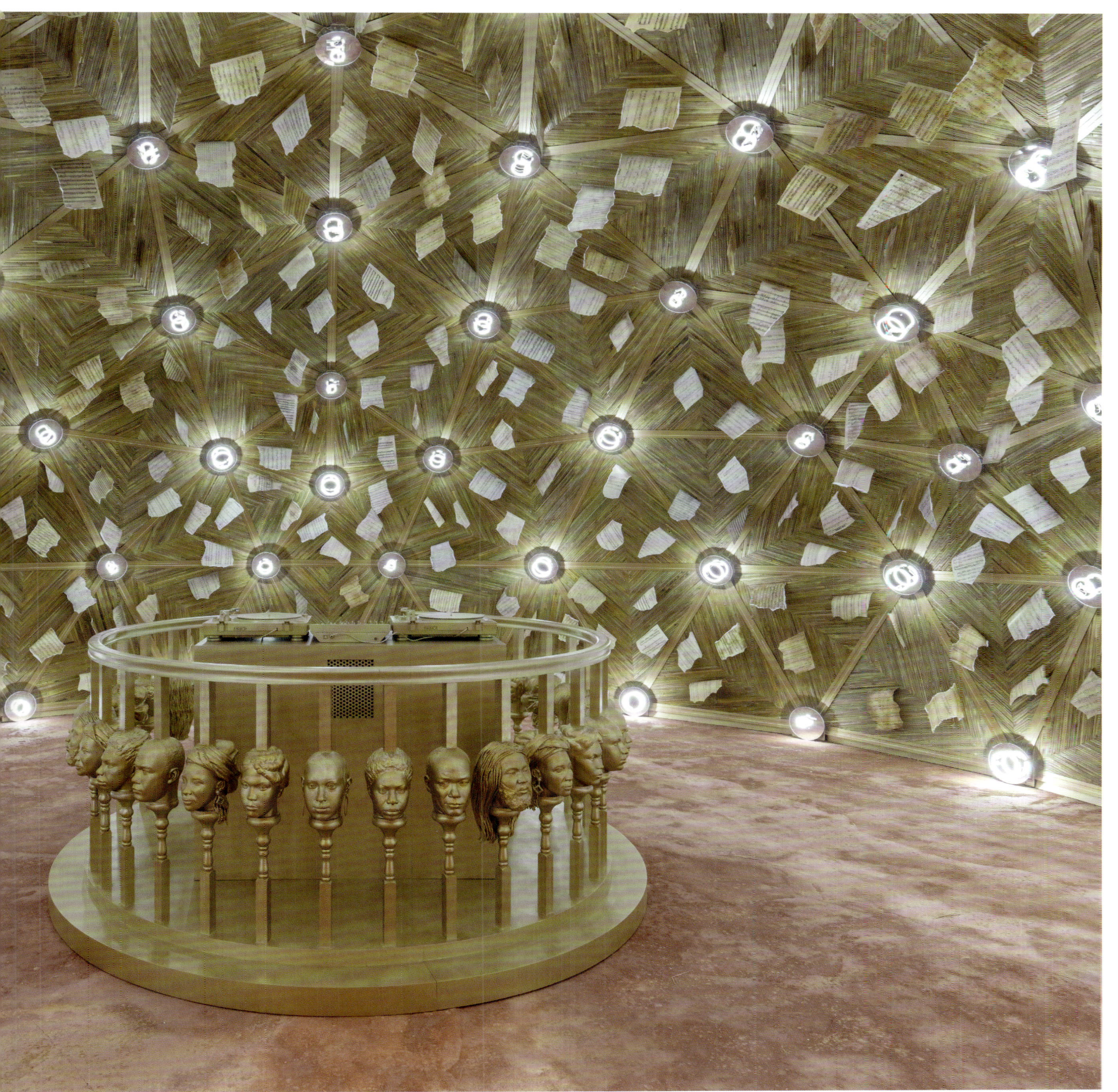

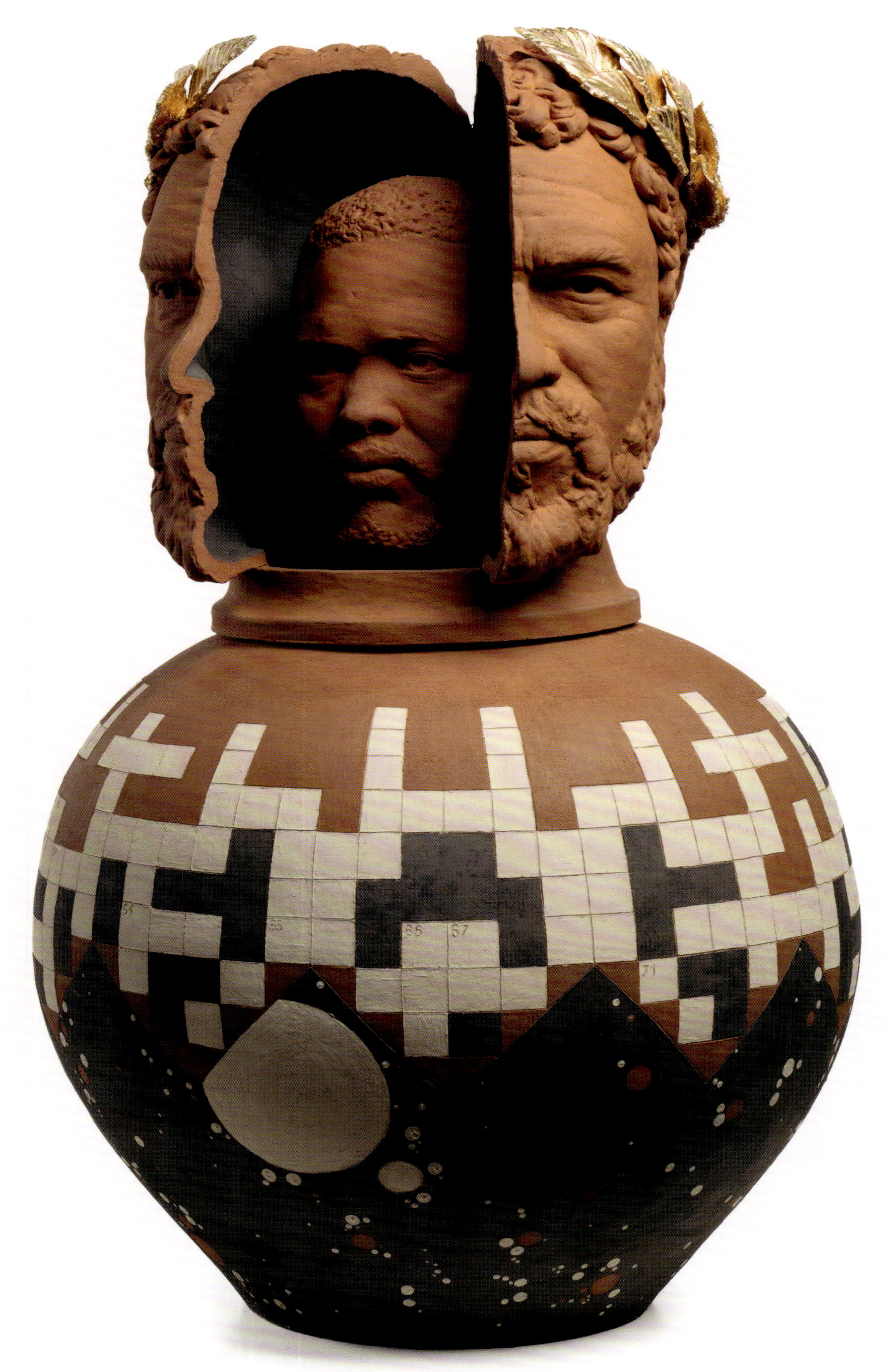

opposite,
INNER ELDER (BIKO AS SEPTIMIUS SEVERUS), 2023
CERAMIC
100 X 60 X 60 CM

next pages, from left,
INNER ELDER (NINA SIMONE AS QUEEN OF SHEBA), 2023
CERAMIC
100 X 60 X 60 CM

INNER ELDER (MARY SEACOLE), 2023
CERAMIC
90 X 60 X 60 CM

Willow's processing power was seen by many in the scientific community as evidence of the accuracy of Deutsch's theories, demonstrating quantum computing as an inherently multiverse-dependent process, while sceptics argue that there are other explanations. This is a debate taking place at the cutting edge of scientific research and discovery. One of the things I find so intriguing about it all is that, in contrast to the limited capacity of Western culture to contend with the existence of parallel worlds, many African cultures have a working relationship with the concept. In my own ethnic group, the Yoruba of Southwestern Nigeria, the existence of multiverses is a foundational principle within the culture and belief system, where the world of the living, the ancestral and the unborn, are believed to exist simultaneously. Rather than seeing the past, the present and the future as discrete and isolated from one another, they are understood as co-existing.

The Yoruba expression 'the child is father of the man' attests to the belief in the circularity of time in Yoruba cosmology and the relationship of continuity between the ancestral, the living and the unborn. The idea of multiple timelines co-existing is made material in Strachan's work, where ancestors who lived in different centuries exist on the same timeline, fusing to become one. I was reminded of this in works like Inner Elder, a series of clay busts where Strachan pairs figures such as South African anti-apartheid activist Bantu Stephen Biko with the Roman Emperor Septimius Severus (born in modern day Libya). In another bust from Inner Elder, the jazz icon Nina Simone's head opens to reveal the legendary Queen of Sheba within. While there are of course differences, the work also reminded me of the Yoruba concept of orí. In Yoruba cosmology, each human being has a personal orí. The spiritual head, or inner head orí inu is housed in the physical head orí ode. This spiritual head is responsible for an individual's fate, which is preordained before birth. Although you still have autonomy in what path you choose to follow, it is believed that your life will be in fuller alignment if you follow the direction of your orí.

There is meaningful synergy between Strachan's remixing of timelines and the sonic innovations for which Tubby should be more widely known, such as the invention of the remix – so central to dance and electronic music (genres that are regularly disassociated from their Black roots). Again, I am struck by the continuities between West Africa and the Caribbean. The primary characteristic of a remix is that it transforms preexisting materials to create something new. In my first book, Don't Touch My Hair, I wrote about the Yoruba oral tradition of oriki – an epistemic and performative tradition that is a cornerstone of Yoruba cultural expression, and which demonstrates the spirit of the remix explicitly. As the scholar Karin Barber explains, oriki is often used in place of the English word 'definition', for oriki are believed to 'encapsulate the essential qualities of entities. But oriki do more than define. They evoke a subject's qualities.

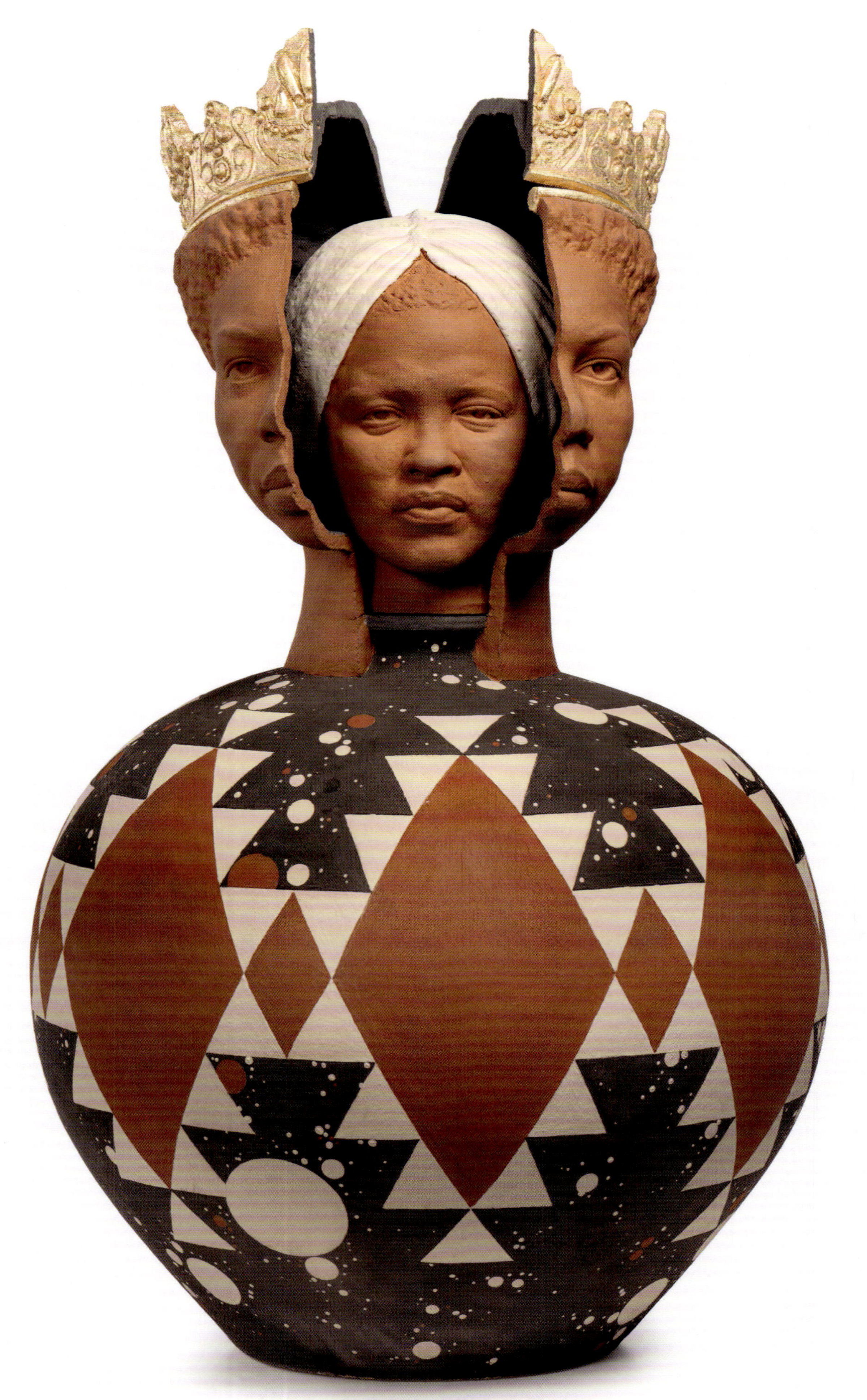

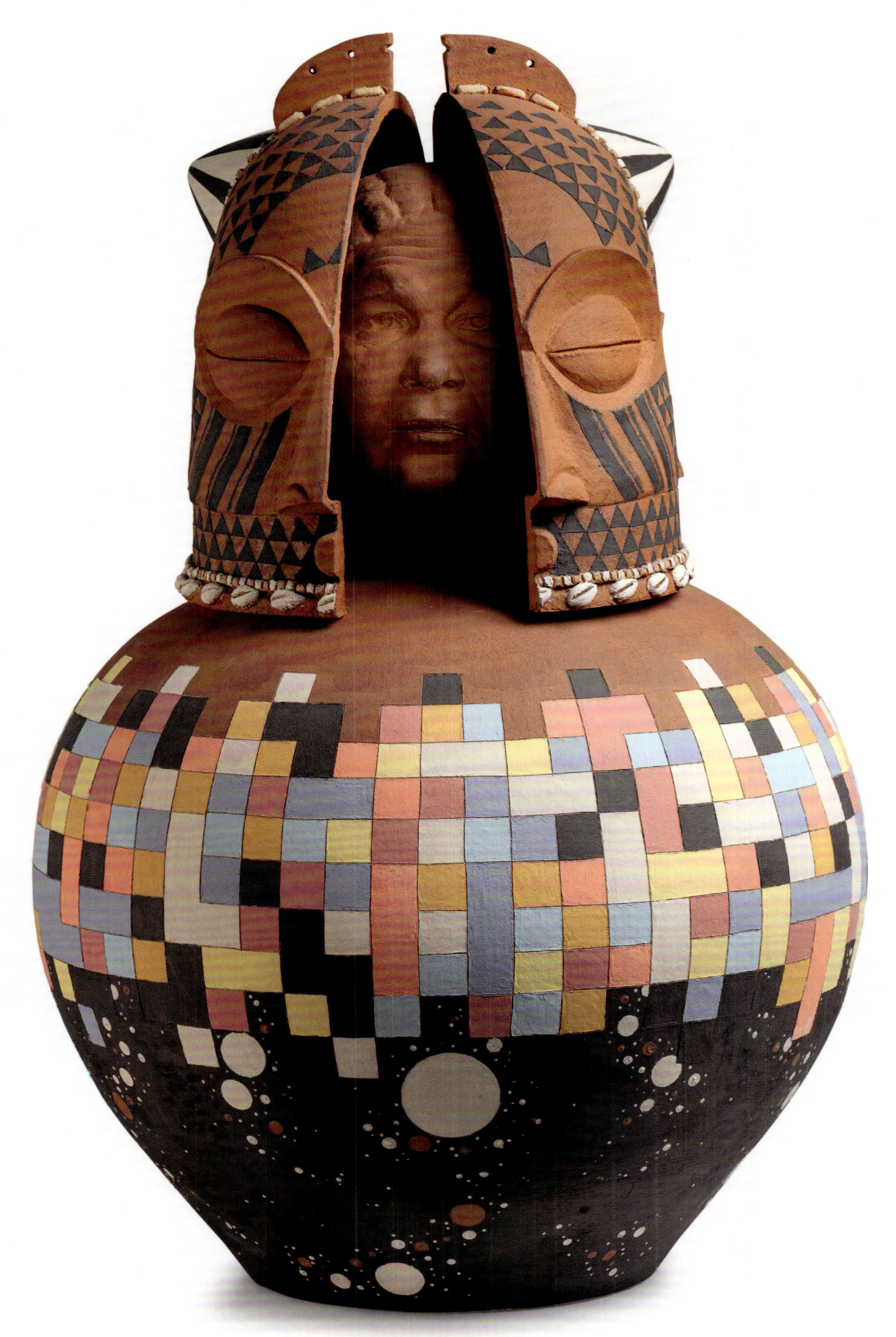

They go to the heart of it and elicit its inner potency.' In her investigation of the role of oriki in Yoruba reckonings with time, as well as culturally significant events, Barber writes:

> At the time of their composition, each oriki refers to the here and now. They encapsulate whatever is noteworthy in contemporary experience ... but because they are valued they are preserved, and transmitted for decades – even centuries ... Oriki are valued all the more for coming from the past, and bringing with them something of its accumulated capabilities, the attributes of earlier powers ... A single performance often contains items composed as much as 200 years apart ... the items from different historical moments are not usually arranged in chronological order, nor are the most ancient units separated from the newest ones. They might be performed in virtually any order and combination. This is not because a chronological ordering is beyond the scope of oriki performers – the oriki of all the successive Obas (Yoruba kings) of Okuku and those of the successive holders of the most senior chiefly title are performed in order – but because oriki performances usually aim at something else. The past is recalled for a different purpose.[4]

The European understanding of 'history' locates the action in an irrecoverable time past. Past events are static, preserved, frozen in aspic. Meanwhile, African-infused forms of enlivening the past have different intentions. In contrast to Eurocentric methods of recording and documenting history, in an African context multiple pasts are weaved skilfully together with the present.[5] I felt this profoundly in Strachan's work and with his approaches to reimagining the past, the present and the future. I immediately recognized his practice as operating within a shared logic that has a connective thread running through African and African diasporic cultural expression, ranging from oriki, to the remix, to black hairstyling culture, not least in the way we see hairstyles that are millennia old, repurposed in communication with and in response to contemporary settings.

In A Map of the Crown, Strachan created black bronze busts with ornate hairstyles sculpted from afro textured hair that he collected from barber shops and salons across the Bahamas. Because the physical head orí ode houses the spiritual head orí inu, the maintenance and grooming of hair is seen as an act of spiritual significance in Yoruba culture, in a way that is identifiable across many African cultures. Given the creative energy that Black communities have poured into hairstyling culture, not to mention the texture of afro hair that lends itself so purposefully to the creation of intricate braided patterns and designs, seeing hair exhibited in this way in the exhibition feels particularly fitting. Strachan describes hair as a 'vehicle for a story of survival'. 'The number of resources that you can find within the confines of your body, especially when you're in a desperate situation,

opposite,
A MAP OF THE CROWN (CONGO CANDLE WICK), 2022
BRONZE, FLOCKED HAIR
177 X 60 X 60 CM

next pages, from left,
A MAP OF THE CROWN (FULANI BLACK), 2024
BRONZE, FLOCKED HAIR
63 X 40 X 33 CM

A MAP OF THE CROWN (MODERN AMERICAN), 2023
BRONZE, FLOCKED HAIR
53 X 27 X 24 CM

A MAP OF THE CROWN (UKUANYAMA NAMIBIA), 2022
BRONZE, FLOCKED HAIR
46 X 22 X 32 CM

A MAP OF THE CROWN (JIMMA ETHIOPIA), 2023
BRONZE, FLOCKED HAIR
71 X 29 X 41 CM

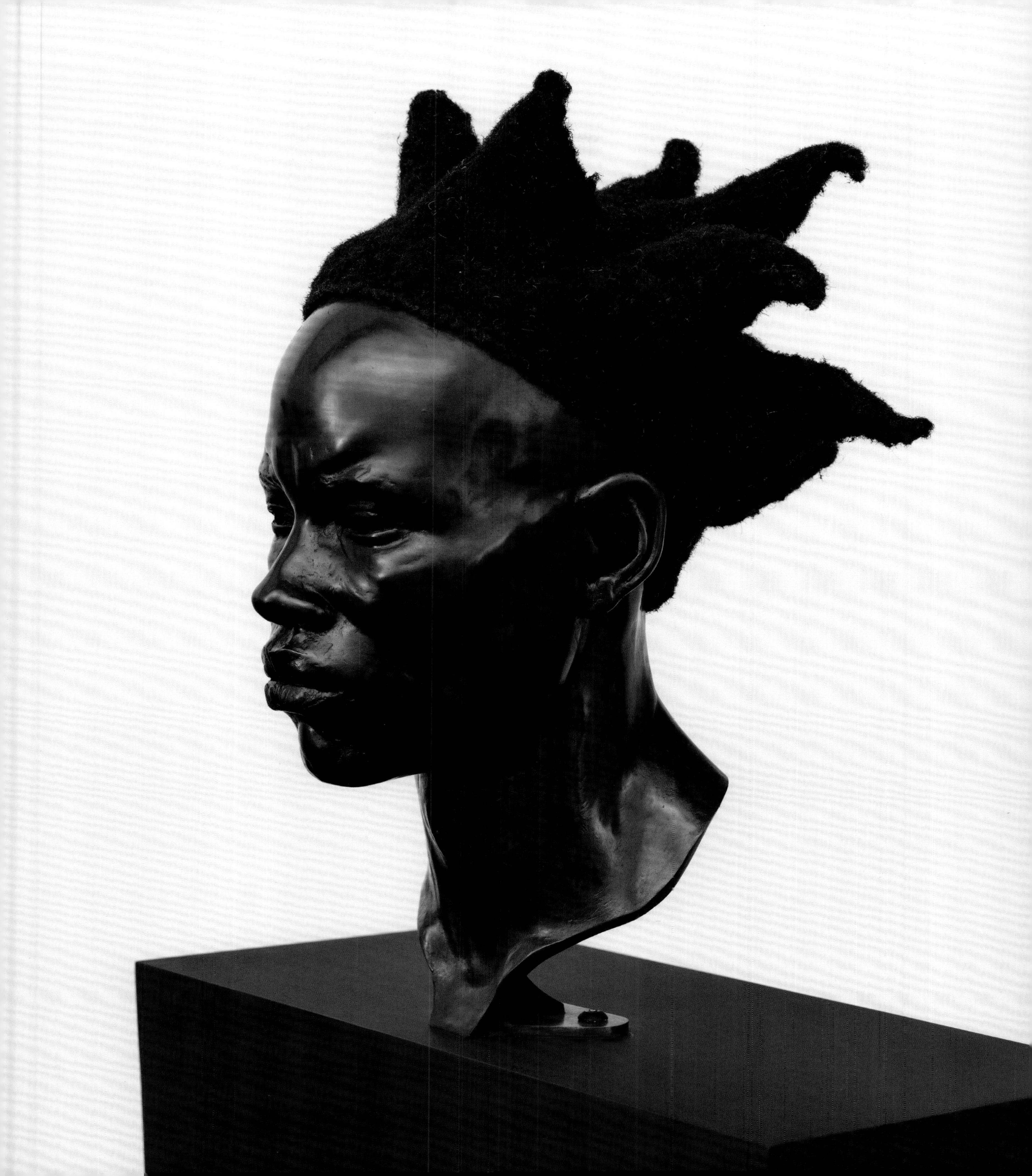

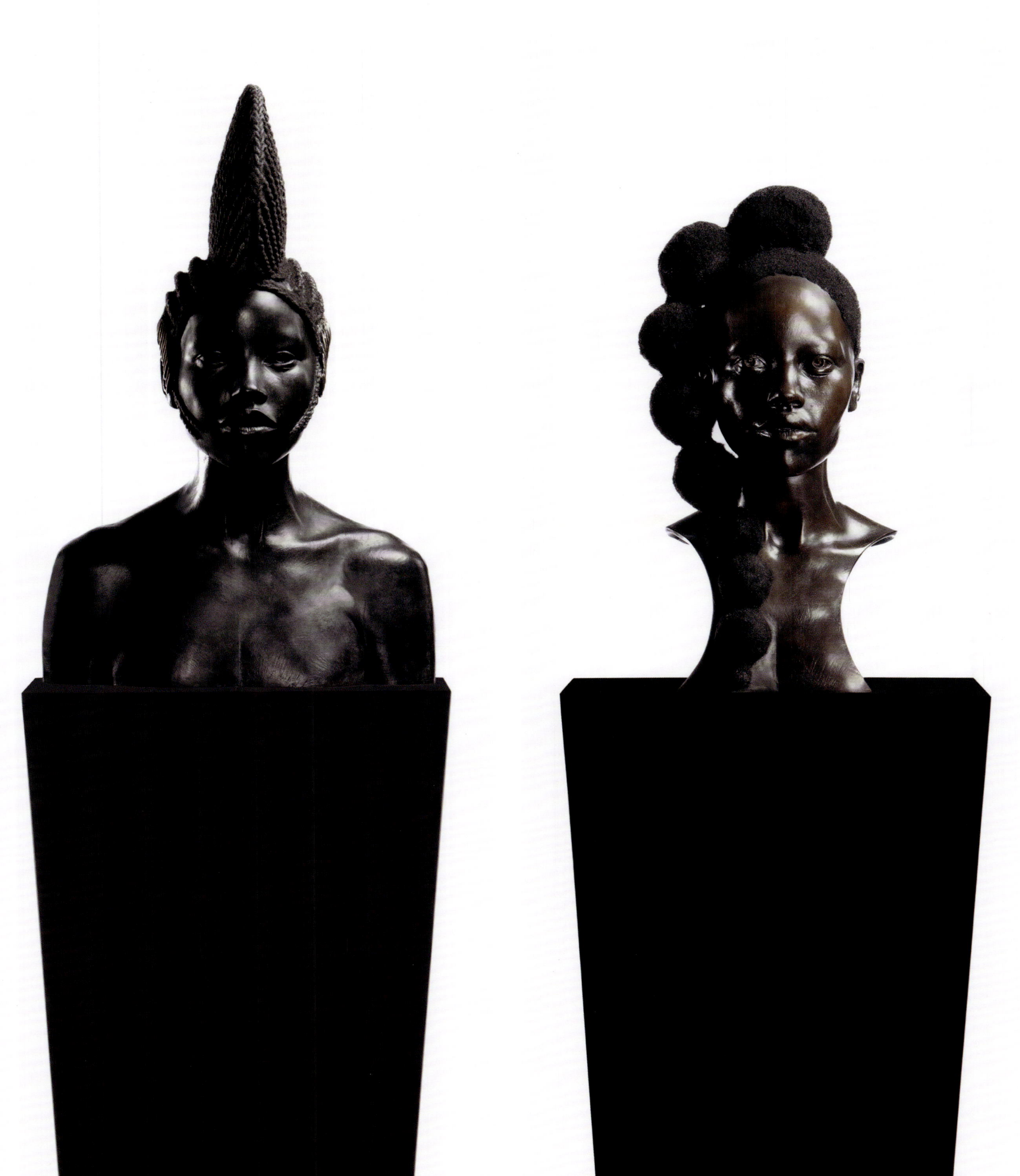

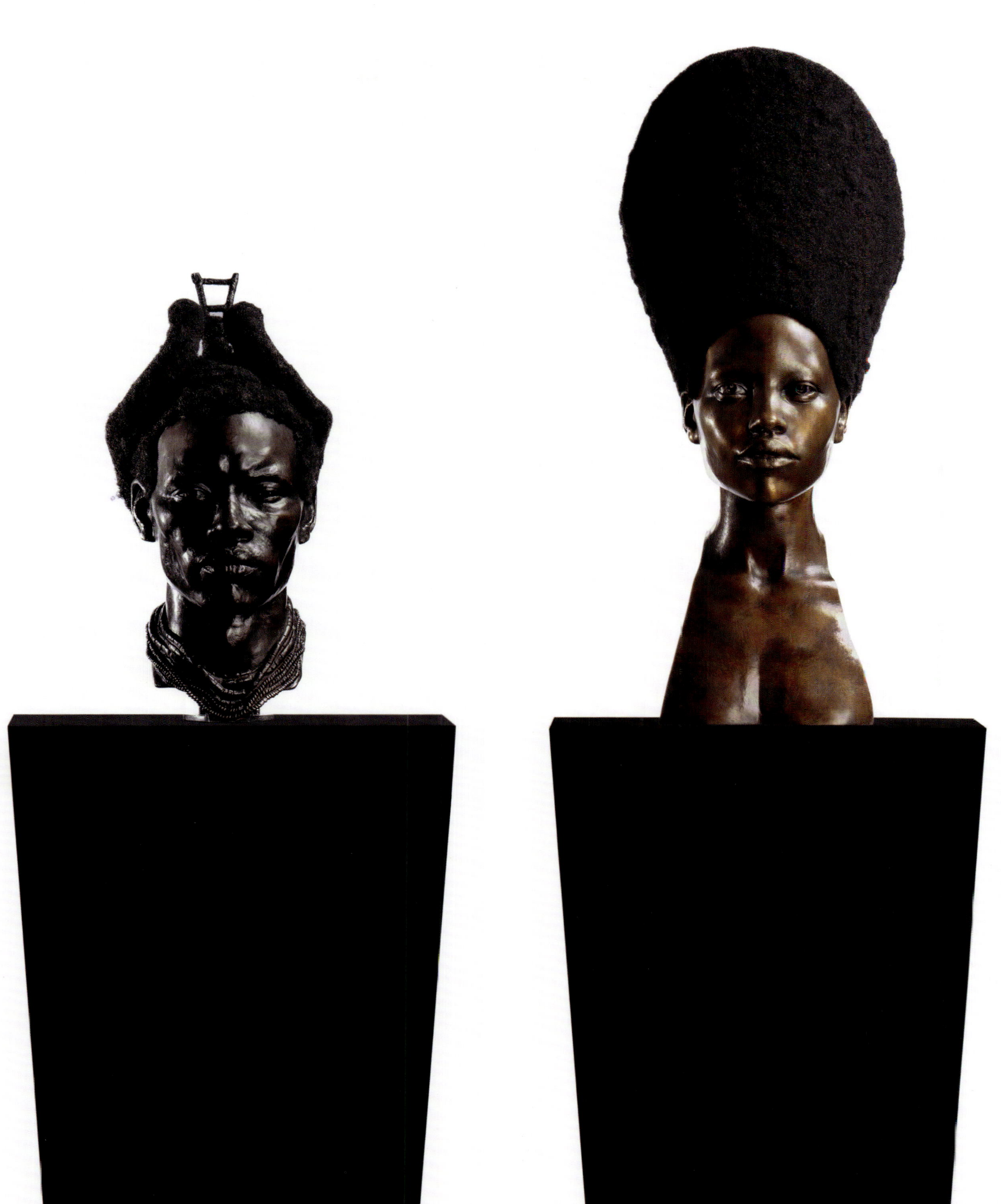

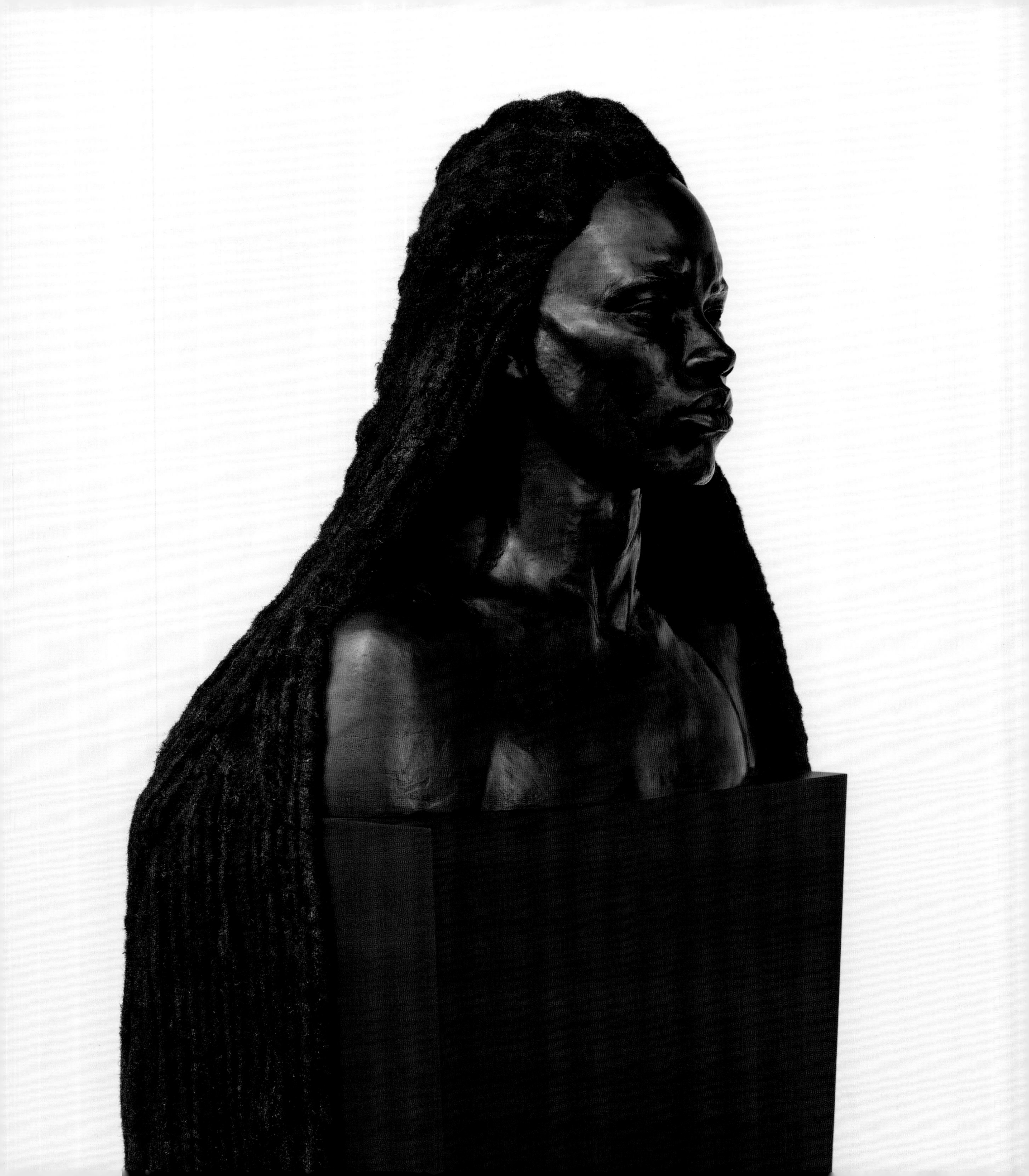

A MAP OF THE CROWN (HIMBA DREADED KNOTS), 2022
BRONZE, FLOCKED HAIR
180 X 60 X 60 CM

is incredible.'[6] The truth of this statement in the context of black hair cannot be overstated. One of the most powerful examples is the story of San Basilio de Palenque in Colombia, often credited as the first free town of the Americas, home to thousands of fugitives who, escaping from plantations in and around Cartagena, went on to find freedom in the Palenque. Central to the success of the Palenque was the existence of an extensive intelligence network in which hair braiding played a pivotal role. Braided hair patterns were utilized as a form of mapping that was unintelligible to the Spanish, constituting an important method of communication. Hairstyles operated as a sort of underground railway where women would encode important messages into hair patterns through which the enslaved could communicate plans regarding escape, and eventually make their way to liberation and freedom in the Palenque.

Strachan's practice defies rigid categorization in yet another way that reflects the logics of African-diasporic art forms. His use of various media, encompassing sculpture, collage, installation, sound and drawing, repudiates the imperial logic of strict categorization, as well as its catastrophic attempts to order the world according to discrete and atomized classification. In contrast, the African and African-diasporic ontologies in which Strachan's work is located tend to be far more holistic and intragrated. Hayward director Ralph Rugoff refers to the 'Invisibility Paintings', collages with titles like Double Consciousness and Self Portrait as King Oba with British Zombies, which incorporate images ranging from various other works by Strachan to those by ancient Egyptians, diagrams and more recent figures from Black history, as visually and conceptually polyrhythmic, a term I love that again references the influence of music in Strachan's art. As Strachan explains 'coming out of the academy,

SELF-PORTRAIT AS KING OBA WITH BRITISH ZOMBIES, 2023
OIL, ENAMEL, PIGMENT AND MUSEUM BOARD ON ACRYLIC PANEL
213 X 213 X 6 CM

whether you're a painter or photographer or a sculptor, you're taught how to organize what you're making into distinct categories. In the Bahamas, we wouldn't care about that. We fundamentally believe in the human capacity to understand a lot of different ways of making and thinking and being all at the same time.'[7]

It's no coincidence that Strachan's studio is called Isolated Labs: his practice is as much informed by scientific research as it is by the mythic, and indeed the sharp distinction between the two is one of the limitations of the binary worldview we have inherited from Western intellectual traditions. While this can be dated at least from Plato and his insistence on the separation of the body and the mind, understanding the world through bifuriaction was further entrenched through the concept of duality conceived of by Rene Descartes, the hugely influential seventeenth-century French philosopher and scientist.

Strachan moves beyond merely theoretical or conceptual engagement with his subject matter, fully immersing himself in embodied experience and practical applications. He has trained, for instance, as both a deep-sea diver and a cosmonaut at Yuri Gagarin Cosmonaut Training Centre in Star City, Russia. When undertaking the gruelling simulations and gravitational exercises carried out by trainee cosmonauts, he comments:

You learn hcw to tolerate stress: you spin, jump, shake, fall and float. You experience intense gravity; then you are weightless. The training was part of Orthostatic Tolerance, a body of work investigating the physiological stress that cosmonauts and deep-sea explorers endure while exiting and returning to the surface of the Earth. Taking part in the

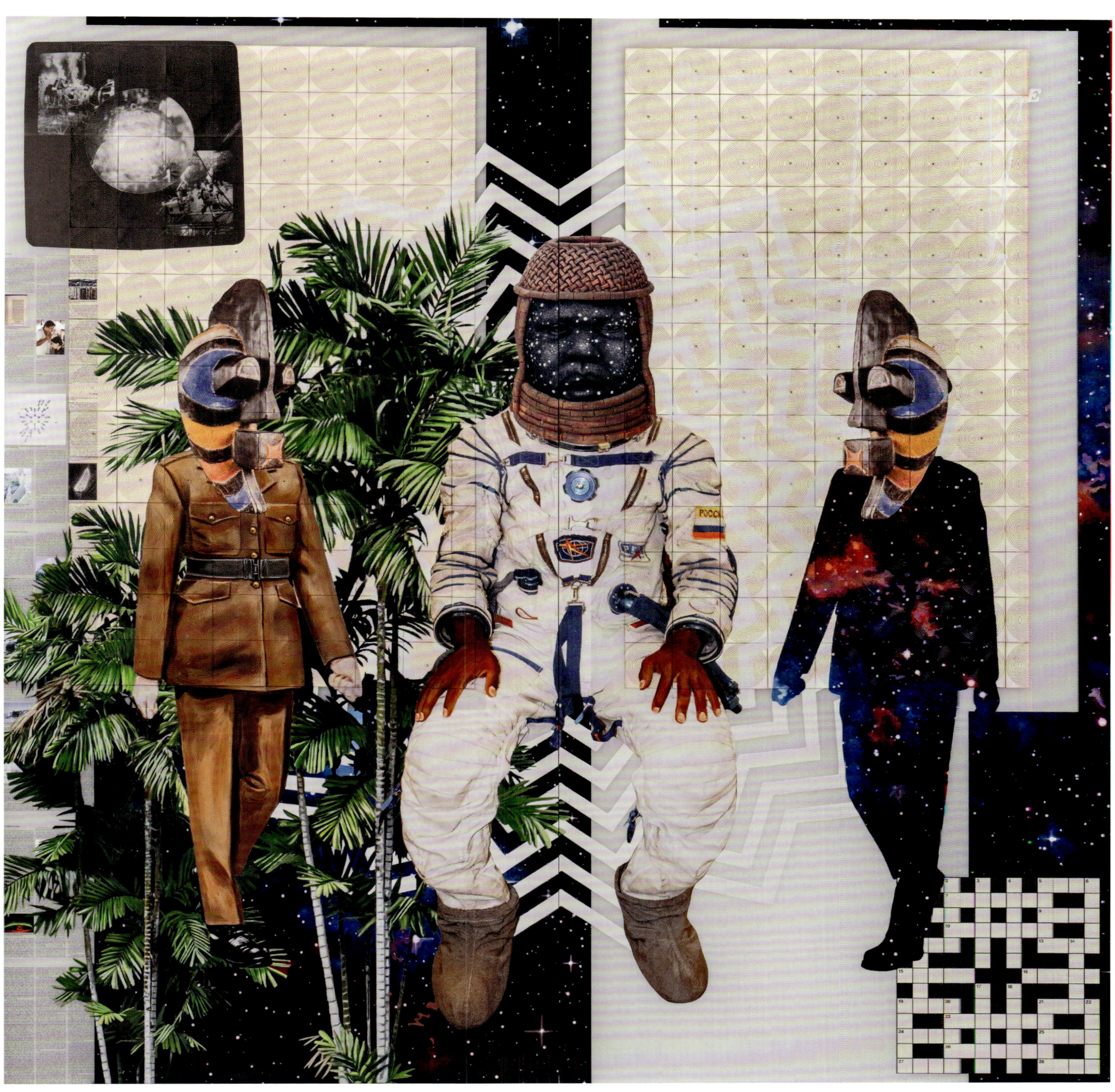

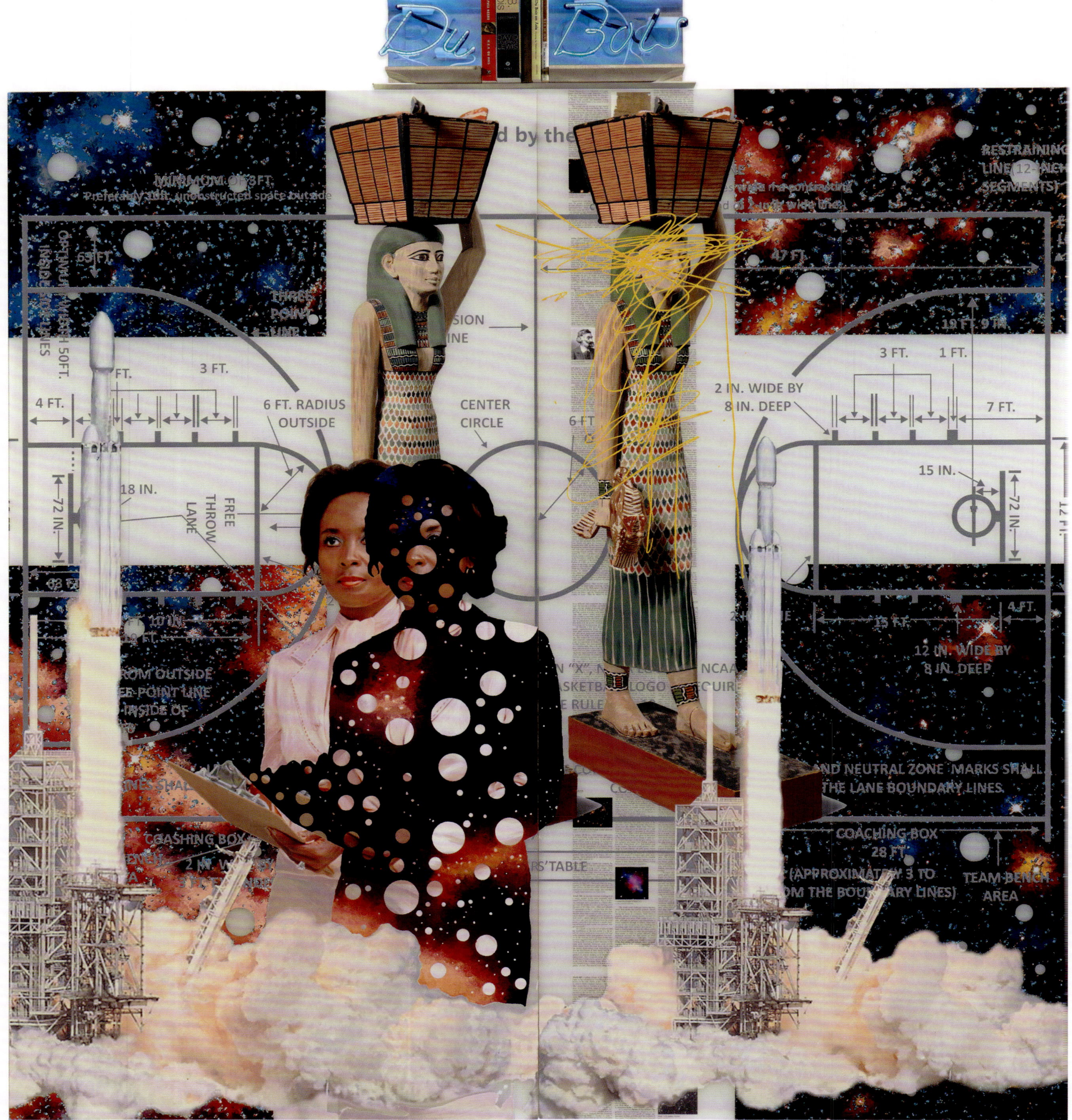
Du Bois
W.E.B. DU BOIS
DAVID LEVERING LEWIS
MINIMUM OF 3FT.
RESTRAINING LINE
SEGMENTS)
47 FT.
19 FT. 9 IN.
3 FT.
1 FT.
2 IN. WIDE BY 8 IN. DEEP
7 FT.
15 IN.
72 IN.
4 FT.
3 FT.
6 FT. RADIUS OUTSIDE
CENTER CIRCLE
6 FT
FREE THROW LANE
18 IN.
72 IN.
12 IN. WIDE BY 8 IN. DEEP
4 FT.
COACHING BOX
28 FT.
TEAM BENCH AREA
COACHING BOX

DOUBLE CONSCIOUSNESS,
2023
OIL, ENAMEL, PIGMENT,
ACRYLIC, MATBOARD, GLUE,
NEON TRANSFORMERS,
LIMESTONE, PAPER, BOOKS
TWO PANELS
EACH 76 X 152 X 5 CM
BOOKEND: 25 X 65 X 18 CM
OVERALL: 178 X 152 X 18 CM

training programmes was also a way to pay homage to black pioneers like Henson, Robert Henry Lawrence Jr, the first African American astronaut and Andrea Motley Crabtree, the first female US Army deep-sea diver.[8]

The ocean is further referenced in Strachan's replica of SS Yarmouth which appears in the exhibition floating on a lake on top of the gallery's Brutalist architecture. This ship was the flagship of the former Black Star Line, the first Black-owned shipping company in North America, established by the Jamaican political activist Marcus Garvey in 1919. The plan was to facilitate international commerce among the African diaspora, as well as to eventually repatriate the descendants of enslaved people by providing a route back to Africa. True to groundbreaking form, Strachan has bought the rights to the Black Star Line and intends to re-establish it.

I often crave abstract non-representational Black art and so deeply appreciate paintings like Self-Portrait as Exploding Galaxy (2023) made of oil, enamel and pigment, the night sky rendered as a brightly coloured explosion of balls of light. This work not only demonstrates Strachan's enduring interest in the cosmos, but in terms of art history, also liberates Black subjectivity from the representational constraints of the violent taxonomy of race in order to reflect the cosmic consciousness of which we are all a part. Strachan's engagement with the cosmos, as well as with the ocean's depths, attends to the gravitational pull of above and below, evidence again of his inherently holistic approach. It reminds us that the cosmos and the ocean are literally a match made in heaven; the ocean's water molecules are composed of hydrogen made in the Big Bang, while the oxygen in them was birthed in a star.

opposite,
BLACK STAR, 2024
INK ON PAPER
29 X 21 CM

next pages,
BLACK STAR, 2024
ALUMINIUM, FIBREGLASS,
STEEL, PAINTED WOOD
543 X 1210 X 200 CM

INSTALLATION VIEW AT
HAYWARD GALLERY, LONDON,
2024

Personally, There is Light Somewhere had a profound effect on me and has led me back to DJing as part of my own practice. In preparation for the public conversation I had with Strachan, programmed within the exhibition's events, I listened to a lot of dub. I grew up with reggae, since my parents were both fans, as well as other Caribbean genres of music (my mother was born and raised in Trinidad), but last summer something I'd been searching for revealed itself and I knew I needed to immerse myself in this sonic universe. Dissatisfied with the corporate and liberal approaches to anti-racism that have become almost default post-2020 and which – being in many instances performative – have unsurprisingly fizzled out, I felt starved of more revolutionary expressions of liberation politics. I was deeply drawn to what Peter Tosh describes as the 'spiritual ingredients' of reggae, and the manner in which the intention and purpose behind the music animates the sound. Dub and roots reggae just felt like the blackest fucking sound I could find. When I use 'black' here, I am not beholden to some essentialist, representational identitarian definition, nor to racial taxonomies, but rather to 'black' as in the characteristics of afro-diasporic art discussed here and evidenced in Strachan's art. Black – not about some notion of 'purity' or return to an 'original Africa' – but rather blackness as innovation, blackness as fugitivity offered as a radical counterpart to inclusivity within oppressive frameworks. Blackness as anti-imperialist and anti-consumerist.

Dub takes extant reggae songs and manipulates them using a mixing board, layering them in aural effects such as reverb and echo.[9] These effects are fundamentally spatial in quality, giving the listener an impression of vast open space. Josh Kun's theories about 'audiotopias' (temporary aural spaces created through music) can be applied here in regard

"THE BLACK STAR LINE," Inc.

MARCUS GARVEY: IN THE EARLY 1920's JAMAICAN BORN PIONEER MARCUS GARVEY HAD A DREAM THAT ANY AFRICAN LIVING IN THE NEW WORLD SHOULD HAVE THE CHANCE TO TRAVEL TO THEIR PLACE OF ORIGIN AFRICA. GARVEY, A POWERFUL ORATOR AND CAPTIVATING LEADER INCORPORATED THE BLACK STAR LINE WITH THE SUPPORT OF 4 MILLION MEMBERS FROM THE FAMED UNIA OR THE UNIVERSAL NEGRO IMPROVEMENT ASSOCIATION.

IN SHORT ORDER GARVEY AND HIS TEAM AMASSED 4 SHIPS AND MADE VOYAGES TO CUBA, HAITI AND THE BAHAMAS. HOWEVER, BEFORE THEY COULD MAKE THE TRANS-ATLANTIC JOURNEY, HIS FREEDOM AND TIME IN AMERICA WAS STOLEN AWAY FROM HIM. GARVEY WAS ACCUSED BY THE FBI OF MAIL FRAUD, WAS JAILED THEN DEPORTED BACK TO JAMICA. NONE OF THE SHIPS MADE IT TO AFRICA. MORE THAN 100 YEARS LATER MOST OF GARVEY'S STORY AND THE LEGACY OF THE BLACK STAR LINE REMAINS INVISIBLE.

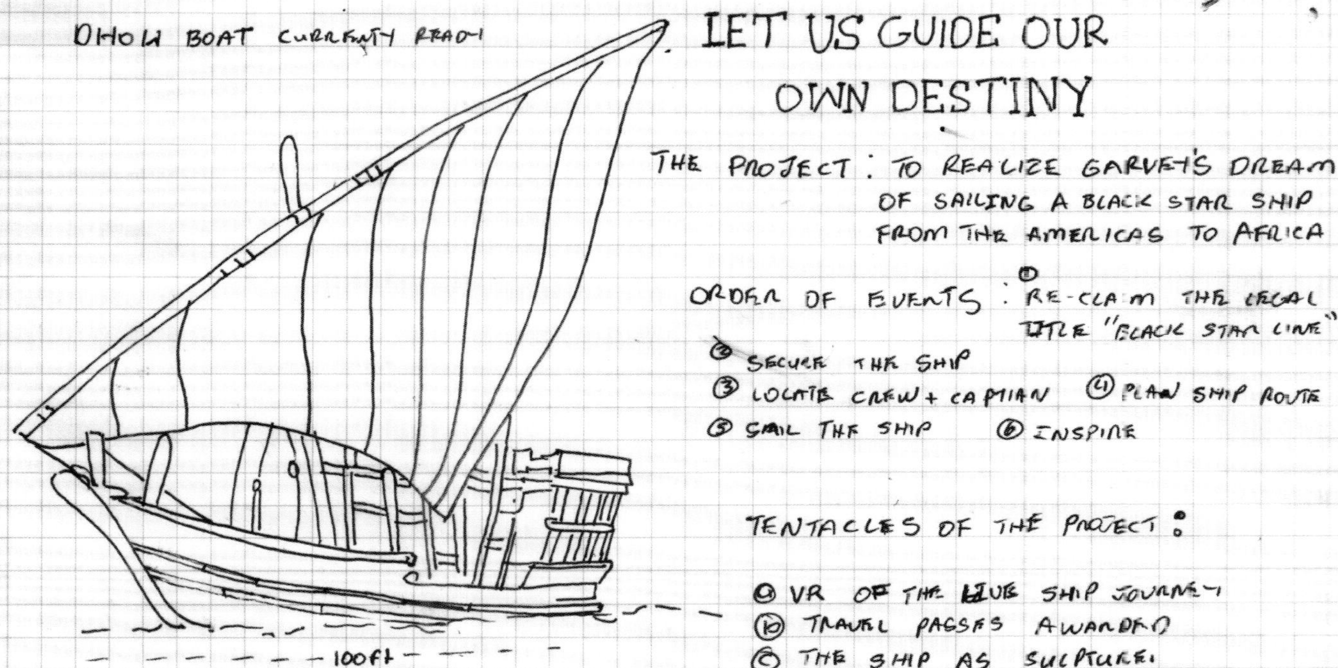

LET US GUIDE OUR OWN DESTINY

THE PROJECT: TO REALIZE GARVEY'S DREAM OF SAILING A BLACK STAR SHIP FROM THE AMERICAS TO AFRICA

ORDER OF EVENTS: ① RE-CLAIM THE LEGAL TITLE "BLACK STAR LINE"
② SECURE THE SHIP
③ LOCATE CREW + CAPTIAN ④ PLAN SHIP ROUTE
⑤ SAIL THE SHIP ⑥ INSPIRE

TENTACLES OF THE PROJECT:

ⓐ VR OF THE LIVE SHIP JOURNEY
ⓑ TRAVEL PASSES AWARDED
ⓒ THE SHIP AS SULPTURE
ⓓ THE SHIP AS FLOATING MUSEUM
ⓔ DOC ON MARCUS GARVEY/BSL
ⓕ EDUCATION OUT REACH/PUBLIC PROGRAMS

*HOLDS 100 PLUS CREW

BUDGET DRAFT—

SHIP	300K
SHIP RENOVATION	300K
18 MEMBER CREW	240K
CAPTIAN	60K
LEGAL	50K
FILM	150K
MANAGMENT	80K
DOCKING	150K
SUPLIES	60K
INSURANCE	70K
EQUIPMENT	50K

"LET MY PEOPLE COME/LET MY PEOPLE GO"

°TIME LINE DRAFT

2021
FEB – BOAT LOCATED
JULY → PARTNERSHIPS FORMED
JULY – BOAT SITE VISIT/CAP SELECTED
AUG – SHIPPING ROUTE DESIGNED
NOV – BOAT PREP

2022
JAN – BOAT MOVES TO BAH
MAR – ROUTE FINAL
APRIL – TICKETS AWARDED
SEPTEMBER – SET SAIL

TOTAL ONE MILLION FIVEHUNDRED + TEN THOUSAND

BSL PROJECT – 2020
TAVARES STRACHAN —

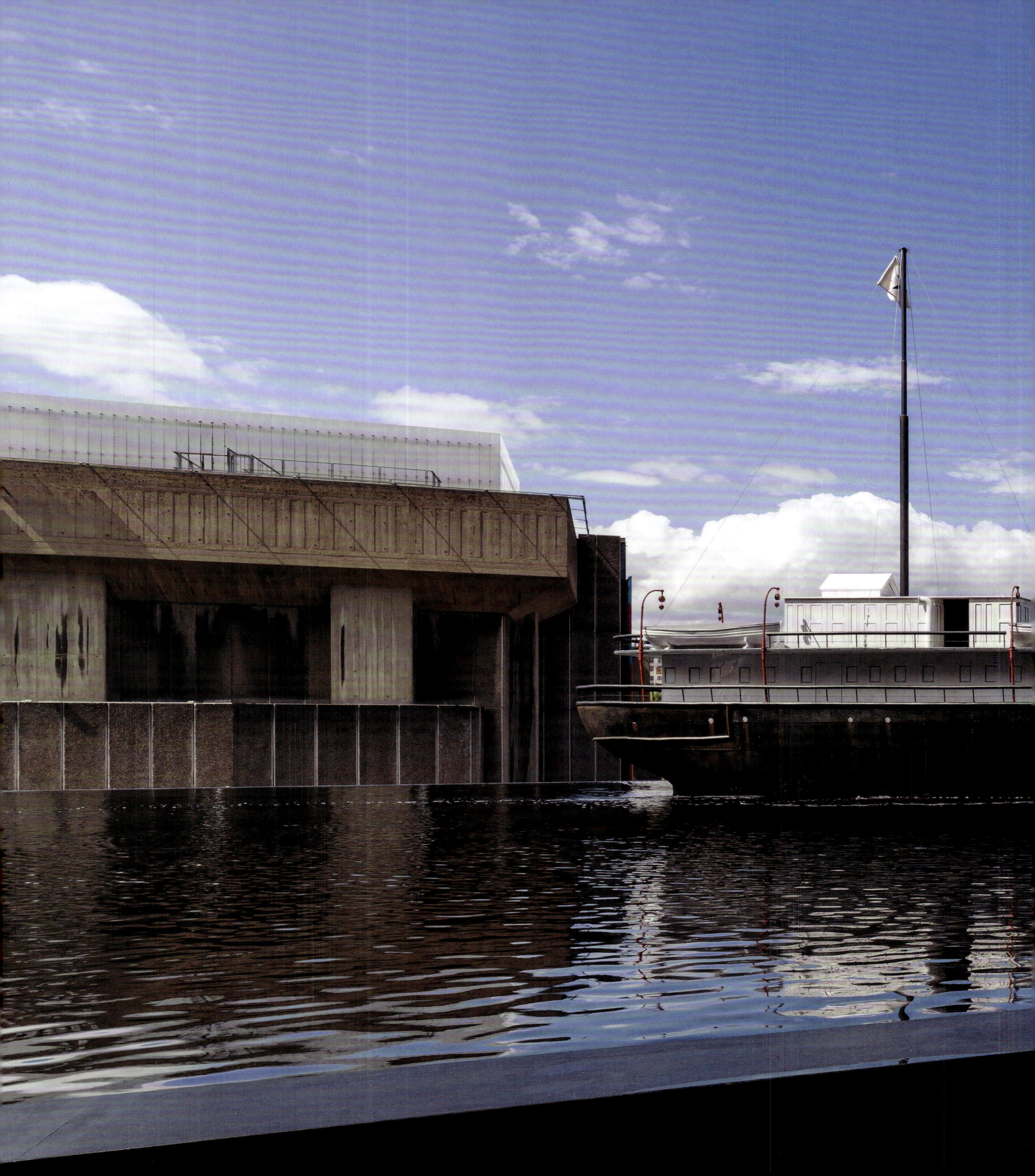

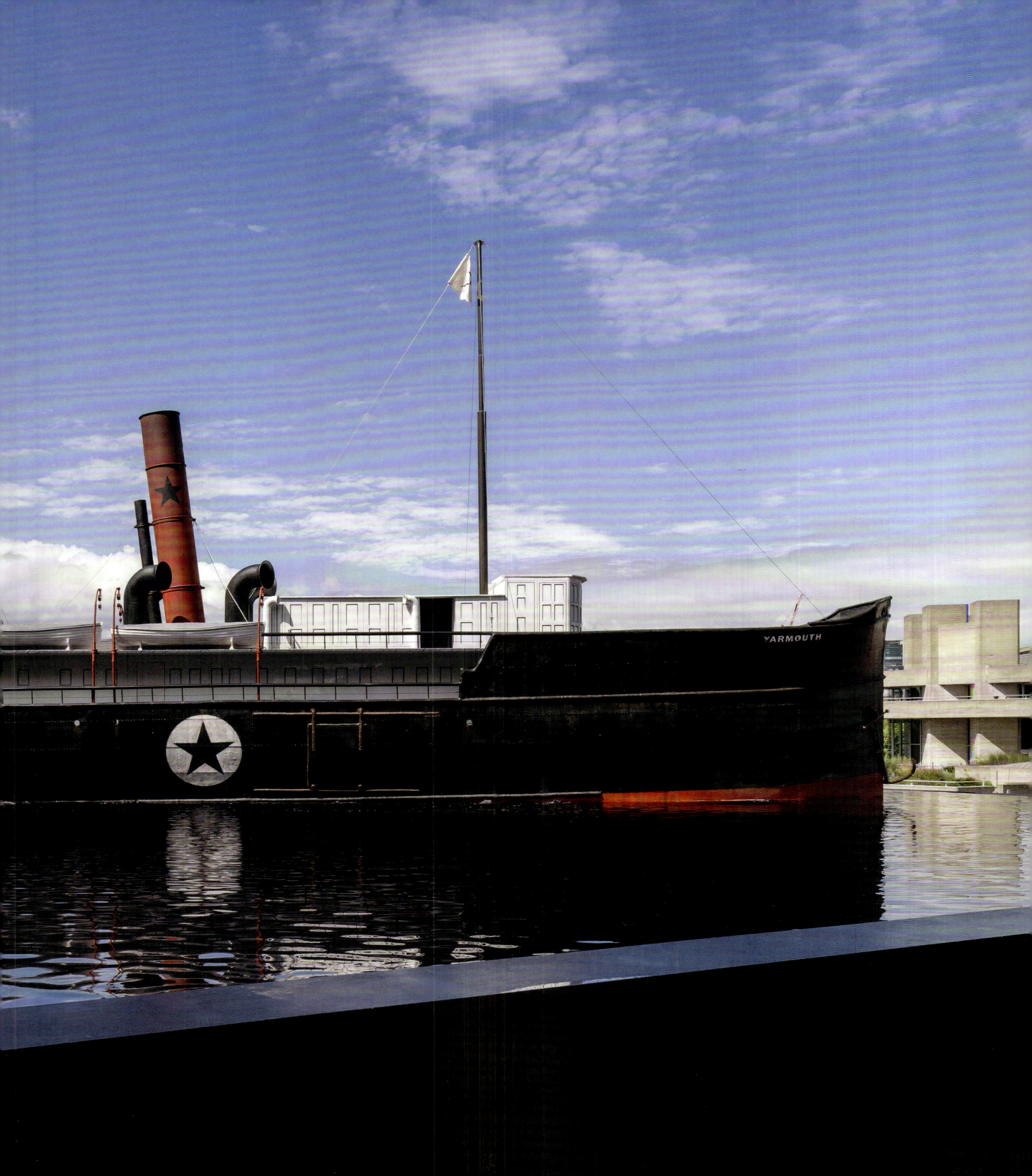
YARMOUTH

United States of Africa, 2022
Oil, enamel and pigment on acrylic
214 x 214 x 5 cm

to the ways in which sonic spaces are said to 'create "new maps" that allow an individual to analyze their current social predicament. These "new maps," therefore, engender a "remapping" of reality, a reconstitutive process that parallels dub's emphasis on modification and alteration'.[10]

Comparable to the relationship of hair-braiding patterns and mapping that allowed enslaved Black people to communicate and ultimately discern paths to freedom in the Palanque, dub remaps, conjuring new spaces that it shapes out of sound, offering escape when the current conditions are untenable.

The architect Mabel O. Wilson defines racism as an environment of constraint, of controlling space, controlling where people are able to go.[11] What alchemy to resist this through the production of alternative, or parallel spaces that we access through our hairstyles, or through soundscapes that exist beyond the jurisdiction of oppression!

One of the most powerful songs I've ever heard and which I have been listening to while writing this essay is 'They Shall Not Die' by Jamaican British reggae artist Sir Collins from the album New Cross Fire Page One (1981). Collins' son Steve was one of the thirteen young black people who were killed at a house party in New Cross in what was believed to be a firebombing, a racially motivated attack after other Black homes and community centres in the area had recently been the target of arson attacks. The title is a defiant chant proclaiming Steve's continued existence, but it is also located in a tradition that sees the drum as a bridge that interfaces with the worlds of the spirits and the living and understands musical intercession as the mechanism or the medium through

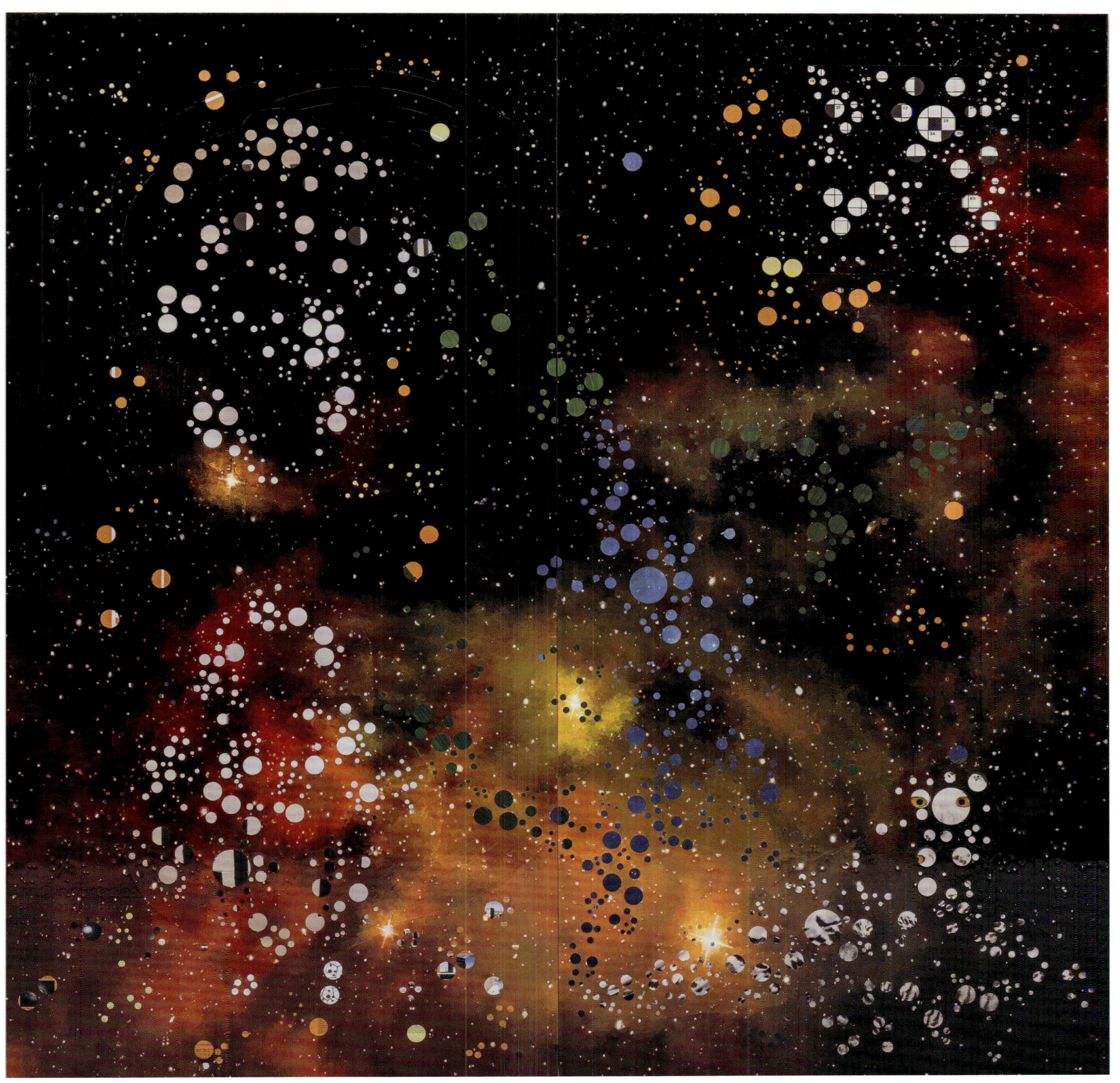

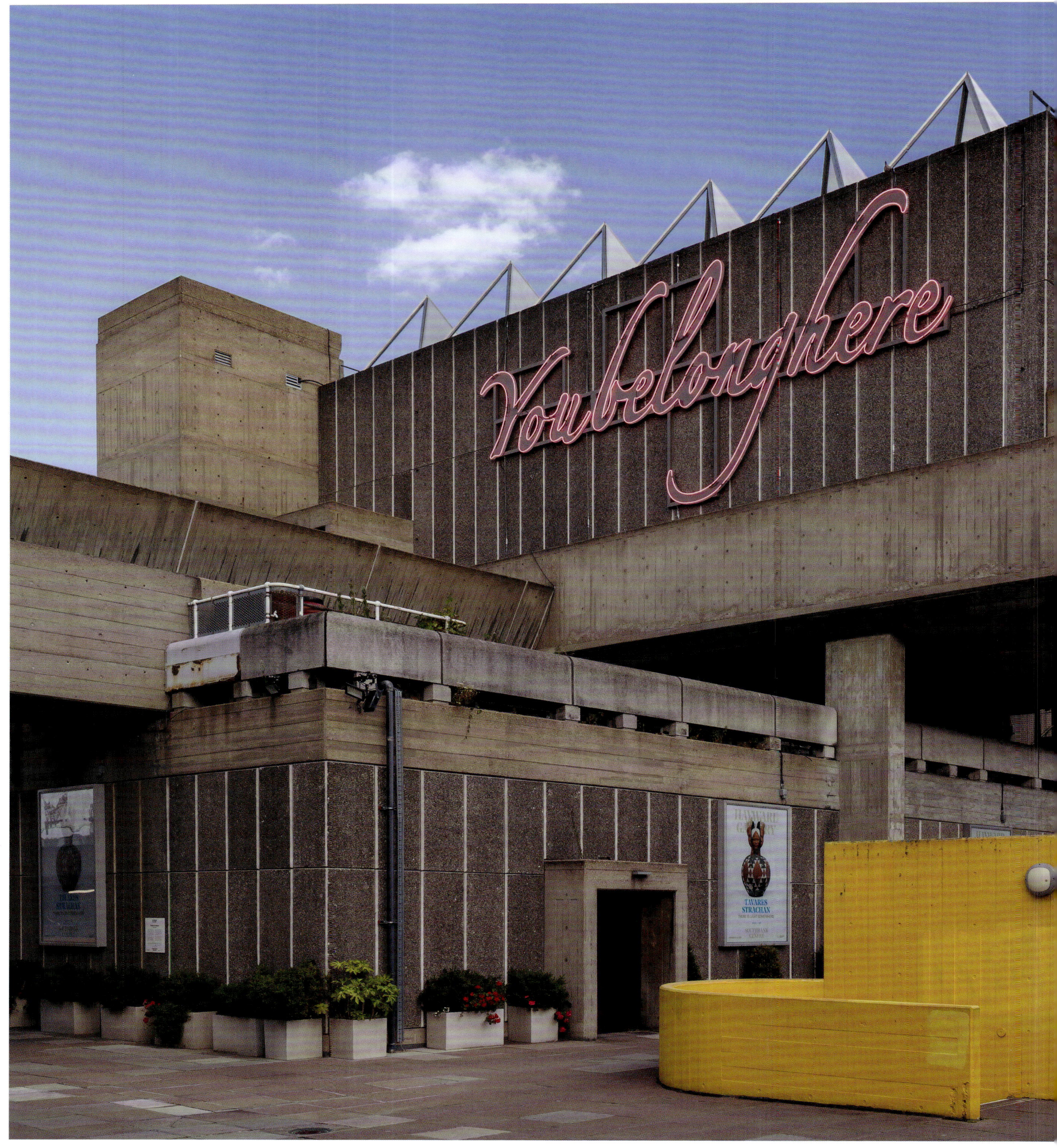
You belong here
TAVARES
STRACHAN

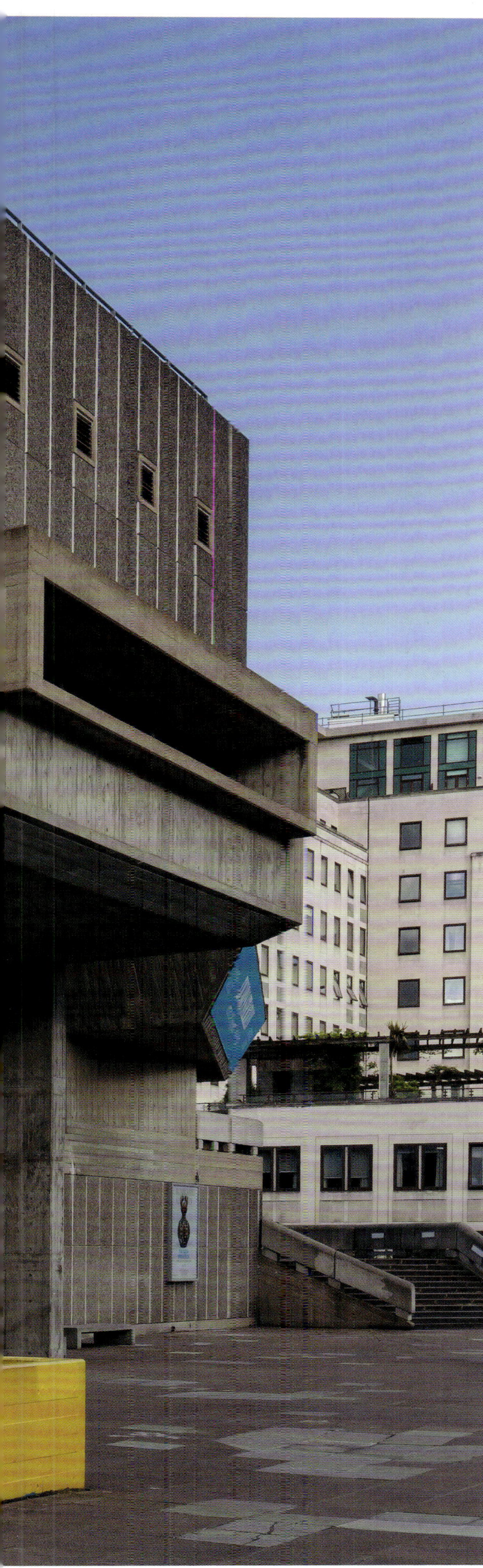

YOU BELONG HERE, 2014
NEON
910 X 2440 CM

INSTALLATION VIEW AT
HAYWARD GALLERY, LONDON
2024

which to communicate with parallel worlds. The Nyabinghi drum that features on the track was developed by Jamaican musician Count Ossie, a fusion of Jamaican kumina drumming (with its Asante roots in Ghana), and songs and rhythms learnt from the Nigerian musician Babatunde Olatunji, whose first name incidentally means father comes again in Yoruba, a name that is frequently given when a baby is born shortly after the death of his father or grandfather (Yetunde is the female equivalent after the death of a grandmother – although generally Yoruba names are gender neutral), reflecting the cultural belief in reincarnation.

Strachan describes his practice as 'ininfinite protest', explaining that 'if you think about protest as a finite act, it can be ended by someone. But if it's an infinite act, and if we all share it, and if we all have a common sense of what protest is and what the goals are, then it cannot be ended'.[12]

Outside the gallery, the declaration You Belong Here is written in neon pink cursive script. Simple yet so profound. We belong here! You belong here, but who are you? And where is 'here' in all the infinitesimal possibilities of the multiverse? Whatever the answer, where such endless possibility exists, I find it not only comforting but hugely exciting to see that we can stake our claim to home, to belonging, wherever we are and that even if the space we are in denies us, even in the face of the most unimaginable hostility, it is abundantly apparent that we have the resources to birth our own worlds – worlds far more full of magic and wonder than those who might reject us could ever even begin to imagine.

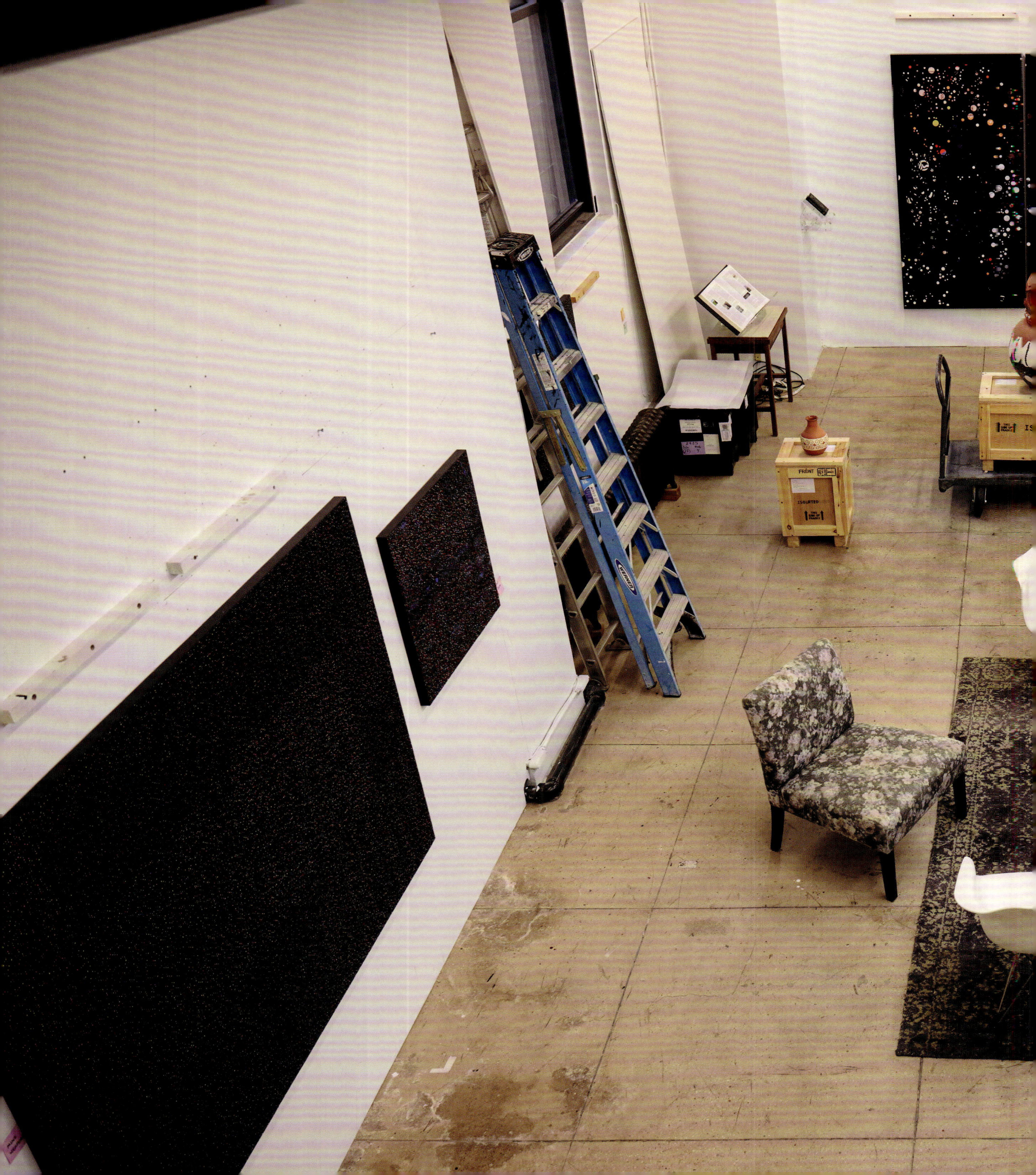

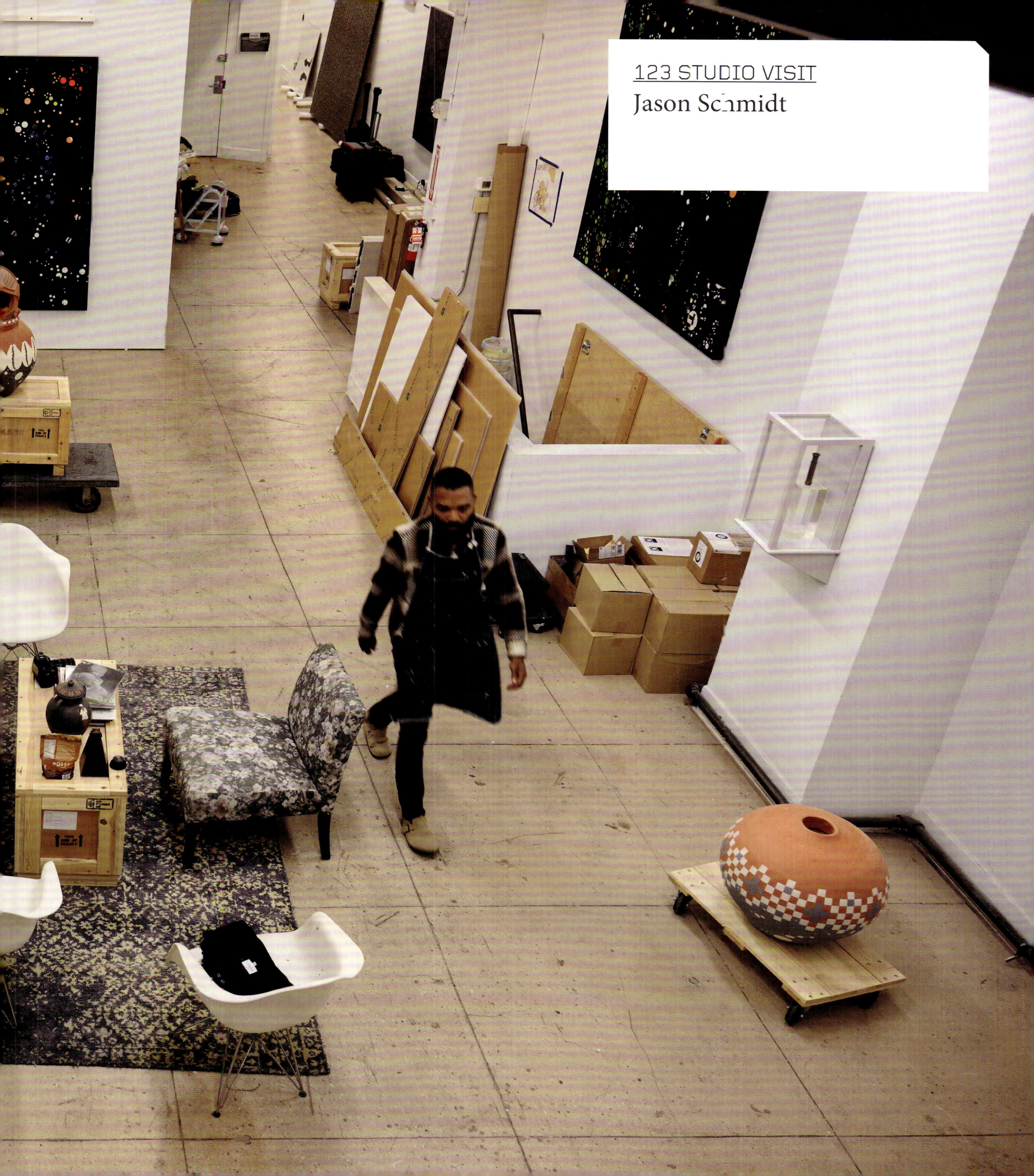

Jason Schmidt

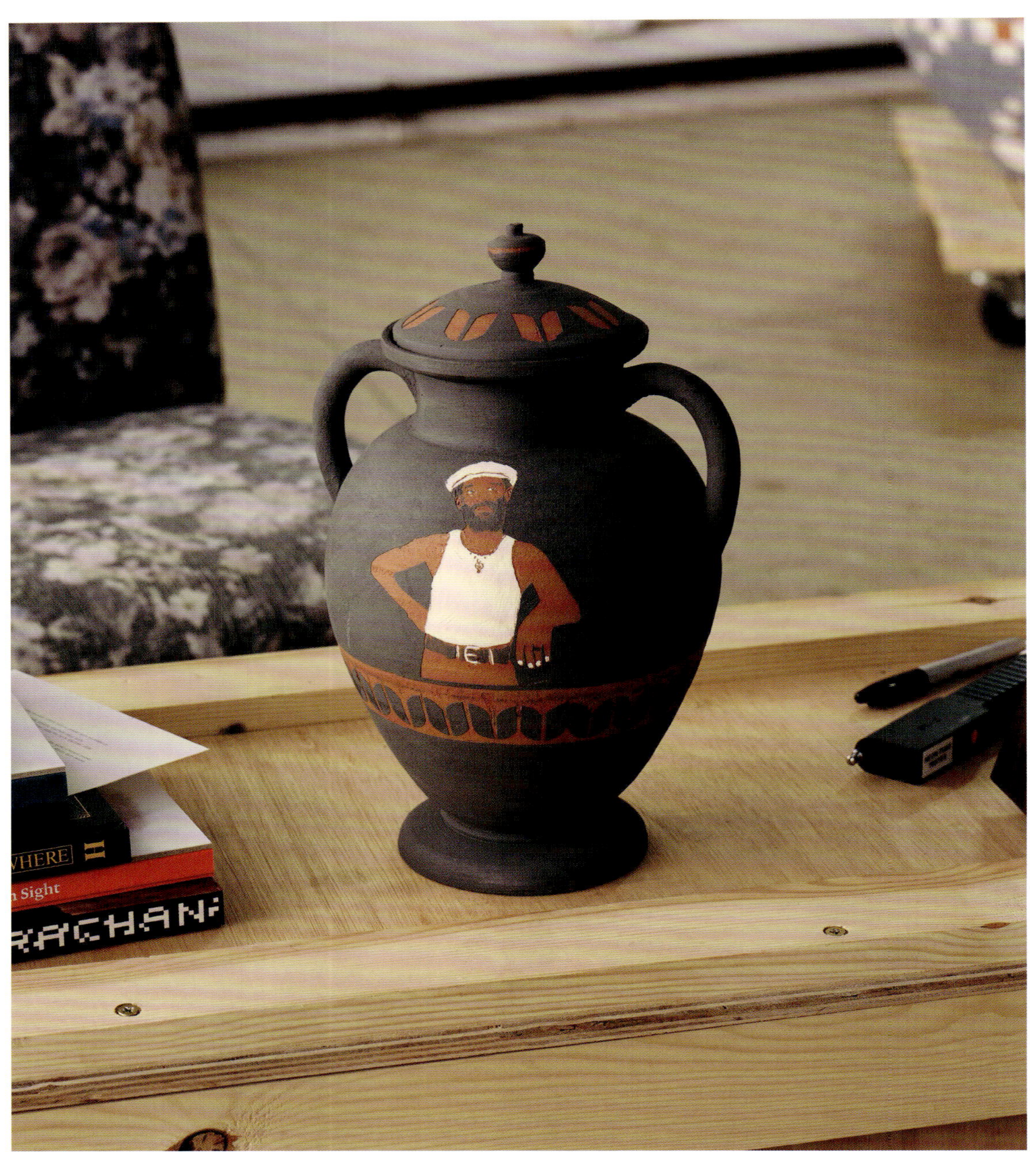

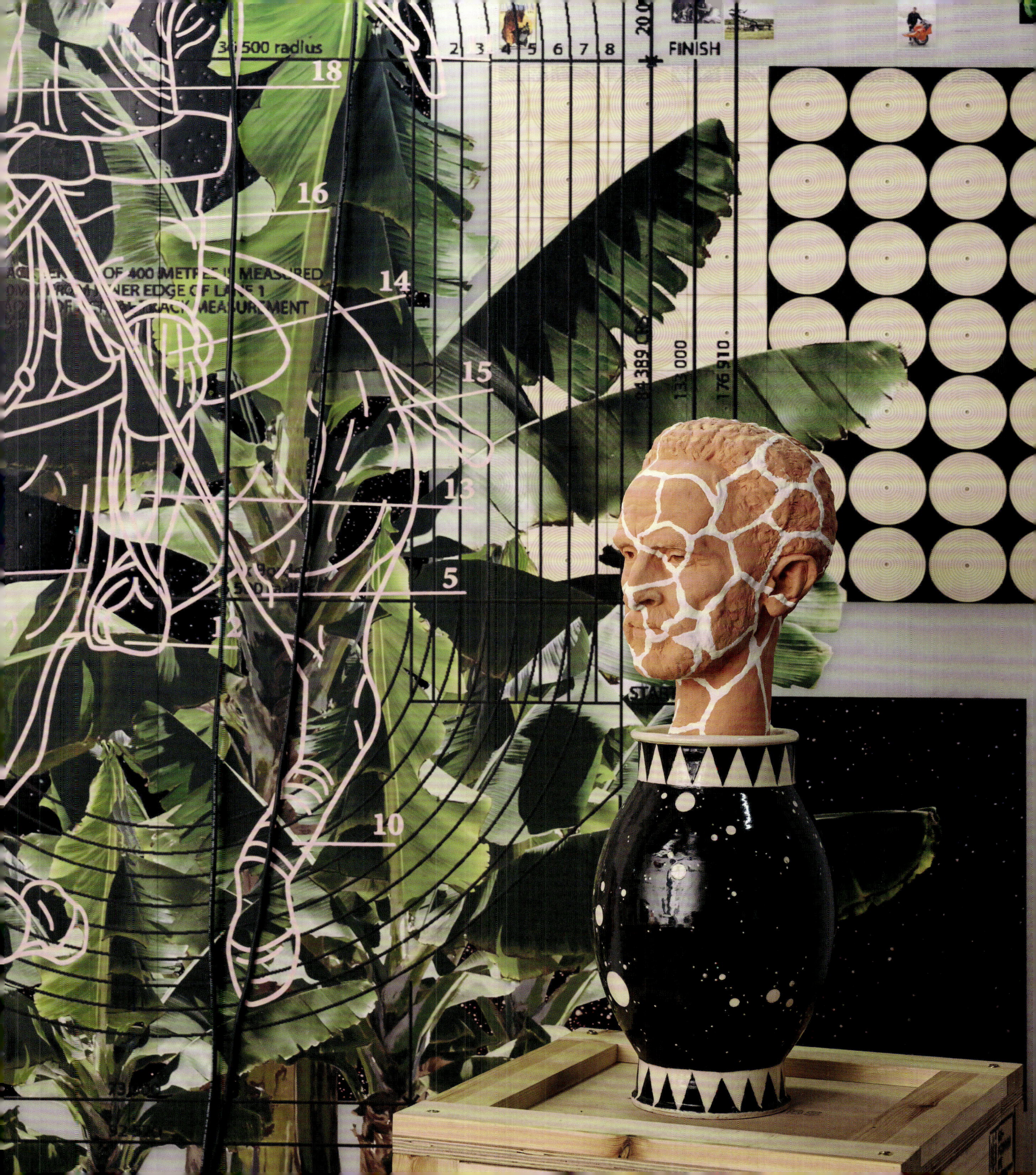

FINISH
2 3 4 5 6 7 8
20
18
16
14
15
13
5
12
10
176 910

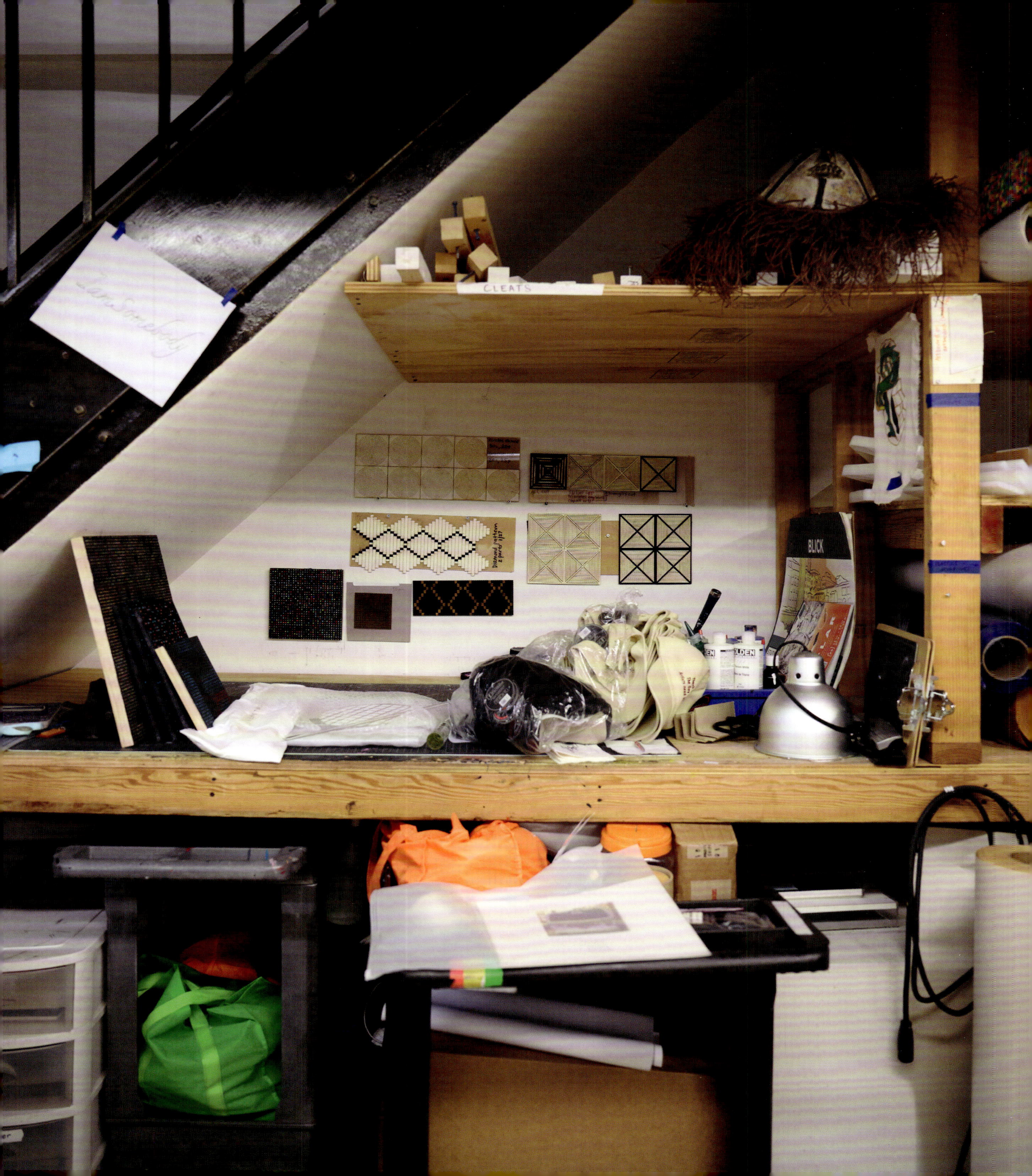

CLEATS
Diamond pattern
2 parts 1/27
BLICK

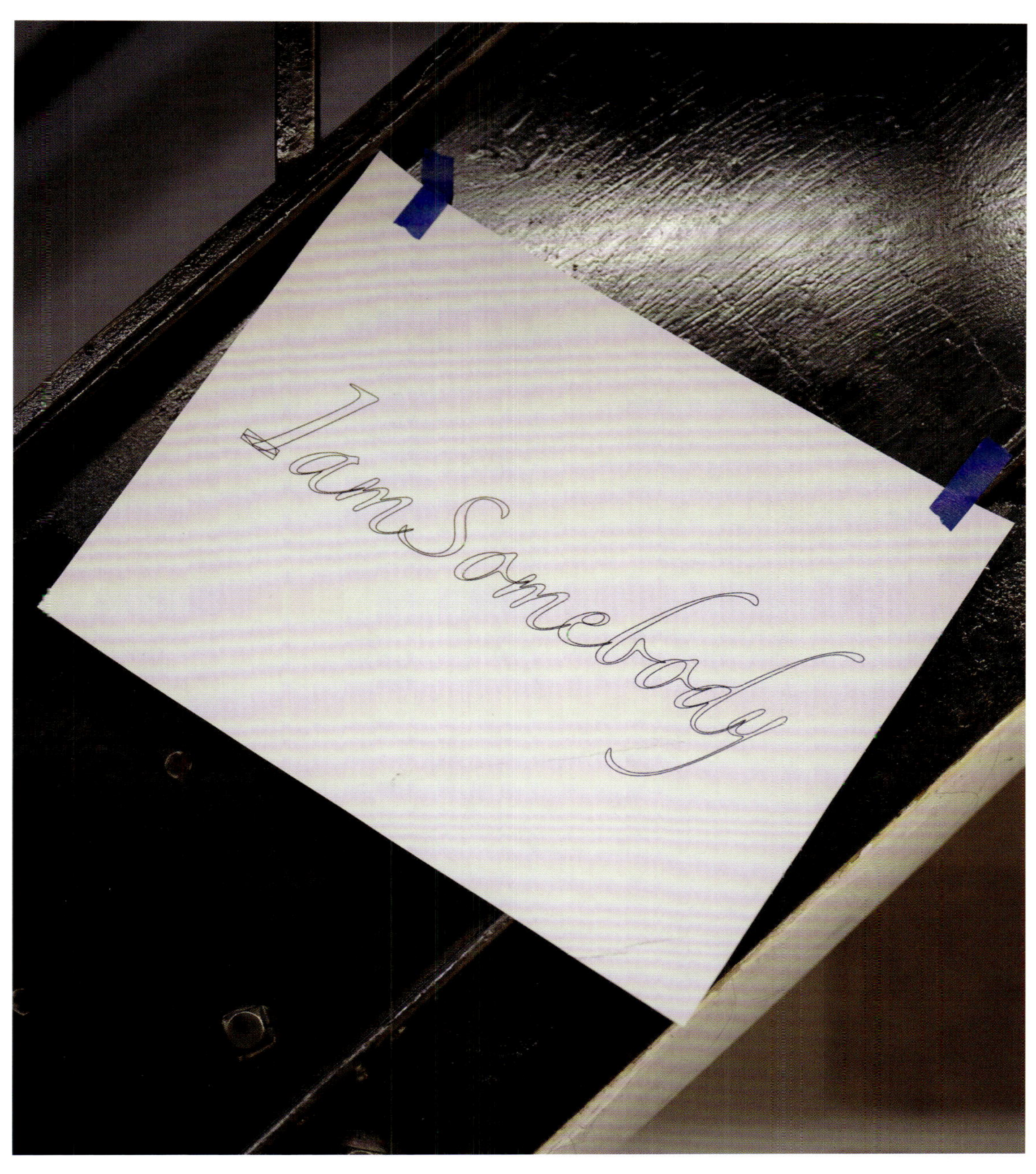
I am Somebody

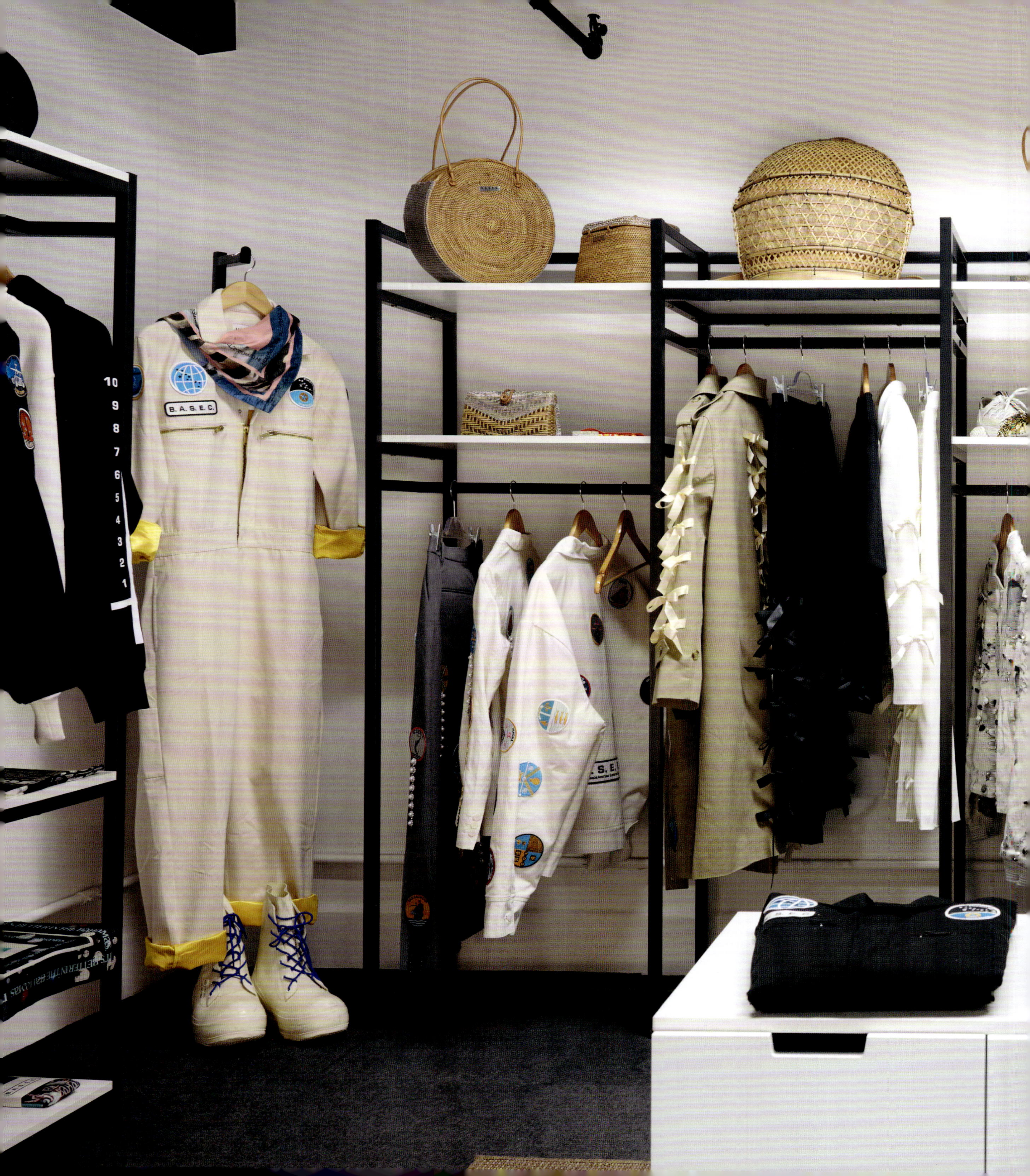
B.A.S.E.C.
10
9
8
7
6
5
4
3
2
1

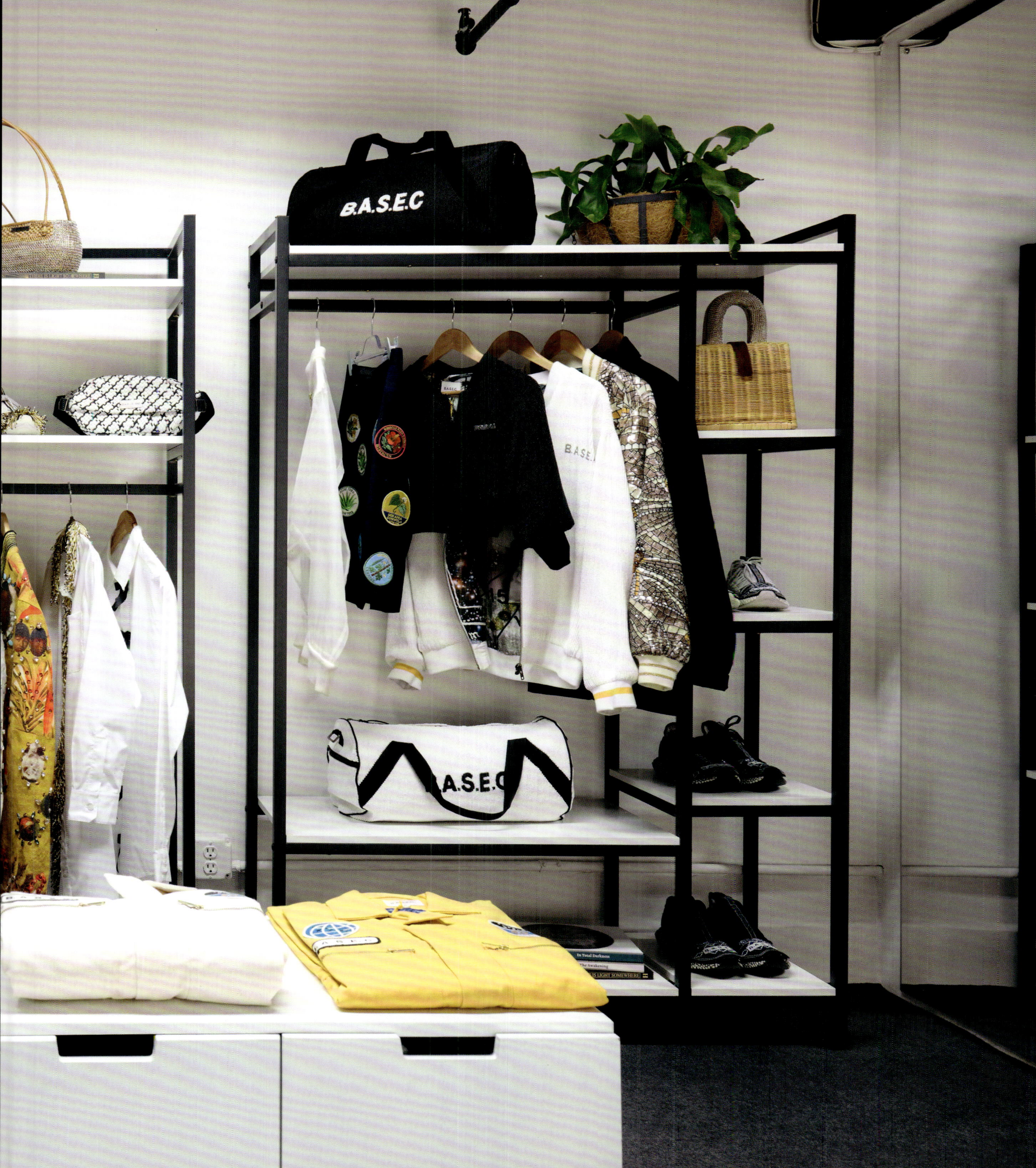
B.A.S.E.C

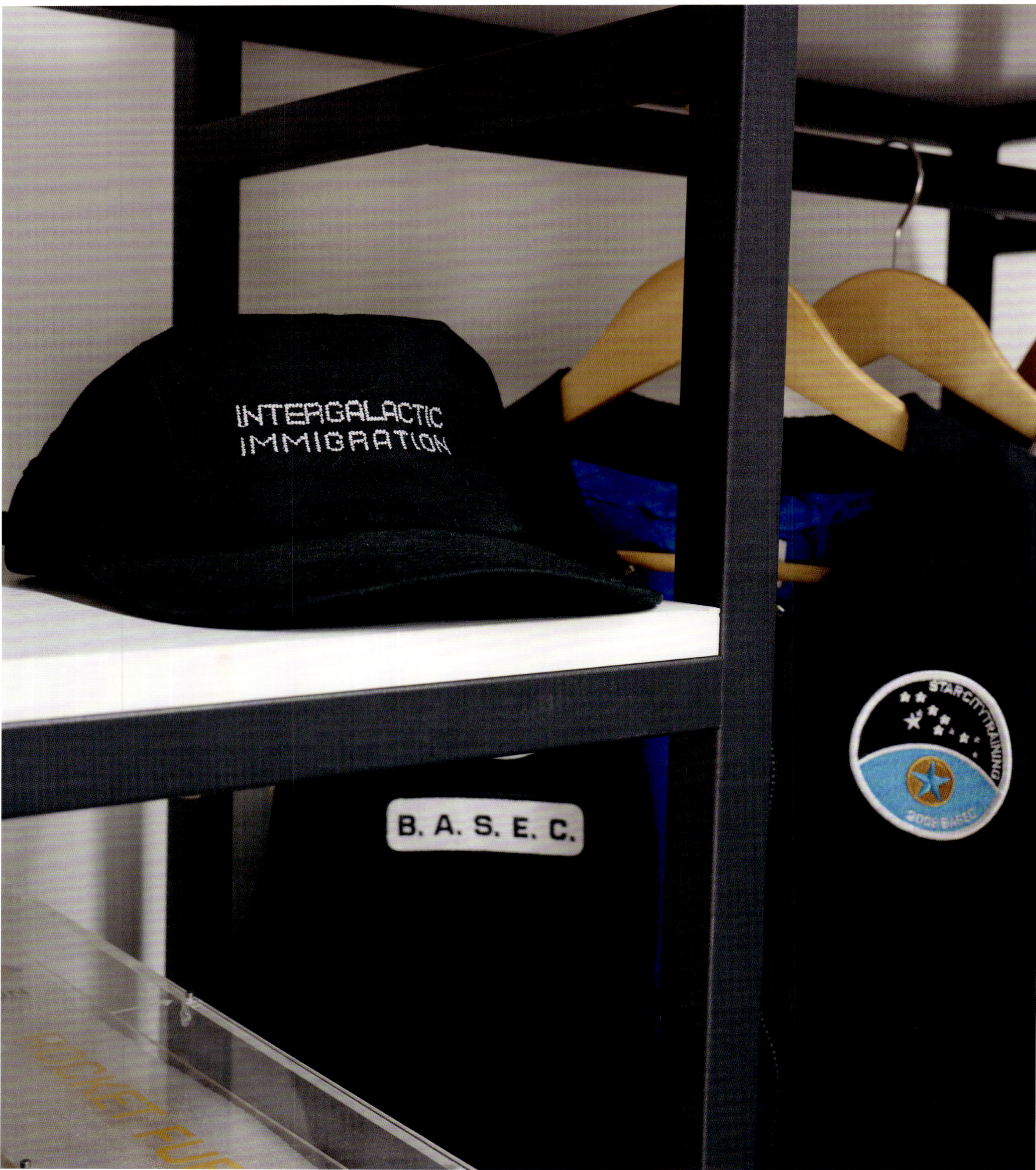
INTERGALACTIC
IMMIGRATION
B. A. S. E. C.
STARCITYTRAINING

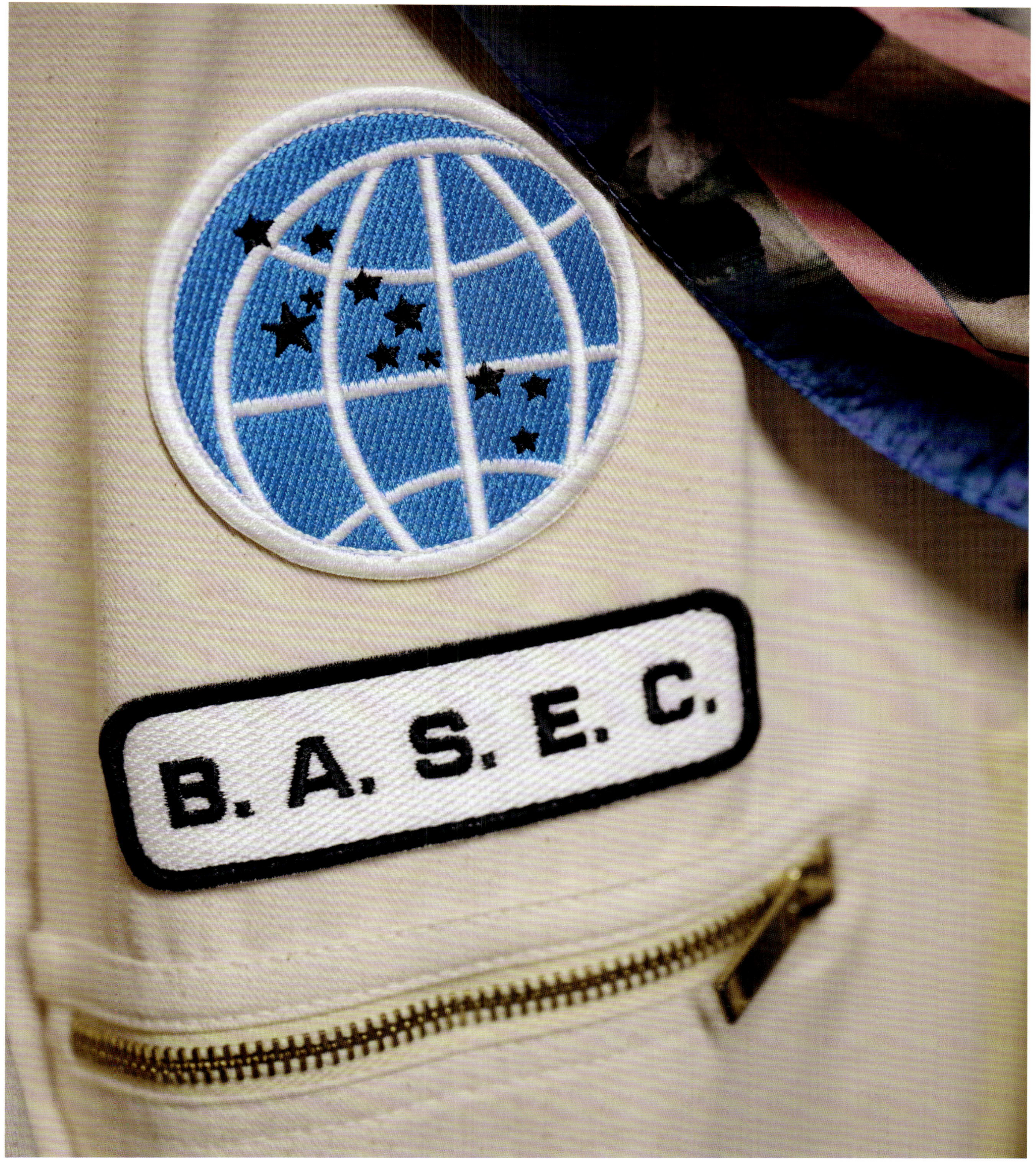
B. A. S. E. C.

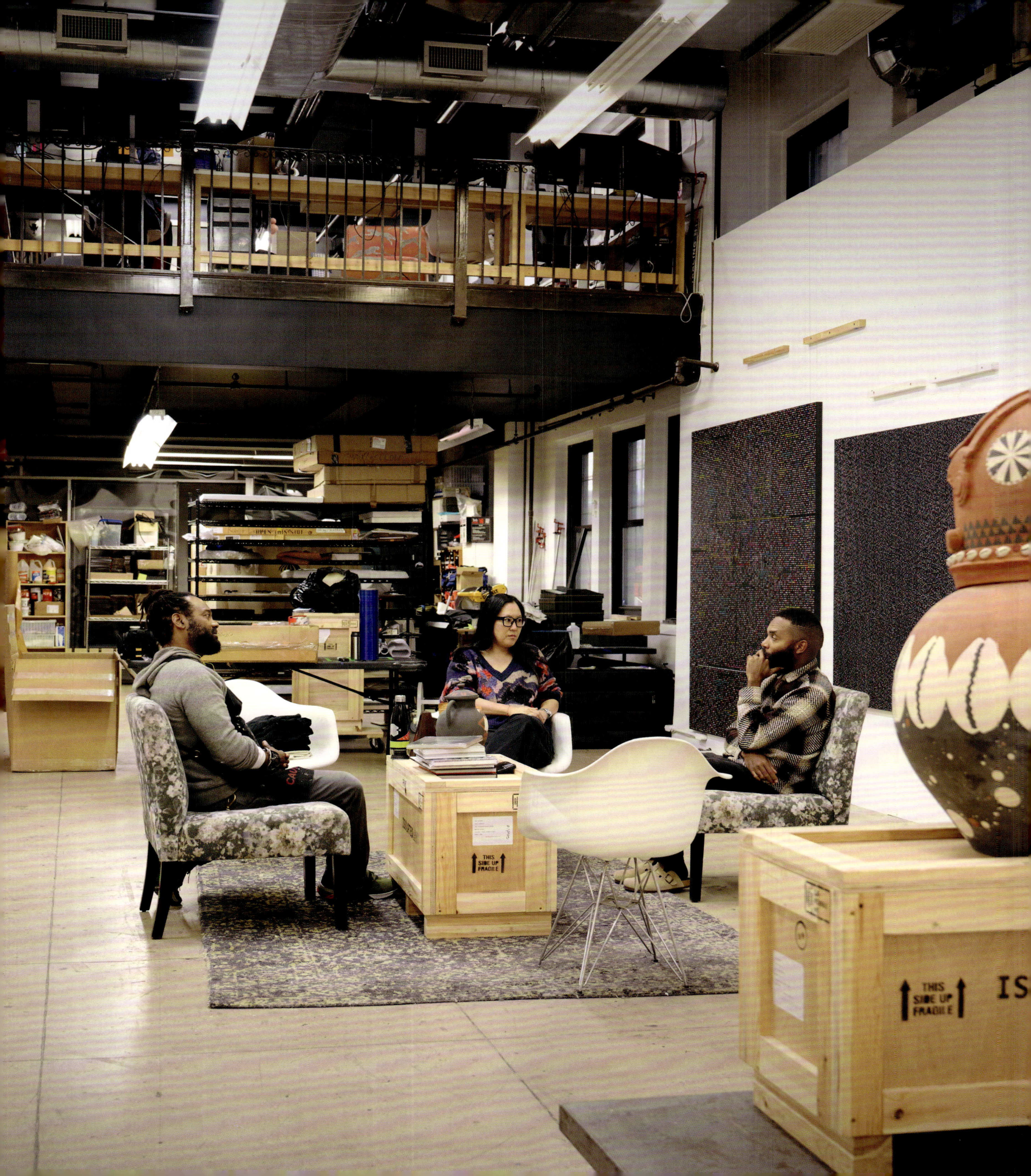
THIS SIDE UP FRAGILE
THIS SIDE UP FRAGILE
IS

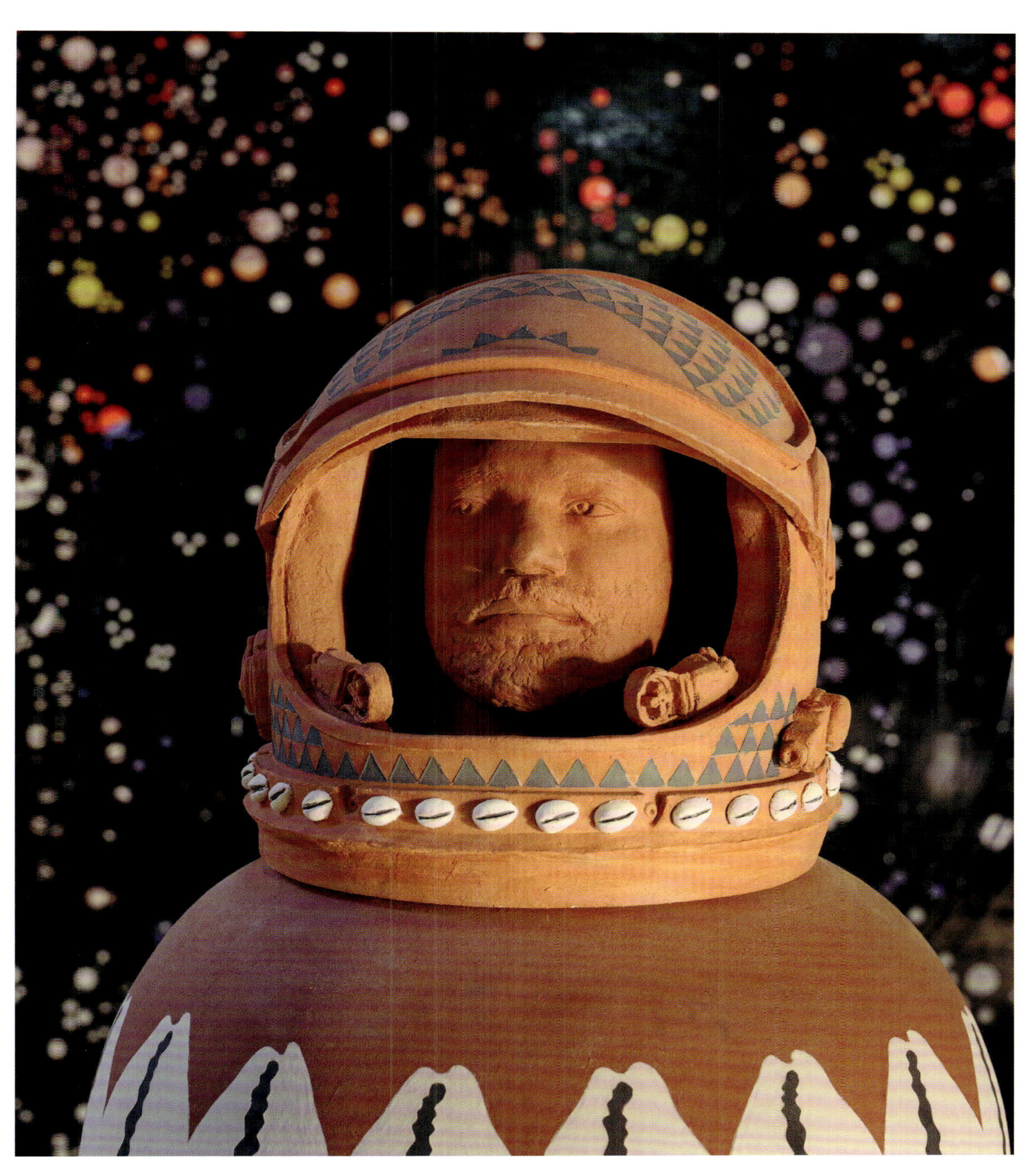

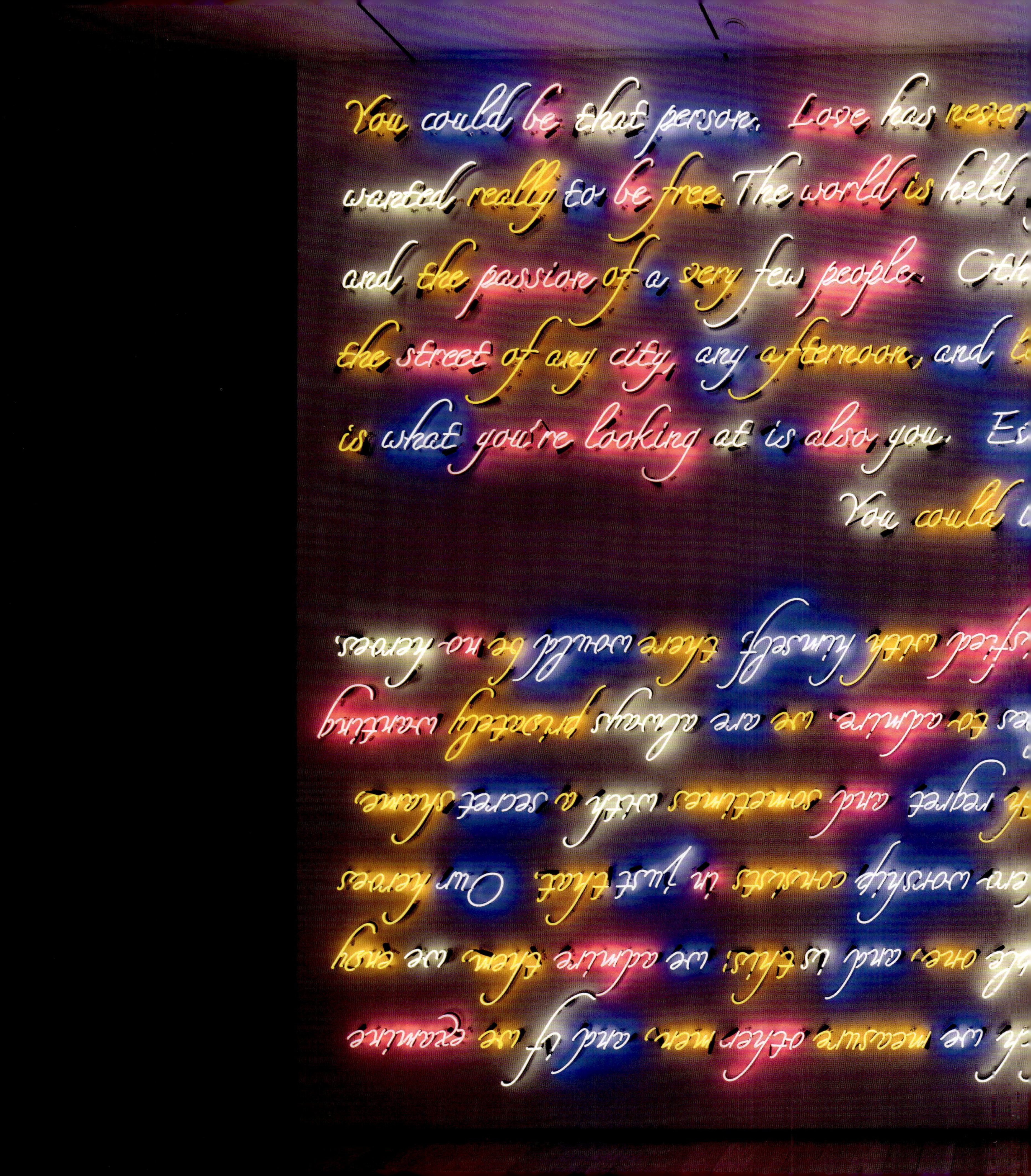

You could be that person. Love has reser

wanted really to be free. The world is held

and the passion of a very few people. Oth

the street of any city, any afternoon, and t

is what you're looking at is also you. Es

You could

h we measure other men, and if we examine

ble one, and is this: we admire them, we envy

ero worship consists in just that. Our heroes

h regret and sometimes with a secret shame

es to admire. we are always privately wanting

sfied with himself there would be no heroes.

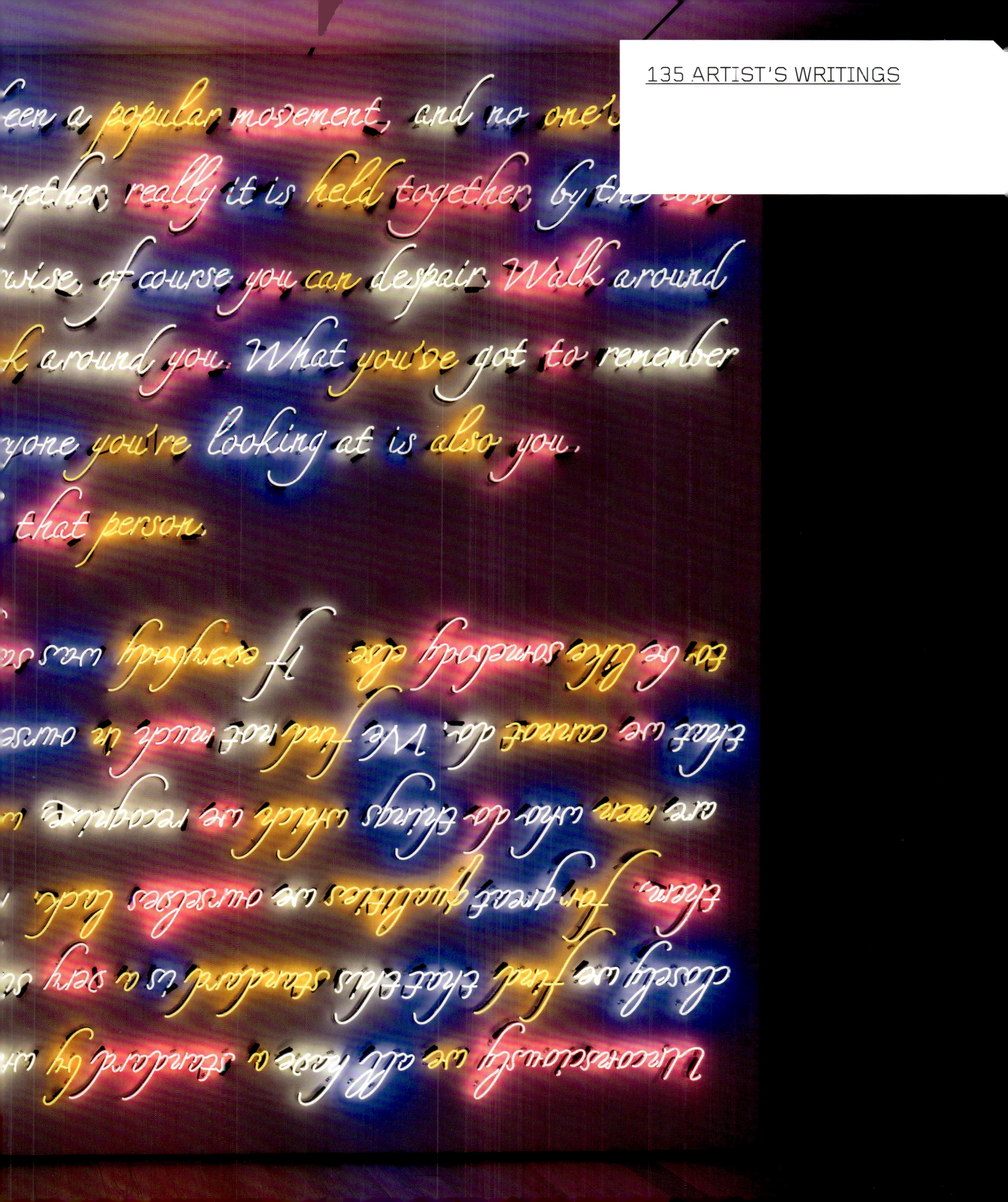

Monologue #1 (The Advocate), 2025

previous pages,
PRIVATELY WANTING TO BE LIKE SOMEBODY ELSE (MARK TWAIN)/THAT PERSON (JAMES BALDWIN), 2025
BLUE, YELLOW, WHITE, AND PINK NEON TRANSFORMERS AND ELECTRICAL COMPONENTS
721 X 533 CM

INSTALLATION VIEW AT THE LOS ANGELS COUNTY MUSEUM OF ART, 2025

We were not born yesterday.
What do you think this is?
I rose from mud and marrow.
We rose from mud and marrow.
Flint sparked, breath stirred, and time noticed us.
We did not ask—we became.
Fire.
Wheel.
Empire.
Bread became an altar.
Stone became scripture.
Memory became law… and lies.
We mapped the stars while shackled to the ground.
We split the atom, and called it peace.
We invented the car.
We invented the telephone.
We invented the television.
We invented the internet.
And we invented the light.
We built cathedrals beside plantations.
We said liberty, meant chains.
We crossed oceans, launched rockets, broke records, broke silence.
And still they ask:
What have you done?
You believe you are insured.
But are you insured from your insurance?
We are the charge.
We've witnessed refinement… barbarism in tailored suits.
Silence mistaken for order,
Profit baptized as progress,
They call survival a crime.
They say the system is broken…
But it runs perfectly—for them.
Still—we rise.
We run.
We endure.
We refuse.
We are not errors.
Not afterthought.
Not a myth.
We were there at the beginning.

Monologue #2 (Inheritance), 2025

You think I do not see?
…I do see
Yes I see for sure.
Every day, behind these mirrors, I watch time return after it is cut away.
They say it is just hair,
But I know—each strand is a river
each curl a root,
each edge a horizon.
Each one of you is ensured.
But are you insured against your insurance?
We were not born yesterday, no.
But yesterday still hums.
I hear it in the stones, stacked upon stones,
in the wind threading through broken branches,
in the echoes that circle long after voices fade.
…Do not mistake this for silence.
Silence is not absence,
Silence is the soil waiting for rain.
…They call me Inheritance because I carry…
The names; the languages; the recipes; the songs.
The ones *scattered* like seeds…
I gather them.
I press them into palms—
I braid them into crowns—
I fold them into cloth.
I hide them in breath, so no storm can *tear* them loose.
You speak of empire, of bread turned altar, stone turned scripture.
But I tell you…
We made scripture too.
Not carved in marble,
but traced in footprints on wet ground,
etched in constellations,
written in the rhythm of bodies that refused to vanish.
They ask: what have you done?
I say:
We bore children and taught them to dream as the sky dreams at dawn.
We took fragments and made them feasts.
We took beats and made them galaxies.
We shaped tomorrow the way rivers shape valleys… slow, certain, unstoppable.
Still they erase…
Still they point to the ledger and say: "you do not belong here."
But ledgers rot.
Bricks crumble.
Time remembers.
The earth remembers us.
The rivers remember us.
The stars remember us—
because we named them, long before glass lenses gave them numbers.
So I say to you, and to all who listen
We are not guests here.
We are not shadows in someone else's house.
We are the *spark* in the fire.
We are the root beneath the monument.
We are the tide that will not turn back.
And hear me now—
we are not done.
Not nearly.
Because I am Inheritance,
and my message is this:
We were here at the beginning.
We will be here at the end.
And we will be the beginning again.

Stone Love (Apollo x Venus – The Sculptor's Argument), 2025

next pages,
THE BARBER SHOP, 2025
PERFORMANCE, INSTALLATION
DIMENSIONS VARIABLE

INSTALLATION VIEW AT
THE LOS ANGELES COUNTY
MUSEUM OF ART, 2025

opposite,
A MAP OF THE CROWN
(UNKNOWN AFRICAN CA. 1960),
2023
BRONZE, FLOCKED HAIR
56 X 55 X 38 CM

Intro:

I KNOW YOU GOT NO ×4
I KNOW YOU GOT NO LOVE

[Verse 1: The Thinker / Present-Day Man]

Hey there to Venus,
Your
arms broke between us
(and) we've
been mourning all evening
long
before you got so cold/I know you got no love
man
can't satisfy you—
carved you
out of myth and pure iron
And
you know i can't waste my prayers
on
marble that's sold as soul—
Hey there Apollo,
your
light left a shadow
we're too
caught in tomorrow
and the
gods of yesterday can't be found
(You)
aiming your arrows
aiming at prophecy
but, logic brings sorrow
to believe in things that you cannot see

STONE LOVE.

[Pre-Chorus: Statues in Chorus]

Clash of the titans-
it's a cycle
reason vs. hunger, a fight to
the death with earthquake, thunder and lightening
(death with, earthquake, thunder and lightening)
Ring the alarm
and watch for silence
Not every god feel guilt or guidance
Eyes like sun, lips like science
I KNOW YOU GOT NO LOVE

[Chorus: Crowd of Mortals]

Cah trust love when it's carved already
Put yuh hands up if yuh still feel empty
×4
You a living girl, he a still-life body
You a fire, him a statue steady
Cah trust god who know everybody—
probably
He got no love.
I know you got no—
I know you got no—
I know you got no—
I know you got no love!
×2

[Verse 2: Venus Responds]

If you change your direction,
don't expect connection
Wheel and pull back, selector—
want perfection
then pay the price
Beauty ain't sacrifice
Still your voice and please recognize—
I lost my arms, but not my insight
You talk to stars
but you fear the night.

[Bridge: Apollo's Rebuttal]

You think I'm cold
because I speak in clarity
But love ain't chaos no
masquerading as charity
You want thunder
but I bring symmetry
You want fire
but I hold divinity
I gave you temples,
you gave me riddles
I asked for meaning
you played the middle
With your heart made of stone
Worse silence you'll ever know
I've seen this times many times before—
It's just DUST AND STONE

[Verse 3: Modern Reflection]

You
wanted to know me—
like
no one ever should
And now that you're lonely—
you
say you misunderstood
But
there's no knight
in
museum glass to help
there's No fight that
time cannot pass all by itself
Just like your sculptor,
you shaped me in the past
halted my motion
meanwhile you moved on fast

[Final Chorus: All Figures Join – Choir of Stone & Flesh]

STONE LOVE
I KNOW YOU GOT NO X4
I KNOW YOU GOT NO LOVE
X4

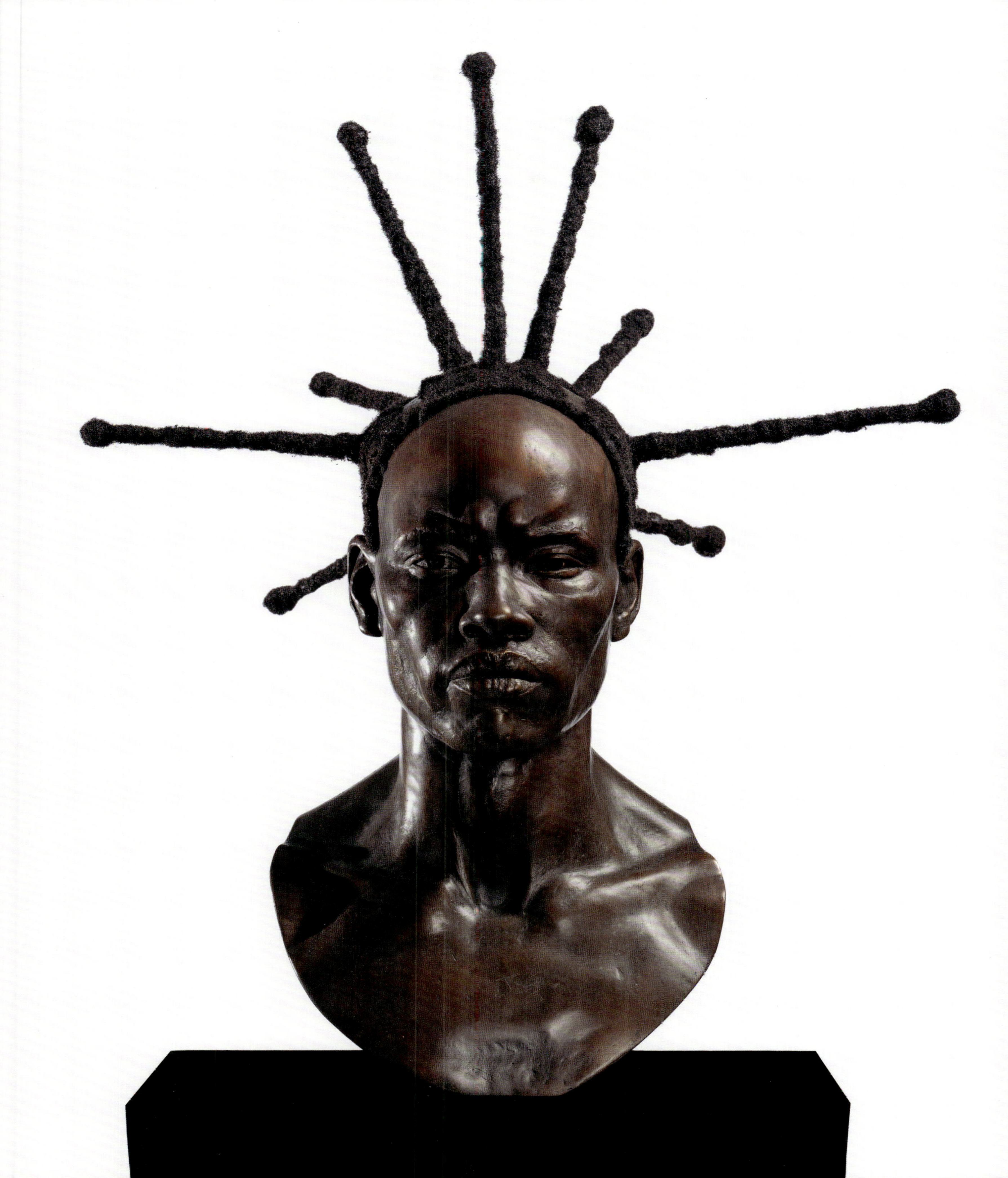

THE BARBER SHOP, 2025
PERFORMANCE, INSTALLATION
DIMENSIONS VARIABLE

The installation includes
HAIR CARE POSTERS 1–7, 2025
DIGITAL SILKSCREEN ON
BURLAP

BROWN SKIN BEAUTY-CUCUMBER LOTION, 2025
CERAMIC
38 X 38 X 38 CM

LUCKY BROWN (SMALL), 2025
CERAMIC
28 X 28 X 28 CM

MIND FIELD NO.5, 2023
FLOCKED HAIR ON CANVAS
152 X 152 CM

MIND FIELD NO.3, 2023
FLOCKED HAIR ON CANVAS
152 X 152 CM

A MAP OF THE CROWN (NYABINGHI), 2025
BRONZE, FLOCKED HAIR
185 X 65 X 50 CM

A MAP OF THE CROWN (SHILLUK), 2025
BRONZE
60 X 49 X 35 CM

A MAP OF THE CROWN (AMASUNZU BLACK), 2023
BRONZE, FLOCKED HAIR
50 X 35 X 30 CM

LUCKY BROWN, 2025
CERAMIC
64 X 60 X 60 CM

MIND FIELD NO.6, 2023
FLOCKED HAIR ON CANVAS
152.4 X 152.4 CM

MADAM JONES SEVEN, 2025
CERAMIC
55 X 55 X 55 CM

VANISHING CREAM, 2025
CERAMIC
6 X Ø 36 CM

HAIR GLORY, 2025
CERAMIC
6 X Ø 36 CM

SWEET GEORGIA BROWN, 2025
CERAMIC
6 X Ø 36 CM

BEAUTIFIES AND SOFTENS, 2025
CERAMIC
6 X Ø 36 CM

INSTALLATION VIEW AT
THE LOS ANGELES COUNTY
MUSEUM OF ART, 2025

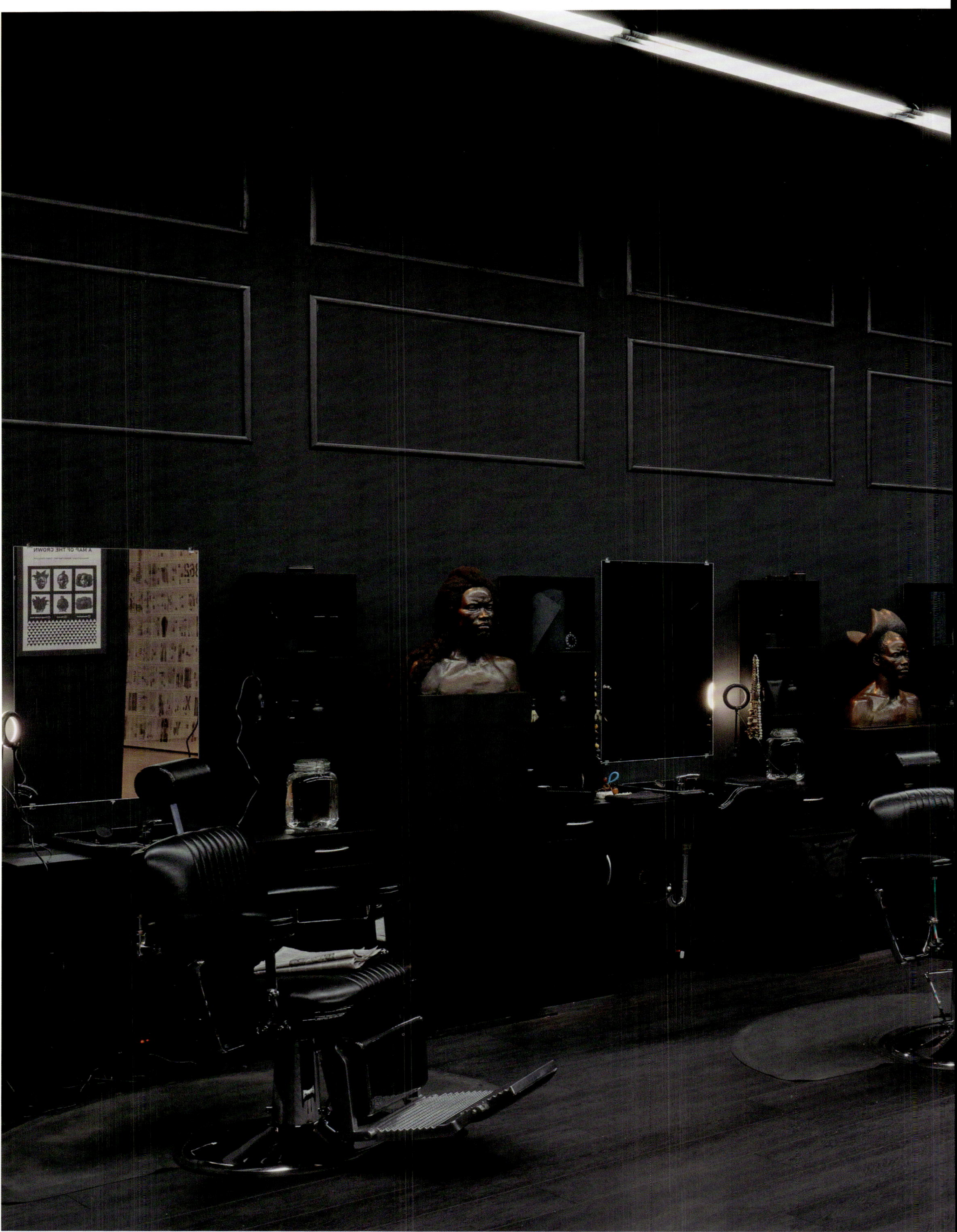

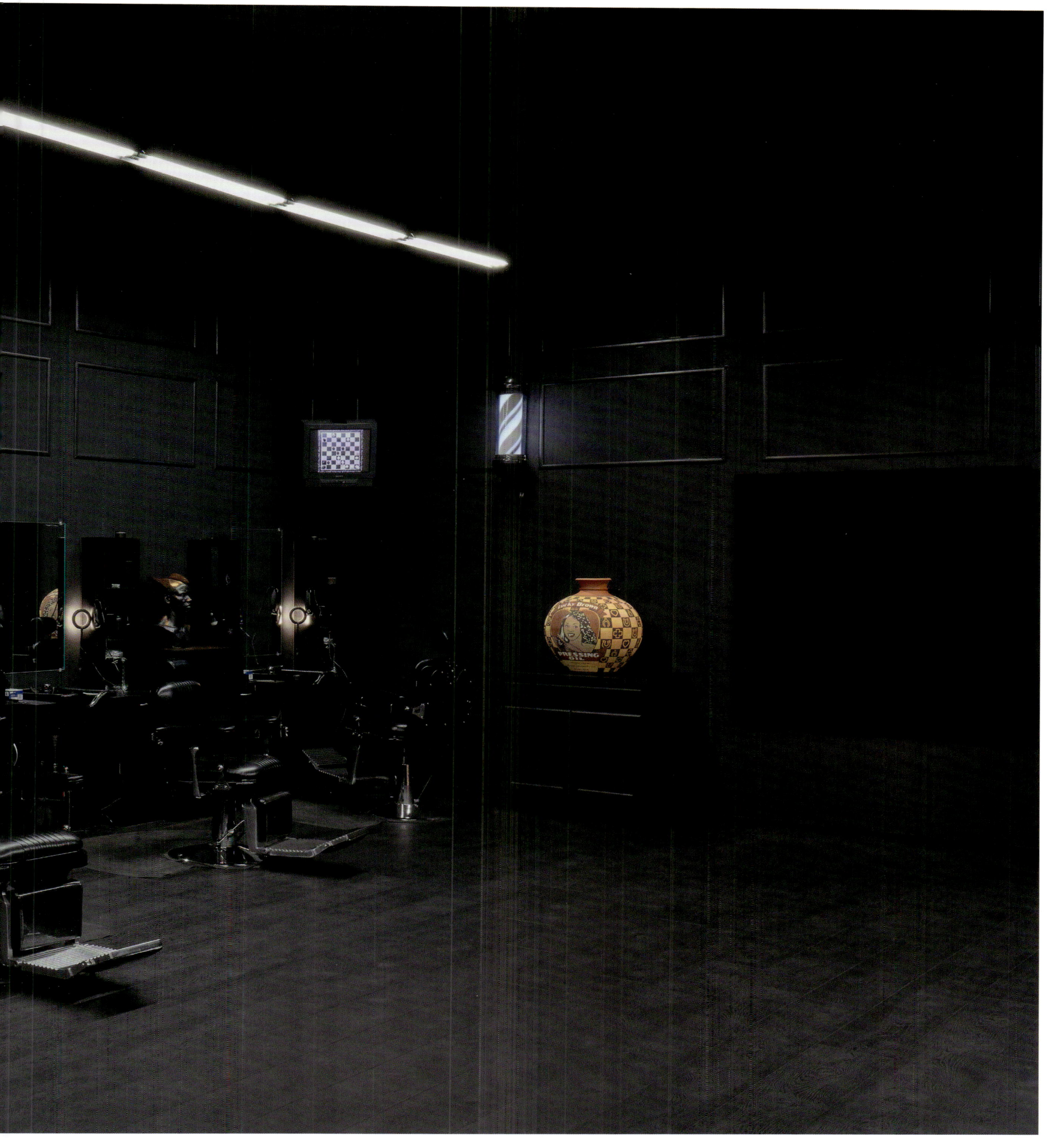
Lucky Brown
PRESSING OIL

A Dreamer's Scheme, 2025

below,
IN PRAISE OF MIDNIGHT (PICASSO × IFE KING), 2025
BRONZE
117 X 28 X 28 CM

opposite, from left,
IN PRAISE OF MIDNIGHT (SIMONE × QUEEN VICTORIA), 2025
RESIN AND STEEL
333 X 114 X 117 CM

IN PRAISE OF MIDNIGHT (TUBMAN × ALLIGATOR), 2025
BRONZE
114 X 46 X 25 CM

A dreamer's scheme
Stash truth keys on a sonic beam
Five hundred years deep, echoes where the shadows gleam
Archives hidden, dressed like they never been—
Silk-wrapped memory, royal threads for the kid within

Murmuring, names on the wind we're recovering
Ancestors whispering, watch how their songs keep surfacing
City of forgotten ones, silence brings apocalypse
Strike at the silence, their voices rise—ain't no stopping this

Mad soul, my sanity leaking like an hourglass
Time in my palm breaks, trying to piece the past
I got ghosts that used to guide you, saints who could've shined through
Now marching with my crew of seekers—our ill truth

Love's Thelonious cutting through your weak construction
Notes bent sideways, turning silence into function
First World, Third World, cosmic improvisation
Hidden chords erupt like a quiet revelation

And when the last note drops, the monuments are rusting—
Love is the weapon, the unseen is combusting.
History on fire, the forgotten stand tall—
Invisible no longer, their names smash the wall.
Drums of the cosmos, the silence is shattered,
The lost take the crown, the lie lies tattered.

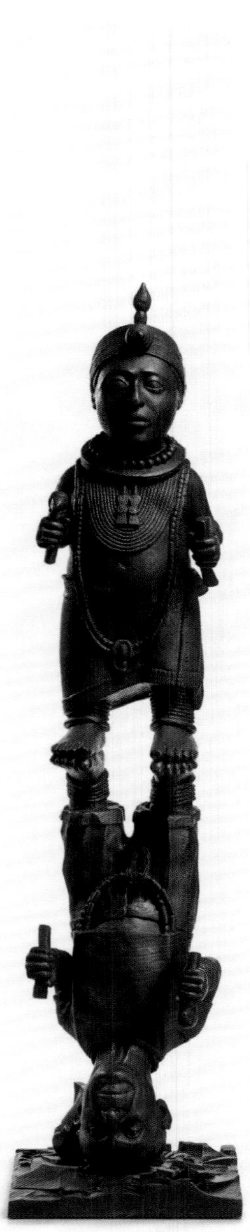

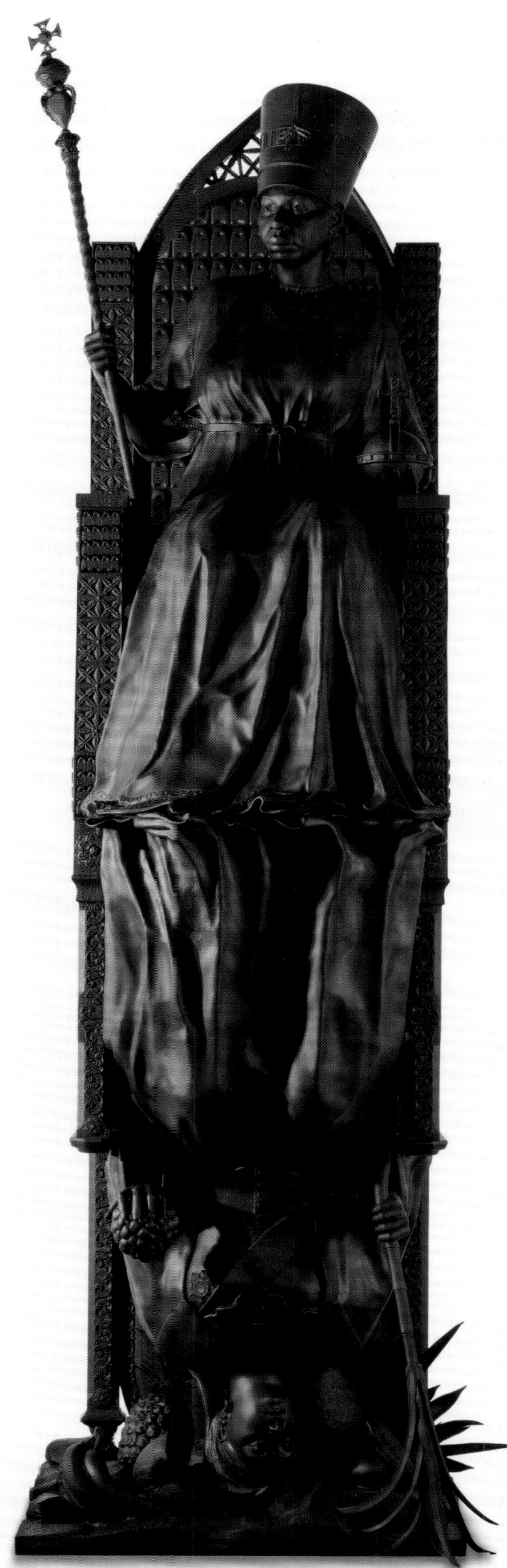

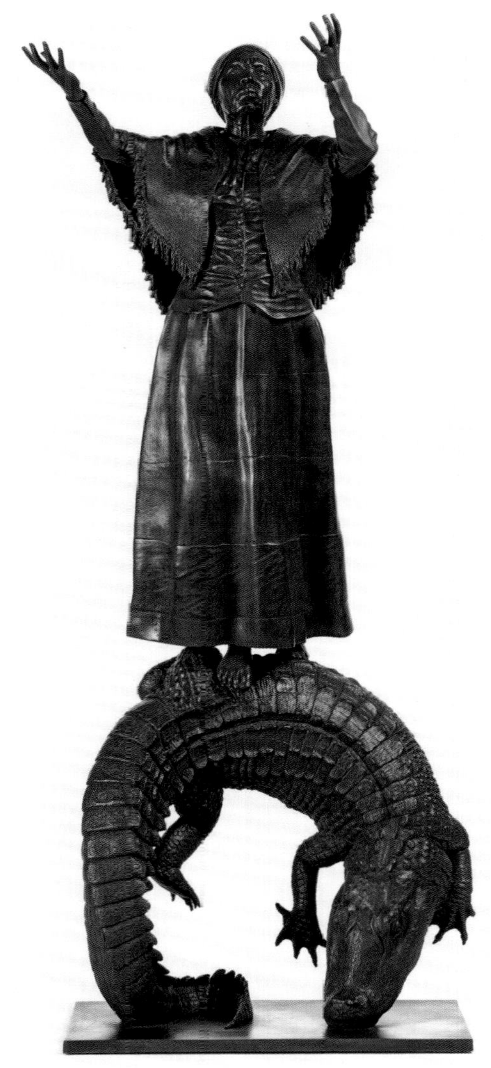

In Praise of Midnight, 2025

IN PRAISE OF MIDNIGHT (CHRISTOPHE x NAPOLEON), 2025
RESIN AND STEEL
485 X 345 X 155 CM

Monuments have always fascinated me. They are not just markers of history but embodiments of power, cultural memory, and contested narratives. In recent years, the debates around monuments have sharpened, underscoring their symbolic weight. I began to wonder: what would happen if we literally turned these forms upside down? I scanned several monuments, digitally inverted them, and used the underside of their plinths—the literal foundations of these historic works—as platforms for new sculptures. The results are hybrid objects that hold two worlds in tension: the celebrated figure of the past and a new figure that redefines the meaning of the monument.

One such work places a full-body cast of an Ife sculpture from West Africa upon the inverted full-body portrait of Pablo Picasso. The sculpture becomes a gesture of reversal, a collision between old and new, African and European, origin and appropriation. Picasso famously drew from West and Central African sculptural traditions—appropriating their forms, masks, and aesthetics as catalysts for modernism, most notably in works like *Les Demoiselles d'Avignon* (1907). By turning him upside down and placing the Ife figure above, the sculpture reframes that historical borrowing, returning primacy to the sources from which modern art once extracted its power. This work in particular is produced at one-third scale, a reference to traditions of African sculpture in which the human head is conceived as one-third of the body's proportion. In this way, the works not only engage with European monumental traditions but also carry within them the sculptural logics of Africa.

Another work juxtaposes the equestrian monument of Napoleon Bonaparte, flipped on its head, with the figure of King Henri Christophe. Christophe was one of the central leaders of the Haitian Revolution, which began in 1791 and culminated in Haiti declaring independence in 1804—the first Black republic in the world, and the first successful revolt of enslaved people in the Western Hemisphere. His presence atop Napoleon reverses the colonial hierarchy: the empire-builder becomes the foundation for the revolutionary.

Around Christophe orbit the legends of other heroes of Haiti's struggle—Toussaint Louverture, the brilliant strategist who shaped the early revolt; Jean-Jacques Dessalines, who declared Haiti's independence and became its first head of state; and Cécile Fatiman, the mambo priestess said to have presided over the Bois Caïman ceremony that sparked the uprising. Their stories blur the line between history and myth, underscoring how monuments themselves often lean toward fiction—embellishing, simplifying, and constructing narratives that may stand far apart from lived experience. My aim is to use sculpture to expose that slippage: to reveal how monuments do not simply record history but actively shape its memory.

For these monumental works, *In Praise of Midnight*, I am less interested in offering answers than in posing questions. What does it mean to reframe monuments not as fixed declarations but as sites of complexity? How do we acknowledge that all human beings—no matter how lionized—are profoundly flawed, contradictory, and layered? By destabilizing traditional forms of heroism and reconstituting them as hybrids, these works insist that our future monuments must reflect humanity's entanglement with fallibility as much as with triumph. These hybrid forms also remind us that if we step back from immediate conflicts and divisions, and take a longer, wider view, we begin to see that we are all part of one singular, unfolding human story.

As much as these works engage history, they also speak to my own joy in the act of making. The experience of casting, inverting, and recombining forms is one of profound pleasure—a sculptor's delight in weight, texture, and transformation. For me, the studio becomes a laboratory where history, fiction, and form collide, and where new possibilities are sculpted into being.

Cast in bronze and resin, these works embody collisions across time and geography. They are not about closure but about opening: monuments reimagined as questions, as contradictions, as fragile gestures that honor the complexity of human life. In the quiet hours of midnight, when the old day ends and the new one has not yet begun, these works invite us to dwell in uncertainty—the space where tomorrow begins.

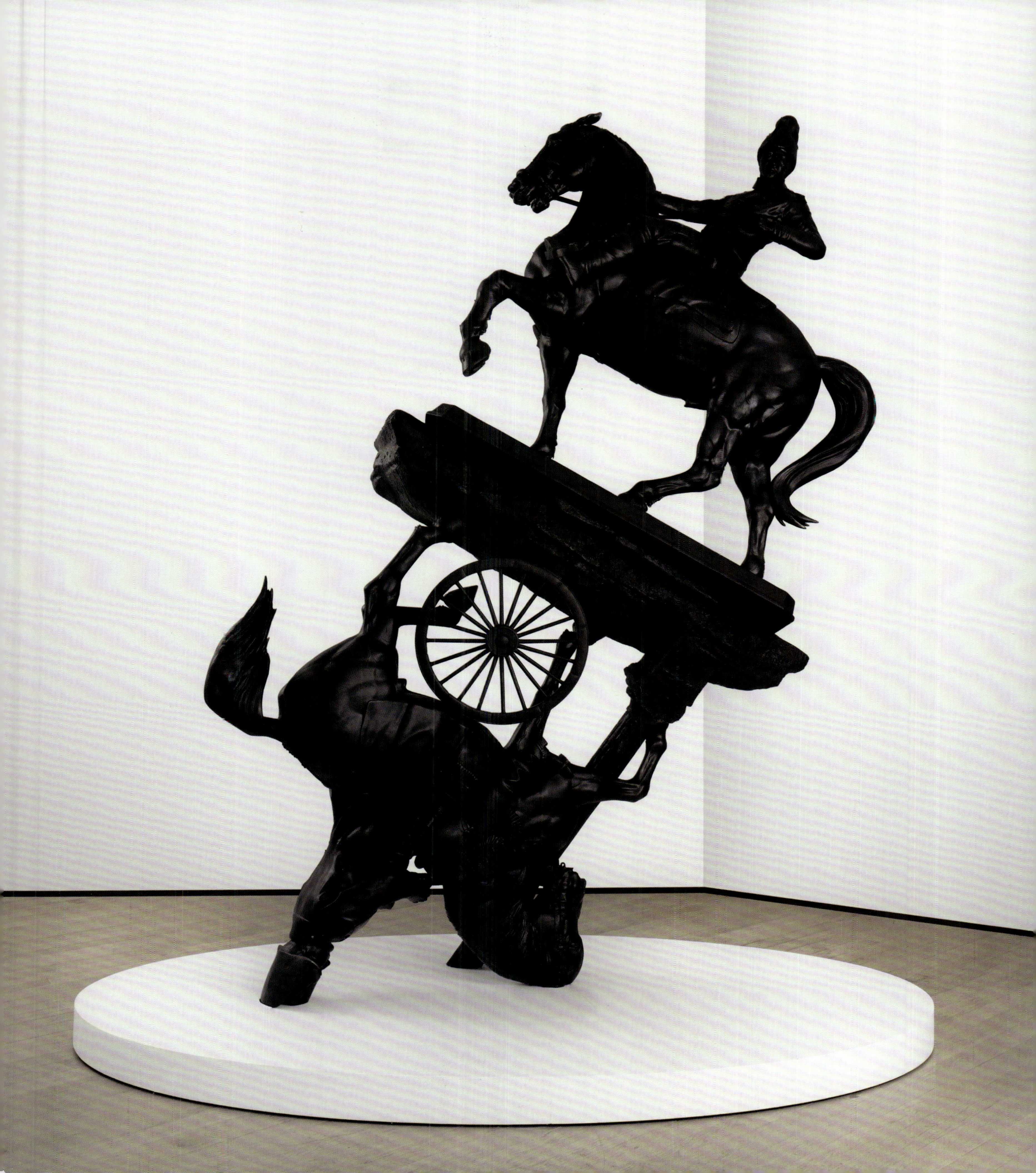

NOTES

next pages,
EXHIBITION VIEW OF
TAVARES STRACHAN: THE DAY TOMORROW BEGAN, LOS ANGELES COUNTY MUSEUM OF ART, 2025

SURVEY: PAGES 071–115

1 Tavares Strachan, in Zoe Lescaze, 'The Artists Whose Medium is Science', *T: The New York Times Style Magazine*, 16 September 2020.
2 Systems Theory developed in the mid-twentieth century via the work of biologist Ludwig von Bertalanffy, sociologist Talcott Parsons, sociologist Niklas Luhmann and others.
3 Jack Burnham 'Systems Esthetics', *Artforum*, vol. 7, no. 1 September 1968, 30–35.
4 See Hans Haacke, 'Artist's Writings: Untitled Statement 1967', in *Hans Haacke*, Walter Grasskamp, Molly Nesbit and Jon Bird (ed.), London: Phaidon Press, 2004, 102–03; and *Hans Haacke: All Connected*, Gary Carrion Murayari and Massimiliano Gioni (ed.) (London: Phaidon Press, 2019), 287.
5 Kynaston McShine, 'Acknowledgements', in *Information* (New York: The Museum of Modern Art, 1970), 1.
6 Kynaston McShine 'Essay', 1970, ibid, 138.
7 The concept of systemic or institutional racism was first developed by Stokely Carmichael (later Kwame Ture) and Charles V. Hamilton in *Black Power: The Politics of Liberation* (New York: Random House, 1967).
8 Alaska's Arctic is ground zero for the world's climate crisis. As a direct result of rising global temperatures, polar ice caps are shrinking, permafrost is receding, and sea ice is declining. According to NOAA's 2023 Annual Climate Report the combined land and ocean temperature has increased at an average rate of 0.11° Fahrenheit (0.06° Celsius) per decade since 1850, or about 2° F in total. The rate of warming since 1982 is more than three times as fast: 0.36° F (0.20° C) per decade. See Rebecca Lindsey and Luann Dahlman, 'Climate Change: Global Temperature', The National Oceanic and Atmospheric Administration (NOAA), 18 January 2024, https://www.climate.gov/news-features/understanding-climate/climate-change-global-temperature
9 Tavares Strachan, quoted in Christian Viveros-Faune, 'Features', *Art Review,* 21 July 2014.
10 Charles F. Kennel and Elena Yulaeva, 'Influence of Arctic Sea-Ice Variability on Pacific Trade Winds', Proceedings of the National Academy of Sciences – PNAS 117 (6), 2020: 2824–34, https://doi.org/10.1073/pnas.1717707117
11 See https://www.basecofficial.com
12 Rev. Ralph Abernathy quoted in Imani Perry, 'The True Cost of the Moonshot', *The New York Times,* 21 July 2019, Section F, 7.
13 Countries with Space Programs, 2024. World Population Review. Retrieved 25 February 2025, from https://worldpopulationreview.com/country-rankings/countries-with-space-programs.
14 Anita Johnson-Patty, Director Global Communications, Bahamas Ministry of Tourism & Aviation,'The Bahamas Makes Giant Leap Into Space Welcoming First International Spacex Landing', Retrieved 3 March 2025, https://www.bahamas.com/pressroom/the-bahamas-makes-giant-leap-into-space-welcoming-first-international-spacex-landing.
15 See the US Embassy & Consulates in China Press statement, 'Marking 29 Years since the Panchen Lama's Disappearance', 18 May 2014, https://china.usembassy-china.org.cn/marking-29-years-since-the-panchen-lamas-disappearance/
16 Erin Jenoa Gilbert, 'Unmasking Marcus Garvey: A Marvelous Real Revolution', in *Tavares Strachan: The Awakening* (London and New York: Marian Goodman Gallery and Isolated Publishing, 2020), 79.
17 Tavares Strachan, 'The disappearing sculpture... | Seated Panchen Lama by Tavares Strachan'(London: Southbank Centre, 2011), https://youtu.be/r3oXfR1IWjE?si=Dd9ya1_Qtrx8NDSf
18 Elspeth F. Garman, 'Rosalind Franklin 1920–1958', Acta Crystallographica. Section D, Biological Crystallography, 76 (7), 2020: 698–701. https://doi.org/10.1107/S2059798320008827
19 Caroline M. Fannin, 'Lawrence, Robert Henry, Jr.', African American Studies Center (Oxford: Oxford University Press, 2013), https://doi.org/10.1093/acref/9780195301731.013.35093
20 Judith Mackrell, 'Alicia Alonso obituary', *The Guardian*, 17 October 2019.
21 Margot Lee Shetterly, 'Mary W. Jackson: NACA/NASA Mathematician and Engineer', https://www.nasa.gov/people/mary-w-jackson-biography/.
22 Maggie M. Cao, 'Tavares Strachan's Subversive Circulations', in Ralph Rugoff, Tavares Strachan, Maggie M. Cao and Ekow Eshun, *Tavares Strachan: There is Light Somewhere* (London: Hayward Gallery, 2024), 51.
23 Tavares Strachan in Christian Viveros-Fauné, 'The Visibility Artist: Tavares Strachan', *The Village Voice*, 27 April 2022.
24 Tavares Strachan, in Adrian Searle and Marian Goodman, 'Tavares Strachan: Sight Unseen', in *Tavares Strachan: In Plain Sight* (London and New York: Marian Goodman Gallery and Isolated Labs), 62.
25 Ellison's famous quote reads: 'I am an invisible man. No, I am not a spook like those who haunted Edgar Allan Poe; nor am I one of your Hollywood-movie ectoplasms. I am a man of substance, of flesh and bone, fiber and liquids – and I might even be said to possess a mind.' By alighting upon the words 'I am a man of substance', the Memphis strikers asserted their presence while referencing the cultural and legal alienation that Ellison expressed in his work.
26 Steve Estes, *I Am a Man: Race, Manhood, and the Civil Rights Movement* (Chapel Hill: University of North Carolina Press, 2005), HeinOnline, https://heinonline-org.ezpprod1.hul.harvard.edu/HOL/P?h=hein.civil/iamn0001&i=144, 136.
27 Ibid., 132
28 Buried inside *Gemini I (Woman King)* are some 100 words including: fearless, virtuous, mighty, eminent, pioneering, legendary and courageous – words often used to describe an individual who is highly respected for their achievements or abilities, unafraid in the face of danger or adversity and possess excellent moral qualities and character.
29 Tavares Strachan, 'The Encyclopedia of Invisibility: A Home for Lost Stories', Tavares Strachan TED2023, April, 2023, video, 10.20, https://www.ted.com/talks/tavares_strachan_the_encyclopedia_of_invisibility_a_home_for_lost_stories?utm_campaign=tedspread&utm_medium=referral&utm_source=tedcomshare
30 Philipp Blom, *Enlightening the World: Encyclopédie, The Book that Changed the Course of History* (New York: Palgrave McMillan, 2005), quoted in Maggie M. Cao, 'Tavares Strachan's Subversive Circulations', in *Tavares Strachan: There is Light Somewhere*, 2024, op. cit., 47.
31 Tavares Strachan, 'Foreword', *Encyclopedia of Invisibility* (New York: Isolated Labs, 2018).
32 The *Encyclopædia Britannica* was first published in 1768, Strachan's work is most closely aligned with the 15th edition, also known as 'Britannica 3', published in 1974, which consisted of 28 volumes in three parts: the *Micropædia* (ready reference and index), *Macropædia* (knowledge in depth), and *Propædia* (outline of knowledge).
33 Tavares Strachan, in 'Tavares Strachan: Beyond the Horizon', interview with Neville Wakefield, *ArtAsia Pacific Almanac*, vol. XV, 2020.
34 Early editions of the *Encyclopædia Britannica* included some of the most distinguished British scholars of the day. By the time of the 15th edition, it was being intentionally complied with a global perspective, with more than 4,000 contributing authors from over 100 countries.
35 Tavares Strachan in 'Tavares Strachan and Amanda Gluibizzi', *The Brooklyn Rail*, June 2022.
36 In fact, two room-sized versions exist: *Six Thousand Years*, 2018 and *Eighteen Ninety*, 2020. *Six Thousand Years* debuted at Regen Projects, Los Angeles and featured 826 individual units. It was displayed as part of the artist's mid-career survey *There is Light Somewhere* at the Hayward Gallery, London, 2024, where the room in which it was installed incorporated 2,078 panels. The alternative version *Eighteen Ninety*, 2020, featuring 1,354 panels, was included in the exhibition *In Plain Sight* at Marian Goodman Gallery, London, 2020.
37 Tavares Strachan in 'Infinite Protest: A Conversation with Tavares Strachan', in *Tavares Strachan: There is Light Somewhere*, 2024, op. cit., 78.
38 Bruce Henderson, 'Who Discovered the North Pole?', *Smithsonian Magazine,* April 2009, https://www.smithsonianmag.com/history/who-discovered-the-north-pole-116633746/
39 Robert Isenberg, 'Matthew Henson: The US' unsung Black explorer', BBC, 19 April 2023, https://www.bbc.com/travel/article/20230418-matthew-henson-the-us-unsung-black-explorer.
40 Presented as part of *Entangled Pasts, 1768–now: Art, Colonialism and Change,* 3 February–28 April 2024, Royal Academy, London.
41 https://www.splcenter.org/presscenter/splc-reports-over-160-confederate-symbols-removed-2020/
42 Craig Owens, 'Representation, Appropriation, and Power', in Craig Owens, and Scott Stewart Bryson. *Beyond Recognition: Representation, Power, and Culture.* University of California Press, 1992, 88.
43 See Louisa Buck, 'Tavares Strachan: I grew up not feeling empowered by art', *The Art Newspaper*, 8 September 2020.
44 Craig Owens, 'The Allegorical Impulse: Toward a Theory of Postmodernism', in Craig Owens, and Scott Stewart Bryson, *Beyond Recognition: Representation, Power, and Culture* (Berkeley: University of California Press, 1992), 53.

FOCUS: PAGES 117–127

1 See Patrick Manning, *Francophone Sub-Saharan Africa: 1880–1985* (New York: Cambridge University Press, 1988).
2 Mikey Dread, cited in Paul Du Noyer, *The Illustrated Encyclopedia of Music* (1st ed.) (London: Flame Tree Publishing, 2003), 356–57.
3 Tavares Strachan, in *Tavares Strachan: There is Light Somewhere*, 2024, op. cit., 82.
4 Karin Barber, *The Anthropology of Texts, Persons and Publics* (New York: Cambridge University Press 1991), 27.
5 See Emma Dabiri, *Don't Touch My Hair*, Penguin, London, 2020.
6 Strachan, 2024, op. cit., 82.
7 Ibid, 79.
8 See Dabiri, 2019, Ibid, 18.
9 John Baker, 'Natural Audiotopias: The Construction Of Sonic Space In Dub Reggae', USF Tampa Graduate Theses and Dissertations, 2009, https://digitalcommons.usf.edu/etd/1842.
10 Ibid.
11 Mabel O. Wilson, in Emanuel Admassu, Anita N Bateman, Mabel O. Wilson and NMutiti Studio, *Where is Africa* (New York: Center for Art, Research and Alliances, 2024), 16.
12 Strachan, 2024, op. cit., 81.

right,
IN PRAISE OF MIDNIGHT (BIKO x CHURCHILL), 2025
BRONZE
213 X 58 X 58 CM

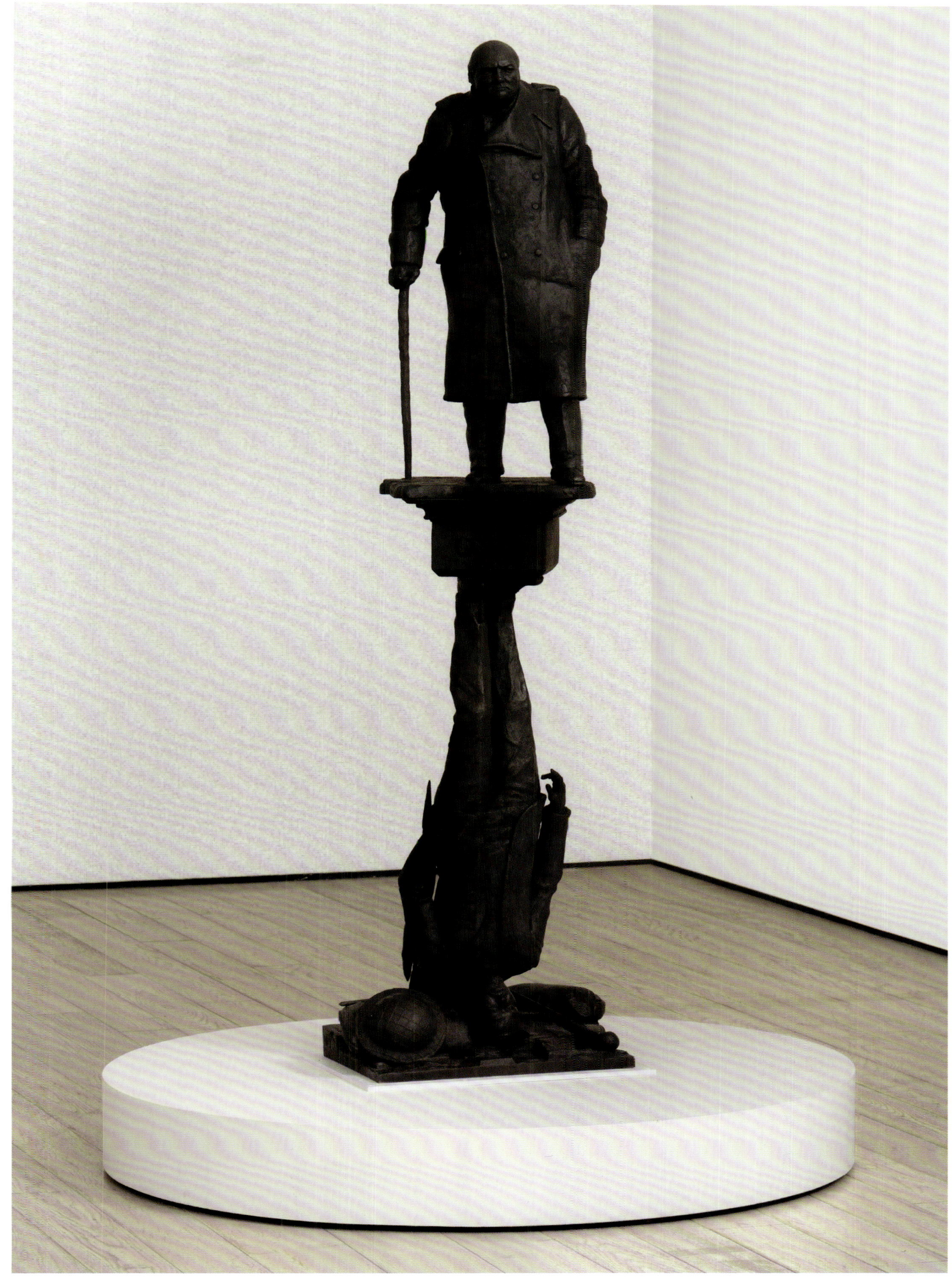

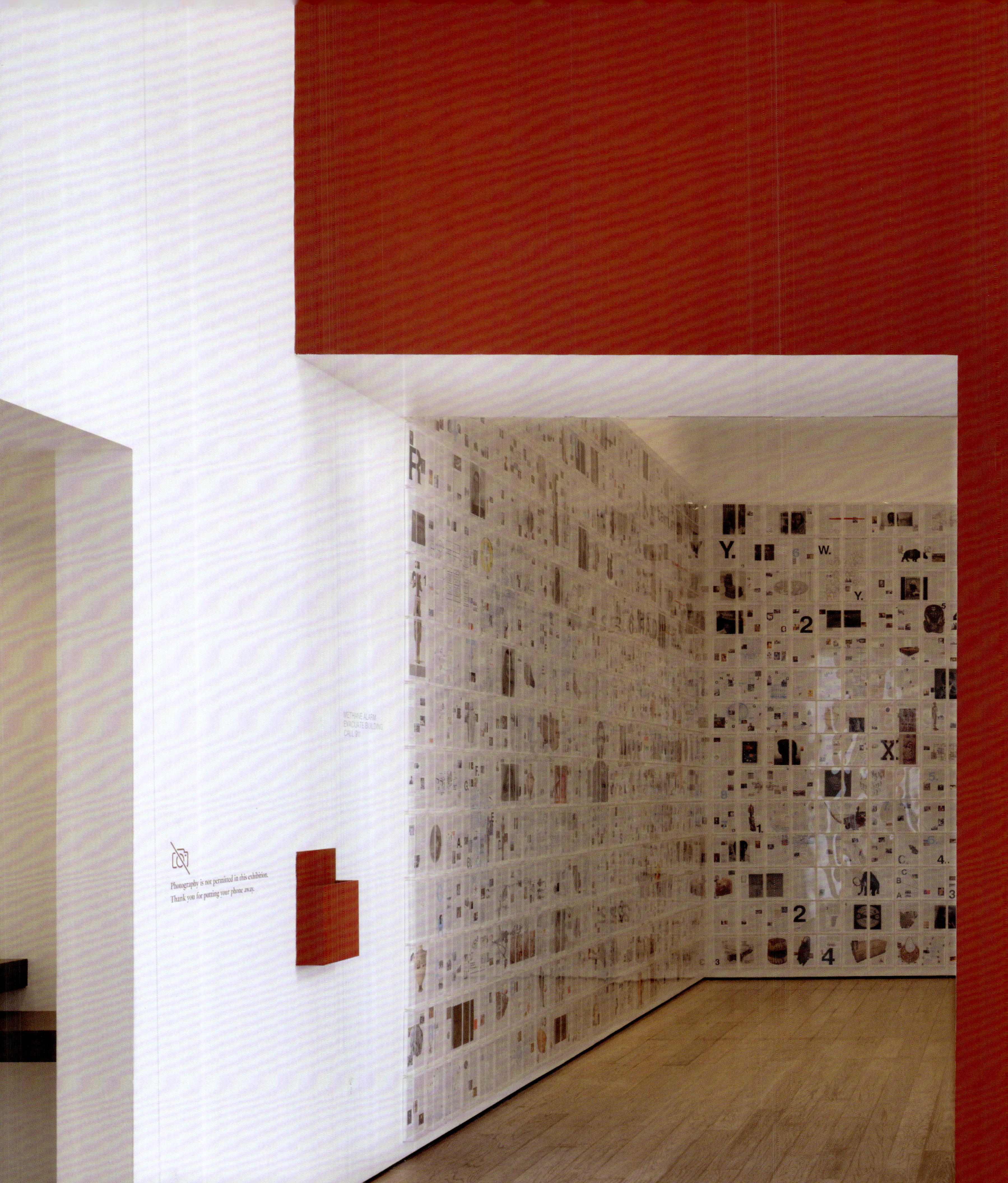
METHANE ALARM
EVACUATE BUILDING
CALL 911
Photography is not permitted in this exhibition.
Thank you for putting your phone away.

TAVARES STRACHAN

THE DAY TOMORROW BEGAN

Tavares Strachan's *The Day Tomorrow Began* is a constellation of artworks and installations that explore different ways we make sense of the past and present. The exhibition begins with *The Encyclopedia of Invisibility*, a compilation of thousands of entries on subjects that have been left out of or erased from mainstream narratives. Strachan is interested in reinventing the ways we preserve information and creating new models for how we access that knowledge.

The media and techniques Strachan uses to create his works bind craft and concept together; there is history in material—whether neon, paint, ceramic, bronze, resin, sound, or video—and in the ways we make things. Rather than being seen in isolation, the objects in this exhibition are brought together in multisensory environments that ask us to reflect on the wholeness of our lived experiences: observed and imagined.

The title of this exhibition—*The Day Tomorrow Began*—can be understood as the specific moment when the future begins, perhaps at the breaking of first light, a time of renewal. It also suggests the continuous and fluid nature of time: yesterday's tomorrow is today, and today will soon be tomorrow's yesterday. We are always in the flow of the past and the future, and how we think about history defines the present, which in turn shapes what comes next. Strachan's practice suggests that there are always new possibilities for the ways in which we experience art, history, ideas, ourselves, each other, and each day. This exhibition is an invitation to those possibilities.

This exhibition was co-organized by the Los Angeles County Museum of Art and the Columbus Museum of Art.

Presented by

HYUNDAI

This exhibition is part of The Hyundai Project at LACMA, a joint initiative between Hyundai Motor Company and LACMA since 2015.

Major support provided by LACMA's Future Arts Collective, the Anthony Pritzker Family Foundation, and Pete and Michelle Scantland.

Generous support provided by Contemporary Projects Endowment Fund, Evanne and Edward Gargiulo, Judelson Family Foundation, and Dr. Marina Ochakoff.

All exhibitions at LACMA are underwritten by the LACMA Exhibition Fund. Major annual support is provided by The David & Meredith Kaplan Foundation and Louise and Brad Edgerton, Edgerton Foundation, with generous annual funding from Tanya Fileva, Mary and Daniel James, Bert Levy Fund, Justin Lubliner, Alfred E. Mann Charities, Kelsey Lee Offield, Maggie Tang, Lenore and Richard Wayne, and Marietta Wu and Thomas Yamamoto.

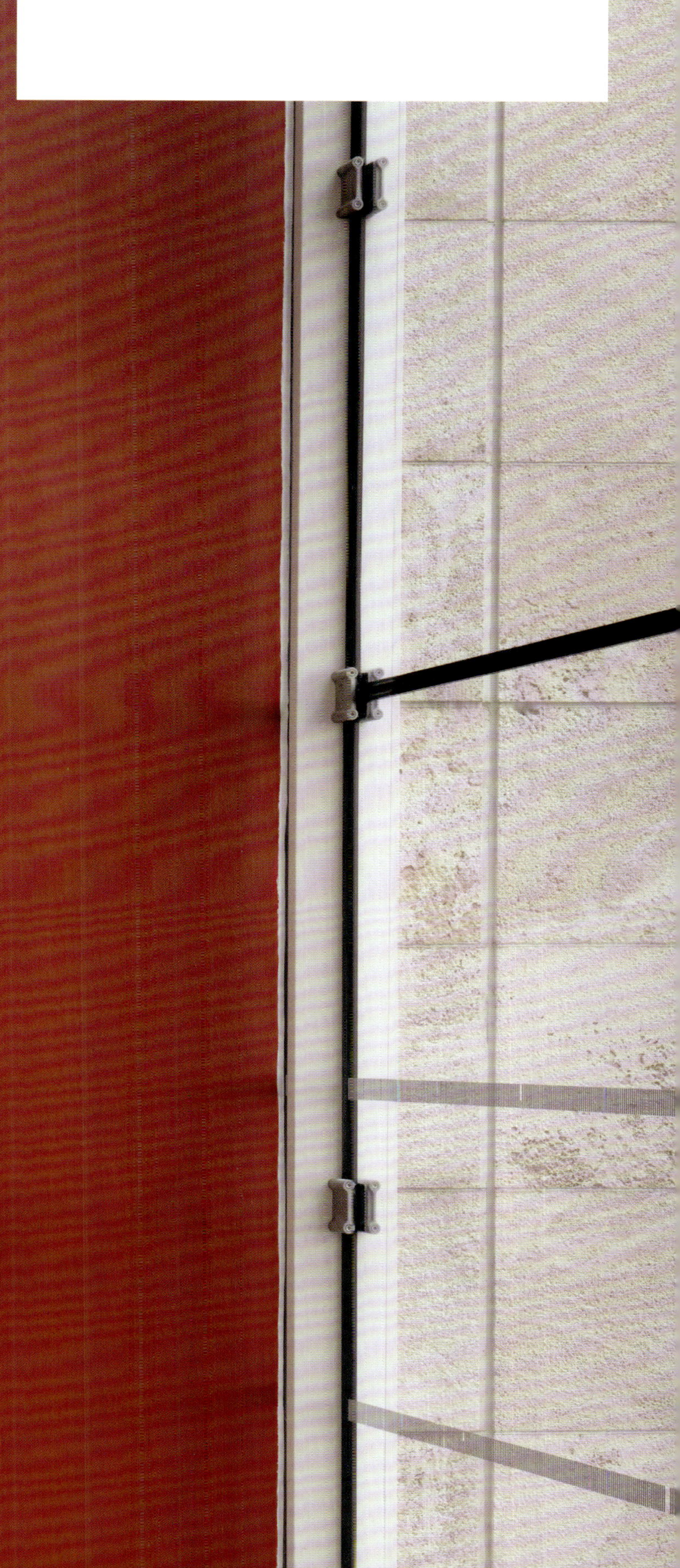

CHRONOLOGY: Tavares Strachan, born in Nassau in 1979.
Lives and works in New York.

SELECTED EXHIBITIONS AND PROJECTS
1998–2005

SELECTED ARTICLES AND INTERVIEWS
1998–2005

1998
'Floyd's Fury',
PRO GALLERY, Nassau (group)

Recipient of the Governor's Award, Nassau

1999
'Reactions',
CENTRAL BANK GALLERY, Nassau (solo)

'Visual Dialogue',
PRO GALLERY, Nassau (group)

'Post Independent Art',
CENTRAL BANK GALLERY, Nassau (group)

2000
'Glass Triennial',
WOODS GERRY GALLERY at RHODE ISLAND SCHOOL OF DESIGN,
(group)

'Shattered Fractions',
COLLEGE GALLERY, Nassau (group)

'On The Edge of Time: Contemporary Art from the Caribbean',
THE INTER-AMERICAN DEVELOPMENT BANK CULTURAL CENTER,
Washington, DC (group)

Joins the Roots Junkanoo Group, Nassau

Recipient of the Queen Elizabeth Arts/Poetry Award, Nassau

2001
'Synergism',
PRO GALLERY, Nassau (solo)

2002
'Mine',
LOMBARD-FREID FINE ARTS, New York (solo)

4th CARIBBEAN BIENNIAL, Santo Domingo (group)

'Meiosis',
SOL GALLERY, Providence, Rhode Island (group)

'Perspectives',
WOODS GERRY GALLERY at RHODE ISLAND SCHOOL OF DESIGN,
Providence (group)

2003
'One-On-One,
PIEROGI 2000, New York (solo)

Obtains a BFA and Distinguished Student Award in Glass at Rhode
Island School of Design

2004
'Nothing Compared To This: Ambient, Incidental And New Minimal
Tendencies In Current Art',
CONTEMPORARY ARTS CENTER, Cincinnati (group)

2005
'Untitled',
SAFN MUSEUM, Reykjavík (group)

SELECTED EXHIBITIONS AND PROJECTS
2006–10

2006
'Where We Are Is Always Miles Away',
THE LUGGAGE STORE, San Francisco (solo)

'Tavares Strachan',
RONALD FELDMAN FINE ARTS, New York (solo)

'Tavares Strachan',
PIEROGI 2000, New York (solo)

'The Distance Between What We Have and What We Want',
ALBURY SAYLE PRIMARY SCHOOL, Nassau (solo)

'School Days',
JACK TILTON GALLERY, New York (group)

Obtains a MFA in Sculpture, Yale School of Art, Yale University

2007
'New York States Of Mind',
QUEENS MUSEUM OF ART, New York, toured to HAUS DER KULTUREN DER WELT, Berlin (group)

'20th Anniversary: In The Fullness Of Time',
THE LUGGAGE STORE, San Francisco (group)

'Connecticut Contemporary',
WADSWORTH ATHENEUM MUSEUM OF ART, Hartford, Connecticut (group)

'From The Fat Of The Land: Alchemies, Ecologies, Attractions',
GRAND ARTS, Kansas City (group)

2008
'Tavares Strachan',
PIEROGI 2000, Leipzig (solo)

'A Hundred Years',
DANIEL WEINBERG GALLERY, Los Angeles (solo)

'InnerOuterSpace',
MATTRESS FACTORY, Pittsburgh (group)

2009
'The Distance Between What We Have and What We Want (Arctic Art Project)',
BROOKLYN MUSEUM OF ART, New York (solo)

'You Can Do Whatever You Like (The Orthostatic Tolerance Project)',
INSTITUTE OF CONTEMPORARY ART, Philadelphia (solo)

2010
'Orthostatic Tolerance: It Might Not Be Such A Bad Idea If I Never Went Home',
MASSACHUSETTS INSTITUTE OF TECHNOLOGY (MIT) LIST VISUAL ARTS CENTER, Cambridge (solo)

'Orthostatic Tolerance: Launching Into An Infinite Distance',
GRAND ARTS, Kansas City (solo)

SELECTED ARTICLES AND INTERVIEWS
2006–10

2006
O'Leary, Mary E., 'Yale artist taking the city to California', New Haven Register, 21 January

Anand, Easha, 'Chunk of New Haven Street Goes West', Yale Daily News, 31 January

Deleveaux, Yolanda, 'Tavares Strachan', The Miami Herald Tribune (Bahamas Edition), The Arts Section, 16 August

Kraft, Jessica, 'New York', Contemporary, no. 86

Huston, Johnny Ray, 'Where We Are Is Always Miles Away', San Francisco Bay Guardian, 15–21 November

Leaverton, Michael, 'Earth Moving', SF Weekly, 15–21 November

Heller, Maxwell, 'Tavares Strachan: Hermetically Sealed', The Brooklyn Rail, December–January

Baker, Kenneth, 'A Whole Lot of Nothing Worthy of Contemplation', San Francisco Chronicle, 2 December

Smith, Roberta, 'More Than You Can See: Storm of Art Engulfs Miami', The New York Times, 9 December

2007
Helfand, Glen, 'Tavares Strachan at the Luggage Store Gallery', Artforum, February

Volk, Gregory, 'Tavares Strachan', Art In America, February

Hromack, Sarah, 'Tavares Strachan', Art Papers, March–April

'The Chickcharney | Mission', Printed Project, June

2009
Smith, Roberta, 'Rewards and Clarity in a Show of Restraint', The New York Times, 19 February

Saltz, Jerry, 'Energy to Burn', New York Magazine, 22 March

Cotter, Holland, 'Yoon Lee, Jonathan Schipper, Tavares Strachan', The New York Times, 16 April

2010
Smee, Sebastian, 'Universe of Possibilities', Boston Globe, 28 May

Thorson, Alice, 'Tavares Strachan', Art in America, June

Viveros, Christian-Fauné, Tavares Strachan', Art Review, July

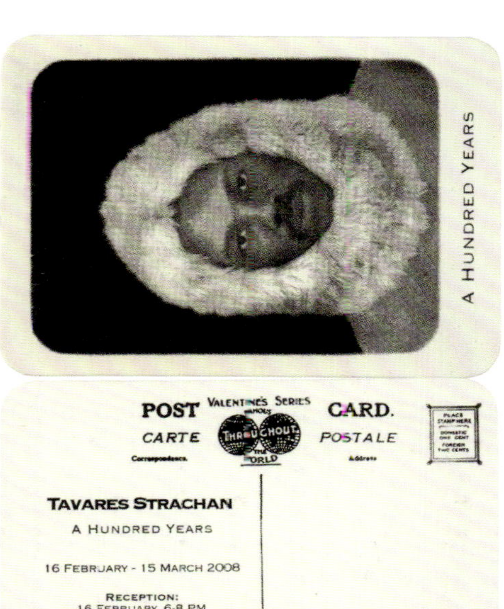

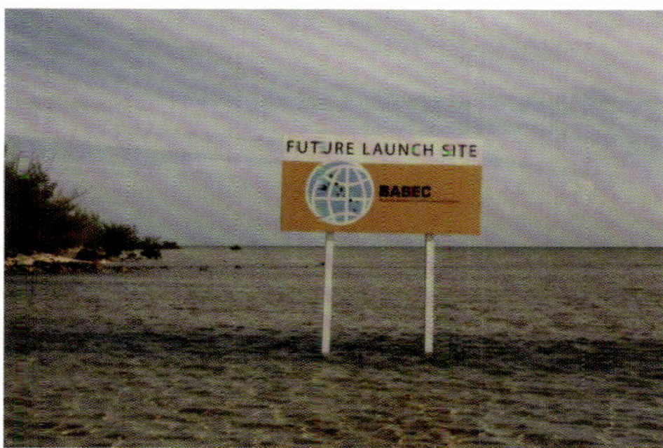

TAVARES STRACHAN seen / unseen

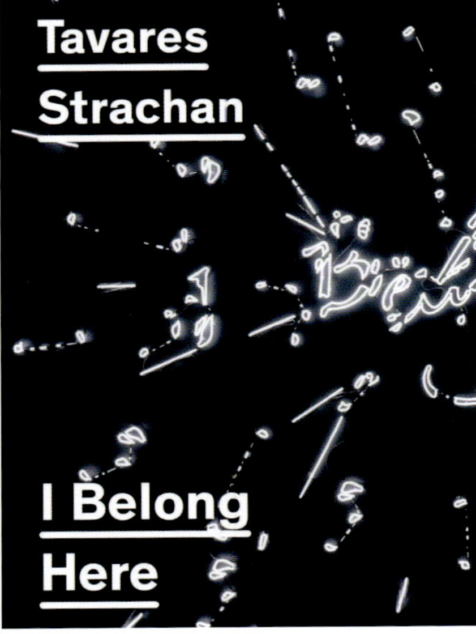

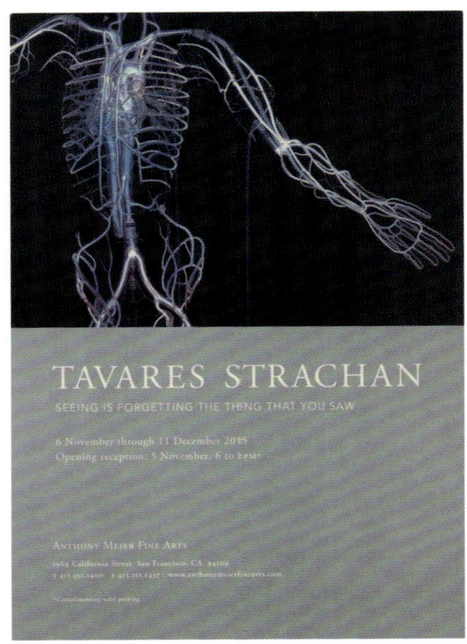

SELECTED EXHIBITIONS AND PROJECTS
2010–17

2010 (cont.)
'Roundabout',
CITY GALLERY WELLINGTON, New Zealand, toured to TEL AVIV MUSEUM OF ART (group)

3rd FOKUS ŁÓDŹ BIENNALE, Poland (group)

2011
'Seen/Unseen',
UNDISCLOSED LOCATION, New York (solo)

'Sometimes Lies Are Prettier',
ROSSI & ROSSI, London (solo)

2012
'Here And Now',
DVIR GALLERY, Tel Aviv (solo)

2013
1st BAHAMAS PAVILION at 55th VENICE BIENNALE (solo)

'Life: On the Moon',
VARIOUS SMALL FIRES, Los Angeles (group)

'Arctic',
LOUISIANA MUSEUM OF MODERN ART, Humlebæk, Denmark (group)

5th MOSCOW BIENNALE OF CONTEMPORARY (group)

'Pataphysics: A Theoretical Exhibition',
SEAN KELLY GALLERY, New York (group)

12th BIENNALE DE LYON (group)

2014
'On The Blue Shore Of Silence',
TRACY WILLIAMS GALLERY, New York (group)

'Bringing The World Into The World',
QUEENS MUSEUM, New York (group)

PROSPECT.3 TRIENNIAL, New Orleans (group)

2015
'How To Make Someone Invisible',
FERGUS MCCAFFREY, St. Barthélemy (solo)

'Seeing Is Forgetting The Thing That You Saw',
ANTHONY MEIER FINE ARTS, San Francisco (solo)

'The Transformation Business',
JANE LOMBARD GALLERY, New York (group)

2016
'Winter 2015: Collected Works',
RENNIE COLLECTION, Vancouver (group)

2017
'Solidary & Solitary: The Joyner/ Giuffrida Collection',
OGDEN MUSEUM OF SOUTHERN ART, New Orleans, toured to BALTIMORE MUSEUM OF ART; SMART MUSEUM, Chicago; NASHER MUSEUM OF ART, Durham, North Carolina; RACLIN MURPHY MUSEUM OF ART, Notre Dame, Indiana (group)

1st DESERT X, Coachella Valley, California (group)

SELECTED ARTICLES AND INTERVIEWS
2010–17

2015
Binlot, Ann, 'An Artful Ode to an Undersung Chemist', T: The New York Times Style Magazine, 6 November

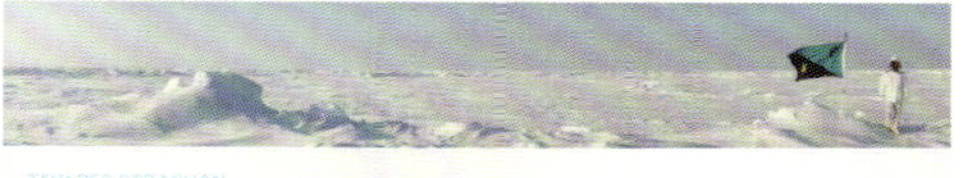

SELECTED EXHIBITIONS AND PROJECTS
2018–20

2018

'Invisibles',
REGEN PROJECTS, Los Angeles (solo)

'The Other Side Of The Sun',
MESTRE PROJECTS, Nassau (solo)

'Always, Sometimes, Never',
FRYE ART MUSEUM, Seattle (solo)

'In Broad Daylight',
BALTIMORE MUSEUM OF ART (commissioned outdoor installation)

1st FAENA FESTIVAL, Miami Beach (group)

57th CARNEGIE INTERNATIONAL, Pittsburgh (group)

'Indicators: Artists on Climate Change',
STORM KING ART CENTER, New Windsor, New York (group)

'Declaration',
INSTITUTE FOR CONTEMPORARY ART at VIRGINIA COMMONWEALTH UNIVERSITY, Richmond (group)

2019

'Smoke & Mirrors,
AF PROJECTS, Los Angeles (group)

'Soft Power: A Conversation For The Future',
SAN FRANCISCO MUSEUM OF MODERN ART (group)

'How The Light Gets In',
JOHNSON MUSEUM OF ART at CORNELL UNIVERSITY, Ithaca, New York (group)

'Far Out: Suits, Habs, And Labs for Outer Space',
SAN FRANCISCO MUSEUM OF MODERN ART (group)

58th VENICE BIENNALE (group)

'The Visible Turn: Contemporary Artists Confront Political Invisibility',
UNIVERSITY OF SOUTH FLORIDA CONTEMPORARY ART MUSEUM, Tampa (group)

2020

'In Plain Sight',
MARIAN GOODMAN GALLERY, London (solo)

'You Belong Here',
THE MOMENTARY CRYSTAL BRIDGES MUSEUM OF AMERICAN ART, Bentonville, Arkansas (permanent outdoor installation)

'Unmastered',
MESTRE PROJECTS Nassau (group)

'We Belong Here',
NEVADA MUSEUM OF ART, Reno (group)

'Winter Light',
HAYWARD GALLERY, London (group)

'The Willfulness of Objects',
THE BASS, Miami (group)

'Bright Golden Haze',
OKLAHOMA CONTEMPORARY, Oklahoma City (group)

'Life During Wartime: Art in the Age of Coronavirus',
UNIVERSITY OF SOUTH FLORIDA CONTEMPORARY ART MUSEUM, Tampa (group)

SELECTED ARTICLES AND INTERVIEWS
2018–20

2018

Ober, Cara, 'Tavares Strachan: In Broad Daylight', Bmore Art, August

Finkel, Orbit Jori, 'Tavares Strachan teams with SpaceX to launch Satellite-Sculpture into Orbit', The New York Times, 13 November

2019

Loos, Ted, 'In San Francisco, Wiedling Influence (Gently) Through Art', The New York Times, 23 October

2020

Wakewfiled, Neville, 'Tavares Strachan: Behind the Horizon', Art Asia Pacific, January–March

Walsh, Brienne, 'The phrase "We are in this together" takes on subversive meaning in Tavares Strachan's art', Forbes, 28 April

Chan, T. F., 'Tavares Strachan's call for unity is written in neon', Wallpaper*, May

Benson, Louise, 'These Are the Artists You Need to Know', Elephant, June

Lescaze, Zoë, 'The Artist Whose Medium Is Science', T: The New York Times Style Magazine, 16 September

Searle, Adrian, 'In Plain Sight review: Tavares Strachan's baffling, thrilling, uplifting visions', The Guardian, 8 September

Buck, Louisa, 'Tavares Strachan: "I grew up not feeling empowered by art"', The Art Newspaper, September

Williams, Gilda, 'Tavares Strachan at Marian Goodman', Artforum, December

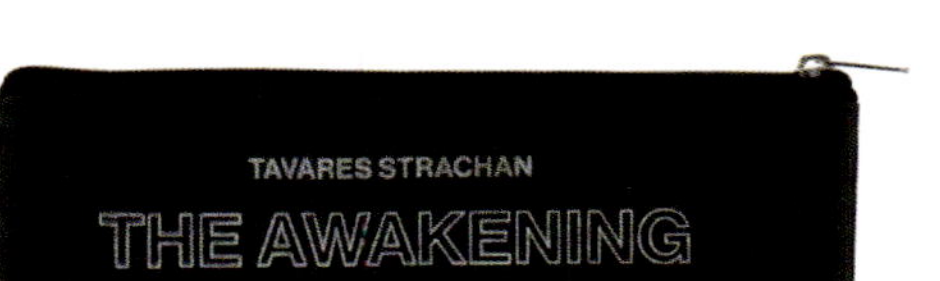

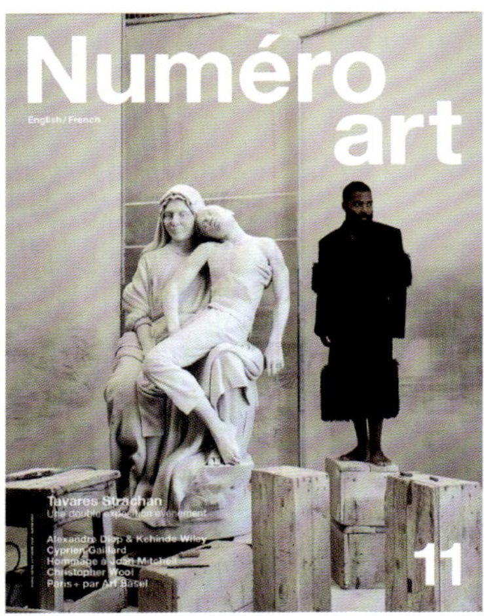

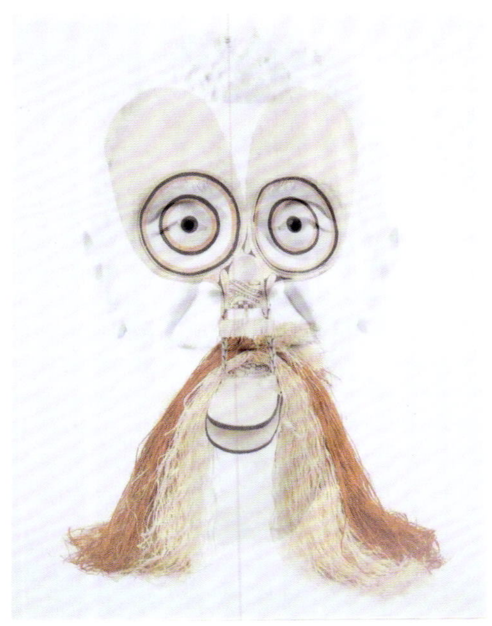

SELECTED EXHIBITIONS AND PROJECTS
2020–2024

2020 (cont.)
'Invisible',
SCIENCE GALLERY, Trinity College Dublinv (group)

'Countermythologies',
NXTHVN, New Haven, Connecticut (group)

2021
'Belong/Brooklyn',
BARCLAYS CENTER, New York (commissioned outdoor sculpture)

1st DIRIYAH CONTEMPORARY ART BIENNALE, Riyadh (group)

2022
'In Broad Daylight',
PERROTIN, Paris (solo)

'In Total Darkness',
GALERIE MARIAN GOODMAN, Paris (solo)

'The Awakening',
MARIAN GOODMAN GALLERY, New York (solo)

'Forecast Form: Art in the Carribean Diaspora 1990–Today',
MUSEUM OF CONTEMPORARY ART, Chicago (group)

'Les Portes du Possible: Art & Science Fiction',
CENTRE POMPIDOU-METZ, France (group)

'Books Revisited',
CENTER FOR BOOK ARTS, New York (group)

'Citing Black Geographies',
GRAY, Chicago and New York (group)

'Flesh And Bones: The Art Of Anatomy',
GETTY MUSEUM, Los Angeles (group)

'Substance – Substances',
CHURCH OF SAN MARTÍN, Arévalo, Ávila, Spain (group)

'The Impermanent Display I',
LUMA, Arles, France (group)

2023
'Do And Be',
PERROTIN, Seoul (solo)

'The Return',
GOODMAN GALLERY, Johannesburg (solo)

'The Irreplaceable Human: Conditions of Creativity in the Age of AI',
LOUISIANA MUSEUM OF MODERN ART, Humlebæk, Denmark (group)

14th SHANGHAI BIENNALE (group)

'Incarnations: Le corps dans la collection du macLYON – Acte 2',
MUSEUM OF CONTEMPORARY ART, Lyon (group)

'One Hundred More Fires | Social Forms: Art as Global Citizenship',
OREGON CONTEMPORARY, Portland (group)

'Schema: World as Diagram',
MARLBOROUGH GALLERY, New York (group)

2024
'Tavares Strachan: Between Me and You',
BLANTON MUSEUM OF ART, Austin (solo)

SELECTED ARTICLES AND INTERVIEWS
2020–2024

2021
Strachan, Tavares, 'Top Ten', Artforum, March

Kooiman, Mirjam, 'Tavares Strachan: Encyclopedia of Invisibility', Foam, no. 59, June

2022
Civin, Marcus, 'Tavares Strachan: Protesting for Goodness' Sake', DAMN, Spring

Kananjian, Dodie, 'The Cosmic Vision of Tavares Strachan', Vogue, April

Viveros, Christian-Fauné, The Visibility Artist: Tavares Strachan', The Village Voice, 27 April

Gluibizzi, Amanda, 'Tavares Strachan', The Brooklyn Rail, June

Park, August, 'Tavares Strachan', W Korea, 25 August

Grau, Donatien, 'Who is Tavares Stravhan, new art star exhibited at Perrotin and Marian Goodman?', Numéro, October

Viéville, Camille, 'LÉveil Selon Tavares Strachan' Le Journal des l'Art, October

Yerebakan, Osman Can, 'How Tavares Strachan's limitless art bends the laws of time and space', GQ, October

Rappolt, Mark, '"We Get to Make Meaning": Tavares Strachan and Stan Burnside', Art Review, November

2023
Park, Han-sol, 'How cosmic vision and lost histories collide in Tavares Strachan's art', The Korea Times, 14 September

Sherwin, Skye, 'The Last Supper recast: artist Tavares Strachan on reimagining Da Vinci's dinner guests', The Guardian, 26 December

2024
Finkel, Jori, "Art Seeks Enlightenment in Darkness, The New York Times, 24 April

SELECTED EXHIBITIONS AND PROJECTS
2024–25

2024 (cont.)
'Magnificent Darkness',
MARIAN GOODMAN GALLERY, Los Angeles (solo)

'Tavares Strachan: There Is Light Somewhere',
HAYWARD GALLERY, London (solo)

'Project a Black Planet: The Art and Culture of Panafrica',
THE ART INSTITUTE OF CHICAGO (group)

'World Without End: The George Washington Carver Project',
CALIFORNIA AFRICAN AMERICAN MUSEUM, Los Angeles (group)

'Invisibility: Powers and Perils | PST ART: Art & Science Collide',
OXY ARTS, Los Angeles (group)

'Entangled Pasts, 1768–Now: Art, Colonialism and Change',
ROYAL ACADEMY OF ARTS, London (group)

'Flight into Egypt: Black Artists and Ancient Egypt, 1876–Now',
THE METROPOLITAN MUSEUM OF ART, New York (group)

'Get in the Game: Sports, Art, Culture',
SAN FRANCISCO MUSEUM OF MODERN ART (group)

2025
'Tavares Strachan: Starless Midnight',
MARIAN GOODMAN GALLERY, New York (solo)

'Tavares Strachan: Supernovas',
KUNSTHALLE MANNHEIM (solo)

'Tavares Strachan: The Day Tomorrow Began',
LOS ANGELES COUNTY MUSEUM OF ART, toured to COLUMBUS MUSEUM OF ART, Ohio (solo)

'Beautiful Collisions',
SOUTH BY SOUTHWEST (SXSW) AT CHRIST CHURCH SPITALFIELD, London (group)

1st BUKHARA BIENNIAL, Uzbekistan (group)

'The Strangers',
ATELIER JOLIE, New York (group)

'Thus masked, the world has a language',
MARIANE IBRAHIM GALLERY, Chicago (group)

SELECTED ARTICLES AND INTERVIEWS
2024–25

2025
Corwin, William, 'Tavares Strachan: Starless Midnight', The Brooklyn Rail, April

Beason, Tyrone, 'A new LACMA exhibit uses art and science to unlock hidden histories', Los Angeles Times, 16 October

Akers, Torey, '"It's about world-making": Tavares Strachan on his expansive new LACMA exhibition', The Art Newspaper, 17 October

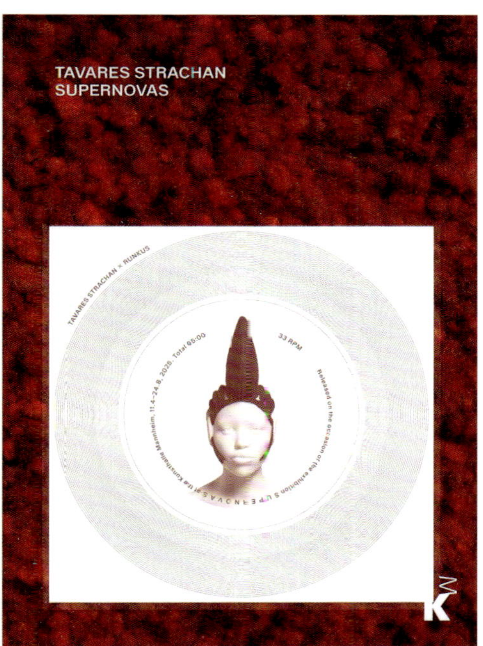

BIBLIOGRAPHY

THE ENCYCLOPEDIA OF INVISIBILITY, 2014–18
DARK BLUE GOAT SKIN LEATHER, FRONTIER OPAQUE PAPER
2400 PAGES
38 X 33 X 13 CM

MONOGRAPHS, EXHIBITION BROCHURES AND ARTIST'S BOOKS

Strachan, Tavares, and Robert Hobbs, The Distance Between What We Have and What We Want, Pierogi Gallery and Ronald Feldman Fine Arts, New York, 2006

Strachan, Tavares, Franklin Sirmans and Maxwell Heller, Tavares Strachan: Orthostatic Tolerance. It Might Not Be Such a Bad Idea if I Never Went Home, Massachusetts Institute of Technology Press, Cambridge, 2010

Strachan, Tavares, Robert Hobbs, Stamatina Gregory and Christian Viveros-Fauné, Tavares Strachan: I Belong Here, Conception, New York, 2013

Strachan, Tavares, Robert Hobbs, Gregory Volk, Franklin Sirmans and Mimi Sheller, Tavares Strachan: Seen/Unseen, Art Asia Pacific, Hong Kong, 2014

Strachan, Tavares, Amanda Hunt, Erica Sellers, Neville Wakefield and Shaheen Merali (ed.), Tavares Strachan: I Am, Isolated Labs, New York, 2017

Strachan, Tavares, The Encyclopedia of Invisibility, Isolated Labs, New York, 2018

Strachan, Tavares, Marian Goodman and Adrian Searle, Tavares Strachan: In Plain Sight, Marian Goodman Gallery and Isolated Labs, New York, 2022

Strachan, Tavares, Emmanuel Perrotin, Romi Crawford, Nancy Spector and Kaitlyn Greenidge, Tavares Strachan: In Broad Daylight, Perrotin, Paris, and Isolated Labs, New York, 2022

Strachan, Tavares, Olivia Anani and Michele Robecchi, Tavares Strachan: In Total Darkness, Marian Goodman Gallery and Isolated Labs, New York, 2024

Strachan, Tavares, Pedro Alonzo, Gavin Delahunty, Erin Jenoa Gilbert and Alysia Nicole Harris, Tavares Strachan: The Awakening, Marian Goodman Gallery and Isolated Labs, New York, 2024

Strachan, Tavares, Ralph Rugoff, Maggie M. Cao and Ekow Eshun, Tavares Strachan: There Is Light Somewhere, Hayward Gallery, London, 2024

Strachan, Tavares, Diana Nawi, Dr. Asfa-Wossen Asserate, Paul Farber, Christina 'Muffin' Fernander, Uncle Harry Gardiner, Paul Holdengräber, Sibahle Mtimkulu and Ella Strachan, Tavares Strachan: The Day Tomorrow Began, Los Angeles County Museum of Art, 2025

Strachan, Tavares, Michele Robecchi, Gavin Delahunty, Emma Dabiri and Jason Schmidt, Tavares Strachan, Phaidon, London, 2026

SELECTED EXHIBITION CATALOGUES AND SURVEYS

Acevedo-Yates, Carla, Forecast Form: Art in the Caribbean Diaspora 1990s–Today, Museum of Contemporary Art, Chicago, and DelMonico Books, New York, 2023

Bause Rubinstein, Heather, and Meyer Raphael Rubinstein, Schema: World as Diagram, Marlborough Gallery, New York, 2023

Blair, Ian, Cameron Shaw, Yael Lipschutz, Ash Arder, Bethel S. Moges, Bridget R. Cocks, Jarvis C. McInnis, Laura Briscoe, Fraser Livingstone and Mark D. Hersey, World Without End: The George Washington Carver Project, California African American Museum, Los Angeles, and Himmer, Munich, 2025

Byrd, Antawan, Elvira Dyangani Ose, Adom Getachew, Matthew S. Witkovsky, KJ Abudu, Sophia Azeb, Bruno Baptistelli, Sandrine Colard, Ntone Edjabe, Fehras Publishing Practices, Brent Hayes Edwards, Sarah Estrela, Merve Fejzula, Tsitsi Jaji, Mpho Matsipa and Musab Younis, Project a Black Planet: The Art and Culture of Panafrica, The Art Institute of Chicago, 2025

Campbell, Diana (ed.), Recipes for Broken Hearts, Bukhara Biennial, Uzbekistan, 2025

Cao, Maggie M., Painting US Empire: Nineteenth Century Art and Its Legacy, University of Chicago Press, 2025

Crawford, Romi, Citing Black Geographies, Richard Gray Gallery, Chicago, 2022

Cazali, Rosina (ed.), 4th Caribbean Biennial/IV Bienal del Caribe, Centro Cultural Cariforo de la República Dominicana, Santo Domingo, 2002

Damasio, Alain, Alexandra Müller, Catherine Dufour, Sabrina Calvo, Kim Stanley Robinson, Michael Roch, Laura Nsafou, Nadia Chonville, Philippe Curval and Ariel Kyrou Les Portes du Possible: Art & Science Fiction, Centre Pompidou Metz, 2022

De Zegher, Catherine, Joseph Bockstein, Vladimir Medinsky, Sergei Kapkov, Gabriel Gorodetsky, Craigie Horsfield, Ruth Herz, Svetlana Boym, Noemi Smolik, Souchou Yao, Pascal Gielen, Alexei Penzinand and Keti Chukhrov More Light, 5th Moscow Biennale of Contemporary Art, 2013

Dunlop Fletcher, Jennifer, Seph Rodney, Katy Siege, AJ Dungo and Megan Rapinoe, Get in the Game: Sports, Art, Culture, San Francisco Museum of Modern Art and Tra Publishing, Miami, 2024

Eshun, Ekow, In the Black Fantastic, MIT Press, Cambridge, Massachusetts, and Hayward Gallery, London, 2022

Figueres, Muni, and Félix Angel, On the Edge of Time: Contemporary Art from the Bahamas, Inter-American Development Bank Cultural Center, Washington, DC, 2000

Fisch, Taylor, and Corina Reynolds, Books Revisited, Center for Book Arts, New York, 2022

Garrido Castellano, Carlos, Forecast Storm: Art in the Caribbean Diaspora 1990s-Today, Distributed Art Publishers, New York, 2023

Kornell, Monique, Thisbe Gensler, Naoko Takahatake and Erin Travers, Flesh and Bones: The Art of Anatomy, Getty Research Institute, Los Angeles, 2022

Lawson, Dhyandra, Michael Govan, Paul Mpagi Sepuya, Dionne Brand, Frida Orupabo, Widline Cadet, Ytasha Womack and Sammy Baloji, Imagining Black Diasporas: 21st-Century Art and Poetics, Los Angeles County Museum of Art and Del Monico, New York, 2025

Levin, Kim (ed.), Printed Project, Issue 07: Unconditional Love, Visual Arts Ireland, Dublin, 2007

Merali, Shaheen (ed.), New York States of Mind: Art and the City, Saqi Books, London, 2008

Martin, Courtney J. (ed.), Mary Schmidt Campbell, Christopher Bedford, Andrianna Campbell, Nicholas Cullinan, Joost Bosland, Jacqueline Francis, Alexis Clark and Elvira Dyangani Ose, Four Generations: The Joyner/Giuffrida Collection of Abstract Art, Gregory R. Miller, New York, 2017

Meta Bauer, Ute (ed.), Rakan Altouq, Aya Albakree, Rose Lejeune, Wejdan Reda, Anca Rujoiu, Ana Salazar Herrera and Rahul Gudipudi, After Rain, Diriyah Biennale Foundation, Riyadh, and Les Presses du Réel, Dijon, 2024

Ng, Elaine W., Roundabout, City Gallery Wellington, New Zealand, and Tel Aviv Museum of Art, 2010

Price, Dorothy, Esther Chadwick, Cora Gilroy-Ware and Sarah Lea, Entangled Pasts, 1768–now: Art, Colonialism and Change, Royal Academy of Arts London, 2024

Rugoff, Ralph (ed.), May You Live Interesting Times, Venice Biennale, 2019

Schaffner, Ingrid, Emmanuel Iduma, Pico Iyer, Maira Kalman, Liz Park and Marcus Rediker, Carnegie International 57th Edition, Carnegie Museum of Art, Pittsburgh, 2019

Sirmans, Franklin, Christine Y. Kim, Rita Gonzalez, Mary McCay and Rickey Laurentiis, Prospect.3: Notes for Now, Prospect New Orleans, and Prestel, New York, 2014

Switzer, Stacy, and Anne Fischer, Problems and Provocations: Grand Arts 1995–2015, Grand Arts, Kansas City, 2016

Tommasino, Akili, Andrea Myers Achi, Makeda Djata Best, Barbara Chase-Riboud, Awol Erizku, Lauren Halsey, Solange Knowles, Iman Issa, Mia Matthias, Julie Mehretu, Kai Mora, Jennifer Newsom, Matthew Shenoda and Fred Wilson, Flight into Egypt: Black Artists and Ancient Egypt, 1876–Now, Metropolitan Museum of Art, New York, 2024

Triscott, Nicola, The Live Creature and Ethereal Things: Physics in Culture, Touchladybirdlucky Studios, London, 2018

Ussing Seeberg, Mathias, Lærke Fydal Jørgensen, Poul Erik Tøjner, Amy F. Ogata, Audre Lorde, Todd Lubart, Thomas Mann and Miguel Sicart, The Irreplaceable Human: Conditions of Creativity in the Age of AI, Louisiana Museum of Modern Art, Humlebæk, Denmark, 2024

Wasko, Ryszard, Adam Klimczak, Ewelina Chmielewska and Lucja Wasko-Mandes, From the Liberty Square to Independence Square, Fokus Łódź Biennale, Poland, 2010

Yan, Gong, Hallie Ayres, Dong Bingfeng, Lukas Brasiskis, Christina Kiaer, Ekaterina Kulinicheva, Jonas Staal, Anton Vidokle, Elena Vogman, Zirong Xiang, Wang Xin, Zhang Zhen and Arseny Zhiyaev, Cosmos Cinema, Shanghai Biennale and Sternberg, Berlin, 2024

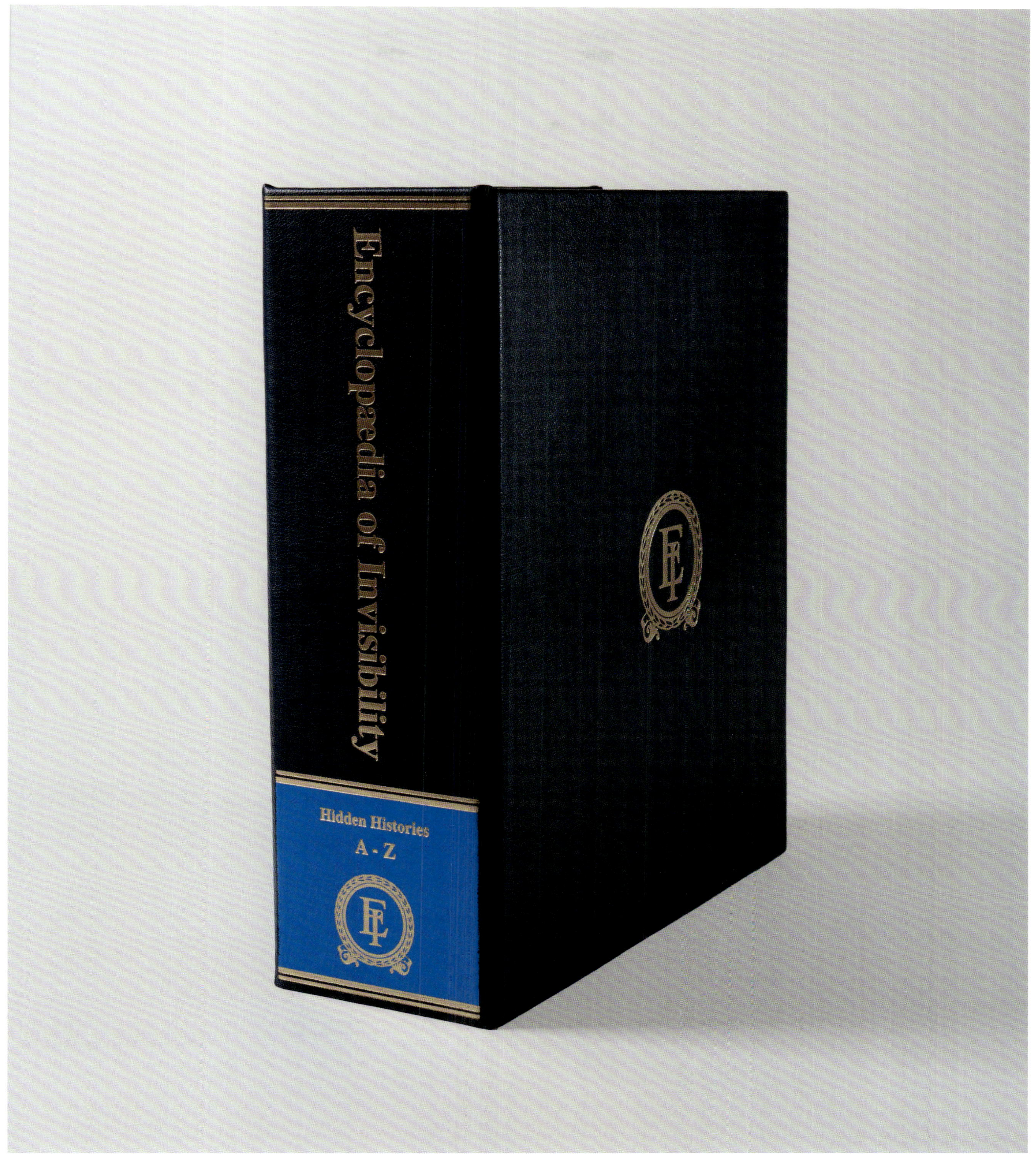
Encyclopædia of Invisibility
Hidden Histories
A - Z

ILLUSTRATED WORKS

A MAP OF THE CROWN (AMASUNZU BLACK), 2023, pages 140–141

A MAP OF THE CROWN (CONGO CANDLE WICK), 2022, page 105

A MAP OF THE CROWN (JIMMA ETHIOPIA), 2023, page 107

A MAP OF THE CROWN (HIMBA DREADED KNOTS), 2022, page 108

A MAP OF THE CROWN (FULANI BLACK), 2024, page 106

A MAP OF THE CROWN (MODERN AMERICAN), 2023, page 106

A MAP OF THE CROWN (NYABINGHI), 2025, pages 140–141

A MAP OF THE CROWN (SHILLUK), 2025, pages 140–141

A MAP OF THE CROWN (UKUANYAMA NAMIBIA), 2022, page 107

A MAP OF THE CROWN (UNKNOWN AFRICAN CA. 1960), 2023, page 139

THE BARBER SHOP, 2025, pages 140–141

BEAUTIFIES AND SOFTENS, 2025, page 2, 140–141

THE BIRTH OF EXUMA (EAGLE TALON), 2024, PAGES 86–87

BLACK STAR, 2024, page 115

BLACK STAR, 2024, pages 116–117

BLAST OFF, 2008–09, pages 44–45

BROWN SKIN BEAUTY-CUCUMBER LOTION, 2025, pages 140–141

CORONATION HUT, 2022, pages, 14, 16–17

THE DISTANCE BETWEEN WHAT WE HAVE AND WHAT WE WANT, 2005–06, pages 42–43

DISTANT RELATIVES (ANDREA MOTLEY CRABTREE), 2020, pages 8, 10, 82, 83

DISTANT RELATIVES (DEREK WALCOTT), 2020, pages 9 10, 84

DISTANT RELATIVES (HENRIETTA LACKS), 2020, page 8

DISTANT RELATIVES (JAMES BALDWIN), 2020, pages 8, 85

DISTANT RELATIVES (MARY J. SEACOLE), 2020, page 9

DISTANT RELATIVES (MATTHEW HENSON), 2020, pages 9, 11

DISTANT RELATIVES (ROBERT HENRY LAWRENCE JR.), 2020, page 9

DISTANT RELATIVES (ROBERT SMALLS), 2020, pages 8, 10, 85

DISTANT RELATIVES (SHIRLEY CHISHOLM), 2020, pages 9, 11

DISTANT RELATIVES (SISTER ROSETTA THARPE), 2020, pages 10, 85

DISTANT RELATIVES (VIVIAN ANDERSON), 2020, pages 8, 85

DOUBLE CONSCIOUSNESS, 2023, page 112

THE ENCYCLOPEDIA OF INVISIBILITY, 2014–18, pages 38–39, 74, 75, 76, 77, 157

ENCYCLOPEDIA ROOM: PANEL PAINTING, 2022, pages 24–25, 70–71, 72–73

ENOCH (DISPLAY UNIT), 2015–17, pages 18–19

EVERY TONGUE SHALL CONFESS, 2023, pages 7, 90–91

THE FIRST SUPPER (GALAXY BLACK), 2023, pages 36–37, 79, 80, 81

FOUR-HUNDRED METER DASH, 2018, page 90

GEMINI 1 (WOMAN KING), 2025, pages 67, 68–69

HAIR CARE POSTERS 1–7, 2025, pages 140–141

HAIR GLORY, 2025, pages 2, 140–141

I AM, 2017, pages 64–65

I AM THROUGH WITH PASSING, 2022, pages 12–13, 15,

I BELONG HERE, 2011, pages 34-35

INNER ELDER (BIKO AS SEPTIMIUS SEVERUS), 2023, page 100

INNER ELDER (NINA SIMONE AS QUEEN OF SHEBA), 2023, page 101

INNER ELDER (MARY SEACOLE), 2023, page 102

IN PRAISE OF MIDNIGHT (BIKO × CHURCHILL), 2025, page 147

IN PRAISE OF MIDNIGHT (CHRISTOPHE × NAPOLEON), 2025. page 145

IN PRAISE OF MIDNIGHT (PICASSO × IFE KING), 2025, page 142

IN PRAISE OF MIDNIGHT (SIMONE × QUEEN VICTORIA), 2025, page 143

IN PRAISE OF MIDNIGHT (TUBMAN × ALLIGATOR), 2025, PAGE 143

INTERGALACTIC PALACE, 2024, pages 96–97, 98–99

JAH RASTAFARI WITH RICE FIELD (STACKED WITH PINEAPPLE, SHIELD, AND FOOTBALL), 2023, pages 88–89

THE LAST SUPPER (A FAREWELL TO THE FLAVOURS WE MIGHT LOSE), 2025, pages 30–31

THE LEGACY, 2023, page 91

LETTER E, 1999, page 6

LIVING ROOM, 2022, pages 24–25, 26–27, 29

LUCKY BROWN, 2025, pages 140–141

LUCKY BROWN (SMALL), 2025, pages 140–141

MADAM JONES SEVEN, 2025, pages 140–141

MATTHEW HENSON (HUNTER'S SHIRT STACKED WITH FOOTBALL AND SPEAR), 2023, page 93

MIND FIELD NO. 1, 2023, pages 58, 59

MIND FIELD NO. 3, 2023, pages 140–141

MIND FIELD NO. 5, 2023, pages 140–141

MIND FIELD NO. 6, 2023, pages 140–141

MIND FIELD NO. 7, 2023, page 57

MIND FIELD NO. 8, 2023, pages 60, 61

OSHUN (RED STAR), 2025, pages 40–41, 62

PRIVATELY WANTING TO BE LIKE SOMEBODY ELSE (MARK TWAIN)/THAT PERSON (JAMES BALDWIN), 2025, pages 134–135

ROCKET LAUNCH ABACO 1, 2010–11, page 46

ROCKET LAUNCH ABACO 2, 2010–11, page 46

ROCKET LAUNCH ABACO 6, 2010–11, page 47

ROCKET LAUNCH ABACO 7, 2010–11, page 47

RUIN OF A GIANT (KING TUBBY), 2024, pages 94, 97

SEATED PANCHEN LAMA, 2011, pages 49, 50–51

SELF-PORTRAIT AS KING OBA WITH BRITISH ZOMBIES, 2023, page 111

SOME LOADS ARE TOO HEAVY TO CARRY ALONE, 2025, pages 32–33

SWEET GEORGIA BROWN, 2025, pages 2, 140–141

THAT PERSON (JAMES BALDWIN), 2025, PAGES 86–87

TRAINING IN 6 PARTS: NEUTRAL DIVE, 2009–10, pages 20–21

UNITED STATES OF AFRICA, 2022, page 119

VANISHING CREAM, 2025, page 2

VANISHING CREAM, 2025, pages 140–141

THE WASH HOUSE, 2025, pages 32–33

THE WASH HOUSE (LARGE), 2025, pages 32–33

THE WASH HOUSE (SMALL), 2025, pages 32–33

WHAT WILL BE REMEMBERED IN THE FACE OF ALL THAT IS FORGOTTEN, 2014–15, pages 53, 54–55

YOU BELONG HERE, 2014, pages 120–121

COMPARATIVE IMAGES

THE ARTIST TRAINING AT THE THE YURI A. GAGARIN RUSSIAN STATE SCIENCE RESEARCH COSMONAUT TRAINING CENTRE, STAR CITY, RUSSIA, 2009–2010. THE PROJECT WAS PART OF THE SERIES BASEC (BAHAMAS AIR AND SEA EXPLORATION CENTER), page 18

JASON GARDNER JUNKANOO IN DA CULTURAL VILLAGE, NASSAU, BAHAMAS, 2016, page 6

RUNKUS PERFORMING AT THE OPENING OF TAVARES STRACHAN: SUPERNOVAS, KUNSTHALLE MANNHEIM, GERMANY, 2025, page 22

PUBLIC COLLECTIONS

THE BASS, Miami

CARNEGIE MUSEUM OF ART, Pittsburgh

GOVERNOR GENERAL'S OFFICE, New Providence Bahamas

LOS ANGELES COUNTY MUSEUM OF ART

THE METROPOLITAN MUSEUM OF ART, New York

THE MOMENTARY | CRYSTAL BRIDGES MUSEUM OF AMERICAN ART, Bentonville, Arkansas

MUSÉE D'ART CONTEMPORAIN DE LYON

MUSEO DE ARTE MODERNO, Santa Domingo

NASSAU INTERNATIONAL AIRPORT (PUBLIC SCULPTURE)

THE QUEENSLAND ART GALLERY & GALLERY OF MODERN ART, Brisbane

RHODE ISLAND SCHOOL OF DESIGN, Providence

SAN FRANCISCO MUSEUM OF MODERN ART

SIR LINDEN PINDLING'S UNITY HOUSE, Nassau

PHAIDON PRESS LTD.
2 COOPERAGE YARD
LONDON E15 2QR

PHAIDON PRESS INC.
111 BROADWAY
NEW YORK, NY 10006

PHAIDON SARL
55, RUE TRAVERSIÈRE
75012 PARIS

PHAIDON.COM

First published 2026

ISBN:
978-1-83729-023-9
Signed Edition:
978-1-83729-232-5
Limited Edition:
978-1-83729-332-2

A CIP catalogue record of this book is available from the British Library and the Library of Congress.

Commissioning Editor
Michele Robecchi

Production Controller
Gif Jittiwutikarn

Design
Melanie Mues, Mues Design, London

Layout
Cantina, London

Printed in China

PUBLISHER'S ACKNOWLEDGEMENTS

We would like to thank Mariko Tanaka, Miho Suzuki and Emma Fasciolo at Isolated Labs, New York; Amanda Singer and Junette Teng at Marian Goodman Gallery, New York. Emma Paterson and Matilda Southern-Wilkins at Aitken Alexander Associates, London; Nathalie Brambilla, James Brown, Clive Burroughs, Raphaële Coutant, Jude Grover, João Mota, Andrew Mott, Michelle Pamisa, Ruby Powers, Tracey Smith, Phoebe Stephenson, Hans Stofregen, Andie Trainer, Clara Ustinov, Elaine Ward, Jonathan Whale, Yuqing Lin.

Photographers: David Blank, Mark Blower, Brooke DiDonato, Claire Dorn, Rebecca Fanuele, Brian Forrest, Jason Gardner, Chris Hoover, Garret Linn, Oliver Parkin, Jason Schmidt, Elon Schoenholz, Miho Suzuki, Lucas Trampe, Ricky Vigil M, Jonty Wilde.

All works are in private collections unless otherwise stated.

ARTIST'S ACKNOWLEDGEMENTS

This publication came into being through the vision of Michele Robecchi and the dedicated team at Phaidon, whose belief in this project carried it forward.

I hold deep gratitude for my extraordinary team – Yiwei Chen, Emma Fasciolo, Barbara Gooding, Miho Suzuki, Mariko Tanaka, Christophe Thompson and Nicholas Zhao – whose care, intelligence and commitment shaped every step of this journey.

At its heart, this work is an act of shared curiosity and collaboration. I am thankful to all those whose contributions, seen and unseen, helped bring this vision into the world.

I am also especially grateful to the exceptional team at Marian Goodman Gallery, with special thanks to Junette Teng.
This publication stands as a testament to collective effort, creative exchange and a faith in art's ability to connect across space and time.

CONTEMPORARY ARTISTS:

Contemporary Artists is a series of authoritative and extensively illustrated studies of today's most important artists. Each title offers a comprehensive survey of an individual artist's work and a range of art writing contributed by an international spectrum of authors, all leading figures in their fields, from art history and criticism to philosophy, cultural theory and fiction. Each study provides incisive analysis and multiple perspectives on contemporary art and its inspiration. These are essential source books for everyone concerned with art today.

MARINA ABRAMOVIĆ KLAUS BIESENBACH, KRISTINE STILES, CHRISSIE ILES **VITO ACCONCI** FRAZER WARD, MARK C. TAYLOR, JENNIFER BLOOMER **AI WEIWEI** HANS ULRICH OBRIST, KAREN SMITH, BERNARD FIBICHER **DOUG AITKEN** DANIEL BIRNBAUM, AMANDA SHARP, JÖRG HEISER **PAWEŁ ALTHAMER** ADAM SZYMCZYK, ROMAN KURZMEYER, SUZANNE COTTER **FRANCIS ALŸS** CUAUHTÉMOC MEDINA, RUSSELL FERGUSON, JEAN FISHER, MICHAEL TAUSSIG **ROSA BARBA** STUART COMER, SHANAY JHAVERI, ÉLISABETH LEBOVICI, JULIE AULT **UTA BARTH** PAMELA M. LEE, MATTHEW HIGGS, JEREMY GILBERT-ROLFE **CHRISTIAN BOLTANSKI** DIDIER SEMIN, TAMAR GARB, DONALD KUSPIT **MONICA BONVICINI** ALEXANDER ALBERRO, JANET KRAYNAK, JULIANE REBENTISCH **LOUISE BOURGEOIS** PAULO HERKENHOFF (WITH THYRZA GOODEVE), ROBERT STORR, ALLAN SCHWARTZMAN **MARK BRADFORD** ANITA HILL, SEBASTIAN SMEE, CONNIE BUTLER **CECILY BROWN** COURTNEY J. MARTIN, JASON ROSENFELD, FRANCINE PROSE **CAI GUO-QIANG** DANA FRIIS-HANSEN, OCTAVIO ZAYA, TAKASHI SERIZAWA **JORDAN CASTEEL** LEGACY RUSSELL, ASMA NAEEM, KATHERINE BRINSON **MAURIZIO CATTELAN** NANCY SPECTOR, FRANCESCO BONAMI, BARBARA VANDERLINDEN, MASSIMILIANO GIONI **VIJA CELMINS** ROBERT GOBER, LANE RELYEA, BRIONY FER **NIGEL COOKE** DARIAN LEADER, TONY GODFREY, MARIE DARRIEUSSECQ **RICHARD DEACON** PIER LUIGI TAZZI, JON THOMPSON, PETER SCHJELDAHL, PENELOPE CURTIS **TACITA DEAN** JEAN-CHRISTOPHE ROYOUX, MARINA WARNER, GERMAINE GREER **MARK DION** LISA GRAZIOSE CORRIN, MIWON KWON, NORMAN BRYSON **PETER DOIG** ADRIAN SEARLE, KITTY SCOTT, CATHERINE GRENIER **STAN DOUGLAS** SCOTT WATSON, DIANA THATER, CAROL J. CLOVER **MARLENE DUMAS** DOMINIC VAN DEN BOOGERD, BARBARA BLOOM, MARIUCCIA CASADIO, ILARIA BONACOSSA **JIMMIE DURHAM** LAURA MULVEY, DIRK SNAUWAERT, MARK ALICE DURANT, KATE NESIN **OLAFUR ELIASSON** MADELEINE GRYNSZTEJN, DANIEL BIRNBAUM, MICHAEL SPEAKS **ELMGREEN & DRAGSET** LINDA YABLONSKY, MARTIN HERBERT, CONNIE BUTLER, JASON SCHMIDT **CERITH WYN EVANS** HANS ULRICH OBRIST, NANCY SPECTOR, DANIEL BIRNBAUM **PETER FISCHLI AND DAVID WEISS** ROBERT FLECK, BEATE SÖNTGEN, ARTHUR C. DANTO **TOM FRIEDMAN** DENNIS COOPER, BRUCE HAINLEY, ADRIAN SEARLE **THEASTER GATES** CAROL BECKER, LISA YUN LEE, ACHIM BORCHARDT-HUME **ISA GENZKEN** ALEX FARQUHARSON, DIEDRICH DIEDERICHSEN, SABINE BREITWIESER **ANTONY GORMLEY** ERNST GOMBRICH, JOHN HUTCHINSON, LELA B. NJATIN, W. J. T. MITCHELL **DAN GRAHAM** BIRGIT PELZER, MARK FRANCIS, BEATRIZ COLOMINA **PAUL GRAHAM** ANDREW WILSON, GILLIAN WEARING, CAROL SQUIERS **SHILPA GUPTA** ALEXANDRA MUNROE, NAV HAQ, ELVIRA DYANGANI OSE **HANS HAACKE** WALTER GRASSKAMP, MOLLY NESBIT, JON BIRD **MONA HATOUM** GUY BRETT, MICHAEL ARCHER, CATHERINE DE ZEGHER, NANCY SPECTOR **SHARON HAYES** JULIA BRYAN-WILSON, JEANNINE TANG, LANKA TATTERSALL **THOMAS HIRSCHHORN** BENJAMIN H. D. BUCHLOH, ALISON M. GINGERAS, CARLOS BASUALDO **JIM HODGES** JANE M SAKS, ROBERT HOBBS, JULIE AULT **JENNY HOLZER** DAVID JOSELIT, JOAN SIMON, RENATA SALECL **RONI HORN** LOUISE NERI, LYNNE COOKE, THIERRY DE DUVE **CAMERON JAMIE** PHILIPPE VERGNE, RALPH RUGOFF, ELENA FILIPOVIC **CHRIS JOHANSON** CORRINA PEIPON, BOB NICKAS, JULIE DEAMER **RASHID JOHNSON** CLAUDIA RANKINE, SAMPADA ARANKE, AKILI TOMMASINO **ILYA KABAKOV** BORIS GROYS, DAVID A. ROSS, IWONA BLAZWICK **ALEX KATZ** ROBERT STORR, CARTER RATCLIFF, IWONA BLAZWICK, BARRY SCHWABSKY **ON KAWARA** 'TRIBUTE', JONATHAN WATKINS, RENÉ DENIZOT **MIKE KELLEY** ISABELLE GRAW, JOHN C. WELCHMAN, ANTHONY VIDLER **MARY KELLY** MARGARET IVERSEN, DOUGLAS CRIMP, HOMI K. BHABHA **WILLIAM KENTRIDGE** CAROLYN CHRISTOV-BAKARGIEV, DAN CAMERON, J. M. COETZEE **JANNIS KOUNELLIS** 'TRIBUTE', PHILIP LARRATT-SMITH, RUDI FUCHS **YAYOI KUSAMA** AKIRA TATEHATA, LAURA HOFTMAN, UDO KULTERMANN, CHATERINE TAFT **CHRISTIAN MARCLAY** JENNIFER GONZALEZ, KIM GORDON, MATTHEW HIGGS **KERRY JAMES MARSHALL** CHARLES GAINES, GREG TATE, LAURENCE RASSEL **PAUL McCARTHY** KRISTINE STILES, RALPH RUGOFF, MASSIMILIANO GIONI, ROBERT STORR **CILDO MEIRELES** PAULO HERKENHOFF, GERARDO MOSQUERA, DAN CAMERON **WILLIAM MONK** ISABELLE GRAW, TERRY R. MYERS, ÀNGELS MIRALDA **WANGECHI MUTU** ADRIENNE EDWARDS, COURTNEY J. MARTIN, KELLIE JONES, CHIKA OKEKE-AGULU **YOKO ONO** LAURIE ANDERSON, ERIKO OSAKA, THIERRY RASPAIL **LUCY ORTA** ROBERTO PINTO, NICOLAS BOURRIAUD, MAIA DAMIANOVIC **JEAN-MICHEL OTHONIEL** GAY GASSMANN, CATHERINE GRENIER, ROBERT STORR **TREVOR PAGLEN** LAUREN CORNELL, JULIA BRYAN-WILSON, OMAR KHOLEIF **JORGE PARDO** CHRISTINE VÉGH, LANE RELYEA, CHRIS KRAUS **NICOLAS PARTY** STÉPHANE AQUIN, STEFAN BANZ, ALI SUBOTNICK, MELISSA HYDE **ADAM PENDLETON** ALEC MAPES-FRANCES, ADRIENNE EDWARDS, ANDRÉA PICARD **RAYMOND PETTIBON** DENNIS COOPER, ROBERT STORR, ULRICH LOOCK **RICHARD PRINCE** ROSETTA BROOKS, JEFF RIAN, LUC SANTE **NEO RAUCH** INGRID MÖSSINGER, RALPH KEUNING, DAVID SALLE **LILI REYNAUD-DEWAR** ÉLISABETH LEBOVICI, DIEDRICH DIEDERICHSEN, MONIKA SZEWCZYK **PIPILOTTI RIST** HANS ULRICH OBRIST, PEGGY PHELAN, ELIZABETH BRONFEN **UGO RONDINONE** LAURA HOPTMAN, ERIK VERHAGEN, NICHOLAS BAUME, JASON SCHMIDT **DAAN ROOSEGAARDE** NICO DASWANI, FUMIO NANJO, CAROL BECKER **STERLING RUBY** KATE FOWLE, FRANKLIN SIRMANS, JESSICA MORGAN **ANRI SALA** HANS ULRICH OBRIST, MARK GODFREY, LIAM GILLICK **DORIS SALCEDO** NANCY PRINCENTHAL, CARLOS BASUALDO, ANDREAS HUYSSEN **WILHELM SASNAL** ANDRZEJ PRZYWARA, DOMINIC EICHLER, JÖRG HEISER **THOMAS SCHÜTTE** JULIAN HEYNEN, JAMES LINGWOOD, ANGELA VETTESE **DANA SCHUTZ** HAMZA WALKER, DAN NADEL, LYNNE TILLMAN **STEPHEN SHORE** MICHAEL FRIED, CHRISTY LANGE, JOEL STERNFELD **ROMAN SIGNER** PAULA VAN DEN BOSCH, GERHARD MACK, JEREMY MILLAR **LORNA SIMPSON** KELLIE JONES, THELMA GOLDEN, CHRISSIE ILES, NAOMI BECKWITH **NANCY SPERO** JON BIRD, JO ANNA ISAAK, SYLVÈRE LOTRINGER **SIMON STARLING** FRANCESCO MANACORDA, DIETER ROELSTRAETE, JANET HARBORD **FRANK STELLA** ANDRIANNA CAMPBELL, KATE NESIN, LUCAS BLALOCK, TERRY RICHARDSON **JESSICA STOCKHOLDER** BARRY SCHWABSKY, LYNNE TILLMAN, LYNNE COOKE, GERMANO CELANT **TAVARES STRACHAN** MICHELE ROBECCHI, GAVIN DELAHUNTY, EMMA DABIRI, JASON SCHMIDT **SARAH SZE** OKWUI ENWEZOR, BENJAMIN H. D. BUCHLOH, LAURA HOPTMAN **WOLFGANG TILLMANS** PETER HALLEY, JAN VERWOERT, MIDORI MATSUI, JOHANNA BURTON **LUC TUYMANS** ULRICH LOOCK, JUAN VICENTE ALIAGA, NANCY SPECTOR, HANS RUDOLF REUST **BERNAR VENET** FLORENCE DERIEUX, BARRY SCHWABSKY, CLAIRE LILLEY **ADRIÁN VILLAR-ROJAS** HANS ULRICH OBRIST, CAROLYN CHRISTOV-BAKARGIEV, EUNGIE JOO **JEFF WALL** THIERRY DE DUVE, ARIELLE PÉLENC, BORIS GROYS, JEAN-FRANÇOIS CHEVRIER, MARK LEWIS **GILLIAN WEARING** RUSSELL FERGUSON, DONNA DE SALVO, JOHN SLYCE **LAWRENCE WEINER** BENJAMIN H. D. BUCHLOH, ALEXANDER ALBERRO AND ALICE ZIMMERMAN, DAVID BATCHELOR **FRANZ WEST** ROBERT FLECK, BICE CURIGER, NEAL BENEZRA **JONAS WOOD** MARK GROTJAHN, HELEN MOLESWORTH, IAN ALTEVEER **YIN XIUZHEN** HOU HANRU, WU HUNG, STEPHANIE ROSENTHAL **LISA YUSKAVAGE** ARIEL LEVY, BARRY SCHWABSKY, LENA DUNHAM **ZHANG HUAN** ROSELEE GOLDBERG, YILMAZ DZIEWOR, ROBERT STORR